The Syro-Aramaic Reading of the Koran

Christoph Luxenberg

The Syro-Aramaic Reading of the Koran

A Contribution to the Decoding of the Language of the Koran

Verlag Hans Schiler

Bibliografische Information der Deutschen Bibliothek:
Die Deutsche Bibliothek verzeichnet diese Publikation in der Deutschen Nationalbibliografie; detaillierte bibliografische Daten sind im Internet über http://dnb.ddb.de abrufbar.

British Library Cataloguing in Publication data:
A catalogue record for this book is available from the British Library.
http://www.bl.uk

Library of Congress control number available:
http://www.loc.gov

Revised and enlarged edition.
Original published 2000 (2004, 2007):
Die syro-aramäische Lesart des Koran
Ein Beitrag zur Entschlüsselung der Koransprache

1st Edition 2007
Editor: Tim Mücke, *textintegration.de*
Cover: J2P, using a page of the
Koran codex 328(a) – Hijazi –
by courtesy of Bibliothèque Nationale de France

Printed in Germany

ISBN-10: 3-89930-088-2
ISBN-13: 978-3-89930-088-8

www.schiler.de

Contents

Index of Koran Suras

FOREWORD

In the year 2000 the first German edition of this study (*Die syro-aramäische Lesart des Koran*) presented to the public a fraction of more extensive investigations on the language of the Koran. A second expanded edition followed in 2004. A third German edition has been published recently.

The basis of this first English edition is the first and, in part, the second German edition. Beyond that, the present English edition contains minor supplements and new findings.

It is hoped that the selection of results made in this publication will provide a stimulus to Koran researchers to begin discussing the methods and interpretations arising from them with regard to the contents of the text of the Koran. From the controversy provoked in the meantime over the language of the Koran, no objectively grounded refutation has emerged in view of the essential findings presented here.

What is meant by *Syro-Aramaic* (actually *Syriac*) is the branch of Aramaic in the Near East originally spoken in Edessa and the surrounding area in Northwest Mesopotamia and predominant as a written language from Christianization to the origin of the Koran. For more than a millennium Aramaic was the *lingua franca* in the entire Middle Eastern region before being gradually displaced by Arabic beginning in the 7th century. It is thought that the Greeks were the first to call Aramaic *Syriac* (as the language of *Assyria* in the time of Alexander the Great[1]). This term was then adopted by the Christian Arameans, who in this way wanted to distinguish themselves from their pagan fellow countrymen. *Syriac* is also the name given by the Arabs in their early writings (for example in *hadith* literature)[2] to this Christian Aramaic, which is an ar-

1 Aramaic as the language of Assyria is attested to in the Old Testament by a historical fact in 701 B.C. (2 Kings 18:26 and Isaiah 36:11; cf. Henri Fleisch, *Introduction à l'Étude des Langues Sémitiques*, Paris 1947, p. 69).

2 Thus according to one tradition (*hadith*) the Prophet is said to have given his secretary, Zayd ibn Thabit (d. 45/665 A.D.), the task of learning *Syriac* and *Hebrew* in order to read him the writings he received in these languages. Cf., for

gument for the importance of this language at the time at which written Arabic originated.

As a written language, and especially in translations of the Bible, which presumably existed as early as the second century of the Christian era,[3] Syro-Aramaic achieved such an influence that it soon stretched beyond the region of Syria to, among other places, Persia. The Christian Syriac literature, which was in its heyday from the 4th to the 7th century, is especially extensive.[4]

With its *Syro-Aramaic reading of the Koran* this study in no way claims to solve all of the riddles of the language of the Koran. It is merely an attempt to illuminate a number of obscurities in the language of the Koran from this particular perspective. The fact, namely, that Syro-Aramaic was the most important written and cultural language in the region in whose sphere the Koran emerged, at a time in which Arabic was not a written language yet and in which learned Arabs used Aramaic as a written language,[5] suggests that the initiators of the Arabic

---

example, Ibn Saʿd az-Zuhrī (d. 230 H./845 A.D.), *aṭ-Ṭabaqāt al-kubrā*, 8 vols. + Index, Beirut 1985, II 358). In the *Encyclopedia of Islam*, Leiden, Leipzig 1934, vol. 4, 1293b, one reads under Zaid b. Thabit: "In any event he was his secretary, who recorded a part of the revelations and took care of the correspondence with the Jews, whose language or writing he is said to have learned in 17 days or less." It should be noted here, however, that the Jews did not speak Hebrew at this time, but Aramaic (Jewish Aramaic).

3 This is attested to by the original Syriac gospels harmony known as "Diatessaron," composed presumably before 172/3 A.D. in Rome by the Syrian Tatian. Cf. Anton Baumstark and Adolf Rücker, *Die syrische Literatur* [*Syriac Literature*], in: *Handbuch der Orientalistik* [*Handbook of Oriental Studies*], ed. Bertold Spuler, vol. 3, *Semitistik* [*Semitistics*], Leiden 1954, II 2. *Die Literatur des altsyrischen Christentums* [*The Literature of Old Syrian Christianity*], p. 171.

4 Cf. on this subject Theodor Nöldeke's *Kurzgefasste Syrische Grammatik*, Leipzig 1898 (second edition), reprint, Darmstadt 1977, Introduction xxxi-xxxiv. [*Compendius Syriac Grammar, Engl. translated by A. Chrichton, London, 1904.*] On the importance of Aramaic or *Syriac* in general, Nöldeke says: "This language was dominant for longer than a millennium in a very extensive area of the Near East far beyond its original boundaries and even served for the less educated neighboring populations as a written language" (xxxi).

5 On this subject Nöldeke says in his sketch *Die semitischen Sprachen* [*The Se-*

written language had acquired their knowledge and training in the Syro-Aramaic cultural milieu. When we consider, moreover, that these Arabs were for the most part Christianized and that a large proportion of them took part in the Christian Syrian liturgy,[6] then nothing would be more obvious than that they would have naturally introduced elements of their Syro-Aramaic cult and cultural language into Arabic. To indicate the extent to which this is the case in the Koran is the task this study has set for itself. The samples contained herein may be considered as representative of a partially attainable deciphering – via Syro-Aramaic (that is, Syriac and in part other Aramaic dialects) – of the language of the Koran.

In this study it has not been possible to look into the entire literature on the subject, since such literature is fundamentally based on the erroneous historical-linguistic conceptions of traditional Arabic exegesis of the Koran and therefore scarcely contributes anything to the new methods presented here. This includes, in particular, the late lexical works of so-called *Classical* Arabic, which, though they may have their value as *reference dictionaries* for post-Koranic Arabic, they are not *etymological* dictionaries[7] which means that they are no help at all in understand-

---

mitic Languages], Leipzig 1899, second edition, p. 36: "Aramaic was the language of Palmyra whose aristocracy, however, was in large part of Arab descent. The Nabateans were Arabs. It is probable that many Arameans lived in the northern part of their empire (not far from Damascus), but further to the south Arabic was spoken. Only Aramaic was at that time a highly respected civilized language which those Arabs used because their own language was not a written language."

6 Notable in this regard is the following, the first Arabic dissertation on the subject, submitted in Tunis in 1995: *Salwā Bā-l-Ḥāğğ Ṣāliḥ-al – ʿĀyub* (سلوى بالحاج صالح ـ العايب): *al-Masīḥīya al-ʿarabīya wa-taṭawwurātuhā min našʾatihā ilā l-qarn ar-rābiʿ al-hiğrī/al-ʿāšir al-mīlādī* (المسيحيّة العربيّة وتطوّراتها من نشأتها إلى القرن الرابع الهجري / العاشر الميلادي): (*Arab Christianity and Its Development from Its Origins to the Fourth Century of the Hegira / Tenth Century of the Christian Era*), Beirut 1997.

7 Included here is the project of the WKAS (*Wörterbuch der klassischen arabischen Sprache* [*Dictionary of Classical Arabic*]), which has been in preparation since 1957. Cf. Helmut Gätje, *Arabische Lexikographie. Ein historischer*

ing the pre-Classical language of the Koran. An etymological dictionary of Arabic continues to be a desideratum. The reason for its lack is probably the notion that the (presumably) older Arabic poetic language and the younger written Arabic are identical. To be consistent, Arabic (due to a number of archaic characteristics) was classified from the point of view of historical linguistics as older than Aramaic. This historical-linguistic error makes understandable much of the criticism, even from competent Semiticists who have expressed their opinions on individual findings in the course of the debate that this study has provoked in Germany and abroad since its first appearance in 2000.

It is here not the place to go into this criticism in detail. This remains reserved for a soon-to-follow publication that will treat morphologically, lexically and syntactically the Aramaic basic structure of the language of the Koran. This English edition has been insubstantially supplemented, in particular by the appending of the index of Koranic passages and terms, the prospect of which was held out to readers in the first German edition.

Berlin, January 2007

Überblick [*Arabic Lexicography: A Historical Overview*], in Historiographia Linguistica XII: 1/2, Amsterdam 1985, 105-147, loc.cit. 126-138 under No. 7, Allgemeines zum 'WKAS' [On the ‚WKAS' in general], with bibliographical information on p. 142 under (B) Secondary Literature.

1. INTRODUCTION

According to Islamic tradition the Koran (in Arabic, قرءان / *Qurʾān*), the sacred scripture of Islam, contains the revelations, eventually fixed in writing under the third caliph ʿUṯmān (Othman) ibn ʿAffān (644–656 A.D.), of the Prophet Muḥammad (Mohammed) (570–632 A.D.), the proclamation of which had stretched over a period of about twenty years (approx. 612–632 A.D.) in the cities of Mecca and Medina.

As the first book written in Arabic known to tradition, the Koran is considered by speakers of Arabic to be the foundation of written Arabic and the starting point of an Arabic culture that flourished intellectually in the High Middle Ages. Moreover, according to Islamic theology its contents are held to be the eternal word of God revealed in Arabic.

Non-Muslims see in the Koran a cultural heritage of humanity. It is from this they derive their interest and justification in studying this literary monument from the standpoint of cultural history and the history of religion, as well as from a philological perspective.

Precisely this philological perspective will be occupying us here, since there is naturally a danger of making false inferences on the basis of a text that, in large parts of the Koran, has not been clarified philologically, as not only Western scholars of the Koran, but also the Arabic philologists themselves admit. Whence derives the fundamental interest, not only of the historian of culture and religion, but also and especially of the philologist, to endeavor, as a matter of priority, to clarify the Koranic text.

A good start in this direction was already made by the Western Koran scholarship of the 19th century. Here, listed in the chronological order of their appearance, are the most important publications looking into the text of the Koran in more detail:

- ABRAHAM GEIGER (1810–1874), *Was hat Mohammed aus dem Judenthume aufgenommen?* [*What Did Mohammed Take from Judaism?*], Bonn, 1833. This Bonn University dissertation documents sources in Jewish literature for a series of Koranic terms and passages.

- THEODOR NÖLDEKE (1836–1930), *Geschichte des Qorâns* [*History of the Koran*], Göttingen, 1860. This publication, recognized among Western experts as the standard work in the field, was preceded in 1856, as the author reports in his *Foreword* (v), by a Latin monograph, *De origine et compositione Surarum Qoranicarum ipsiusque Qorani*. It later experienced a revision, in a second edition, by the following editors: Teil I (*Über den Ursprung des Qorāns*) [Part I (*On the Origins of the Koran*)] and Teil II (*Die Sammlung des Qorāns*) [Part II (*The Collection of the Koran*)] by Friedrich Schwally, Leipzig, 1909 and 1919, respectively, and Teil III (*Die Geschichte des Korantexts*) [Part III (*The History of the Koran Text*)] by G. Bergsträßer and O. Pretzl, Leipzig, 1938 (cited in the following as: *GdQ*).
- SIEGMUND FRAENKEL (1855–1909), *De vocabulis in antiquis Arabum carminibus et in Corano peregrinis*, Leiden, 1880. In this summarized dissertation, Fraenkel, a student of Nöldeke, produces a list of Koranic expressions borrowed for the most part from Aramaic. The author subsequently followed up on this first study with a more extensive study in which additional Koranic expressions are discussed: *Die aramäischen Fremdwörter im Arabischen* [*The Foreign Words of Aramaic Origin in Arabic*], Leiden, 1886 (cited in the following as: *Aramäische Fremdwörter* [*Aramaic Foreign Words*]).
- KARL VOLLERS (1835–1909), *Volkssprache und Schriftsprache im alten Arabien* (Kapitel 5: "Die Sprache des Qorāns") [*Vernacular Language and Written Language in Ancient Arabia* (Chapter 5: "The Language of the Koran")], Strasbourg, 1906 (cited in the following as: *Volkssprache und Schriftsprache* [*Vernacular Language and Written Language*]). In this monograph Vollers, on the basis of a minutely precise philological analysis of a series of Koranic forms, argues that the Koran was originally composed in a Western Arabic dialect (of Mecca and Medina) and only later, in the second half of the second century of the Hiğra/Hegira (*loc. cit.* 183), reworked by Arabic philologists and adapted to the classical linguistic form of Old Arabic poetry.

- THEODOR NÖLDEKE, *Neue Beiträge zur semitischen Sprachwissenschaft* (S. 1–30): Zur Sprache des Korāns, I. Der Korān und die *ᶜArabīja*; II. Stilistische und syntaktische Eigentümlichkeiten der Sprache des Korāns; III. Willkürlich und mißverständlich gebrauchte Fremdwörter im Korān [*New Essays on Semitic Linguistics* (pp. 1–30): On the Language of the Koran, I. The Koran and ᶜArabīya, II. Stylistic and Syntactic Peculiarities of the Language of the Koran, III. Arbitrary and Confusing Use of Foreign Words in the Koran], Strasbourg, 1910 (cited in the following as: *Neue Beiträge* [*New Essays*]). In his introduction Nöldeke, to whom Vollers had dedicated the preceding study, dismisses Vollers' thesis as erroneous and, despite admitting the existence of dialectal variations, pronounces himself in favor of the ᶜArabīya (the classical Arabic language) in the Koran. He ends the second chapter, however, by concluding that the good linguistic common sense of the Arabs has almost completely protected them from imitating the characteristic peculiarities and weaknesses of the language of the Koran. According to Nöldeke, the Koran constitutes a literature for itself, which is without real predecessors and which has also had no successors, and the Koran passages and individual Koranic expressions that have been added by later Arab writers as decoration are nothing but linguistic oddities (*op. cit.* 22 f.).
- JACOB BARTH (1851–1914), *Studien zur Kritik und Exegese des Qorāns* [*Studies contributing to criticism and exegesis of the Koran*], in: *Der Islam* 6, 1916, pp. 113–148. In this article J. Barth attempts to read critically certain isolated passages of the Koran based exclusively on his comprehension of Arabic. In so doing, Barth was one of the first scholars who dared occasionally to change the diacritical dots of the canonical text of the Koran. In all Barth was successful in only four cases in reestablishing the original or authentic reading (Sura 37:76 (78); 12:9; 9:113 (112); same reading in 66:5).
- IGNAZ GOLDZIHER (1850–1921), *Die Richtungen der islamischen Koranauslegung* [*The Trends in Islamic Koranic Exegesis*], Lei-

den 1920. In the first chapter of this work (pp. 1–52) Goldziher treats neutrally of the emergence of the controversial readings of the Koran according to Islamic tradition, but without proposing any alternative textual criticism. This monograph draws attention to the uncertainty of the *textus receptus* on which Islamic Koranic exegesis is based.

- JOSEF HOROVITZ (1874–1931), *Koranische Untersuchungen* [*Koranic Investigations*], Berlin, 1926. In the first section of this study Horowitz deals thematically with selected Koranic terms; in the second he discusses Koranic proper names.
- ALFONS MINGANA (1881–1921), *Syriac Influence on the Style of the Kur'ān*, in: Bulletin of the John Rylands Library 77–98, Manchester, 1927 (cited in the following as: *Syriac Influence*). In this essay Mingana, an East Syrian by birth, takes up both of the aforementioned authors and faults their analyses for the insufficiency of their criticism of the Koran text itself. By drawing attention to the Syro-Aramaic influence on the style of the Koran, he to a certain degree builds a bridge between Vollers' thesis of the dialectal origin of the Koran and the classical thesis advocated by Nöldeke. But the examples he provides in the essay to support his view were probably of little help in its gaining general acceptance since their number fell far below what in part had already been identified by Arabic philologists, and even more so by Western Koran scholars, as borrowings from Aramaic and Syriac. Although the route of research he had proposed would have been an entirely appropriate way to approach the solving of the mystery of the language of the Koran, the lack of conviction in reconstructing it has probably had as a consequence that no other scholar of the Koran has pursued it further.
- HEINRICH SPEYER (1897–1935), *Die biblischen Erzählungen im Qoran* [*The Biblical Stories in the Koran*], Breslau (?), 1931, reprint Hildesheim, 1961. This work continues in a much larger scope the work by Geiger mentioned at the outset. The author succeeds in providing impressive proof of the existence of a number of biblical passages in the Koran, not only from the canonical

Bible, but also from Jewish and Christian apocrypha and literatures. Although the listing of Koranic expressions in Index II does contribute further to their clarification, these expressions are not subjected to closer philological analysis. Probably for this reason Jeffery, in the next work, seems not to have taken any notice of Geiger's book.

– ARTHUR JEFFERY (1893–1959), *The Foreign Vocabulary of the Qur'ān*, Baroda, 1938 (cited in the following as: *The Foreign Vocabulary*). In this work Jeffery essentially summarizes the philological investigations of foreign words in the Koran published in Europe up to 1938 and at the same time also takes into account the opinions of the Arabic philologists and commentators of the Koran. His work, however, restricts itself to the purely etymological presentation of these expressions without arriving at meanings divergent from those accepted by either the Arab commentators or the modern European translators of the Koran. Of the approximately three hundred words (including around fifty proper names), those of Aramaic and Syro-Aramaic origin predominate. An examination of a series of those foreign words found by Jeffery to be of non-Aramaic origin has revealed that this is in part based on a misreading or misinterpretation of the Koranic expressions; some of these expressions will be discussed individually to the extent permitted by the scope of this work.[8]

In fact, Mingana's contribution to our understanding of the *Syriac influence on the style of the Koran* – never since refuted by Western Koran scholars – could have furthered Koranic studies had anyone taken up and consistently pursued the theoretical guidelines he proposed nearly three quarters of a century ago. The examples given to support his thesis, however, were obviously inadequate. Still, Mingana cannot be far from the truth with his statistical rough estimate of the foreign language portion of the Koran. On a scale of 100, he divides up this portion as

8 See the following examples to صراط (*ṣirāṭ*), قصر (*qaṣr*), سطر (*saṭara*), صيطر (*ṣayṭara*) and اضطر (*iṭṭarra*) below p. 226 ff.

follows: 5% Ethiopic, 10% Hebrew, 10% Greco-Roman, 5% Persian and nearly 70% Syriac (= Syro-Aramaic) including Aramaic and Christian Palestinian (cf. op. cit. 80). The evidence he provides for this he then divides into five categories: (a) proper names, (b) religious terms, (c) expressions of ordinary language, (d) orthography, (e) sentence constructions and (f) foreign historical references.

While the items listed under (a), (b), and (d) (I, II, and IV) are for the most part sufficiently well known, the examples cited for (c) turn out to be relatively few, considering that it is, after all, precisely the expressions of ordinary language that make up the brunt of the language of the Koran. Category (e) (V), on the other hand, is examined from four points of view, which could, in itself, have served as the basis of a more in-depth investigation. A prerequisite for an investigation of this kind, however, would be a mastery of both the Syro-Aramaic and the Arabic language at the time of the emergence of the Koran. Finally, in (f) (VI), it is essentially a question of a thematic examination of the text of the Koran in which the author, at times with convincing results, follows up, in particular, on the above-mentioned work by Speyer.

– GÜNTER LÜLING, *Über den Ur-Qurʾān. Ansätze zur Rekonstruktion vorislamischer christlicher Strophenlieder im Qurʾān* [*Regarding the Original Koran. Basis for a Reconstruction of Pre-Islamic Christian Strophic Hymns in the Koran*], Erlangen 1974 (2nd ed., Erlangen 1993).[9] This study is, after that of Jacob Barth's, a further, more extensive attempt to elucidate obscure passages of the Koran by changing certain diacritical dots. Lüling's thesis depends on the one hand on the supposition of an "Ur-Qurʾān" (Original Koran), in which the author sees, not without reason, Christian hymns, which he then undertakes to reconstruct. On the other hand, as to his philological method for elucidating obscure passages of the Koran, Lüling supposes a pre-Islamic *Christian Arabic*

9 Revised and enlarged English version: Günter Lüling, *A Challenge to Islam for Reformation. The Rediscovery and reliable Reconstruction of a comprehensive pre-Islamic Christian Hymnal hidden in the Koran under earliest Islamic Reinterpretation*. Delhi, Motilal Banarsidass, 2003.

koine, but one whose essential nature he fails to define. However, by basing himself on an essentially theological argument to achieve the goal of reconstruction and elucidation, Lüling only occasionally succeeds and is, on the whole, unable to solve the enigma of the language of the Koran. His merit is, however, to have re-posed the question of the nature of the language of the Koran. The kernel of his thesis of a Christian "Original Koran" would have engendered further research, had it not been rejected categorically by the representatives of this discipline in Germany.

2. Reference Works

The present study has originated impartially, i.e. independently of the works of Western scholarship listed above, as well as of Koran-related Arabic philology and exegesis. They would also, in all probability, have been detrimental to the method, which has gradually been worked out here in the course of this study, for research into the language of the Koran, and will thus only be referred to for comparative purposes during the philological discussions of individual passages in the Koran. In the discussion of the Koranic expressions requiring clarification, the following Arabic reference works have been consulted:

(a) the most important Arabic commentary on the Koran by *Ṭabarī* (d. 310 H. / 923 A.D.), which also takes into account earlier Koran commentaries: Abū Ǧaᶜfar Muḥammad b. Ǧarīr aṭ-Ṭabarī, *Ǧāmiᶜ al-bayān ᶜan taʾwīl āy al-Qurʾān* (30 parts in 12 vols.), 3rd ed., Cairo, 1968 (cited below as *Ṭabarī* / *Tabari* followed by the part and page number);

(b) the principal Arabic lexicon, لسان العرب *Lisān al-ᶜarab* of Ibn Manẓūr (1232–1311 A.D.), based on the Arabic lexicography begun in the second half of the 8th century with كتاب العين *Kitāb al-ᶜayn* by *al-Ḫalīl b. Aḥmad* (d. circa 786 A.D.):[10] Abū l-Faḍl Ǧamāl ad-Dīn Muḥammad b. Mukarram b. Manẓūr al-Ifrīqī al-Miṣrī, *Lisān al-ᶜarab* ("*Tongue*" *of the Arabs*), 15 vols., Beirut, 1955 (cited in the following as *Lisān* with the volume number, page number and column letter, a or b).

Furthermore, for comparative purposes, the translations of the main most recent representatives of Western Koran scholarship will be given in the following order – Richard Bell (English), Rudi Paret (German) and Régis Blachère (French) – based on the following editions:

10 Cf. Stefan Wild, *Das Kitāb al-ᶜAin und die arabische Lexikographie* [*The Kitāb al-ᶜAin and the Arabic Lexicography*], (Wiesbaden, 1965) 1 ff., 58 ff., and specifically on the *Lisān al-ᶜArab* 87-90.

- Richard Bell, *The Qur'ān. Translated, with a critical rearrangement of the Surahs*, vol. I, Edinburgh, 1937, vol. II, Edinburgh, 1939.

  – *A Commentary on the Qur'ān*, vols. I & II, Manchester, 1991.
- Rudi Paret, *Der Koran: Übersetzung*, 2nd ed., Stuttgart, Berlin, Cologne, Mainz, 1982.

  – *Kommentar und Konkordanz*, Stuttgart, 1971.
- Régis Blachère, *Le Coran* (*traduit de l'arabe*), Paris, 1957.

(Cited in the following as: Bell, Paret or Blachère [vol.] and page.)

To verify the readings interpreted according to Syro-Aramaic, the following Syro-Aramaic lexicons will be used:

- Payne Smith, ed., *Thesaurus Syriacus*, tomus I, Oxonii 1879; tomus II, Oxonii 1901 (cited in the following as: *Thes./Thesaurus* volume and column).
- Carl Brockelmann, *Lexicon Syriacum*, Halis Saxonum, 1928.
- Jacques Eugène Manna, *Vocabulaire Chaldéen-Arabe*, Mosul, 1900; reprinted with a new appendix by Raphael J. Bidawid, Beirut, 1975 (cited in the following as: *Mannā* and column).

The translations cited will show how these Western scholars of the Koran have understood the Koran passages in question, even after a critical evaluation of the Arabic exegesis. The expressions that are to receive a new interpretation will in each case be underlined. This will then be followed by the proposed translation according to the Syro-Aramaic understanding, and also in some cases according to the Arabic understanding, accompanied by the corresponding philological explanations.

3. The Working Method Employed

The aim of this work was in the first place to clarify the passages designated in Western Koran studies as *obscure*. However, apart from the previously unrecognized Aramaisms, the investigation of the overall Koranic language, which is considered to be indisputably Arabic, has uncovered, so to speak as a by-product, a goodly number of not insignificant misreadings and misinterpretations, even of genuinely Arabic expressions. Precisely in relation to the latter, it has turned out again and again that the meaning accepted by the Arabic commentators of the Koran has not at all fit the context.

In such cases the reference works of Arabic lexicography, which originated later and were thus, in their developed form, unknown to the earlier commentators of the Koran, have often been able to set things straight. In this regard it should be noted that in his large Koran commentary *Ṭabarī* invariably refers to the oral Arabic tradition, but not once to a lexicon of any kind. Only occasionally, in order to explain an unclear Koranic expression, does he quote verses from Arabic poetry, but these comparisons are often misleading since the vocabulary of this poetry differs fundamentally from that of the Koran.

As a departure from traditional Western methods of interpretation, which for the most part rely closely on the Arabic tradition, in the present work the attempt is made for the first time to place the text of the Koran in its historical context and to analyze it from a new philological perspective with the aim of arriving at a more convincing understanding of the Koranic text. The results will show that perhaps even more passages have been misunderstood in the Koran than those whose uncertainty has been conceded by previous Koran commentators and translators. Beyond this, the analysis will in part reveal considerable deficits in the previous interpretation of many aspects of the syntactic structure of the language of the Koran. The major points of the acquired method, which has evolved in the process of the detailed textual analysis, will be presented in the following.

The canonical version of the 1923/24 Cairo edition of the Koran will serve as the textual basis. Koran citations, orthography (without vowel signs) and verse numbering refer to this edition. This modern Koran edition differs from the earlier Koran manuscripts as a result of the subsequent addition of a large number of reading aids worked out for the faithful by Arabic philologists over the course of the centuries. Included among these are, in the first place, the so-called diacritical dots, serving to distinguish the equivocal and ambiguous letters in the early Arabic alphabet. These twenty-two letters requiring clarification will be discussed in more detail below.

Starting from the understanding that the Arabic readers, in view of the fact that the basic form of the earlier Koranic manuscripts is not easy to decipher even for educated Arabs, have for the most part correctly read today's accepted version of the Koran, this version is fundamentally respected in the forthcoming textual analysis following the principle of *lectio difficilior*. Only in those instances in which the context is obviously unclear, in which the Arabic commentators of the Koran are *at the limit of their Arabic*, in which it is said over and over again in *Ṭabarī* اختلف أهل التأويل في تأويل ذلك "*the commentators disagree on the interpretation* (*of the expression in question*)," or, not infrequently, when the listing of a series of speculations both in *Ṭabarī* and in the *Lisān* is concluded with the remark والله أعلم (*wa-l-lāhu aʿlam*) (*God knows it best* – or in plain English, *God only knows* what the expression in question really means!), only then will the attempt be made, while paying careful attention to the given context, to discover a more reasonable reading. The procedure employed in doing so will be as follows:

(a) For an expression designated as *obscure* by the Western Koran translators, a check is first made in the Arabic commentary of *Ṭabarī* to see whether one or the other of the cited interpretations ignored by the Western Koran translators does not, in fact, fit better in the context. Namely, it occasionally happens that the Arabic tradition has kept an accurate or an approximate memory of an earlier Aramaic expression. If this is not the case, then

(b) in the *Lisān* the Arabic expression in question is examined for possible alternative semantic meanings, since *Ṭabarī* and the earlier Arabic commentators did not have an aid of such scope at their disposal and in any case in his commentary *Ṭabarī* never refers to any Arabic lexicon whatsoever. This step also occasionally results in a better, more fitting sense. However, if the search remains unsuccessful, then

(c) a check is made to see whether there is a homonymous[11] root in Syro-Aramaic whose meaning differs from that of the Arabic and which, based on a consideration of objective criteria, clearly fits better in the context. In a not insignificant number of cases this Syro-Aramaic reading produced the better sense. Here one must see to it that according to the context the two homonyms can occur both in the Arabic and in the Syro-Aramaic meaning. Then, if this check leads nowhere,

(d) an attempt is made in the first place to read the Arabic writing differently than in the Cairo version of the Koran by changing the diacritical points, which were not there originally and which were later and perhaps erroneously added. Not infrequently it can be determined that the Arabic readers have apparently falsely read an expression in itself genuinely Arabic because they lacked the appropriate background information. However, if all of the possible alterations do not result in a sense that fits the context, then

(e) the attempt is made, while changing the diacritical points, to make out an Aramaic root beneath the Arabic writing. In an almost incalculable number of cases this has been successful to the extent that the Aramaic expression has given the context a decidedly more logical sense. However, if this attempt also fails, then

(f) a final attempt is made to reconstruct the actual meaning of the apparently genuine Arabic expression by translating it back into Aramaic by way of the semantics of the Syro-Aramaic expression. This attempt exceeds in importance, extent and level of difficulty the discovery of actual Aramaisms (or Syriacisms) for, as there are still no Arabic-Aramaic dictionaries, the researcher must here depend solely on his or her own knowledge of (the) lan-

11 I.e. etymologically related.

guage(s).[12] In the process, what appear to be genuinely Arabic expressions can be divided into: (1) loan formations and (2) loan translations (or calques).

(g) Another category involves, in turn, those for the most part genuine Arabic expressions that are neither susceptible to plausible explanation in the *Lisān* nor explainable by translation back into Syro-Aramaic, either because they have a completely different meaning in modern Arabic or because their basic Arabic meaning is unknown. In such cases the important lexical works by the East Syrian physicians *Bar ʿAlī* (d. 1001) and *Bar Bahlūl* (mentioned in a document in 963)[13] occasionally provide information on their real meanings. These Syro-Aramaic lexicons were created in the 10th century, presumably as a translating aid for Syrian translators of Syriac scientific works into Arabic, as Syro-Aramaic was being displaced more and more by Arabic.[14] The Syro-Aramaic-(*Chaldean-*)Arabic dictionary of *Mannā* mentioned at the outset, by taking into account, among other lexicons, that of *Bar Bahlūl*, continues to a certain extent this tradition of Eastern Syrian lexicography. The Arabic vocabulary that these lexicons employ for the explanation of Syro-Aramaic words and expressions is of eminent importance here, especially when, as an equivalent of a Syro-Aramaic expression, several Arabic synonyms are listed, of

---

12 With its appended *Index latinus* Brockelmann's *Lexicon Syriacum* does offer a stopgap, however.

13 Anton Baumstark, *Geschichte der syrischen Literatur* [*History of Syrian Literature*] (Bonn, 1922) 241. It is said of *Bar ʿAlī* in the same work that he worked as an eye doctor and spoke Arabic. On the importance of these works, Baumstark writes (242): "The work by B. Bahlûl, which was later on often published in a combined edition with the other and which is especially valuable due to its exact citation of sources, was also geared from the start to the explanation of foreign words of Greek origin and enriched by objective erudition of a philosophical, scientific and theological nature. Naturally, a considerable element of the West Syrian scholarly tradition begins to make itself felt in the complicated textual history of this codification of Eastern Syrian lexicography…".

14 Cf. Theodor Nöldeke, *Die semitischen Sprachen* [*The Semitic Languages*], 2nd edition (Leipzig, 1899) 43.

which one or the other occasionally occurs in the Koran. In this respect, the *Thesaurus Syriacus* has proven to be a veritable treasure trove whenever it cites, although irregularly, at least relatively often, the Arabic explanations of the Eastern Syrian lexicographers.[15] In this way it has been possible, thanks to the *Thesaurus Syriacus*, to explain many an obscure Koranic expression. A systematic exploration of the Arabic vocabulary in these early Eastern Syriac lexicons, however, would bring even more to light. Also, the early Christian-Arabic literature of the Eastern Syrians,[16] until now ignored by Koran scholars, yet whose Arabic vocabulary reaches back, in part at least, to the pre-Islamic usage of the Christian Arabs of Mesopotamia and Syria, would lead to more convincing results than the so-called *Old Arabic* – though for the most part post-Koranic – poetry, whose vocabulary is extremely inappropriate and misleading for understanding the Koran.[17]

This is namely the case when misunderstood Koranic expressions are used improperly or in a completely different context in this poetry and then cited as authentic evidence for the interpretation of these same Koranic expressions by the later Arabic philologists. This inner-Arabic methodology proper to later Arabic lexicography consists in explaining obscure expressions, for the most part speculatively and in the absence of other literature, on the basis of the often hard to unravel context of earlier Arabic poetry,

---

15 Payne Smith refers to a) BA.: *Jesu Bar-Alii Lexicon Syro-Arab.*, potissimum e cod. Bibl. Bodl. Hunt. xxv. b) BB.: *Jesu Bar-Bahlulis Lexicon Syro-Arab*, e cod. Bibl. Bodl. Hunt. clvii, Marsh. cxcviii.

16 Thus, for example, Nöldeke (*loc. cit.* 43) refers to the learned metropolitan of Nisibis, Elias bar Schinnājā (975 – c. 1050 A.D.), who had written "his works intended for Christians either in Arabic or in parallel columns of Arabic and Syriac, i.e. in the spoken language and in the language of the learned."

17 For example, Nöldeke says in this regard (*loc. cit.* 53): "Admittedly the poems of the Arab heathen period were only recorded significantly later and not at all without distortion," and further (58), "In particular the literature of satirical and abusive songs has with certainty introduced many arbitrary and in part quite strangely devised expressions into the (Arabic) lexicon."

in the course of which a borrowing from a foreign language is only sporadically identified correctly. Western scholars of the Koran have not considered these circumstances with sufficient scepticism. Although one often notes the clumsiness of the Arabic commentators, it is mostly without being able to help them out. Compared to this, the fully mature Syro-Aramaic – especially theological – literature existing long prior to the Koran and the reliably traditional semantics of the Syro-Aramaic vocabulary – even after the Koran – offer an aid that, on the basis of the results of this study, will prove to be an indispensable key to the understanding, not only of the foreign-language vocabulary, but also of what is considered to be the Arabic vocabulary of the language of the Koran.

(h) Now and then one also finds genuine Arabic expressions that have been misread and misunderstood because, though they are written in Arabic script, they have been produced orthographically according to the Syro-Aramaic phonetic system and are to be pronounced accordingly, so that one can only identify them as meaningful Arabic expressions in this roundabout way. An example that will be discussed more fully below (p. 111 ff., Sura 16:103; 41:40, Koranic يلحدون *yulḥidūn* is a misreading of يلحزون = Syriac ܠܓܙܘܢ phonetically Arabic يلغزون *yalġuzūn*) gives a first hint of the assumption that the original Koranic text was written in *Garshuni* (or *Karshuni*), that is to say Arabic written in Syriac letters. Further evidences corroborating this hypothesis will be given with empiric accuracy in a forthcoming publication.[18]

18 Cf. the anthology published in the meantime, ed. by Karl-Heinz Ohlig: *Der frühe Islam. Eine historisch-kritische Rekonstruktion anhand zeitgenössischer Quellen* [*The Early Islam. A Historic-Critical Reconstruction on the Basis of Contemporary Sources*], Berlin, 2007, p. 377–414: C. Luxenberg, *Relikte syro-aramäischer Buchstaben in frühen Korankodizes im ḥiǧāzī- und kūfī-Duktus* [*Relics of Syro-Aramaic letters in Early Koran Codices in Ḥiǧāzī and Kūfī Style*]. A previous example was provided in a prior anthology, ed. by Karl-Heinz Ohlig / Gerd-R. Puin: *Die dunklen Anfänge. Neue Forschungen zur Ent-*

These are the essential points of the working method that has resulted from the present philological analysis of the Koranic text inasmuch as it has involved an analysis of individual words and expressions. Added to this are problems of a syntactical nature which have cropped up in the course of the textual analysis and which have been discussed in detail, case by case. The examples that follow in the main part of this study may be seen as putting this method to the test.

But beforehand it seems necessary to introduce non-Arabists to the problem of Koranic *readings*. This set of problems is connected in the first place with the virtually *stenographic* character of the early Arabic script, which for this reason is also called *defective script*. This can per-

---

stehung und frühen Geschichte des Islam [*The Obscure Beginnings. New Researches on the Rise and the Early History of Islam*], Berlin, 2005, 2006, 2007, p. 124–147, C. Luxenberg: *Neudeutung der arabischen Inschrift im Felsendom zu Jerusalem* [*New Interpretation of the Arabic Inscription within the Dome of the Rock in Jerusalem*]. In this contribution the author has shown that the Arabic letter لـ /L in the word لبدا (traditional reading *libadan*) in Sura 72:19 is a mistranscription of the Syriac letter ܥ / *ʿayn* that the copyist has confused with the quite similar Syriac letter ܠ /L. No wonder that the Koran commentators in East and West were perplexed in the face of this riddle. So Bell translates (II 611 f.) this verse (وانه لما قام عبد اللــه يدعوه كادوا يكونون عليه لبدا) following the Arab commentators, as follows: "And that, when a servant of Allah stood calling upon Him, they were upon him almost in swarms [note 3: The meaning is uncertain. The "servant of Allah" is usually taken to be Muhammad, and "they" to refer to *jinn*, which is possible if angels now speak].
However, to solve this puzzle we just need to restore the original Syriac spelling ܥܒܕܐ that leads to the Arabic reading عبدا / *ʿibādan* (*servants of God*) instead of the meaningless لبدا / *libadan* (allegedly "*in swarms*"). The philological discussion with regard to the context of the verses 18–20 had as result the following understanding:
18. and that the *worship* belongs (only) to God; so along with God you shall not invoke any one; 19. and that, when the *servant of God* (i.e. Jesus, Son of Mary – cf. Sura 19:30, where the child Jesus, immediately after his birth, says about himself: اني عبد اللــه "*I am the servant of God!*") had *risen* (from the dead) going on to invoke Him, they (i.e. the people) almost would have worshiped him (as God); 20. he *said* (NB – not *say*): I invoke indeed my Lord and do not associate with Him any one! (Cf. Sura 5:117).

haps be best explained by the following outline of the chronological origins of the Arabic script.

4. THE ARABIC SCRIPT

Except for a few pre-Islamic 4th–6th century A.D. inscriptions stemming from northern Ḥiǧāz and Syria,[19] the Koran is considered to be the first book ever written in Arabic script. The early form of the Arabic letters and the type of ligatures employed suggest that the Syro-Aramaic cursive script served as a model for the Arabic script.[20]

Both scripts have the following in common with the earlier Aramaic (and Hebrew) script: the writing runs from right to left; in principle the letters designate the consonants with only two letters serving to reproduce the semi-long and long vowels *w*/*ū* و and *y*/*ī* ي as so-called *matres lectionis*.

Later on, the *alif* / ا, which in Aramaic only serves in certain cases as a long *ā*, mainly when final, but occasionally also as a short *a*, was introduced by the Arabs as a third *mater lectionis* for a long *ā*, in general and also in context.

To the extent that this writing reform was also carried out in the text of the Koran,[21] the consequences for certain readings were inevitable.[22] An initial marking of the short vowels *a*, *u* and *i* by points, likewise modeled upon the earlier Syro-Aramaic vocalization systems – according to which the more lightly pronounced vowel (*a*) is indicated by a point

19 Cf. Adolf Grohmann, *Arabische Paläographie* [*Arabic Paleography*], vol. I (Vienna, 1967), vol. II (Vienna, 1971) 16 f., and Nāǧī Zayn ad-Dīn, مصور الخط العربي (*Muṣawwar al-ḫaṭṭ al-ʿarabī* [*Illustrated Presentation of the Arabic Script*]) (Baghdad, 1968) 3 f.

20 As to this still discussed thesis see John F. Healy, *The Early History of the Syriac Script. A Reassessment.* In: *Journal of Semitic Studies* XLV/1 *Spring 2000*, p. 55-67. The question whether the Arabic script is of Syriac *or* Nabatean origin (p. 64 f.) – or a combination of both – is ultimately of minor relevancy, since a next study will prove that the prototype of the Koran, as mentioned above, was originally written in *Garshuni* (or *Katshuni*), i.e. Arabic with Syriac letters.

21 According to R. Blachère the exact time at which this writing reform took place cannot be established (*Introduction au Coran*, 1st edition, 93 f.).

22 The examination of single words will show that the incorrect insertion of the *alif* ا (for long *ā*) has on occasion resulted in a distortion of the meaning.

above and the more darkly pronounced vowel (*e*/*i*) by a point below the consonant, to which was added in Arabic a middle point to mark the *u* – is said to have been introduced as the first reading aid under ʿAbd al-Malik ibn Marwān (685–705).[23]

The real problem in the early Arabic script, however, was in the consonants, only six of which are clearly distinguishable by their form, whereas the remaining 22, due to their formal similarities (usually in pairs), were only distinguishable from each other by the context. This deficiency was only gradually removed by the addition of so-called *diacritical dots*. The letters to be differentiated by points together with their variants depending on their position at the beginning, in the middle or at the end of a word, connected or unconnected (and accompanied by their Latin transcription), appear as follows (whereby it should be noted that six letters are connected with the preceding letters on the right, but not with the letters following them on the left):

ṯ ثثث ث / *t* تتت ت / *b* ببب ب
ḫ خخخ خ / *ḥ* ححح ح / *ǧ* ججج ج
ḏ ـذ ذ / *d* ـد د
z ـز ز / *r* ـر ر
š شـــشـــش ش / *s* ســـســـس س
ḍ ضضض ض / *ṣ* صصص ص
ẓ ظظظ ظ / *ṭ* ططط ط
ġ غغغ غ / ʿ(ʿ*a*/ ʿ*u*/ ʿ*i*) ععع ع
q ققق ق / *f* ففف ف
(final) *ā* ـى ى / *ī* / *y* ييي ي / *n* ننن ن

By taking into account the last letter as a final *ā* as opposed to the variant *ī* and if one imagines that all of the diacritical points above and below the letters are non-existent, we would even have 23 varieties that could occasion misreadings. Added to this are the possibilities of mixing up the optically similar groups of letters د /*d*, ذ / *ḏ*, and ر /*r*, ز / *z* as well as of confusing those of the latter group with the و /*w* / *ū*, further,

23 R. Blachère, *Introduction au Coran* 78 ff.

of confusing the phonetically proximate phonemes هـ / *h* and حـ / *ḥ* and mistaking the guttural عـ / *ʿa* / *ʿu* / *ʿi* for the stop (*hamza*) ء / *ʾa* / *ʾu* / *ʾi* that was introduced later on as a special symbol.

Occasionally the voiceless س / *s* has been mistaken for the corresponding emphatic sound ص / *ṣ*, something which, though trivial when considered in purely phonetic terms, is nonetheless significant etymologically and semantically. In individual cases, a confusion has also occurred between the final ه /-*h* as the personal suffix of the third person masculine and the same special symbol accompanied by two dots ة /-*t* used to mark the feminine ending (a^{tun}), as well as between the connected final ن /*n*, the connected ـى / *y* with a final *a* and even the connected final ـر /*r*. In one case, the three initial peaks in the voiceless ـسـ /*s* were even taken to be the carriers of three different letters and were – regrettably for the context – provided with three different diacritical points (e.g., ـسـ /*s* = نبتـ /*n-b-t*).[24]

In comparing the letters that are distinguishable by means of diacritical points with those that are unambiguous due to their basic form – these are the letters:

ا ـا (as *ā* or as the so-called *hamza* bearer أ أ إ *ʾa* / *ʾu*/ *ʾi*)
ك ككك ك / *k*, ل للل ل / *l*
م ممم م / *m*, ه ههه ه / *h*, و ـو / *w* or *ū*

– one would have, considered purely in mathematical terms, a ratio even worse than 22 to 6 if one takes into account further sources of error, the extent of which can not yet be entirely assessed.

Compared to the Aramaic / Hebrew and the Syro-Aramaic alphabet, whose letters are unambiguous (except for the ܕ / *d* and ܪ / *r*, which because of their formal similarity are distinguished from each other by a point below or above the letter, which may in turn have served as a model for the subsequently introduced and further developed punctuation system of the Arabic script), the early Arabic script was thus a kind

24 On the transcription of Aramaic loan words, see Siegmund Fraenkel, *Die aramäischen Fremdwörter im Arabischen* [*The Foreign Words of Aramaic Origin in Arabic*] (Leiden, 1886; rpt., Hildesheim, New York, 1982) xvii ff.

of shorthand that may have served the initiates as a mnemonic aid. More, it would seem, was also not required at the beginning, since reliable *lectors* or *readers* (قراء / *qurrā*ʾ) were said to have heard the proclamation of the Koran directly from the Prophet and learned it by heart.

5. The Oral Tradition

According to Islamic tradition, the Koran was handed down by an unbroken chain of *lectors*, in part by notable contemporaries of the Prophet, such as Ibn ʿAbbās (d. at 73 in 692 A.D.) and early authorities, such as Anas Ibn Mālik (d. at 91 in 709 A.D.). They are also said to have contributed considerably to the fixing of the Koranic text and to have retained their authority as Koran specialists even long afterwards.[25]

This is contradicted, though, by the report that ʿUṯmān had gotten the "sheets"[26] (of the Koran) from Ḥafṣa, the Prophet's widow, and used them as the basis of his recension. This was the "fixed point backwards from which we must orient ourselves."[27]

In any case the Islamic tradition is unable to provide any date for the final fixing of the reading of the Koran by means of the introduction of the diacritical points, so that one is dependent on the general assertion that this process stretched out over about three hundred years.[28]

Only the long overdue study and collation of the oldest Koran manuscripts can be expected to give us more insight into the development of the Koranic text up to its present-day form. In this regard Koran scholars will always regret that the historical order issued by Caliph ʿUṯmān, conditioned as it was by the political circumstances at the time, has resulted in the irretrievable loss of earlier copies of the Koran.[29]

25 Blachère 102 ff.

26 *Ṭabarī* reports of *one* sheet, however, on which ʿUmar had written down the notes collected by the companions of the Prophet: وكان عمر كتب ذلك في صحيفة واحدة (cf. *Ṭabarī* I 26 f.).

27 Nöldeke-Schwally, *Geschichte des Qorāns* [*History of the Koran*] II 21.

28 Blachère 71.

29 *Ṭabarī* I 27 f.

6. The Arabic Exegesis of the Koran

In the history of Koran exegesis there has been no lack of attempts to provide ever new interpretations of the irregular and occasionally rhythmical rhyming prose of the Koran text. In his *Geschichte des Qorāns* [*History of the Koran*] cited at the beginning, Theodor Nöldeke gives an overview both of the creators of the Arabic exegesis, with Ibn ʿAbbās[30] (cousin of the Prophet, d. 68 H./687 A.D.) and his disciples, and of the extant Arabic commentaries of Ibn Isḥāq (d. 151/786) and Wāqidī (d. 207/822), of Ibn Hišām (d. 213/828), of Buḫārī (d. 256/870) and of Tirmiḏī (d. 279/829).[31]

Although the Islamic exegesis refers to Ibn ʿAbbās as its earliest authority, he himself appears never to have written a commentary, considering that he was only twelve years old at the death of the Prophet.[32] This seems all the more to be the case since the Prophet himself – according to Islamic tradition – is said to have responded with silence to the questions of his contemporaries on the meaning of particular verses of the Koran. Thus, among other things, it was reported of some who were in disagreement over the reading of a Koran Sura:

> "We thereupon sought out the messenger of God – God bless him and grant him salvation – and met him just as ʿAlī was conversing with him. We said: 'We are in disagreement over a reading.' Whereupon the messenger of God blushed – God bless him and grant him salvation – and spoke: 'Those who have preceded you went to ruin because they were in disagreement with each other.' Then he whispered something to ʿAlī, whereupon the latter spoke to us: 'The messenger of God – God bless him and grant him salvation – commands you to read as you have been instructed'; (the version following this adds): 'Each (reading) is good and right'."[33]

---

30 *GdQ* II 163.

31 *GdQ* II 170 f.

32 Régis Blachère, *Introduction au Coran* (Paris, 1947) 225 f.

33 *Ṭabarī* I 12 f.

In the introduction to his Koran commentary, *Ṭabarī* (224/25–310 H./839–923 A.D.) lists a series of variant statements concerning the confusion of the first readers of the Koran, all of which at bottom agree with each other. Thus, among other statements, he gives the following, which is traceable back to Ubayy:

> "Two men were arguing over a verse of the Koran, whereby each maintained that the Prophet – God bless him and grant him salvation – had taught him to read it so and so. Thereupon they sought out Ubayy in order for him to mediate between them. However, he contradicted both of them. Whereupon they sought out the Prophet together. Ubayy spoke: 'Prophet of God, we are in disagreement over a verse of the Koran and each of us maintains that you taught him to read it so and so.' Whereupon he spoke to one of them: 'Read it out to me,' and this one read it out to him. Whereupon the Prophet said: 'Correct!' Then he asked the other to read it out to him, and this one read it out differently than his friend had read it out. To this one too the Prophet said: 'Correct!' Then he spoke to Ubayy: 'Read it out yourself as well,' and Ubayy read it out, but differently than both. Yet to him too the Prophet said: 'Correct!' Ubayy reported: 'This gave rise to such a doubt in me with regard to the messenger of God – God bless him and grant him salvation – as that of heathens!' And he continued: 'However, because the messenger of God – God bless him and grant him salvation– noticed from my face what was occurring in me, he raised his hand and struck me on the breast and said: 'Pray to God for protection from the accursed Satan!' To this Ubayy said: 'Then I broke into a sweat'."[34]

34 *Ṭabarī* I 18.

7. THE SEVEN READINGS

This evidenced embarrassment on the part of the Prophet, which, as reported, evinced considerable doubts about his mission among some of his contemporaries, is explained in the Islamic tradition by the following sequence:

Gabriel had at first commanded the Prophet to read the Koran in *one reading*, but upon the Prophet's imploring indulgence for his people and Michael's support, Gabriel, in consideration of the variety of Arabic dialects, had granted the Prophet *two*, then according to different reports *three*, *five*, *six* and finally *seven readings*, all of them valid as long as verses dealing (for example) with God's mercy did not end, say, with His meting out divine judgment – and vice versa – that is, as long as a given reading did not result in an obvious contradiction.[35] Finally, at the behest of Caliph ʿUṯmān and for the preservation of dogmatic unity among the Muslims, the controversy over the actual meaning of the disputed *seven readings* was resolved once and for all in favor of *one* reading by means of the fixing of the Koran in writing.[36] *Ṭabarī*, however, seems not in the least to have been concerned that in the establishment of the canonic version of the Koran the lack of any diacritical points or other vowel signs made *one* reading a fiction. By his time (the 10th century A.D.) the consonant text of the Koran already appears to have been fixed by the diacritical points introduced in the meantime (or by the oral interpretation that had prevailed in the meantime).

But when and according to what criteria or according to what tradition these points were introduced, and to what extent the originators disposed of the necessary philological and also, considering the biblical content of the Koran, of the necessary theological competence, for such questions the historical critique of *Ṭabarī*, though he was considered a scholar in his day, do not seem to have been adequate. He begins as a matter of course from the premise that there had been nothing to critici-

35 *Ṭabarī* I 18-26.

36 *Ṭabarī* I 26-29.

ze to that point about the established reading of the Koran and does not allow any other variant readings – at least where the original consonant text is concerned. He does, to be sure, permit divergent readings, but only when vocalic indicators are lacking in the original text and only if the variants in question are supported in the Islamic tradition by a majority or minority of commentators, in which case he usually gives precedence to the majority interpretation.

What exactly, though, is to be understood by what *Ṭabarī* calls the سبعة أحرف (*sabʿat aḥruf*) (*seven letters*), whether by that the consonants are meant, or the vowels, or both at the same time, on this subject *Ṭabarī* says nothing, especially considering the fact that Ubayy does not identify the disputed reading. However, because there are twenty-two consonants in the Arabic alphabet distinguishable by diacritical points (in a given case either with or without points), these can scarcely be meant. On the other hand, if one understands أحرف (*aḥruf*) simply as *bookmarks*, then it would be more plausible to understand them as the missing *vowel signs*. This all the more so since the *Thes.* (I 419), for ܐܬܘ / ܐܬܘܬܐ (*ātū* / *ātūtā*), although it cites حرف (*ḥarf*) under (2) *particula*, lists among other things under (3) *litera alphabeti*, ܐܬܘܬܐ ܕܢܩܫܬܐ (*ātūtā da-nqaštā*) (= *accentuation mark*) *vocalis* (BHGr. 351v).

Though one could argue against this that this late piece of evidence from the Syriac grammar of Bar Hebraeus[37] (1225/6–1286), likely modeled on the Arabic grammar of *Zamaḫšarī* (1075–1144), is poorly suited to explain حرف (*ḥarf*) in the sense of *vowel sign*, it is still permitted to see in the number *seven* a reference to the *seven vowels* of the Eastern Syrians mentioned by Jacob of Edessa (c. 640–708) in his Syriac grammar ܬܘܪܨ ܡܡܠܠܐ ܢܗܪܝܐ (*turrāṣ mamllā nahrāyā*) (*The Rectification of the Mesopotamian Language*).[38]

These seven vowels were collected by Jacob of Edessa in the model sentence ܒܢܝܚܘ ܬܗܝܢ ܐܘܪܗܝ ܐܡܢ [39] (*b-nīḥū teḥēn Ōrhāy emman*) =

37 Cf. Baumstark, *Geschichte der syrischen Literatur* [*History of Syrian Literature*] (Bonn, 1922) 317.

38 Baumstark 254.

39 *Mannā* 13.

(*ī* / *ū* / *e* / *ē* / *ō* / *ā* / *a*) (*"May you rest in peace, Edessa, our Mother!"*).[40]

Insofar as *Ṭabarī* also mentions the variant reading خمسة أحرف (*ẖamsat aḥruf*) (*five letters*), a corresponding allusion may thereby be given to the five Greek vowels introduced by the Western Syrians.[41] This would be important, at least in terms of Koranic pronunciation, to answer the question as to whether it was not arbitrary that the post-Koranic Classical Arabic system of vowels was fixed at the three basic vowels *a*, *u*, *i* (for short and long).

In terms of comparison, the at least five vowels of the modern-day Arabic dialects of the Near East in the former Aramaic language area provide a better lead than the uncertain pronunciation of the so-called Old Arabic poetry, from which, moreover, for whatever reason, the Koran distances itself (Sura 26:224; 36:69; 69:41). In this connection, Theodor Nöldeke also remarks:

> "We don't even have the right to assume that in Proto-Semitic there were always only three dynamically distinct vowels or vocal spheres."[42]

Final ی *(yā') as a Marker for final ē*

In any case, the Arabic tradition documents the existence of the vowel *e* to the extent that it designates by the term إمالة (*imāla*) the modification of *ā* to *ē* as a peculiarity of the Arabic dialect of Mecca. However, from

---

40 I.e. "*our capital*" or the "*city in* which *we grew up*" (cf. *Thes.* I 222).

41 Cf. Baumstark, *GSL* 255. On the vowel system of the Eastern and Western Syrians, see also Carl Brockelmann, *Syrische Grammatik* [*Syriac Grammar*] (Leipzig, 1960) 9, as well as Theodor Nöldeke, *Kurzgefasste syrische Grammatik* [*Compendious Syriac Grammar*], 2nd edition, Leipzig, 1898 (reprint, Darmstadt, 1977) 7 f. On the five vowels in Lihyanite, see A. J. Drewes, *The Phonemes of Lihyanite*, in: *Mélanges linguistiques offerts à Maxime Rodinson* (Supplément 12 aux comptes rendus du groupe linguistique d'études chamito-sémitiques), (offprint, Paris, n.d.) 165 ff.

42 Theodor Nöldeke, *Beiträge zur semitischen Sprachwissenschaft* [*Essays on Semitic Linguistics*], Strasbourg, 1904, 33.

this one can make conclusions about the pronunciation not only of Arabic, but especially of Aramaic loanwords. For example, keeping just to proper names, whose pronunciation is taken to be certain, the transliterated name ميكيل (= *Michael*), which faithfully reproduces the Syro-Aramaic written form ܡܝܟܝܠ,[43] should not be pronounced ميكال / *Mīkāl*,[44] as it is vocalized in the modern Cairo edition of the Koran (Sura 2:98), but *Mīḵāēl* according to the Syro-Aramaic pronunciation. The same applies for the name جبريل, which should not be pronounced *Ǧibrīl*, as the Cairo edition reads today (Sura 2:97, 98 and 66:4), but as a transliteration of the Syro-Aramaic ܓܒܪܝܠ (with the more common spelling ܓܒܪܐܝܠ) *Gabriēl*.

Of the Arabic expressions, one can mention, for example, بلى, which the modern Koran reads in twenty-two passages as *balā*, although the pronunciation *balē* (or *bále* – with the accent on the first syllable) is still attested today, among other places, in the Arabic dialects of the Mesopotamian region and in Bedouin dialects. The *Lisān* (XIV 88b) even refers explicitly to the fact that the final ى in بلى, like أنّى (*annē*) and متى (*matē*), can be pronounced with an *imāla* (*balē*).

In his chapter entitled *"Die wichtigsten orthographischen Eigentümlichkeiten des othmanischen Textes"* [*The Most Important Orthographical Peculiarities of the Othmani Text*] (*GdQ* III 26 ff.), Nöldeke goes into more detail on this phenomenon. According to Nöldeke, the use of the final ى cannot be explained (in these cases) on the basis of etymology. On that basis, one can instead deduce a particular pronunciation of the vowel. Words like أنّى were not pronounced with a pure *ā*, but with a "*tendency towards yāʾ* (= *ē*)" (*imāla naḥwa l-yā*), and thus as a long or short *e*. This explanation is supported not only by the orthography, but also by the rhyme.[45]

---

43 Cf. *Thes.* II 2088, which gives this written form in addition to the more common ܡܝܟܐܝܠ. On the other hand, with the pronunciation remaining the same, the variant given in Nöldeke ميكال (see the following note) corresponds to the Hebrew spelling מיכאל.

44 Cf. Nöldeke, *GdQ* III 17.

45 *Ibid.* 37.

Also belonging here among the Koranic proper names is موسى , which the Cairo edition reads as *Mūsā*, whereas according to the Syro-Aramaic form ܡܘܫܐ (in Hebrew משה) *Mōšē* (in Western Syriac *Mūšē*) would be the pronunciation.

On the Spelling of عيسى (*ʿĪsā*)

On the other hand, it is doubtful whether one can explain the name عيسى (read in the Cairo edition as *ʿĪsā*) on the basis of an assimilation to موسى *Mūsā*, as S. Fraenkel has done (*WZKM* IV 335 ff.), even though Horovitz backs this view by remarking "how fond indeed the Koran is elsewhere of name pairs and of the assimilation of one name to another."[46] In other words, although for موسى the pronunciation *Mōšē* is attested, for عيسى the pronunciation *ʿĪšē* / *ʿĪsē* is not. Though it is possible in this case that this is based on the Eastern Syrian name *ʾĪšōʿ* (for Jesus), it is scarcely imaginable, as Horovitz says (*loc. cit.*), that "*its final* ʿ[ayn] … *has shifted its position.*"

Arguing against both this thesis and Landauer's thesis, mentioned by Horovitz (in Nöldeke *ZDMG* XLI 720, note 2), of an assimilation to Esau, is the final *ō* in ܝܫܘܥ / *ʾĪšōʿ* (whose final ʿ / ܥ is usually not pronounced by the Eastern Syrians) and the final *ū* in ܥܝܣܘ / *ʿĪsū* (or the final *aw* in Hebrew עשו *ʿEsaw*). Meanwhile, what comes closest to the spelling عيسى orthographically is the Biblical name ܐܝܫܝ (in Hebrew ישי / אישי), *ʾĪšay* (David's father / Jes. Sir. 45:25; Is. 11:1,10).

Here one must bear in mind that among the Eastern Syrians the initial ʿ / ܥ is frequently weakened and produced exactly like the *ʾi* with an initial glottal stop, while the final ʿ / ܥ totally disappears. This pronunciation is to this extent identical with that of the Mandaeans, who use a ʿ/ ע to reproduce the initial *ʾi* and leave off the final ʿ/ܥ , as is also attested by Nöldeke in his *Mandäische Grammatik* [*Mandaic Grammar*][47] (§ 55,

---

46 Cf. Josef Horovitz, *Koranische Untersuchungen* [*Koranic Investigations*] (Berlin, Leipzig, 1926) 128.

47 Theodor Nöldeke, *Mandäische Grammatik* [*Mandaic Grammar*], Halle an der Saale, 1875 (reprint Darmstadt, 1964).

p. 56), and precisely in connection with the name עשו / *ʾĪšō* "Jesus" = ܝܫܘܥ / *ʾĪšōʿ*.

This finding is interesting not only because it once again points to the Eastern Syrian region, but also and especially because it raises the question – relevant to the history of religion – as to whether with the name عيسى (= ישי / ܐܝܫܝ = *ʾĪšay*) the Koran has intended the connection between the historical *Jesus* and *Isai*, a genealogical ancestor of his, named in Isaiah 11:1,11 and Luke 3:32, or whether it consciously or unconsciously confused ܝܫܘܥ / *ʾĪšō* (ʿ) with ܐܝܫܝ / *ʾĪšay* or perhaps took them to be dialectal variants of one and the same name.[48]

That in any case the modern Koran reads عيسى = *Īsā* is with certainty the result of post-Koranic phonetics, especially considering the fact that this name does not appear in Old Arabic poetry, as Horovitz (*loc. cit.* 129) remarks. The Koranic spelling does correspond, on the other hand, to the Eastern Syriac orthography and the phonetics of Biblically documented names. This is why عيسى is certainly not to be read *ʿĪsā*, but rather *ʾĪšay*.

Therefore, the fact that, especially in Mandaic, the ʿ / ܥ / ע is used to reproduce the initial plosive ʾ in place of the originally weak initial ܝ / י /*y* (and not simply as Horovitz falsely believes [*loc. cit.*], in citing Nöldeke, "*for the designation of ī*") is important in explaining historically the later introduction by Arabic philologists of the *hamza* (i.e. *glottal stop*) symbol (which is actually an initial عـ / *ʿayn* reduced in size).

In the examples given by Nöldeke (*loc. cit.* §55), the ע / ʿ does replace the initial י /*y*, but what is crucial is that it is supposed to indicate the *glottal stop preceding the vowel,* something which Nöldeke, however, does not especially emphasize. This becomes clear, though, on the basis of examples in which the ע / ʿ also replaces an initial ܐ / א, the articulation of which always starts with a glottal stop; thus Mandaic עית or עת is written for Syro-Aramaic ܐܝܬ (*ʾīṯ*) (*there is*). This is particularly evi-

48 It is well known that among Western Syrians the pronunciation *ō* was used for long *ā* in contrast to the pronunciation *ā* among the Eastern Syrians. As Mingana has already pointed out in *Syriac Influence* 83, the Eastern Syriac pronunciation is to be assumed in the Koran.

dent in the examples cited by Nöldeke in §16 (p. 15) where initial א and ע alternate and have the same function: אמראת and עמראת (*ʾamraṯ*) "*she said*"; אזלאת and עזלאת (*ʾazlaṯ*) "*she went*," etc.

According to this pattern, then, the spelling عيسى is to be realized like Mandaic עישי = אישי / ܐܝܫܝ = إيشي / *Īšay*. Finally, one should not fail to mention the fact that the name ܐܝܫܐ / *ʾĪšā*, presumably created from ܐܝܫܝ / *ʾĪšay* by monophthongizing the final diphthong, is widespread among Eastern Syrians today. The possibility can thus not be excluded that the Koran considered this name, common among the Aramean Christians of its day, to be a variant form more suitable to the Arabic pronunciation than the actual name ܝܫܘܥ / *ʾĪšōᶜ* (*Jesus*), which is realized in the Eastern Syriac dialect as *ʾĪšō* (or *ʾĪšo* with the accent on the first syllable). But even in this case the initial عـ in عيسى is to be understood as the *glottal stop* before the initial *ī*, and hence: عيسى = إيشى / *ʾĪšay* > إيشا / *ʾĪšā*.[49]

Final ا (*alif*) *and Final* ه (*h*) *as Markers for Final ē*

However, the Arabic philologists could no longer know that the vowel *e* / *ē* can be designated not only by a final ى / *y*, but also occasionally by a final ا / *ā*. Such cases can be found, among other places, for example, in sentences in which the verb is in dual or plural, but the corresponding subject, on the face of it and seen from the point of view of Arabic morphology, is singular.

Apparent inconsistencies of this sort can be easily removed, though, when one knows that singular and plural endings in Syro-Aramaic remain for the most part unchanged graphically, whereas phonetically they

---

49 According to this, the monophthongization of the final diphthong *ay* need not necessarily end in *ē* as Nöldeke assumes. The other alternative would be, as in the present case, the substitutive lengthening of the vowel *a* : *ay* > *ā*. We can find another example of this in the name ܣܝܢܝ / *Sīnay* (Hebrew סיני), which became the Arabic سينا / *Sīnā* (in a hypercorrect pronunciation with an unjustified vowel stop سيناء / *Sīnāʾ*). On the basis of this phonetic law one could also explain the original name of Abraham's wife, *Sarai*, which according to Genesis 17:15 was, at God's behest, henceforth to be *Sara*.

are inflected in the masculine from *ā* to *ē*. We encounter such endings, for instance, in Sura 11:24 and 39:29 where in each case the Koran has similes with two opposing examples followed by this question:

هل يستويان مثلا

The modern Koran reads *hal yastawiyān*^{i} *maṯala*^{n} (literally): *"Are the two equal to each other as example?"* It is understandable that the later readers of the Koran could not otherwise interpret the final ا in مثلا (< Syro-Aramaic ܡܬܠܐ / *maṯlā*) than as تمييز (*tamyīz*) (accusative of specification), in accordance with the rules of Arabic grammar first created toward the end of the 8th century. However, if one were instead to read مثلا as a transliteration of the Syro-Aramaic plural ܡܬ̈ܠܐ (*maṯlē*) "*the examples*" (= الأمثال / *al-amṯāl*) (since there is no dual in Syro-Aramaic except for the dual suffix of the two-numbers ܬܪܝܢ / *trēn* [masc.], ܬܪܬܝܢ / *tartēn* / [fem.], and ܡܐܬܝܢ / *māṯēn* / (*two hundred*) and the emphatic ending makes the Arabic definite article ال / *al-* superfluous), the sentence would yield a coherent meaning: "*Are the two examples somehow equal?*" (and not "Are the two equal *as example*?"). According to this, when translated into modern-day Arabic (and taking into account the Koranic dual), the sentence would then read: هل يستويان المثلان (in Classical Arabic: هل يستوي المثلان / *hal yastawī l-maṯalān*).

Besides the fact that the Arabic verb استوى / *istawa* (in the VIIIth verbal stem) is also derived from the Syro-Aramaic verb with the same meaning ܐܫܬܘܝ / *eštwī*, the Koran here combines the Arabic dual in the verb with the Syro-Aramaic plural in the subject. In this passage, مثلا is therefore not to be read as the Arabic singular *maṯala*^{n}, but as the Syro-Aramaic plural ܡܬ̈ܠܐ / *maṯlē* (with an *imāla* to the ى / *y*).

Furthermore, we find a similar final *ē* in the plural of ساجد (*sāǧid*) (< Syro-Aramaic ܣܓܕ / *sāgeḏ*), whose unusual Classical Arabic plural formation سجدا (*suǧǧad*^{an}) (occurring 11 times in the Koran in Sura 2:58, 4:154, 7:161, 12:100, 16:48, 17:107, 19:58, 20:70, 25:64, 32:15, and 48:29) again turns out to be a transliteration of the Syro-Aramaic plural form ܣܓ̈ܕܐ (*sāgḏē*). The Koranic spelling سجدا is thus to be pronounced not *suğğad^an*, but in conformity with the common pronunciation of vernacular Arabic: *sāğdē* (= ساجدين / *sāğidīn* > *sāğdīn*).[50]

Sura 6:146

Another example is provided to us by الحوايا (*al-ḥawāyā*) (Sura 6:146), a reading that is considered uncertain,[51] but whose meaning (*innards*) has been correctly suspected even though the ـحـ in it (whose form in the early Koran manuscripts corresponds initially to the Syro-Aramaic ܓ / *g*) has been misread as an Arabic ـحـ / *ḥ*. As a transliteration of the Syro-Aramaic plural ܓܘܝܐ (*gawwāyē*>*gwāyē*),[52] الحوايا should read – based on the Syro-Aramaic expression – الجوايا / *al-ğawwāyē*.

Here, in accordance with the original Syro-Aramaic pronunciation, one can also assume that the ending (with an *imāla* to the ى / *y*) was probably pronounced *al-ğawwāyē*, especially since this expression is neither traditional in Arabic nor correctly recognized in the Koran itself. On closer examination of the two readings, one discovers first of all that the *Lisān* (XIV 209b), referring to this passage in the Koran and citing al-Farrā᾽ (761–822), explains حوايا (*ḥawāyā*) in the same way as *Ṭabarī* (VIII 75f.), who quotes thirteen authorities for the meaning "*intestine, large intestine.*" What is surprising in this is that under the root جوا (*ğawā*) the *Lisān* (XIV 157b) has exactly the meaning that coincides with the here correct Syro-Aramaic meaning. This is how it explains it: وجوّ

---

50 Some critics, who, in accordance with post-Koranic Classical Arabic grammar, take this plural form as genuinely Arabic, generally overlook the historical-linguistic environment in which the Koranic text came into being. More details to this plural will follow in a next study.

51 Rudi Paret, *Kommentar* [*Commentary*], at the conclusion of his remarks on Sura 6:146: "The interpretation of the expression *ḥawāyā* is uncertain."

52 *Thes.* (I 667) gives under ܓܘܝܐ (*gawwāyā*): ܗܕܡܐ ܒܪܝܐ ܘܓܘܝܐ (*haddāmē barrāyē w-gawwāyē*) *membra externa et interna* (*the external and internal extremities / organs*); and on page 668 under *gwāyā:* (*1*) *id quod intus est, viscera, intestina* (*that which is inside, intestines, inner organs*), (from the Syrian lexicographers): ܓܘܝܐ (*gwāyā*): جوف: بطن. احشاء. داخل ما في الجوف. الباطن و البطن . Pl. ܓܘܝܐ (*gwāyē*) *viscera* (*intestines*), ܟܐܒܐ ܕܓܘܝܐ (*kēḇā dagwāyē*) (*gastric complaint, dysentery*).

كل شيء: بطنه وداخله وهو الجوّة أيضاً (*said of anything, ǧaww or ǧawwa*[t] *means its interior and inside*).

There can be no doubt that the *Lisān*, with the masculine جوّ (*ǧaww*) and the feminine-looking جوة (*ǧawwa*ᵗ), is reproducing nothing more than one and the same Syro-Aramaic masculine form, once in the *status absolutus* or *constructus* ܓܘ (*gaw*), and another time as the phonetic transcription of the *status emphaticus* ܓܘܐ (*gawwā*), whereby in this case the Arabic final ة (*a*ᵗ) is to be pronounced as *ā* insofar as it is taking on the function of a *mater lectionis* in the place of the Syro-Aramaic final ܐ / *ā*. The later Koran readers were no longer aware that this final ة was originally thought of as a final ه / *h* = *ā*(*h*) to mark a *status emphaticus*, as this is also the case in Biblical Aramaic[53] and Jewish Aramaic.[54]

Only after introduction of the post-Koranic Classical Arabic grammar was this final ه / *h* misinterpreted as a feminine ending (ة / *tāʾ marbūṭa*, which is considered a special symbol in the Arabic alphabet) and provided with the two originally lacking dots of the actual ت / *t*, which on the other hand suggests an adaptation of the graphically similar-looking Aramaic (or Hebrew) letters ה and ת as variants for designating the feminine ending of the Hebrew *status absolutus* or *constructus* (see for example גנה *gannā* / גנת *ginnaṯ* or *gannaṯ*[55]).

Carl Brockelmann has already drawn attention to this parallel and to the Koranic spelling of the feminine ending with ت in the *status constructus*, e.g. نعمت الله (instead of نعمة الله *niʿma*ᵗᵘ *l-lāh* "the blessing of God") (cf. Carl Brockelmann, *Arabische Grammatik* [Leipzig, 1960] 81, §66a, note). This becomes even clearer on the example in the Koran of

53 Franz Rosenthal, *A Grammar of Biblical Aramaic* (Wiesbaden, 1963) 8 (5): "אהוי may be used as vowel letters (par. 10). א and ה are used for final *ā* or *ē*, ו for *ū* or *ō*, and י for *ī* and *ē*. Final *ē*, which occurs very rarely, is indicated by ה."

54 *Cf. Michael Sokoloff*, A Dictionary of Jewish Palestinian Aramaic (*Ramat-Gan*, ²1992) 133 a: גנה (*gannā*), *det.* גנתה (*gannᵊtā*).

55 Cf. Wilhelm Gesenius, *Hebräisches und aramäisches Handwörterbuch über das Alte Testament* [*Concise Dictionary of Old Testament Hebrew and Aramaic*] (Berlin, Göttingen, Heidelberg, ¹⁷1959) 145 b.

the alternating feminine ending – at times in ة (actually ه / *h* = *ā*), at other times in ت / *at* – of جنة (*ǧanna*) (*garden, paradise*) and جنت (*ǧannat*), respectively, which the later Arabic readers took to be a plural form and read as جنات (*ǧannāt*). Insofar as it is here a question of *paradise*, the word in Syro-Aramaic is always in the singular, namely in the combination جنت عدن (11 times in the Koran, according to the modern reading: *ǧannāt ʿadn*) = ܓܢܬ ܥܕܢ (*gannaṯ ʿḏen*) (*the Garden of Eden = Paradise*; *Thes.* I 743).

Even in the remaining genitive combinations جنت (*ǧannat*) is always to be understood as singular. On the other hand, determined with the Arabic article *al-* and probably to be pronounced with a pausal ending, الجنة (*al-ǧanna*) is clearly in the singular in 52 passages in the Koran, but understood as plural الجنات (*al-ǧannāt*) in one single passage (Sura 42:22). Perhaps it is as a result of an inconsistently executed orthographic reform and of a misunderstood text that جنت (to be read *ǧannat*) appears correctly in the Koran 18 times in the *status constructus*, whereas جنة *ǧanna(t)* appears in this function at least five times (presumably because the later writers of Arabic could no longer comprehend the real meaning of these variants).[56]

Namely, there is otherwise no way to explain to what extent the sound ه / *h*, which is a component of the Arabic alphabet, can also function both as a final *t*, primarily in designating a feminine ending, and for certain masculine endings in singular and plural. Hence we must assume that originally words ة/s in the Koran that ended in *a*/ه *(a)h* – later spelled with two dots as ة *(a)t* – were as such indeclinable, as the alternating orthography of جنه (*ǧanna*) / جنت (*ǧannat*), لعنه (*laʿna*) / لعنت (*laʿnat*), نعمه (*niʿma*) / نعمت (*niʿmat*) suggests.

This is best illustrated on the example of a well-known Arabic term taken up with the masculine Syro-Aramaic emphatic ending *ā*: الخليفة *al-*

56 See in this regard Régis Blachère, *Introduction au Coran* (Paris, 1947) 154 f., where he speaks, however, laconically about the reading *ǧannāt* in "two or three passages." See further Werner Diem, *Untersuchungen zur frühen Geschichte der arabischen Orthographie* [*Studies on the Early History of Arabic Orthography*]. III. *Endungen und Endschreibungen* [*Endings and Their Spellings*], in Orientalia, vol. 50 (1981) 378, § 195.

ḫalīfa(tu), which in English is correctly translated by *the caliph*. Namely, if one reads the Arabic case ending, e.g. in the nominative *al-ḫalīfatu*, it would be like saying "the caliphette (*female*)" in English. At the same time, خليفة (actually خليفه , without the points over the ـه , or خليفا *ḫalīfā*) is nothing other than the phonetic transcription of the Syro-Aramaic substantivized masculine passive participle *ܚܠܝܦܐ (*ḥlīpā*) (*he who is put in the place of, substitute, deputy, successor*), i.e. a *status emphaticus* with a final *ā*, which is not common in Arabic. Later on, this was misunderstood as a pausal pronunciation of the feminine ending *at* and the word was additionally provided with the Arabic article *al*. The Arabic خ / *ḫ* in خليفه renders mirely the vernecular Eastern Syriac pronunciation of the ح (*ḥ* > *ḫ*).

Furthermore, one encounters similar Syro-Aramaisms in such still commonly used expressions as طاغية / *ṭāġiya(tun)* (< Syro-Aramaic ܛܥܝܐ / *ṭāʿyā* / *misled, led astray*, in Arabic with secondary *ġ*, misunderstood as *"tyrant,"* in addition to the Arabic correct active participle طاغ / *ṭāġ*^{in} [57]), as well as in such analogous formations as علامة / *ʿallāma-(tun)* (*an outstanding scholar, an "authority"*), داهية / *dāhiya(tun)* (*a shrewd, cunning person*), whose apparently feminine ending is explained by the Arab philologists للمبالغة as a mark of *"exaggeration, emphasis*."

This misinterpretation is also given by Carl Brockelmann in his *Arabische Grammatik* [*Arabic Grammar*] (*loc. cit.* 82, § 66c): "The feminine ending … (also) serves as a mark of *emphasis*, e.g. علامة (*ʿallāma*^{tun})'*a know-it-all*' from the adjective علام (*ʿallām*^{un}), § 55a." Brockelmann, however, will surely have been aware that this supposedly feminine ending, pausally pronounced, is nothing other than the reproduction of the Aramaic emphatic ending *ā*, which here has nothing to do

57 The same Aramaic root *ṭʿā* was borrowed twice into Arabic, firstly as the above-mentioned *ṭaġā* with the secondary sound correspondence *ʿayn* / *ġ*, and secondly as the semantically corresponding root *ḍāʿa* with sonorization of the first radical, possibly due to its unaspirated articulation. This latter phenomenon has hitherto been overlooked by scholars dealing with Semitic linguistics and will be treated in more detail in a later publication. The semantic identity of Arabic *ḍāʿa* and Aramaic *ṭʿā* is a strong argument against the interpretation as "*tyrant*."

either with the *feminine* or with an *emphasis*, but which has nevertheless been interpreted by the Arabic grammarians, in ignorance of Syro-Aramaic, as such a marker. The same applies to his concluding remark: "Such forms are sometimes also applied to persons, as in راوية (*rāwiya*^{tun}), '*traditionary*'; خليفة (*ḫalīfa*^{tun}) '*deputy, successor*'."

Also deserving of further attention is the reference to § 55a (*Arabische Grammatik* [*Arabic Grammar*] 68) in which Brockelmann says the following about these "emphasizing forms": "فعّال (*fa*^{cc}*āl*) intensive form of فاعِل (*fā*^{c}*il*) and other verbal adjectives, e.g. كذّاب (*kaḏḏāb*) '*lying*'; this form can derive tradesman names from *nomina*, e.g. خبّاز (*ḫabbāz*) '*baker*' from خبز (*ḫubz*) 'bread'." Brockelmann himself shows that he was well aware that these forms were Syro-Aramaisms in his *Syrische Grammatik* [*Syriac Grammar*] 70, § 131, where he explains *nominal stem formations* of the type *qaṭṭāl* as intensive adjectives and vocational names for the most part from *pe*^{c}*al.*[58]

In the canonical version of the Koran, once كاذبة (*kāḏiba*^{tun}) occurs (Sura 56:2) and another time كذبة (*kāḏiba*^{tin}) (Sura 96:16), each read with a hypercorrect feminine and case ending. In Syro-Aramaic, however, both passages are to be read, as above, as ܟܕܒܐ / *kaddāḇā*. But what is thus meant is not Arabic كذّاب / *kaḏḏāb* and كاذب / *kāḏib*, respectively, in the sense of "*liar*," but Syro-Aramaic in the modern Arabic understanding of مكذّب / *mukaḏḏib* "*denier*."

In individual instances the final ه /-*h* was presumably also used to designate the Syro-Aramaic plural ending *ē*, as is made clear, for example, in the orthography of سفره (Sura 80:15) = ܣܦܪ̈ܐ (*sāp̄rē*) (*writer*), but especially in the plural form of *angel* / ملئكه / = ܡܠܐܟ̈ܐ / *malāḵē* (68 times in the Koran). One can see from both cases that the final ه / *h* is not meant as a final ة / *t* but as a final *ē*. Since both endings are borrowed from Syro-Aramaic, the reading with the case vowel (سفرة / *safara*^{tin} or الملئكة / *al-malā*^{ʾ}*ika*$^{tu / ti / ta}$) can hardly be based on a certain Arabic tra-

58 Cf. also in this regard Th. Nöldeke in his *Syrische Grammatik* [*Syriac Grammar*] 70, § 115, where he says concerning these forms as *nomina agentis* that they belong to verbs of the simple stem *peal* and of the doubling stem *pael*, e.g. ܟܕܒܐ (*kaddāḇā*) (> كذّاب / *kaḏḏāb*^{un}).

dition, whereas the Syro-Aramaic expression is attested in both cases, in the latter even, among other places, in the modern Arabic of the Near East (مليكه / *malāykē*).

Excursus: On the Morphology of ملائكة / ملايكه (*malāʾika* = *malāykē*)

This word, which has been identified in Western Koranic research as a foreign word,[59] is most likely borrowed from Aramaic. The grammatical form of the singular already makes this clear: Arabic *malāk* is namely nothing other than the pausal form of the Syro-Aramaic substantivized passive participle *malāḵā*. Here, the lengthening of the central *ā* results, after the dropping of the original central *hamza* (**mala'aḵ*), from the combination of the two consecutive short *a*. If this root were originally Arabic, the passive participial form of the IVth Arabic verbal stem would have to be *mul'ak* and not *mal'ak* (like *mursal* and not *marsal*).

Meanwhile, the final *h* in the Koranic plural form *malāykē* orthographically reproduces the Aramaic plural ending *ē*. This Aramaic final *h*, which was falsely provided with two diacritical points and misinterpreted as *tā' marbūṭa* by later Arabic philologists, has nothing to do with the final *t* of the corresponding Ethiopic plural form. That this final *h* before a personal suffix (as in مليكته / ملئكته / *malāykatuhu* / *malā'ikatuhu*, Sura 2:98,285; 4:136; 33:43,56) (or in *status constructus*) is nevertheless realized as *t*, occurs by analogy to the feminine ending, from which the Arabic linguistic consciousness no longer differentiates the phonetically homonymous Aramaic plural ending (nor likewise the masculine Aramaic *status emphaticus*). The *Lisān* (XIII, 134b) gives us an example of the latter case with the masculine name طلحه / *Ṭalḥā*, whose final *h* is transformed into a *t* (of the "feminine") before a personal suffix, so that

59 Cf. A. Jeffery, *The Foreign Vocabulary*, 269f. See further: W. Wright, *A Grammar of the Arabic Language*, Third Edition, Vol. I, Beirut 1974, 230 (under 2); Jacob Barth, *Die Nominalbildung in den semitischen Sprachen* [*Noun Formation in the Semitic Languages*], Second Edition, Leipzig 1894 (Reprint Hildesheim 1967), 483 (among others).

one has: هذا طلحتنا / *hāḏā Ṭalḥatunā, this is our Ṭalḥa(t).* Until now, however, no one in Arabistics or Semitistics has investigated how the central *y* lacking in the Syro-Aramaic plural form *malāḵē* and inserted in the Arabic *malāykē* comes into being.

The most plausible explanation seems to be the following: According to the more recent Arabic feel for language, the unaltered adoption of the Syro-Aramaic plural form ملاكه / *malākē* would in Arabic be felt to be the feminine singular of the masculine form ملاك / *malāk*. To avoid this, the Arabic feel for language looked for an analogy in the system of Arabic plural formation and found one in the pattern of the substantivized passive participle *faʿīl*, which forms the plural in Classical Arabic as *faʿāʾil* (but actually as *faʿāyel*).

The *Lisān* (X, 481b f.), which correctly gives the root of *malāk* under لأك / *la'aka*, also confirms this explanation by stating (482a, 2 f): والجمع ملائكة، جمعوه متمّما وزادوا الهاء للتأنيث *"the plural is malāʾika* (actually, however, *malāykē*), *one* (at first) *formed the plural perfectly* (i.e. *correctly*) (namely *malāʾik*)[60] *and then added the h to it as sign of the feminine* (namely *malāykē*)." From this one sees that the Arabic philologists were unable to explain to themselves this Syro-Aramaic final *h*, which marks a masculine plural ending, any other way than as a characteristic feature of the *feminine*, which is out of the question here.

To sum up: If J. Barth (*op. cit.*, 483) characterizes this final *h* in foreign words in Arabic as *compensation*, for which, among others, he cites ملائكة / *malā-ʾika* (*malāykē*), it must be said that it is not this final *h*, which in current Arabic usage is correctly received as an Aramaic plural ending, but the inserted medial *y* that serves as a *compensatory element* for the clarification of the Arabic plural form.

We thus have a typical mixed form composed of elements (a) of the primary Aramaic, and (b) of the secondary Arabic plural formation.[61]

---

60 The *Lisān* cites actually this plural form under the root ملك / *malak* (X 496a -6) and refers here to a verse of Umayya b. Abī ṣ-Ṣalt.

61 J. Barth comes fairly close to this explanation when he notes in connection with the formation of such double plurals arising from mixed forms in Arabic and Ethiopic (*loc. cit.* 483): "Both languages often form new plurals on the basis of broken plurals. The process of these formations is then once again subject to the

This is only one example for many critics who uncritically, in terms of philology and history of language, take traditional erroneous notions as their starting point. Further explanations relating to Koranic orthography and morphology follow elsewhere.

To be added, then, to the final ه / *h* as a rendering of the Aramaic emphatic ending *ā* is the final ا / *ā* as the regular emphatic ending in Syro-Aramaic. This final ا / *-ā*, which in Arabic, in contrast to the earlier Aramaic, marks the indetermination of nouns, adjectives and participles exclusively in the accusative (but remarkably does not appear on a ة / *-t* or ت / *-t* suffix), has in many passages of the Koran been interpreted as accusative under its various grammatical aspects (such as حال / *ḥāl* "*accusative of condition*," تمييز / *tamyīz* "*accusative of specification*," etc.) in terms of the later Arabic grammar.[62] But in some Koran passages this

---

formal rules of the normal plural formation. The individual form belongs in the Arab(ic) and Eth(iopic) grammar."

One must add here that in the case of ملائكة / *malāʾika* (= *malāykē*) one ought not to take as one's starting point the secondary Arabic broken plural, but instead the regular Syro-Aramaic plural. There thus subsequently arose, for the reasons presented, out of an originally regular external Syro-Aramaic plural an internal (broken) Arabic plural, which resulted in a new type of Arabic plural. The further extent to which Aramaic has contributed to the variety of Arabic plural formation will be examined in a forthcoming essay. Moreover, on this example the deficit of a linguistic-historical grammar of Classical Arabic becomes apparent.

62 Typical in this respect is the account mentioned by K. Vollers (*Volkssprache und Schriftsprache* [*Vernacular and Written Language*] 183) concerning ʿĪsā b. ʿOmar (d. 149 H.), who as a "reformer" of the grammar (of *Naḥū*) was said to have had a conspicuous preference for the accusative. This funny remark is in reality significant, for it confirms to a certain extent the suspicion that the Arabic "accusative ending" in ا / *ā* as a sign of indetermination is in the end nothing other than a substratum of the Syro-Aramaic emphatic ending, which at the origins of written Arabic had already lost its originally determining function. As a sign of indetermination it therefore presented itself to the early Arab grammarians as an alternative to the determining Arabic particle الـ / *al-*, which in turn confirms the hypothesis that originally it was probably Christian Arabs of Syria and Mesopotamia who, as the originators of written Arabic, imported elements of their Syro-Aramaic cultural language into the so-called Classical Arabic.

final ا / *ā* occurs in such disharmony to the Arabic syntax that as an Arabist one is compelled to view it as faulty Arabic. Theodor Nöldeke, for example, expresses his surprise as follows in the second part of his chapter, "*Zur Sprache des Korāns* – II. *Stilistische und syntaktische Eigentümlichkeiten der Sprache des Korāns* [*On the Language of the Koran* – II. *Stylistic and Syntactic Peculiarities of the Language of the Koran*]" in his *Neue Beiträge zur semitischen Sprachwissenschaft* [*New Essays on Semitic Linguistics*] (Strasbourg, 1910), page 11:

> إنّني هديني ربّي الى صراط مستقيم ديناً قيماً ملّة ابرهيم حنيفاً وما كان من المشركين in Sura 6:162 is quite rough, since following the construction of هدى with الى is one with the accusative [note 2: دينا and ملة are not, as one might think, accusatives of state or condition]; then comes an accusative of state and a clause of state to the effect that he (Abraham) was a righteous (man), no idolater.

Here Nöldeke is right to draw attention to the fact that in the case of دينا (*dīna*^{n}) and ملة (*milla*^{ta}) it is not a question, as some have thought, of an *accusative of state*. In other words, his point is that the accusative ending here (instead of the expected genitive) is in obvious contradiction to the rules of Classical Arabic grammar. Nöldeke, however, surely must have been able to recognize that what we have here is not incorrect Arabic, but correct Syro-Aramaic. Namely, if one compares the Koranic spelling with the Syro-Aramaic equivalents (دينا قيما = ܕܝܢܐ ܩܝܡܐ / *dīnā qayyāmā* = *permanent, constant* – in this context: *straight precept* or *rule*),[63] it becomes clear that here the Arabic ending is a faithful render-

63 *Thes.* II 3532: ܩܝܡ (*qayyām*), ܩܝܡܐ (*qayyāmā*) (1) *permanens, durans*. Now one could dispute the etymology of Arabic دين / *dīn* < Syro-Aramaic ܕܝܢܐ / *dīnā*. C. Brockelmann (*Lexicon Syriacum*) lists the word under two forms with the following information: (a) (145a ult. f.): " ܕܝܢܐ (*dīnā*) (AR [dialectis aramaeis commune], ut h. דין ex acc. *dēnu*, *dīnu* = ar. دَين , äth. *dain*, min. qat. דין , Jens., acc. e sum. *di?* Haupt ZDMG **63** 506, Zimm 23); (b) (151b 5): ܕܐܝܢ, ܕܝܢ (pers. *daena*, *dīn* ex elam. *dēn* e bab. *dēnu* Jens in Horn Grundr p. 133 n 2) religio...." Yet the Persian form *daena* with the diphthong *ae*, as preserved in Arabic *dayn* (*loan, debt*, the reimbursing of which is an *obligation*, *right and*

ing of the Syro-Aramaic *status emphaticus*, which is the reason this ending as such cannot be inflected. Therefore, in this respect it is not to be understood as a sign of the accusative, but rather the word here is grammatically in the genitive, which is why the next word, standing in apposition to it, ملة (*milla*), must likewise be in the genitive and not, as the modern Koran reads, in the accusative (*milla*^{ta}). Yet here too the case vowel is actually superfluous since ملة (*milla*), as a loanword from Syro-Aramaic ܡܠܬܐ (*mell*ṯ*ā*) in the *status constructus*, was in all probability pronounced ملة ابرهيم / *millat Abrāhām* (and not *Ibrāhīm*)[64] – corresponding to the Syro-Aramaic ܡܠܬ ܐܒܪܗܡ / *mellaṯ Abrāhām.*[65]

---

proper), and the Aramaic emphatic ending, points rather to a borrowing from the Semitic. In the Koranic context دينا قيما (*dīnan qayyiman* = *dīnā qayyāmā*) is, in imitation of صراط مستقيم (*ṣirāṭ mustaqīm*), rather to be understood in Arabic in the sense of دين قويم (*qawīm*) or مستقيم (*mustaqīm*) (*straight, proper and lawful conduct*).

64 On the meaning of the originally unpointed letter carrier intimated as a little peak in the Koran (here read as *ī* instead of *ā*), see below p. 72 ff.

65 Under the meanings of the Syro-Aramaic ܡܠܬܐ (*mellṯā*) (whose basic meaning is "*word*") *Mannā*, 400a, cites in Arabic under (3): شريعة . ميثاق . عهد (*šarīʿa, mīṯāq, ʿahd*) (*law, alliance, covenant*). Thus, what must be meant is the *covenant* that, according to Gen. 17:2 ff., God (El Schaddai) entered into with Abraham, but actually the *word* that He gave him. Whence the meaning *word* = *covenant.* As a Syro-Aramaic loanword ملة (*milla*) was not correctly understood in Arabic and was interpreted as everything from "*faith*" and "*religious sect*" to "*nation.*" *Mannā*, 142b, also explains ܕܝܢܐ (*dīnā*) (2): سنة . شريعة (*sunna, šarīʿa*) (*law, rule, precept*) and (9): دين . مذهب . عقيدة (*dīn, maḏhab, ʿaqīda*) (*religion, confession, belief*) with a synonymous meaning. The latter is late in Arabic (cf. C. Brockelmann, *Lexicon Syriacum,* 145a ult., who refers to Accadian *dēnu, dīnu*). In the *Pšiṭṭā* the expression in Gen. 17:2 is ܩܝܡܐ (*qyāmā*) *"covenant"*. We encounter this term in the Koran in Sura 5:97:

جعل الله الكعبة البيت الحرام قيما للناس

Our Koran translators have understood this expression قيما (< Syro-Aramaic ܩܝܡܐ / *qyāmā*) as follows: (Paret 99): „Gott hat die Kaʿba, das heilige Haus zum Unterhalt (?) [W (literally): Bestand (*qiyām*)] für die Menschen gemacht,…". (Blachère 147): «Allah a institué la Kaaba, Temple Sacré se dressant (?) pour les hommes,…» [note 97: *La nourriture qui s'y trouve.* Text.: et sa nourriture.]. (Bell I 108): 98a. "Allah hath appointed the Kaʿba, the Sacred House, as a standing (institution) for the people,…".

As concerns the attribute حنيفا (*ḥanīfā*), in whose ending the Arabic Koran readers saw an accusative of condition – similarly puzzling to Nöldeke – this again has nothing to do with the Arabic accusative; on the contrary, it is a question here too of the Syro-Aramaic *status emphaticus* ܚܢܦܐ (*ḥanpā*), whose ending in this case is a sign of determination: ܚܢܦܐ (*ḥanpā*) = الحنيف (*al-ḥanīf*) (and not, as in the Arabic reading, حنيفا / *ḥanīfa*^{n}).

On the Meaning of حنيف (*ḥanīf*)

In accordance with the Syro-Aramaic meaning of ܚܢܦܐ (*ḥanpā*)[66] (*heathen*), the expression is to be understood as an epithet for Abraham. As a rendering of ܐܒܪܗܡ ܚܢܦܐ (*Abrāhām ḥanpā*), this could be translated into what today is considered the correct Arabic form, ابرهيم حنيفا , or roughly ابرهيم الحنيف (*Ibrāhīm al-ḥanīf* = *Abraham the heathen*). The fact that in the Koran this expression is regularly in the *Arabic accusative* proves precisely that it had been taken up in its Syro-Aramaic form and become an established epithet for Abraham. But what is meant by this epithet, "*the heathen,*" is that Abraham, who actually was a *heathen*, believed precisely as such in the one God. It is also thanks to this special merit that *heathen* as Abraham's epithet has acquired a positive significance, so that in the later Islam it was interpreted as an attribute of Abraham in the sense of "*being of pure faith.*"

Already the Koran transfers this epithet to the "faith" itself (actually the *rule of conduct*, the *guiding principle*) when it says in Sura 30:30: فاقم وجهك للدين حنيفا "so turn (unswervingly) to the *ḥanīf* faith (actually

With his epithet (institution) Bell has approximately guessed the conjectured sense; with "*standing*," however, he has understood the word *qiyām*^{an} itself according to its meaning in Arabic. For it is only the Syro-Aramaic meaning ܩܝܡܐ (*qyāmā*) "*covenant*" that lends the verse its real intent: "God has made the Kaʿba, the sacred house, as a covenant for the people."

66 *Thes*. I 1322. Grammatically this form is an early passive participle of the first stem *pəʿal* which is still preserved in a number of Syro-Aramaic adjectives and substantives, whereas the Koranic form حنيف / *ḥanīf* accords with the Syro-Aramaic paradigm of the regular formation of passive participles of the same stem.

to the '*heathen*' *rule of conduct* = to the *guiding principle* of Abraham the '*heathen*')." Here too حنيفا (*ḥanīfa*ⁿ) is not an Arabic accusative of condition ("turn ... *as a ḥanīf*"), as it has been misinterpreted, among others by the Koran translators, in accordance with the Arabic idea. What is therefore of importance here in terms of the history of religion is the observation that the Arabicized form الدين الحنيف (*ad-dīn al-ḥanīf*) (actually "*the heathen rule of conduct*") has been reinterpreted positively and has become the epitome of the "*pure faith,*" the "*true religion.*"

Nöldeke had already correctly traced the Arabic حنيف (*ḥanīf*) back to the Syro-Aramaic ܚܢܦܐ (*ḥanpā*) "heathen." Still, in terms of its Koranic usage (*loc. cit.* 30), he says the following:

> "It is difficult to say, however, how the other meanings emerged from this original meaning. One must consider, though, that the naïve Arab heathens had no idea of the nature of other religions and thus could easily have misunderstood and falsely employed such expressions."

But the fact that the Koran consciously links this term with Abraham can be inferred from the stereotypical clause that comes after Abraham's epithet, the "*heathen*" (حنيفا) (Suras 2:135; 3:67,95; 6:161 and 16:120, 123): وما كان من المشركين. Now if this appositive is translated literally, "<u>and</u> he was not one of the idolaters," one has here missed the connection with *ḥanīf*, "*heathen.*" For in reality, this subordinate clause conceals within itself a contradiction to the appositive "*heathen.*" This only becomes clear, however, when one takes an adversative function as the basis for the introductory conjunction و / *wa;* only then is the sentence given its correct meaning. With regard to Abraham, who was a "*heathen,*" this additional clause then says, "he was (as a *heathen*) *nonetheless* not an idolater!" Therefore what is meant is: Abraham was indeed (by birth) a *heathen*, but he was no *idolater*!

The idea that Abraham as a *heathen* already believed in God and was therefore no longer an *idolater* is pre-Koranic and we encounter it in a similar way in Saint Paul. In his Epistle to the Romans (4:9–12) Abraham's faith was already imputed to Abraham *before the circumcision* (hence when he was still a *heathen*). Through this he is said to have become the father of all those who as the *uncircumcised* (and thus as *heathens*) believe.

Koranic Arabic and Koranic Aramaic

As someone thoroughly familiar with Syro-Aramaic, Nöldeke ought surely to have been able to recognize the nature of the Koranic language, had he only not expressed himself as follows, during the controversy over the language of the Koran initiated by Karl Vollers, on the side of the advocates of the *ᶜArabīya* (the classical Arabic language):

> "And thus it remains that the Koran was written in the ᶜArabīja, a language whose area was broad and which naturally exhibited many dialectal dissimilarities. Such are also reflected in the Koranic readings, and such have also been preserved, unchanged or transformed, in modern dialects." (*ibid.* 5)

The fact, however, that in the case of these dissimilarities it is a question not only of dialectal variants of the Arabic language, but in particular of borrowings from the civilized Aramaic language nearby, is evidenced by many further features in the Koran. Precisely this final ا /-*ā*, which evoked surprise in Nöldeke, is especially striking. So, for example, in Sura 2:26 and 74:31 it says ماذا اراد الله بهذا مثلا "(But) what does God aim at with this parable." According to the Arabic understanding "parable" is in the accusative of specification demanded by its final ا /-*ā* . Accordingly the verse is then understood: "(But) what does God aim at with that *as* parable."

It should no longer come as a surprise that the Koran frequently combines grammatical forms of Arabic and Syro-Aramaic, since at the time the Koran originated Syro-Aramaic was the most widespread written language of a civilized people in the Orient, and there was still no Arabic grammar. The extent to which the Koran follows different rules than those of the subsequent grammar of so-called Classical Arabic is demonstrated by another example in which the number twelve is not followed by a singular – as it would normally be according to the rules of Arabic – but by a plural. For example, it is said in Sura 7:160: وقطعنهم اثنتي عشرة اسباطا (*wa-qaṭṭa ʿnāhum ʾi<u>t</u>nata<u>y</u> ʿašrata ʾasbāṭan*) "And we divided them into twelve *<u>tribes</u>*", instead of the Arabic اثني عشر سبطا (*ʾi<u>t</u>na<u>y</u> ʿaša<u>r</u>a sib<u>ṭ</u>an*) twelve *<u>tribe</u>*. This, too, would be characterized as false according to the rules of Arabic, but as fully correct according to the rules of Syro-Aramaic.[67]

Moreover, this raises the question as to whether in this case the ا /-*an* ending, explained as a kind of *accusative of specification* according to the rules of Arabic, does not come instead from a Syro-Aramaic plural ending in *ē*. This, because the Arabic rule, according to which the nouns following numbers between eleven and ninety-nine must be (a) in the *singular* and (b) in the *accusative*, is not exactly logical. A more logical explanation would be that such a phenomenon interpreted formally in Arabic as a *singular* with an *accusative ending* was originally a Syro-Aramaic *plural ending*. This, in turn, would mean that the Arabic explanation is *secondary* and not at all *classical*. A similar case would be the *singular* prescribed in Arabic after the number one hundred, which is contradicted by the plural following the number three hundred in Sura 18:25 (ثلث مائة سنين "three hundred <u>years</u>"), although an attempt has been made with the current Koran reading *<u>t</u>alā<u>t</u>a miʾat<u>in</u> sinīna* to uncouple the number three hundred from "*years*" and to suggest the reading "*in years*" in order to cover up this Arabic *irregularity*, which in reality is perfectly correct Syro-Aramaic.

The same is true for the phoneme *ō*, which is lacking in Classical Arabic, but documented in the Koran. On this Nöldeke remarks:

> "This spelling of the *ā* with ى is opposed to another, limited to a few specific words, with و . Since the grammarians expressly remark that the pronunciation of the Ḥiğāz (Hijaz) in these words is broader (تفخيم ، تغليظ) and tends toward the و (*imāla naḥw al-wāw*), we have to assume that the vowel here was pronounced

67 See Th. Nöldeke, *Kurzgefasste syrische Grammatik* [*Compendious Syriac Grammar*], with an appendix prepared by Anton Schall (Darmstadt, 1977), 95, §§ 151, 152.

[long] *å* or *ō*. These words are: صلوة ، زكوة [Footnote 2: In both these words the vowel is probably influenced by the vowel of the Aramaic original forms צלותא זכותא (Schwally); cf. Nöldeke, *Neue Beiträge* (*New Essays*) 25, 29]; مشكوة ، حيوة، Sura 24:35 [Footnote 3: Ethiopic *maskōt* (actually *maškōt* is more likely), Nöldeke, *Neue Beiträge* (*New Essays*) 51]; نجوة Sura 40:44 and منوة Sura 53:20 [Footnote 4: Also Nabatean מנותו (Schwally)], as well as الربوا [Footnote 5: Sura 30:38 has transmitted many a ربًا (the only passage with nunation, cf. p. 38 above)]. Here the spelling with و applies only if the word is without a suffix, whereas with the addition of a suffix the vowel is indicated by ا or is written defectively."[68]

As cited here by Nöldeke, these words, in which the و according to Arabic tradition was probably originally pronounced as *ō*, do not exhaust the other examples that occur in the Koran. To be mentioned would be formations based on the Syro-Aramaic type *pāʿōlā*, which Nöldeke himself defines as follows in his *Syriac grammar* (*op. cit.*, 68, § 107):

"The *nomina agentis* can be formed with ܘ on the basis of the 2nd root from any active participle of the simple verbal stem (Peal): ܩܛܘܠܐ (*qāṭōlā*) "murderer," ܩܝܘܡܐ (*qāyōmā*), ܓܠܘܝܐ (*gālōyā*), etc."

Accordingly, سجود , which in four passages is intended as an infinitive (Sura 48:29, 50:40, and 68:42,43), should in two other passages be understood as a rendering of the plural form of the Syro-Aramaic *nomen agentis* ܣܓܘܕܐ (*sāḡōḏē*) (without the emphatic ending) (Sura 2:125: للطائفين و العكفين و الركع السجود and Sura 22:26: للطائفين و القائمين و الركع السجود). The meaning "*those who prostrate themselves*" for السجود is

68 Th. Nöldeke, *GdQ* III 41. On the same subject, see A. Spitaler, "*Die Schreibung des Typus* صلوة *im Koran. Ein Beitrag zur Erklärung der koranischen Orthographie* [*The Writing of the Type* صلوة *in the Koran: A Contribution to the Clarification of Koranic Orthography*]," in the *Wiener Zeitschrift für die Kunde des Morgenlandes* [*Viennese Journal of Oriental Studies*], vol. 56, Festschrift for W. Duda (Vienna, 1960) 212-226.

clear from the context of the two passages. The fact that the *Lisān* (III 204a) gives for the active participle ساجد (*sāǧid*) (= ܣܓܕܐ / *sāg̱dā*) both سجود (*suǧūd*) (= ܣܓܘܕܐ / *sāgōḏē*) and سجّد (*suǧǧad*) (= ܣܓܕܐ / *sāg̱dē*) as plural forms is with certainty traceable to these unrecognized Koranic Syriacisms. These uncommon, arbitrarily vocalized and odd-sounding plural formations have also never been accepted in Arabic usage. The plural form سجّدا (*suǧadda*ⁿ) occurring in eleven passages in the Koran is obviously the transliteration of ܣܓܕܐ (*sāg̱dē*), which again gives us an indication of the pronunciation *ē* for certain ا endings that come from Syro-Aramaic plural forms. By comparison, in eleven other passages the Koran uses the correct and today still common Arabic plural forms, الساجدون (*as-sāǧidūn*) (once) and الساجدين (*as-sāǧidīn*) (ten times).

Another expression corresponding to the ܩܝܘܡܐ (*qāyōmā*) cited above by Nöldeke as an example of the type *pāʿōlā* is القيوم (Sura 2:255, 3:2 and 20:111), vocalized *al-qayyūm* in the modern Koran, but in Syro-Aramaic *qāyōmā* [69] and thus to be read *al-qāyōm* in Arabic.

To these *nomina agentis* Nöldeke (*op. cit.* §107) adds a few substantives such as ܝܪܘܪܐ (*yārōrā*) "*jackal*" and ܦܬܘܪܐ (*pāṯōrā* /*pāṯū-rā*) "*table*." This, in turn, gives us a clue towards clarifying a substantive, heretofore considered a puzzle, which occurs in the Koran in Sura 74:51, قسورة, and which in the modern Koran is read *qaswara*.

---

69 Karl Ahrens, *Christliches im Qoran* [*Christian Elements in the Koran*], *ZDMG* 84, new series, vol. 9 (1930): 44, refers here to Dan. 6:27. In the corresponding passage of the *Pšiṭṭā*, ܩܝܡ / *qayyām*) is in the *status absolutus* and is used verbally, ܩܝܡ ܠܥܠܡܝܢ (*qayyām l-ʿālmīn*): "(*he is*) *existent* = *he exists for ever.*" In the Koran passage in question, القيوم is attributive and corresponds orthographically to the form ܩܝܘܡܐ / *qāyōmā*). Although this expression is usually used as a substantive (in the sense of *head, administrator*), the *Thes.* (II 3532) also refers to the Eastern Syrian lexicographers, who, among other things, cite as its Arabic equivalent قائم ، ثابت (*qāʾim, ṯābit*). Whence the meaning "*he who is living, he who is constant*" (i.e. *he who is constantly living*) for الحي القيوم (*al-ḥayy al-qayyūm* / *al-qāyōm*).

Sura 74:51

In context, the verses 49 to 51 say:

فما لهم عن التذكرة معرضين / كانهم حمر مستنفرة /
فرت من قسورة

In this connection, the disputed word *qaswara* has been understood by our translators as follows:

> (Bell II 619): 50. "What is the matter with them that they from the reminder turn away; 51. As if they were startled asses fleeing from a lion?"

> (Paret 490): 49: "Warum wenden sie [Note: D.h. die Ungläubigen] sich von der Erinnerung [Note: D.h. von der mahnenden Botschaft des Korans] ab, 50: (scheu) wie aufgeschreckte (Wild)-esel, 51: die vor einem mächtigen (Löwen) fliehen?"

> (Blachère 625): 49 "Qu'ont-ils eu à se détourner du Rappel (*tad̲kira*) 50 comme des onagres effarés 51 qui ont fui devant un lion?"

For قسورة (*qaswara*), Jeffery (*Foreign Vocabulary* 31 f.) first refers to *Ṭabarī* who on the basis of a tradition going back to Ibn ᶜAbbās explains the word as *Ethiopic* in the meaning of "*lion.*" A check of the lexicons, however, shows that there is nothing of the kind in either Aramaic or Ethiopic. Examining the problem in more detail, he continues (35 f.):

> A word like قسورة in lxxiv, 51, is a puzzle at the present day, so that it is no wonder if it gave some trouble to the early exegetes. It is usually taken to mean *lion*, and as-Suyūṭī quotes authorities for its being an Abyssinian word. There is no such word, however, in Ethiopic or any of the later Abyssinian dialects… As far as one can see there is nothing in any of the other languages to help us out, and perhaps the simplest solution is to consider it as a formation from قسر (*qasara*), though the great variety of opinions

> on the word given by the early authorities makes its Arabic origin very doubtful.

In any event, on this point Jeffery is right, for the word is Syro-Aramaic, appearing in the *Thes.* (II 3681) under the variant ܩܘܣܪܐ (*qusrā*) and explained by the East Syrian lexicographers as "*asinus decrepitus*" ("*an ass that is decrepit, wasting away*"):

> ܩܘܣܪܐ ܚܡܪܐ ܣܒܐ ܕܠܐ ܡܣܝܒܪ ܛܥܢܐ (*qusrā: ḥmāra sāḇā ḏ-lā m-saybar ṭaʿnā*), (Arabic): حمار هرم ما يحمل (*an old ass that is incapable of carrying loads*).

It thus turns out that the word is a dialectal form of the actual root ܩܨܪ (*qṣar*) (= Arabic قصر *qaṣura* "*to be incapable, to not be able*," as opposed to قسر / *qasara* "*to force, to compel*"). Under this root the *Thes.* (II 3707) again gives the expression as an additional variant, accompanied by the same explanation from the Eastern Syrian lexicographers[70]

70 Interestingly, the *Lisān* (V 104b) refers to the inhabitants of *Baṣrā*, who are said to have called an outcast ابن قوصرة (*ibn qawṣara*, but actually *ibn quṣrā*). Ibn Durayd, however, considers the expression non-Arabic (لا أحسبه عربيا). In fact, pronounced ܩܘܣܪܐ / *qusrā*, it is still used today contemptuously in the sense of "*failure, incapable*" in New Eastern Syriac dialects (e.g. among the Ṯyārī in Iraq).
Finally, it should be mentioned that the Koranic spelling قسورة (pronounced *qasōrā* / *qasūrā*) can denote an early Aramaic form of passive participle as explained by Th. Nöldeke in his *Syrische Grammatik* [*Syriac Grammar*] (p. 69): "With a short vowel of the first and *ū* (*ō*) of the second radical" (§ 113): "The short vowel was *a* (more often in adjectives) or *u* (more often in abstractions). Between *ū* and *ō* no specific difference seems to exist; ܘ݁ (*ō*) is presumably secondarily tinted from ܘ݂ (*ū*) (– or vice versa). A small number of them have the sense of a passive participle (as in Hebrew): ܪܚܘܡܐ (*rḥūmā*) "*beloved*," f. ܪܚܘܡܬܐ (*rḥūmtā*); ܣܢܘܐܐ (*snūā*) "*hated*" ܣܢܘܐܬܐ, ܣܢܘܬܐ (*snūṯā*) "*unloved wife*";… ܫܡܘܥܬܐ (*šmuʿtā*) "*rumor*",… ܠܒܘܫܐ (*lḇūšā*) "*garment*"; etc.
Forms of passive participles like these also occur in a few examples in the Koran, e.g.: رسول (*rasūl*) "*sent = messenger,* " طهور (*ṭahūr*) "*purified = pure*" – as in Sura 25:48, وانزلنا من السما ما طهورا (*and We have sent down from the heaven pure water*), and Sura 76:21, وسقاهم ربهم شرابا طهورا (*and their Lord will give them to drink a pure beverage*), where the passive sense of طهورا (*ṭahūrā*) (*purified*) appears clearly in comparison with the passive participle of

and the corresponding Latin translation: ܩܘܨܪܐ (*quṣrā*)*: asinus e senectute decrepitus qui onus sustinere non possit* (*an old, exhausted ass incapable of carrying a burden*).

Now, if the Syro-Aramaic – perhaps *metathetically* created – dialectal variant exemplifies the genuine meaning of the Koranic expression, it can be noted in favor of the Koranic form قسورة that the Koran has preserved the more classical Syro-Aramaic form. Namely, this coincides exactly with the *nomina agentis* described above by Nöldeke. Thus, according to the basic form *pāʿōlā,* قسورة is not to be read as *qaswara*, as it has been read until now, but as *qāsōrā* .

As to the meaning of this expression in the Koranic context, it can be said that the comparison to a frightened ass, in referring to those who turn away from the Koranic admonition, is explainable in two ways: (a) either one runs away from something that represents a real danger (say, from a *lion* – and that would be logical), or (b) one runs away from something which by its very nature cannot involve a threat. The latter is here the case. With this metaphor the Koran wants to say that there is nothing frightening about its admonition. It therefore compares those who nevertheless turn away from it in fright to asses who let themselves be scared away, not, say, by an intimidating lion, indeed not even by a *normal* ass like themselves, but of all things by a *hoary, feeble and decrepit* ass about which there is no longer anything threatening at all.[71]

Concerning the term أحرف (*aḥruf*) (*letters / bookmarks*), the Arabic tradition ultimately is not incorrect to have taken it purely and simply as a

---

the second stem مطهرة (*muṭahhara*) (instead of طاهرة / *ṭāhira*) in Sura 2:25, 3:15, 4:57, 80:14, 98:2. However, in the case of قسورة the Syro-Aramaic *nomen agentis* (pronounced *qāsōrā*) is to be assumed, as explained above, since in modern Arabic the actually corresponding form is the active participle of the first stem قاصر (*qāṣir*) (*incapable, unable*).

71 If قسورة (ܩܣܘܪܐ / *qāsōrā*) was taken here to be a *lion*, whereas it is in fact a *hoary, feeble ass*, the spelling حمار (read in Arabic *ḥimār*) was understood in Sura 2:259 as "*ass*" where the Koran, with the Syro-Aramaic ܓܡܪܐ (*gmārā*), means the *perfection* of human beings raised to life from the dead (see below p. 191 ff.).

synonym of قراءات (*qirāʾāt*), *variant readings*, to the extent that it has related them not just to the missing vowels, but also – and especially – to the defective writing of the basic consonant form of the original Koranic text before this text became fixed, in the course of a process lasting centuries, in the *one* variant reading of the currently accepted canonical version.

Yet, the Prophet is said to have remained silent for the most part, not only about the variant readings themselves, but also about the meaning of individual verses of the Koran. There is, for example, a report of the following statement by *ʿĀʾiša* (Aisha), the youngest wife of the Prophet:

> "The Prophet – God bless him and grant him salvation – had the habit of interpreting nothing from the Koran except for a few verses that Gabriel – may salvation be upon him – had taught him."[72]

It is therefore no wonder that the earliest commentators on the Koran were also unable to know any better, which led *Ṭabarī*, the author of the most substantial Arabic Koran commentary to date, to exclaim:

إني لأعجب ممن قرأ القرآن ولم يعلم تأويله ، كيف يلتذ بقراءته ؟

> "Yet I am surprised at anyone who reads the Koran without being able to interpret it: How on earth can he take pleasure in reading it?"[73]

The encyclopedic work of *Ṭabarī* (consisting of 30 parts in the Cairo edition) is characterized by Theodor Nöldeke as a turning point in the history of the interpretation of the Koran. Among Muslims his commentary is considered an incomparable achievement:

> "It is indeed, due to the wealth, variety and reliability of the communicated material, the most informative interpretive work that the Mohammedan world has ever produced."[74]

---

72 *Ṭabarī* I 37.

73 Cited by *Mahmoud Muhammad Shaker* in his introduction to the Koran commentary of *Ṭabarī* (Cairo 1374 H./1955) vol. I 10.

74 Th. Nöldeke, *GdQ* II 172 f.

As Paret remarks in his *Encyclopedia of Islam* article, in this commentary *Ṭabarī* has

> "collected for the first time the ample material of traditional exegesis and thus created a standard work upon which later Koranic commentators drew; it is still a mine of information for historical and critical research by Western scholars."[75]

75 R. Paret in *Enzyklopaedie des Islām*, vol. 4 (Leiden, Leipzig, 1934) 626a.

8. Western Koranic Studies

Without intending to go into a detailed history of the origins of Western Koran studies, which emerged around the middle of the 19th century, some indication will be given here of the actual results of this Koranic research as represented by the translations of Western Koran scholars. August Fischer provides an overview of the subject in his essay, "*Der Wert der vorhandenen Koran-Übersetzungen und Sura 111* [*The Value of the Existing Koran Translations and Sura 111*]."[76] On dealing with the task of translating the Koran, Fischer remarks:

> "A Koran translation is no easy task. The renowned Arabists, scholars such as Reiske, Sacy, Fleischer, De Goeje, Nöldeke, and Goldziher, among others, have avoided it, at least partially because they knew of its great difficulties. Most of the previous Koran translators have been second-, indeed even third- and fourth-rate Arabists. [77]

This was August Fischer's opinion in 1937. However, with the more recent Koran translations by the Briton Richard Bell,[78] the Frenchman Régis Blachère,[79] and the German Rudi Paret,[80] we in the meantime have translations by Arabists of the first rank. Yet despite their scholarly meticulousness, these translations have also contributed little to an essential improvement of our understanding of the Koran. With their *ap-*

76 *Berichte über die Verhandlungen der Sächsischen Akademie der Wissenschaften zu Leipzig. Philolog.-histor. Klasse* [*Records of the Proceedings of the Saxon Academy of Sciences at Leipzig: Philological-Historical Division*], vol 89, no. 2 (1937) 3-9.

77 Cited from Rudi Paret, ed., *Der Koran*, Wege der Forschung [Directions of Research], vol. 326 (Darmstadt, 1975) 7.

78 Richard Bell, trans., *The Qurʾān: Translated, with a critical rearrangement of the Surahs*, vol. I (Edinburgh, 1937), vol. II (Edinburgh, 1939).

79 Régis Blachère, trans., *Le Coran, traduit de l'arabe* [*The Koran Translated from Arabic*], (1st ed. 1947/50, 2nd ed. 1957; Paris, 1966).

80 Rudi Paret, trans., *Der Koran, Übersetzung von Rudi Paret* [*The Koran: Translation by Rudi Paret*], (1962; Stuttgart, Berlin, Köln, Mainz, 1982).

paratus criticus they have merely confirmed the problems identified by August Fischer. He summarizes the major difficulties a Koran translator has to cope with as follows:

1. A considerable number of words and sentences in the Koran are obscure and ambiguous.
2. The numerous allusions in the Koran are hard to interpret and their clarification in the Arabic tradition is contradictory and inadequate, so that in such cases only internal criteria can be of further assistance.
3. There is no systematic or chronological ordering of the Suras.
4. There is a lack of a real *textus receptus* with secure bookmarks. The imperfection of the script in the old Koran manuscripts permits numerous variant readings. The Arabic commentaries on the Koran differ considerably one from the other and not infrequently provide more than half a dozen[81] possible interpretations for one obscure passage in the Koran. All the same, one can by no means do without these commentaries.

   The result is that one is never able to be sure of understanding the Koran in all of its details. A conscientious translator of the Koran will instead always have to work with numerous question marks and lists of the various possible interpretations.[82]

The Koran translators, and in particular Rudi Paret, have fulfilled these requirements and at the same time revealed the limits of Koran studies. Yet it must be granted to Western scholarship that, thanks to its historical-critical methods, it has released the study of the Koran from its inflexibility and made considerable advances, more so from a theological-historical than from a philological perspective. The works of principal interest to this study were cited at the outset.

81 According to Régis Blachère, *sometimes up to a dozen* (see his *Introduction au Coran* [Paris, 1947] xxxii).

82 *Der Koran*, ed. Rudi Paret (Darmstadt, 1975) 7 f.

9. The Language of the Koran

Although justifiable doubts have been entertained concerning the reliability of the oral transmission, considering the fact that, as mentioned above, *Ṭabarī* reports several times that the Prophet was not accustomed to expressing himself either on disputed readings or on the meaning of individual verses or Suras in the Koran, there has nevertheless until now been no doubt among the specialists about the language of the Koran, since after all it is said in ten passages in the Koran itself that it was sent down, i.e. revealed, in *Arabic* (Suras 12:2, 13:37, 16:103. 20:113, 26: 195, 39:28, 41:3, 42:7, 43:3 and 46:12).

However, since Arabic at the time at which the Koran originated still possessed no standardized written language, but instead consisted of spoken dialects, it was naturally assumed that the language of the Koran was identical with the dialect of the Prophet and his sib, the Qurayš in Mecca. In *Ṭabarī*[83] this view is grounded on the following verse of the Koran (Sura 14:4):

وما أرسلنا من رسول إلا بلسان قومه ليبين لهم

> "We have never sent a messenger but in the language (i.e., speaking the language) of his people, that he may explain (the message) to them."

Given this statement it must come as a surprise that the Prophet – as reported in *Ṭabarī* – was supposedly unable to explain this language to his contemporaries. Also concerning Saʿīd ibn al-Musayyab, one of the seven scholars of Medina (d. 712), *Ṭabarī* reports that in response to questions about a Koranic verse he "*kept quiet as if he had heard nothing*" (سكت كأن لم يسمع). To another such knowledge-hungry individual he responded: "Do not ask me about a verse of the Koran; rather ask him who maintains that nothing of it remains concealed from him," by which he was referring to ʿIkrima[84] (a companion of the Prophet who

83 *Ibid.* 29.

84 *Ibid.* 28.

died in 634). The fact that even after the Prophet nobody has succeeded in penetrating the final mystery of this language for as long as the Koran has existed has led in the Islamic tradition to the belief that the language of the Koran is of heavenly origin and thus finally unfathomable for mortals. With the term إعجاز (*iʿǧāz*) (on the basis of Suras 2:23, 10:38, 11:13) the Islamic tradition does indeed characterize the Koran as a *miracle* that cannot be imitated by mortals, but this may refer in general to the human inability to understand the Koran completely into its last detail.

Yet when the Koran speaks of the "*Arabic language,*" one can well ask what language it was talking about at the time of its origin. Faithful to Islamic tradition, which has always encouraged the *search for knowledge* (طلب العلم), and keeping in mind the well-known sayings of the Prophet العلم نور "*Knowledge is light*" and اطلبوا العلم ولو في الصين "*Seek knowledge, and be it in China,*" *Ṭabarī* takes the view that philologists (أهل اللسان) are fundamentally authorized to explain the language in which the Koran was sent down (اللسان الذى نزل به القرآن) because outside of them nobody else is capable of acquiring a knowledge of it (لا توصل إلى علم ذلك إلا من قبلهم), in so far as they are able to provide irrefutable and philologically verifiable arguments for the explanation and interpretation of this language (وأوضحهم برهانا فيما ترجم وبيّن من ذلك مما كان مدركا علمه من جهة اللسان), and regardless of who the interpreters in question may have been (كائنا من كان ذلك والمفسر المتأول).[85]

In the sense of *Ṭabarī* we therefore intend in the following – by taking a philologically prior linguistic phase as a starting-point – to undertake the experiment of reading the text of the Koran differently than the Arabic commentators of the Koran have done it, partially according to an understanding of the Arabic of their time and partially with recourse to Old Arabic poetry. Only on the basis of the results of this linguistic analysis may one judge whether it actually also leads to a better understanding of the Koranic text or not.

85 *Ibid.* 41.

10. FROM SYRO-ARAMAIC ܩܪܝܢܐ (*qəryānā*) TO ARABIC قرءان (*qurʾān*)

The present study is based on the elementary finding that the term *Koran* (قرءان / *qurʾān*) holds the key to the understanding of the Koranic language. Whereas, namely, the Arabic philologists in the interpretation of the word قرءان (*qurʾān*), whose Arabic origin they do not doubt, have not made up their minds yet between the verbal roots قرن (*qarana*) (*to bind, to put together*) and قرأ (*qaraʾa*) (*to read*),[86] it was first recognized in Western Koranic studies that cultural terms like قرأ (*to read*) – and accordingly also كتب (*kataba*) (*to write*) – could not be Arabic in origin. As Theodor Nöldeke says in his *Geschichte des Qorāns* [*History of the Koran*] (I 31–34):

> "Now, since a cultural word like 'read' can not be proto-Semitic, we may assume that it migrated into Arabia, and indeed probably from the north. ... Now, because Syriac has besides the verb קרא the noun *qeryānā*, and indeed in the double sense of *ἀνάγνωσις* ([the act of] *reading, reading aloud*) and *ἀνάγνωσμα* (*reading or lesson, reading matter*), the assumption gains in probability, in connection with what has just been said, that the term Qorān is not an inner-Arabic development out of the synonymous infinitive, but a borrowing from that Syriac word with a simultaneous assimilation to the type fuʿlān."[87]

Nöldeke's probable assumption of the Syriac origin of *qurʾān* has in the meantime become so well accepted in Western Koranic research that the

86 Cf. Nöldeke, *GdQ* I 32, note 3.

87 *Ibid.* 33 f. Furthermore, it remains to be seen whether *fuʿlān* is a genuinely Arabic type. The fact is that in practice the nominal form *qurʾān* has never become generally accepted, though it is cited by the Arabic lexicographers as a variation of the common infinitive *qirāʾa* and also actually occurs in this function in the Koran. One can also identify the non-Arabic origin in the fact that in Arabic usage *Qurʾān* is only understood as a proper name used to designate the holy scripture of Islam.

indication of its Christian-Aramaic origin has today become a matter of course in the standard Western encyclopedia of Islam,[88] whereas this has been completely ignored by both the earlier and modern Islamic exegetes. Thus Erwin Gräf accurately defines the Koran as follows:

> "The Koran, according to the etymological meaning of the word, is originally and really a liturgical text designed for cultic recitation and also actually used in the private and public service. This suggests that the liturgy or liturgical poetry, and indeed the Christian liturgy, which comprises the Judaic liturgy, decisively stimulated and influence Mohammed."[89]

As an ecclesiastical *terminus technicus* (*technical term*), the Koran thus corresponds originally to the *lectionarium* (*lectionary*) still used in Western Christianity today as a liturgical book containing excerpts from scripture to be read aloud during the service.

If it has now been established that the Arabic *qur'ān* is a direct borrowing from the Syro-Aramaic *qəryānā*, then the question must be asked as to the extent to which – in Nöldeke's words – the assimilation of *qur'ān* to the type *fu'lān* has taken place.

Information on this subject is provided for us by the Islamic tradition. Thus the *Lisān* (I 128b f.) records a statement reaching back from *aš-Šāfi'ī* by way of a traditionary chain to *Muǧāhid*, *Ibn 'Abbās* and *Ubayy*, according to which the Prophet had pronounced قرءان (*qur'ān*) without a *hamza*, i.e. without the glottal stop before the *ā* (long a), قران (*qurān*). On the basis of the *alif* and *hamza* signs (اء), which were gradually introduced as a reading aid, but scarcely before the middle of the 8th century,[90] the later Arabic readers, who were no longer familiar with the Prophet's original pronunciation, *qəryān*, went on the assumption that قرءان (*qur'ān*) was to be pronounced without the *hamza*, simply قران (*qurān*). In doing so they ignored the view widely held in the Arabic tra-

88 See, for example, the article al-Kur'ān in *The Encyclopaedia of Islam*, vol. 5 (Leiden, 1986) 400.

89 *ZDMG* 111, new series no. 37 (1962): 396-398.

90 Blachère says in his *Introduction au Coran* 94 that it is impossible to establish more precisely the point in time at which this writing reform took place.

dition according to which the *hamza* was pronounced *softly* in the Arabic dialect of Mecca. This does not at all mean in this case, however, the absence of the *hamza* without replacement, but its realization as a soft يـ / *y*. Accordingly, the pronunciation of the Prophet documented by Islamic tradition must have been قريان (*qəryān*), a pronunciation that exactly corresponds to that of the Arabic-speaking Aramaic Christians of Syria and Mesopotamia. This is also said by the *Thesaurus* with a reference to the Eastern Syrian lexicographers as follows: "Ap. lexx. القريان ܩܪܝܢܐ (*qəryānā: al-qəryān*); it. القرءة . القريان " (*Thes.* II 3716). In this case the vowel *e* in *qəryān* is to be produced, in accordance with the oral tradition of the Eastern and Western Syrians (usually in a single closed syllable), as a so-called *murmur vowel* (dark *ə* or *"shwa"*).

The *hamza* spelling in the medial and final position adopted according to the will of later Arabic philologists against the documented pronunciation of the Prophet has finally had as a consequence that the original Syro-Aramaic pronunciation *qəryān* has been abandoned in favor of the Arabicized pronunciation *qur'ān* (following the pattern of فرقان *furqān* < ܦܘܪܩܢܐ / *purqānā*).[91]

Consequences of the Orthographic Transformation of *qəryān* to *qur'ān*

The Arabic transcription of Syro-Aramaic ܩܪܝܢܐ (*qəryā-nā*) must originally have been pronounced قرين (*qəryān*). Until now, however, research on old manuscripts of the Koran has been unable to establish this spelling. In today's spelling قرءان (*qur'ān*) it is generally recognized that both the *hamza* and the *alif* ا / *ā* (long a) are secondary. In two passages (Suras 12:2, 43:21) the canonical version of the Koran gives evidence of the earlier written form with an accusative ending قرنا (*qur'ān^{an}*), as has already been pointed out by Nöldeke (Bergsträßer-Pretzl) (*GdQ* III 43).[92]

---

91 Thus what Nöldeke called the *fu'lān* type would not exactly be Arabic.

92 Further reference is made, under note 3, to earlier manuscripts of the Koran with the spelling القرن (*al-qurān*) and قرنا (*qurān^{an}*).

Yet even if the extant manuscripts of the Koran have until now not confirmed the presumed spelling قرين (*qəryān*), the original Syro-Aramaic term suggests this written form. Accordingly, one can imagine the following four phases in the transformation of the Arabic orthography to today's accepted canonical spelling قرءان (*qur'ān*): (1) قرين (original pronunciation: *qəryān*); (2) defective spelling: قرن (pronunciation: *qurān*); (3) full spelling قران (same pronunciation: *qurān*); and last of all (4) with the inserted *hamza*: قرءان (accepted pronunciation: *qur'ān*).

This hypothesis is based on the assumption that in a first post-Koranic orthographic reform the Arabic philologists no longer recognized the real meaning of the little peak of the letter carrier يـ /*y* in قرين (*qəryān*) as a defective spelling for *yā*. On the basis of the pronunciation of the Prophet (*qurān*), as documented according to Arabic tradition, they must have read the spelling قرين as "*qarīn*." Whence the removal, without replacement, of the يـ /*y*, from which emerged, in a second phase, the defective spelling قرن with the pronunciation *qurān*. The introduction of the alif ا as a *mater lectionis* for *ā* (long a) logically led, in a third phase, to the full spelling قران [93] (with the same pronunciation: *qurān*). The

93 Cf. W. Diem, *Untersuchungen zur frühen Geschichte der arabischen Orthographie* [*Studies on the Early History of Arabic Orthography*]. I. *Die Schreibung der Vokale* [*The Spelling of the Vowels*], Orientalia, vol. 48 (1979). In § 62 (252) under number 3, W. Diem gives the spelling at Sura 10:61 قران *Qurān* < *Qur'ān* among the types "in which the written form has been retained unaltered." In § 64 (253) he accordingly counts the spelling قرنا (12:2; 43:3 *Qurānā*) among the "few spellings" in which the *alif* "would have been expected etymologically." Just as doubtful is the allegedly primary spelling السيات (4:18 etc. *as-sayyiyāt* < *as-sayyi'āt* "the evil deeds"), whose secondarily inserted *alif* has distorted the original spelling, سنيت, as the transliteration of the Syro-Aramaic ܣܢܝܬܐ (*sanyāṯā*) (*Thes*. II 2669: *plerumque ut subst. usitata, facinora, scelera, vitia*; Ap. lexx.: السيئات ، القبايح ، الذنوب / *as-sayyi'āt* / *"disgraceful, wicked deeds, vices"*). The basis for this reading is the following facsimile edition of the Koran Manuscript No. 328(a) in the *Bibliothèque Nationale de France*: *Sources de la transmission du texte coranique* [*Sources of the Transmission of the Text of the Koran*] eds. François Déroche et Sergio Noja Noseda, vol. 1, *Les manuscrits de style ḥiǧāzī* [*Manuscripts in the ḥiǧāzī Style*], Le manuscrit arabe 328(a) de la Bibliothèque Nationale de France [Arabic Manuscript No. 328(a) in the Bibliothèque Nationale de France] (Paris, Bibliothèque Nationale de

acceptance of the hamza resulted finally, in a fourth phase, in what is today the common spelling in the canonical edition of the Koran, قرءان or قرآن (with the pronunciation *qurʾān*).

However, if the Arabic tradition according to which the Prophet said *qurān* is correct, then this would lead to the understanding that the Koran readers of the first generation did not read the little middle peak ـيـ in the original spelling قرين as *y* or *ī*, but as long *ā*. Later copyists, interpreting this peak as a long *ī*, would have then omitted it as an apparently incorrectly written character. Previously, however, it was known (for etymological reasons) that the little peak only functioned in Koranic orthography to indicate the long vowel *ā* in the reproduction of a secondary *ā* in a final position for *tertiae yāʾ* roots before suffixes (e.g. بنيها = بناها / *banā̱-hā* in Sura 79:27).

The conjecture that the little peak ـيـ for indicating a long *ā* was not exclusively used for a secondary *ā* in *tertiae yāʾ* verbs before suffixes, but was used in other cases as well during the first phase in the editing of the Koran, does not depend solely on earlier Koran manuscripts for its confirmation. On the contrary, evidence can already be provided now on the basis of a few misread words in the modern Cairo edition of the Koran.[94] Of these the following examples may suffice:

France, 1998). As opposed to the spellings السيات (*as-sayyiʾāt*) (Sura 4:18), سياتكم (*sayyiʾātikum*) (Sura 4: 31; 5:12) and سياتهم (*sayyiʾātihim*) (Sura 3:195) in the Cairo edition of the Koran, the Paris Ms. 328(a) has (without diacritical points): السنيت ، سنيتهم ، سنيتكم . According to Koranic orthography, for these spellings a *hamza* carrier is out of the question. The *Lisān* cites this root both under شنا (*šanā*) (XIV 444b) and under شنأ (*šanaʾa*) (I 101b ff.), each with the same original meaning (*to hate*). See also the spellings reproduced under chapter 6 (55) in connection with the "orthography of the Lewis palimpsest" in Th. Nöldeke (Bergsträßer-Pretzl), *GdQ* III.

94 This observation, made by the author in a lecture in 1996, was the startingpoint for the initiative to make microfilms of the Koranic fragments of Sanaa in the expectation that one would there be able to find further proofs. These microfilms have been available since 1998. Subsequently, a first (and till now sole) confirmation has been provided there by the spelling of the word اليه (= الاه = اله / *ilāh*) (*god, deity*), where the middle peak marks the long *ā* as *mater lectionis*, however without any alteration of the meaning (see G.-R. Puin, *Über die*

Sura 41:47
Example 1: ءاذنك (*ā*ḏ*annāk*ᵃ)

ويوم يناديهم اين شركاى قالوا اذنك ما منا من شهيد

Following the understanding of the Arabic commentators,[95] our Koran translators have rendered the underlined expression in the context of the cited part of the verse as follows:

(Bell II 481): "We protest to Thee, there is not amongst us a witness."

(Paret 400): "Und am Tag (des Gerichts), da er ihnen [d.h. den Ungläubigen] zuruft: 'Wo sind (nun) meine (angeblichen) Teilhaber?', sagen sie: 'Wir geben dir (hiermit) Bescheid: Unter uns ist kein Zeuge (der die Wahrheit unserer früheren Aussagen bestätigen könnte).'"

(Blachère 510): "Sache qu'il n'est, parmi nous, nul témoin."

An Arab with a normal feel for the language senses here right away that there is something "clumsy" about the final clause. That in this context آذن (*āḏana*) is supposed to mean "*to inform*" is a pure invention of the Arabic commentators, who could not figure out any other way to explain this misread word. Namely, in the spelling اذنك the upper dot of the ـنـ / *n* has been falsely placed. The apparent ignorance of the later Arabic readers with regard to the real meaning of the originally unpointed little

---

Bedeutung der ältesten Koranfragmente aus Sanaa (Jemen) für die Orthographiegeschichte des Korans [On the Importance of the Oldest Koran-fragments of Sanaa (Yemen) for the History of Koranic Orthography], "*Neue Wege der Koranforschung*" [*New Ways of Koranic Research*], 2, in: *magazin forschung* [*magazine research*], Universität des Saarlandes [University of the Saarland], I, 1999, p. 37-40). The other examples quoted there from the standard edition of the Koran, however, require some rectification. A first discussion concerning the spelling and the etymology of both Syro-Aramaic ܣܛܢܐ (*sāṭānā*) (> Hebrew שׂטן / *sāṭān*) and Koranic شيطن (*šayṭān*) will follow below.

95 *Ṭabarī* (XV 1 f.) reads آذناك (*āḏannāk*ᵃ) and gives the following explanations: أعلمناك (*aʿlamnāk*ᵃ) (*we inform you*), أطعناك (*aṭaʿnāk*ᵃ) (*we obey you*), with the note: أطلعناك (*aṭlaʿnāk*ᵃ) as a synonym for أعلمناك (*aʿlamnāk*ᵃ).

hook ـنـ , which here stands for a long *ā*, is to blame for this. If the oral tradition had not been broken, the later Arabic readers would quite certainly have been able to recognize this well-known Arabic adverbial expression (although borrowed from Syro-Aramaic ܗܝܕܟ / *hāydēḵ* [< **hāy-d-hayk* > **hāy-d-hēḵ*], with secondary vowel reduction and darkening > * *ᵊddayk*, with following monophthongization of *ay* > *ā* = * *ᵊddāk* > Arabic *ᵊḏḏāk* / *iḏḏāk*.[96] Namely, the misread ـنـ / *n* when read as a long *ā* results in the reading إذاك (*then, whereupon*) (actually إذ ذاك *īḏ ḏākᵃ*), which can also be written in modern Arabic in the contracted form إذاك (see, for example, H. Wehr, *Arabisches Wörterbuch* [*Arabic Dictionary*]). According to this reading the passage cited above (this time *in Arabic*) can now be understood as follows:

> "On the day when he will call to them, 'Where are they (now), my associates?' they will <u>*then*</u> answer: 'None of us *professes*[97] (to these) any longer'."

Sura 68:13
Example 2: عتل (*ʿutull*)

In this context a list is made of the negative behaviors of an infidel. Included among them is the character trait described in Sura 68:13–14:

عتل بعد ذلك زنيم / ان كان ذا مال وبنين

On the basis of the wavering understanding of the Arabic commentators,[98] our Koran translators have translated this continuous double verse as follows:

---

96 Cf. *Thes.* I 1002, where to the Syriac ܗܝܕܟ (*hāydēḵ*) corresponds the Chaldaic (i.e. in this case vernacular Eastern Syro-Aramaic) אדּך (*əddāḵ*) > Arabic إذذاك or إذاك (*iḏḏāk*).

97 Arabic شهيد (*šahīd*) does not just have the meaning of "*witness*." The Arabic شهادة (*šahāda*), meaning "*confession of faith*," is also a borrowing from the Syro-Aramaic ecclesiastical term ܣܗܕ (*sheḏ*) (*to testify*, actually *to admit publicly*, from which ܣܗܕܐ / *sāhḏā* "*martyr, confessor*" also comes).

98 *Ṭabarī* XXIX 23-27.

(Bell II 597): 13. "Gross, but yet highly-esteemed,[99] 14. Because he has wealth and children."

(Paret 477): 13: "und der überdies ein Grobian (?) ist und sich (überall) eindrängt (?) (*ʿutullin baʿda ḏālika zanīmin*) 14: (auf Grund der Tatsache), daß er (ein großes) Vermögen und (viele) Söhne hat !"

(Blachère 608): 13 "arrogant et par surcroît, bâtard ! 14 Ne lui obéis pas [*parce*] qu'il est riche et a des fils [*pour le soutenir*]!"

1. The misread ـتـ / *t* in the spelling عتل (pronounced *ʿutull*) is responsible for the different translations of this word by our Koran translators (Bell: "*gross*"; Paret: "*Grobian*"; Blachère: "*arrogant*"). Only Blachère, with "*arrogant,*" has even come close to guessing the real sense correctly from the context. The meaning "*arrogant, overbearing*" is actually yielded only by the reading عال (*ʿālin*). That the later Arabic readers incorrectly placed two dots (ـتـ) over the medial peak intended as a long *ā* and came up with the meaningless reading عتل (*ʿutull*) is precise confirmation of the assumption that an oral tradition no longer existed at the time of the fixing of the Koranic text. And this, even though this genuinely Arabic expression occurs in singular and plural in this meaning in four other passages in the Koran (Suras 10:83; 44:31; 23:46; 38:75). There, however, the original peak has been replaced by the subsequently inserted *alif* ا as a *mater lectionis* for long *ā*. Thus these passages were read correctly. But in the case of Sura 68:13 this meaning was obviously not recognized. The misreading of the spelling as it was left in its original form, however, is to be explained in particular by the absence of an oral tradition.

The realization that the peak was often not just provided with false dots, but from time to time also replaced by an *alif* ا / *ā*, is of importance for Koranic studies for the understanding of many a misreading.

---

99 [Note 1]: "Or 'adopted' from an ignoble family, which is said to refer to Walīd b. Maghīra. But the word is probably from *zanama* to mark a well-bred camel by cutting a part of the ear and letting it hang down."

For whereas with the canonical edition of the Koran it is only necessary to imagine the dots as absent, in the case of the *alif* ا the problem is that a *primary* is not readily distinguishable from a *secondary alif*, especially considering the fact that, in examining them, both Arabic and Syro-Aramaic (and occasionally Hebrew) linguistic components must be considered each time. But that the later insertion of the *alif* by incompetent editors has led to the distortion of many a word would, in view of the unsure or absent oral tradition, only be a logical consequence.

2. Our Koran translators have rendered the spelling زنيم (*zanīm*) in just as contradictory a fashion as the Arabic commentators (Bell: "*highly-esteemed*"; Paret: "*der sich (überall) eindrängt*"; Blachère: "*batard*"). Given the way the word has been misread (*zanīm*), one would be most likely to see it as an active masculine Hebrew plural participle זנים (*zōnīm*) (*whoring, engaging in prostitution*).[100] However, because the Koranic context speaks of a single individual, such a Hebrew plural form is out of the question.

Some information about this is provided for us by the following statement given as indirect speech in Verse 14: ان كان ذا مال وبنين "that he has wealth and children." This statement, however, presupposes a verb, which the misreading of زنيم (*zanīm*) has distorted. Here, too, the absence of an oral tradition has resulted in the Arabic readers' not knowing what to do with this spelling. Whence the arbitrary reading زنيم (*zanīm*), whose just as adventurously imagined meanings H. Wehr, for example, (in his *Arabisches Wörterbuch* [*Arabic Dictionary*]) gives, without further examination, as "*low, base; bastard, son of a bitch; stranger, one who does not belong to something.*"

One cannot blame the Arabic readers, however, if behind the spelling زنيم they were unable to imagine a Syro-Aramaic verb form. Namely, if in its place we read رتيم (*ratīm*), what results is the transliteration of the Syro-Aramaic ܪܛܝܡ (*rṯīm*) in *status absolutus*. For it the *Thesaurus* (II 3997) gives the following definition under the verbal root ܪܛܡ (*rṯam*):

100 Cf. W. Gesenius, *Hebräisches und aramäisches Handwörterbuch* [*Concise Dictionary of Hebrew and Aramaic*] 201b.

“enunciavit, spec. indistincte et submissa voce locutus est” (*to say, to pronounce, especially to speak unclearly and quietly*).

In the case of the Koranic form, it is a question of a Syro-Aramaic passive masculine participle with an active meaning, as Theodor Nöldeke explains in his *Syrischen Grammatik* [*Syriac Grammar*] (§280):

> “Some *participia* of the form ܦܥܝܠ (*pʿīl*) are used in an active meaning: in part this is based on the fact that the *verba* involved could be doubly transitive; in part it is caused by the analogy to forms having a related meaning.”

This Koranic example should be added to those listed by Nöldeke. The attributive passive participle ܪܛܝܡܐ (*rṭīmā*) is also explained actively by the *Thesaurus* (*loc. cit.*) with “*blaesus, balbutiens*” (*lisping, stammering,* metaphorically: *twaddling*). With the now no longer common phrase ما رتم بكلمة (*mā ratama bi-kalima*)[101] (*he didn't speak a word*) and الرتم : الكلام الخفي (*ar-ratam : to speak quietly*) Arabic has preserved a memory of the Syro-Aramaic expression.

Based on this analysis, the double verse from Sura 68:13–14 is now to be read:

عال بعد ذلك رتيم / ان كان ذا مال وبنين

(*ʿālin baʿda ḏālika ratīm / an kāna ḏā mālin wa-banīn*)

According to the Syro-Aramaic reading, it should thus be understood as follows:

> “*arrogant* furthermore *twaddling* 14. that (even without God) he has wealth and children!”

---

101 Cf. *Lisān* XII 226a; the same under رثم (*raṯama*): الأرثم (*al-arṯam*): هو الذي لا يصحّح كلامه ولا يبيّنه (*one who speaks inarticulately*).

Sura 18:9
Example 3: الرقيم (*ar-raqīm*)

In a recent article[102] James A. Bellamy has been the latest to deal with this expression, heretofore considered an unsolved problem in Koranic studies. Taking as a starting point an error on the part of a copyist, he proposes the reading الرقود (*ar-ruqūd*) (*the sleeping* [boys]) in place of the substantive recorded in the canonical version of the Koran الرقيم (*ar-raqīm*) (roughly, *memorial tablet*). In its context this verse reads:

ام حسبت ان اصحب الكهف والرقيم كانوا من ايتنا عجبا

The German translator Paret (238) renders this verse as follows:

> "Or do you think that the people of the cave and the inscription (*? ar-raqīm*) [Note: The interpretation of *ar-raqīm*(*i*) is very uncertain] was (one) of our signs, about which one should be (especially) surprised?"

Blachère (318) renders "ar-Raqîm" as a place name and refers to the contradictory explanations of the commentators. Bell (I 275) does the same and adds the following comment (footnote 1):

> "Much difference of opinion prevails as to the identity of ar-Raqīm, some holding it to be the name of the mountain or the village associated with them, others that it is the name of the dog. Torrey suggests that it is a misreading of Decius as written in Hebrew characters; E. G. Browne, *Oriental Studies,* p. 459."

The thought that, to introduce this legend of the seven sleepers one would expect a corresponding expression, is in itself correct. For the former contested reading والرقيم (*wa-r-raqīm*), J.A. Bellamy proposes the following emendations: (1) removal of the conjunction و / *wa* as superfluous; (2) removal of the medial يـ / *ī* as having resulted from inattentiveness or a blot; (3) changing the final م / *m* into a و *w* / *ū*, and (4) insertion of a presumably omitted final د / *d.* Thus we would have the

102 In the *Journal of the American Oriental Society* 111.1 (1991) 115-117.

reading evidenced in Verse 18 رقود (*ruqūd*) (*sleepers*) as the plural of راقد (*rāqid*) (*sleeping male*). Instead of the previous reading اصحب الكهف و الرقيم (*the people of the cave and the inscription*), one would then have اصحب الكهف الرقود (*the sleeping people of the cave*).

However, by proposing four emendations to a word made up of a total of five letters (if we ignore the article الـ /*al-*), J.A. Bellamy spoils a consideration that is otherwise plausible in its approach. In contrast, the principle of *lectio difficilior* would be better served if we had to change just *one* letter.

The key is here provided to us by precisely that little middle peak that J.A. Bellamy has considered either faulty or only a blot, but which here stands for a long *ā*. Then we would need only to read the probably misread final م /*m* as a final د /*d*. Namely, experts of the Ḥiğāzī manuscripts know that the pronounced ring-shaped final م is produced on the line without the vertical infralinear extension. Nonetheless, one cannot in the first place make a mixing up of final د /*d* and final م / *m* responsible for the misreading. Much more likely is the assumption that later Arabic copyists could no longer recognize the peak ـيـ as a long *ā*. Interpreted as a long *ī*, they must have read و الرقيد (*wa-r-raqīd*), a form that doesn't exist in Arabic at all. The next best alternative was therefore to make a final م / *m* out of the final د / *d*.

That the latter letter was occasionally confused with the Arabic ر / *r* , on the basis, however, of an earlier transcription from Syriac script (due to the identically formed letters ܕ / *d* and ܪ / *r* distinguishable only by the upper and lower dots, respectively), will find itself substantiated in a subsequent study. An initial case first became conspicuous in the following discussion of the spelling يلحدون (*yulḥidūn*) instead of يلغزون (*yalġuzūn* / *yulġizūn*) from Sura 16:103. Two more examples from the Cairo edition of the Koran can be provided as confirmation of this phenomenon:

a) Concerning the transcription of an originally Syriac ܕ / *d* as an Arabic ر / *r:* Such a mistake is encountered in the word ركزا (*rikzā*) (allegedly: *soft voice*) instead of the Syriac ܕܘܟܪܐ = Arabic ذكرا (*ḏikrā*) (*memory*) from Sura 19:98:

وكم اهلكنا قبلهم من قرن هل تحس منهم من احد او تسمع لهم ركزا

Bell (I 291) translates according to Arab commentators: "How many a generation have We destroyed before them! Dost thou perceive of them a single one or hear of them a whisper?"

The word ركزا (*rikzā*) is transcribed in the facsimile of the *ḥiğāzī* Koran codex Or. 2165 (fol. 1– 61), published by the British Library in 2001, as ركرا (*rkra*) (without diacritical points) (fol. 50b, 11). This spelling provides us with a typical example of the unpointed Arabic rendering of the identically shaped Syriac consonants ܕ / *d* and ܪ / *r*, but which with the respective lower and upper dots should have been rendered in Arabic as د / *d* and ر / *r* . Provided with the diacritical dots, the first ر in the Arabic spelling ركرا would thus correspond to the Syriac ܕ / *d*, the second ر to the Syriac ܪ / *r* (and not to the Arabic ز *z*). In this way the original reading ذكرا (*ḏikrā*) can be restored. This also results etymologically and semantically in a sense that fits better to the context. Namely, that ركز (*rikz*) would mean a *whispering*, a *soft voice*, is a pure invention of the Arab commentators, who were unable to come up with anything more suitable in connection with the preceding verb سمع (*samiʿa*) (*to hear*). If one hears something, it must be a voice, they must have thought. At the same time one can also *hear* of someone, that is, learn something about him. Insofar is ذكر (*ḏikr*) here to be understood as *remembrance* of the deceased, whose *memory* continues to exist even after their passing away. The verse cited above is therefore to be corrected and understood as follows:

هل تحس منهم من احد او تسمع لهم ذكرا

"Dost thou perceive of them a single one or hear of them any *mention*?"

b) Concerning the transcription of an originally Syriac ܪ / *r* as an Arabic د / *d* : One such example (among others) is to be encountered in the heretofore *hapax legomenon* طود (allegedly *ṭaud*) from Sura 26:63. Following the Old Testament account Moses is commanded to strike the sea with his staff; there then follows:

فانفلق فكان كل فرق كالطود العظيم

Bell (II 356, 63): "… and it [the sea] clave asunder; each part became like a cliff mighty."

Although the word has been understood correctly here, only Paret (303) gives it in parentheses (*ṭaud*), by means of which he wants to indicate that the word in itself is unusual.[103] The unique mistaken writing of this well-known word through the mistranscription of the Syriac ܪ / *r* as Arabic د / *d* is all the more astonishing since the otherwise correctly transcribed طور (*ṭūr* < Syro-Aramaic ܛܘܪܐ / *ṭūrā, mountain*) occurs ten times in the Koran (Sura 2:63,93; 4:154; 19:52; 20:80; 23:20; 28:29,46; 52:1; 95:2). The corresponding Arabic expression is used once in connection with the sea (Sura 11:42); there it is said of Noah's ark that it sailed في موج كالجبال (*fī mawǧ ka-l-ǧibāl*) "between waves (high) as *mountains*."

c) Since the Arabic letters د / *d* and ر / *r* are clearly distinguishable in the early Koran manuscripts in the Ḥiǧāzī as well as in the Kūfī style,[104] a primary mutual mixing up of these letters is only conceivable on the basis of an original mistranscription of the equivalent Syriac letters ܕ / *d* and ܪ / *r* from an original composed in Syriac

---

103 In fact طود (*ṭaud*) is not only *unusual*, it does not exist in Arabic at all. A supposed verbal root طاد (*ṭāda*) from which a fictitious seventh stem إنطاد (*inṭāda*) is derived with an equally imaginary meaning *"to rise in the air, soar up,"* as quoted, for example, by H. Wehr [*A Dictionary of Modern Written Arabic* (Arabic-English), edited by J. Milton Cowan, Wiesbaden 1979, 669a], and the excogitated modern Arabic word منطاد (*munṭād*) plural (*manāṭīd*) *"balloon, blimp; zeppelin, dirigible"* that results, also shows the basis on which *Classical Arabic* is partly grounded. The *Lisān* (III 270a) explains الطود (*aṭ-ṭaud*) as الجبل العظيم (*al-ǧabal al-ʿaẓīm*) (*a towering mountain*). But herewith it actually just explains the mistranscribed Syro-Aramaic word ܛܘܪܐ (*ṭūrā* > Koranic Arabic طور / *ṭūr*), which the *Lisān* (IV 508b) explains with the same meaning: والطور: الجبل (*ṭūr* i.e. a *mountain*).

104 See in the Appendix in the CD copy 0585 from the Koran manuscript of Samarkand, line 2, the kufic ر / *r* in the word فرق / *farq* and the د / *d* in the word كالطود / *ka-ṭ-ṭauḍ* (*recte:* كالطور / *ka-ṭ-ṭūr*) (Sura 26:63).

script (*Garshuni*/*Karshuni*). In turn, only in this roundabout way can one explain the Arabic misreading of the final *d* (by mistranscription written incorrectly as a final *r*) as final *m*. The occasionally remarkable similarity of the final *r* (here instead of the final *d*, and the final *m* in early Kufic Koran manuscripts (caused by insufficiently careful transcription) can finally be illustrated with the help of a few examples from the Koran manuscript of Samarkand (cf., e.g. in the Appendix ر / *r* and م / *m* in the spelling يمريم / *yā-Maryam* in the corresponding passage from Sura 3:45, CD 0098 (see p. 348), according to the copy of sheet 95, -2).[105] This determination provides us with the graphical proof of a reconstructible mixing up of final *r* (written incorrectly from final *d*) and final *m* in a *second stage* of the Arabic transcription of the Koranic corpus in the Kufic style. This would mean that the Kufic Koran manuscript of Samarkand belongs, not to the first, but at the earliest to a second generation of the Arabic handing down of the Koran. It nevertheless contains in itself sufficient graphical evidence for a Syriac original version of the Koran text, as will be explained.

In so far as the Arab readers did not have the historical background information as to the Syriac scripture of the early Koran, they may have seen within the Arabic scripture system no other alternative than the reading و الرقيم (*wa-r-raqīm*) instead of و الرقيد = و الرقاد (*wa-r-raqīd* = *wa-r-ruqād*). Although this reading also didn't seem very reasonable, at least it was known to exist in Arabic. In cases of doubt, such undefinable words nevertheless have the advantage of becoming interpreted as proper names or place names that cannot be verified, evidence of which is also provided by the commentaries in question. The analogous method of interpretation employed by Arabic philologists will have struck anyone who has worked in particular on Old Arabic poetry.

105 The author has to thank Tariq Ismail for providing a CD copy of the Koran codex of Samarqand [SAMARKANDSKII KUFICHESKII KORAN – Coran coufique de Samarcand écrit d'après la tradition de la propre main du troisième Calife Osman (644–656) qui se trouve dans la Bibliothèque Impériale Publique de St. Petersbourg. Edition faite avec l'autorisation de l'Institut Archéologique de St. Petersbourg (facsimile) par S. Pissaref. St. Petersbourg. 1905].

However, if one reads instead of و الرقيد (*wa-r-raqīd*) و الرقاد (*wa-r-ruqād*), then the problem is already solved. As the nominal form of رقد (*raqada*) (*to sleep*), the *Lisān* (III 183a) gives النوم (*an-nawm*) (*sleep*) as a definition of الرقاد (*ar-ruqād*). Read like this, Sura 18:9 makes the following sense:

ام حسبت ان اصحب الكهف والرقاد كانوا من ايتنا عجبا

"Do you think, say, that the people of the cave and <u>sleep</u> were strange among our signs?"

Example 4: التورية (*at-tawrāt*)

To the designation of a long *ā* with a little peak (ـيـ) in the interior of a word C. Brockelmann names as the only exception the foreign word تورية (*tawrāt*) (Torah) (*Arabische Grammatik* [*Arabic Grammar*], §2 [*d*], note 2, p. 7). On the other hand, Theodor Nöldeke, in his *Geschichte des Qorâns* [*History of the Koran*],[106] had suspected the pronunciation تورِيّة (*tawrīya*). In his *Untersuchungen zur frühen Geschichte der arabischen Orthographie* [*Studies on the Early History of Arabic Orthography*][107] W. Diem contradicted him and found a more detailed elucidation of the traditional reading *tawrāh* (249) faulty. He rejected the derivation from Hebrew תורה (*tōrā*) that A. Jeffery[108] and J. Horovitz[109] assert by referring to J. Wellhausen,[110] who would have expected the Arabic *tawrah* as the equivalent of the Hebrew feminine ending *–ā* , whereas the Koranic spelling with *yā͗* , in which K. Vollers[111] saw an *imāla* from *ā* to *ē* as a variant of *Torah*, is not modeled on the Hebrew spelling תורה. Against the suggestions by F. Schwally,[112] R. Köbert[113]

---

106 *GdQ* (Göttingen, [1]1860) 255.

107 I. *Die Schreibung der Vokale* [*The Spelling of the Vowels*], in: Orientalia, vol. 48 (1979) 207-257, on التوريه *at-tawrāh*: 248-250.

108 *Foreign Vocabulary* 95 f.

109 *Koranische Untersuchungen* [*Koranic Studies*] 71.

110 *Volkssprache und Schriftsprache* [*Vernacular and Written Language*] 102.

111 *Skizzen und Vorarbeiten* [*Sketches and Preliminary Studies*] 6 (Berlin, 1899) 259.

112 *GdQ* III 40, note 3.

and A. Fischer[114] involving the drawing in of the Jewish-Aramaic or Aramaic אוריתא (*ōrāytā*) and the hypothetical "hybrid form" תוריתא (*tōrāytā*), from which the Arabic التورية (*at-tawrīya*) would have emerged, he asserts that in this case the Arabic form in the final position **tawrāyah* should have resulted and not the actual spelling *tawrāh.*

In fact, W. Diem believes he has found the solution in G. Dalman's[115] realization that in a part of the Jewish-Aramaic dialects "the Nisba ending of the feminine *–āytā* experienced a shortening of the *ā* and monophthongization of the thus created diphthong *ay* to *ē*." From this phenomenon (*āytā* > *aytā* > *ēṯā*), which is also well known in East Aramaic dialects, there would have emerged from a hypothetical Aramaic form **tō-rāytā* / **tōraytā* / **tōrēṯā* the only possible choice in Arabic, a word ending in *–āh*, and thus *tawrāh.*

Apart from his giving no further evidence for this alleged form, W. Diem has apparently overlooked the fact that in Arabic another frequently documented structural type ending in *-īya* lends itself more readily to the Aramaic Nisba ending *-āyā* / *-āytā* than the one he has proposed. Parallels such as the Syro-Aramaic ܝܘܡܝܬܐ (*yawmāytā*) = Arabic يوميّة (*yawmīya*) (*daily*), ܒܪܝܬܐ (*barrāytā*) = برّيّة (*barrīya*) (*outside, to be found in the country*), ܓܘܝܬܐ (*gawwāytā*) (*inner, to be found inside*) = جوّية (*ğawwīya*) (*related to the air or atmosphere*)[116] are only a few popular examples. In the Koran in Sura 19:26 a further example is provided for the Syro-Aramaic ܐܢܫܝܐ (*a*)*nāšāyā* by the Arabic انسيا / *insīyā* for the equivalent masculine ending, though here one could also make a claim for the necessity to rhyme.

If for the reasons given by W. Diem (*op. cit.* 248) a borrowing from the Hebrew תורה / *tōrā* is now out of the question for the Koranic spell-

113 *Zur arabischen Rechtschreibung* [*On the Arabic Orthography*] 331.

114 Brünnow-Fischer, *Arabische Chrestomatie* [*Arabic Chrestomathy*], glossary s.v.

115 *Grammatik des jüdisch-palästinischen Aramäisch* [*Grammar of Jewish-Palestinian Aramaic*] (Leipzig, ^{2}1905) 193.

116 The shift in meaning of Syro-Aramaic ܓܘܐ (*gawwā*) (*interior*) to Arabic جو (*ğaww*) (*air, atmosphere*) in Classical Arabic (see below page p. 221 f.) was probably caused by the misinterpretation of this Syro-Aramaic expression in Sura 16:79.

ing توريه (with the accepted canonical pronunciation *tawrāt*), nevertheless another reading than his proposed *tawrāh* must be taken into consideration. On the basis of the Syro-Aramaic term ܐܘܪܝܬܐ (*ōrāytā*), the Arabic ending *–īya* suspected by Th. Nöldeke can at first be confirmed. The initial peak ـتـ / *ta* later provided with two dots according to Arabic tradition cannot be considered as certain because a "hybrid form" combining the initial sound of the Hebraic and the final sound of the Syro-Aramaic term *tōrāytā* has not been documented. But if the Arabic written characters توريه seem rather to argue in favor of the assumption that the Syro-Aramaic ܐܘܪܝܬܐ (*ōrāytā*) served as a model, then اوريه (*awrīya* / *ōrīya*) would have been expected in the Arabic transcription. Considering this, how else is the initial sound of توريه read as ـتـ / *t* to be explained?

An important indication for a plausible explanation is provided by Th. Nöldeke in his *Neue Beiträge zur semitischen Sprachwissenschaft* [*New Studies to Semitic Linguistics*]. In the chapter entitled *"Wechsel von anlautendem w or Hamza und j"* [*"The Alternation of Initial w or Hámza and j"*] (202–206), he gives a series of such examples from Hebrew, Aramaic and Arabic. As a Koranic variant to آسن (*ʾāsin*) (Sura 47:15), he mentions, among others, the variant يسن (*yāsin*). In the Index (206) he compiles the following additional examples: أتم / يتم (*atam* / *yatam*), أتن / يتن (*atan* / *yatan*), أصر / يصر (*aṣar* / *yaṣar*), and أفن / يفن (*afan* / *yafan*).

There are a few examples of this in Syro-Aramaic, precisely in the case of proper names. Well known first of all is the pronunciation *Yešūᶜ* (among the Western Syrians) and *ʾĪšōᶜ* (among the Eastern Syrians) for *Jesus*. One could also mention ܐܘܪܫܠܡ (*Ūrišlem*) (Jerusalem) in Syriac and ܝܪܘܫܠܡ (*Īrušlēm*/*Yīrušlēm*) in Christian-Palestinian (*Thes.* I 101; 1630). Also of interest is the Syrian lexicographers' explanation for the Aramaic names of the *Jordan*, which the *Thes.* (I 1584) renders as follows: ܝܘܪܕܢܢ (*Yurdnān*): ܐܘܟܝܬ ܐܘܪܕܢܢ (i.e. *Urdnān*) ܗ: (i.e.): ܢܘܗܪܐ ܕܢܚ ܠܢ (*nuhrā dnaḥ lan*) (*the light has appeared to us*), in addition to the Arabic variant: الأردن (*al-ʾUrdunn*).

Finally, we find in the Koran itself a further example in the name ياجوج (*Yağūğ*) (Sura 18:94; 21:96), whose initial *y* alternates with the *a* of the Syro-Aramaic spelling ܐܓܘܓ (*Agōg*/*Agōḡ*).[117]

On the Spelling of ياجوج (*Yağūğ*) and ماجوج (*Mağūğ*)

With this pair of names we would have one example, among others in the Koran, of the use of the *alif* as *mater lectionis* (vowel letter) for short *a* in accordance with the Aramaic writing tradition. Whereas A. Jeffery (*loc. cit.*, 288) sees in this *alif* a long *ā* (*Yājūj* / *Mājūj*), the Cairo edition takes it to be a *hamza* carrier and reads: *Ya'ğūğ wa- Ma'ğūğ*.

Arguing against both these readings is (a) the Syro-Aramaic pronunciation, whose *a* in both cases[118] is short; (b) the defective spelling without *alif* in the recently published facsimile of the Koran codex Or. 2165 of the British Library,[119] where in both cases (Sura 18:94 / Folio 47a, 18; Sura 21:96 / Folio 58a, 2) one finds يجوج (*Yağūğ*) and مجوج (*Mağūğ*); (c) the confirmation of this pronunciation in today's usage in the Middle East where these two names are familiar as a *standard quotation.*

As a further example of an *alif* in a medial position for a short *a* the word مائدة, that the Cairo edition reads as *mā'ida* should for the time being suffice. In the Arabic dialect of northern Mesopotamia, however, this word is still commonly used today in the pronunciation *mayde*. As a consequence, the Koranic spelling ought to have been *mayda.*[120]

---

117 Cf. *Thes.* I 23.

118 Although the *Thes.*, II 2003, gives two vowel variants for ܡܓܘܓ (*Māgōg* / *Māgōḡ* and *Magōg* / *Magōḡ*), the latter variant predominates.

119 François Déroche, Sergio Noja Noseda (eds.), *Sources de la transmission manuscrite du texte coranique.* I Les manuscrits de style ḥiğāzī. Volume 2, tome I. Le manuscrit Or. 2165 (f. 1 à 61) de la British Library, Fondazione Ferni Noja Noseda, Lesa 2001.

120 Th. Nöldeke, *NBsS* (*Neue Beiträge zur semitischen Sprachwissenschaft* [*New Essays on Semitic Linguistics*]), Strasbourg 1910, 54 f., is starting from the pronunciation *mā'ida* when he explains: "The word was then usually and often

compressed into ميدة (*mayda*)," which, however, in reality corresponds to the original Koranic pronunciation. But the borrowing of this word from Ethiopic (see A. Jeffery, *loc. cit.*, 255 f.) is doubted by Nöldeke, who then remarks (55): "Finally, it is not even clear at all that the Ethiopic word is of Semitic origin." This recently gave rise to the following attempt at a new interpretation: Manfred Kropp, *Viele fremde Tische, und noch einer im Koran*: Zur Etymologie von äthiopisch *mā'əd(d)e* und arabisch *mā'ida* [*Many Strange Tables, and Another One in the Koran:* On the Etymology of Ethiopic *mā'əd(d)e* and Arabic *mā'ida*], in *Oriens Christianus*, 87, 2003, 140-143. The evidence of this or a similar commodity in Ethiopic, Arabic and now also in the Greco-Roman cultural area would only suggest the Latin etymology of the word being discussed if a Latin basic meaning of a corresponding Latin verbal root were demonstrated. Although *mā'ida* / *mayda* is not attested in written Aramaic, the verbal root and its basic meaning can be determined from standard Aramaic, which will be gone into elsewhere. Yet M. Kropp is right about the falsely assumed etymologies in Arabistics of Arabic *qaṣr* from Latin *castrum* and Koranic *ṣirāṭ* from Latin *strata*, since Arabic *qaṣr* (originally *fortress, citadel*) cannot be explained from the basic meaning of the homonymous Arabic verbal root *qaṣura* (*to be short*). However, if we bring in the phonetic variants of the Syro-Aramaic verbal root ܓܙܪ / *gzar* (*to cut, to cut off*), whose basic meaning shows the two roots to be allophones, there arises from the substantive ܓܙܝܪܬܐ / *gzirtā* derived from it, according to *Mannā* (102b), the meaning: (a) (under 4) حجر منحوت مربع (*a square-cut stone*), (b) in reference to the notched coping of a wall (under 9): افريز البناء (*battlement*) (in Brockelmann, *Lexicon Syriacum*, 112b, 5. *pinna muri*). The latter meaning was then applied to the defensive wall, the defensive tower and / or the entire fortress. Arabistics' previously assumed derivation from Latin *castrum* / *castellum* (> English *castle*, German *Kastell*, French *château*) is thus turned on its head, since even the Latin verb *castrō* (*to castrate*) makes clear its dependence on the basic meaning of the Syro-Aramaic verb. However, in the case of the Latin transcription one must start from the standard Aramaic and/or Arabic form *qaṣr*, since the voiceless emphatic sound *ṣ* is rendered in Latin by a combined *st* . A further example of this is the Koranic صراط / *ṣirāṭ* < Syro-Aramaic ܣܪܛܐ / *serṭā* (*line* = *way*), whose emphatic initial *s* is in turn rendered in Latin by *st* (= *strata*) (see below p. 226 ff.). As already discussed, this is demonstrated by the rendering of city names such as that of the city of بصره / ***Buṣra*** south of Damascus, which is rendered in Greek and Latin as *Βοστρα* / *Bostra*. In one case the emphatic *ṣ* is rendered by the sound combination *ps*. Thus the Greek / Latin transcription of the city ܡܨܝܨܬܐ / ***Maṣṣiṣtā*** is *Mopsuestia* (*Thes.* II 2195).

Instead of the previous pronunciation *tawrāh* / *tawrāt* for the Koranic spelling تورية, we would accordingly have criteria for the pronunciation *yōrīya* / *yūrīya*, in an Arabicized pronunciation perhaps *yawrīya*. The weak point in this argumentation, however, remains the fact that (at least until now) no evidence has been given of the existence of an Aramaic or Syro-Aramaic variant such as יוריתא / ܝܘܪܝܬܐ (*yōrāytā*).

On the other hand, our foundations are strengthened if in the case of the spelling توريه we read the medial peak يه as the phonetic rendering of the Hebrew feminine ending *–ā* (as finally transmitted) to designate the long *ā*. Namely, contrary to Diem's assumption, the Koran does not always render the foreign orthography faithfully in the case of borrowed proper names. An example of this is the orthography of the name Abraham, which in the Cairo Koran edition is written ابرهيم (*Ibrāhīm* = *Abrāhām*) in fifty-four passages and ابرهم (*Abrāhām*) in fifteen passages (see below the example 5, p. 93).

However, it has appeared meanwhile that such an assumption as to the spelling of توريه / يوريه is erroneous, inasmuch as the Koran does not provide any example for the usage of a double *mater lectionis* يه / *yh* to mark the final *ā*, considering the fact that, according to the Aramaic (and Hebrew) orthographical tradition, in this case only the final ـه / *h* fulfils this function. This consideration led us to undertake further investigations to determine the real reading of the little peak ـيـ before the final ـه / *h*. The results can now be presented in what follows.

On the new interpretation of the spelling تورية *(Tawrāh / Tawrāt)* = يورية *(Yawrīya / Yōrīya)*

Taking up once more the Koranic name beginning with *y* يجوج (*Yağūğ*), we have here a parallel for the Syriac spelling ܐܓܘܓ (= arabisch أجوج *Ağūğ*), which would justify an initial *y* for the Koranic spelling يورية (*Yawrīya*) for Syro-Aramaic ܐܘܪܝܬܐ (*Ōraytā*) (= arabisch اورية / *Awrīya* / *Ōrīya* / *Ūrīya*).

In the first German edition of this study (p. 68 ff.) this well-founded reading was temporarily set aside because until then no evidence of it could be given. In the meantime, it not only seems obvious through the reference to the above-mentioned parallel; it can also be substantiated, thanks to the *Mandaic Grammar* (*MG*) of Nöldeke,[121] Namely, in the first chapter on *Schrift und Lautlehre* [*Writing, Phonetics and Phonology*], he remarks under § 6 (p. 7) (3):

> An example of initial *spiritus lenis* with *u, o* is עו: עוראיתא = אוריתא (*Ōraytā*) "Thora"; עור = אור (name of the worst devil, from Hebrew אור (*ūr*) "Feuer");... This עו ,however, can in some circumstances also be *ew, iw* ...

That עוראיתא can accordingly not only be pronounced *Ōraytā*, but in some circumstances also *Yōraytā*, is in turn supported by the Mandaic dictionary.[122] There (p. 191a) the spelling given by Nöldeke as an example עור is rendered alternatively under both pronunciations: "YUR = AUR II (= ʿUR II) *to shine*"; further: "YWR = AWR (=ʿWR) *to blind, to dazzle with light.*" Another example of the initial *y* is provided to us by Nöldeke in the *MG* (§ 62 [5]) with the spelling **יורא** (*yōrā / yūrā*) "*shine.*"

With these examples the Mandaic writing tradition again helps us to solve the riddle of the Koran spelling تورية . Consequently, from now on we can be certain that this spelling should no longer to be read as *Tawrāh / Tawrāt*, but as *Yawrīya / Yōrīya /Yūrīya.*

Now what makes this reading into a certainty is not only the initial *y* which was heretofore unexpected in research on the, but in particular the ending ية , in which Nöldeke had correctly expected the pronunciation *īya.* The argumentation in the first German edition of this study in favor of the reading *Tawrāh / Tawrāt*, according to which the next to the last little peak can be seen as *mater lectionis* for long *ā*, is erroneous since the final *h* fulfills precisely this function.

In other words, as a rule two *matres lectionis*, one following immediately after the other for one and the same function, contradicts the Koranic and Aramaic writing tradition. For this reason the ending *īya* is

121 Theodor Nöldeke, *Mandäische Grammatik*, Halle an der Saale 1975 (Reprint Darmstadt 1964).

122 E. S. Drower, R. Macuch, *A Mandaic Dictionary*, Oxford 1963.

to be confirmed. Thus for the Koranic spelling يوريه the result is clearly the reading *Yawrīya* or *Yōrīya* / *Yūrīya*.

In the light of this misreading of a presumably familiar name, the question can be asked as to how the Arabic reader was able to arrive at such a misinterpretation of the Koranic orthography. The answer can only be that, for the lack of an oral tradition, they allowed themselves to be told by Jewish informants that in Hebrew the word is *Tōrā*, even though in Jewish-Aramaic (as in Syro-Aramaic) this is pronounced אורייתה (*Ōraytā*/*Ōrētā*) (*status absolutus* אורייה /*Ōrayyā*/*Ōrīyā*).[123]

The fact that the Arabic exegetes transferred this reading to a differently pronounced Koranic spelling is reminiscent of the Biblical principle of כתיב /*ktīḇ* (so *written*) and קרא /*qrē* (differently *read*). This appears to be the principle that A. Jeffery (*loc. cit.* 95 f.) is following when – despite the 18 times in which the spelling التورية occurs in the Cairo version of the Koran – he renders this word in the modern Arabic transcription (توراة / *Tawrāt*) and reads it *Taurāh*. Just as rashly did Jeffery agree with the Western Koran scholars who had argued for a direct borrowing from Hebrew, whereby he rejected Fraenkel's consideration, which, with its presumption regarding an Aramaic borrowing, was closer to the truth.[124]

With his comprehensive knowledge of the Aramaic dialects, in particular of Mandaic, Theodore Nöldeke, however, would certainly have had the competence to cope with the riddle of this Koranic orthography had he concerned himself more closely with the text of the Koran.

---

123 Cf. Michael Sokoloff, *A Dictionary of Jewish Palestinian Aramaic*, Ramat-Gan, second printing 1992, 42b.

124 Thus Jeffery writes (*op.cit.* 96): "Western scholars from the time of Marraci, *Prodromus*, I, 5, have recognized it as a borrowing direct from the Heb. (Note 2: So de Sacy, *JA*, 1829, p. 175; Geiger, 45; von Kremer, *Ideen*, 226 n.; Pautz, *Offenbarung*, 120, n. 1; Hirschfeld, *Beiträge*, 65; Horovitz, *KU*, 71; *JPN*, 194; Margoliouth, *ERE*, x, 540), and there is no need to discuss the possible Aram. Origin mentioned by Fraenkel, *Vocab*, 23 (Note 3: Fischer, *Glossar*, 18a, however, suggests that it may be a mixed form from the Heb. תורה (*Tōrā*) and Aram. אוריתא (*Ōraytā*); cf. also Ahrens, *ZDMG*, lxxxiv, 20, and Torrey, *Foundation*, 51.). The word was doubtless well known in Arabia before Muḥammad's time, cf. Ibn Hishām, 659."

Example 5: On the spelling of ابرهيم *(Ibrāhīm = Abrāhām)*[125]

In the case of this name the Arabic readers have proceeded in the opposite fashion: Whereas in the preceding spelling التورية they have falsely seen in the next to the last little peak a *mater lectionis* for long *ā* (instead of *y* or. *ī*), for the spelling ابرهيم they have taken the next to the last little peak to be a *mater lectionis* for long *ī* instead of for long *ā*. This is all the more surprising since the name *Abraham* must have been quite familiar to them.

That with the spelling ابرهيم the reading *Abrāhām* is intended is supported by the fifteen passages in the Cairo edition of the Koran with the defective spelling ابرهم (*Abrhm*). This faithfully renders the Hebrew and Syro-Aramaic written form אברהם / ܐܒܪܗܡ and is to be read as "*Abrāhām.*"[126] The partial full spelling ابرهيم occurs in fifty-four passages in the Cairo version. Here the fact that it is not the first long *ā*, but the second that is indicated by a little peak, can be explained by the Koran writer's wanting in this way to emphasize the *accented syllable* (*Abrahám*).

Sura 12:88
Example 6: مزجية (allegedly *muzǧāt*)

This is actually an example of a little peak that has been misread and taken to be a long *ā*. W. Diem explains (*op. cit.* § 57):

> "In the spelling of the feminine singular forms ending in *–āh* constructed from *tertiae infirmae* roots, sometimes *yā'* and some-

125 In A. Jeffery, *op. cit.* 44-46.

126 As Th. Nöldeke (Bergsträßer-Pretzl), *GdQ*, III, 17, remarks (in note 1): "What is meant by the shorter spelling (ابرهم) is the pronunciation ابراهام (*Abrāhām*) (this, according to the Damascene ibn ʿĀmir, is considered certain in Sura 2; other passages are still in dispute)." Also concerning these two variants on p. 98: "16:124 ابرهيم :ابرهم [Note 3: Not listed by Mingana]; this may be a difference in spelling, but may also represent the form ابراهام (*Abrāhām*) that appears in the Othmanic text." The effort expended by A. Jeffery, *Foreign Vocabulary*, 44-46, to explain this orthography was therefore unnecessary.

times *alif* is encountered. The spellings familiar to me are: مزجيه 12,88 *muzǧāh* (*zǧw*) "little"; ... . Of these spellings, مزجيه corresponds to expectations, since for the undocumented masculine form *muzǧā* of spellings like مسمى *musammā* (§ 45) one can infer a spelling with a final *yā'* that, in accordance with § 56, could then be retained for the spelling of the feminine."

Indeed, one could have spoken of the " مزجيه *muzǧāh* type" if this word had not been misread. That *mediae geminatae* and *tertiae infirmae* roots can be variants of one and the same root is a well-known phenomenon in Syro-Aramaic and Arabic. But the fact that the three verbal forms attributed to the root (زجا زجو) in the Koran (Suras 17:66; 24:43; 12:88) have actually been misread (the first two from the Arabic رجأ *raǧa'a* and أرجأ / *arǧa'a* "*to hold up*," the third from the Syro-Aramaic ܪܓܝ / *raggī* "*to make damp or wet*") and falsely interpreted as the *mediae geminatae* root زج / *zaǧǧa* (*push, throw*), raises the question whether the *tertiae infirmae* root زجا / *zaǧā* / *zǧw* was not adopted into the Arabic lexicography with the same meaning as the root زج / *zaǧǧa* on the basis of this misreading (cf. both roots, e.g. in H. Wehr, *Arabisches Wörterbuch* [*Arabic Dictionary*]).

With far too much confidence, A. Jeffery says of مزجاة / *muzǧāt* (*Foreign Vocabulary* 33 f.) that it is "undoubtedly genuine Arabic." But one ought not to take the Arabic commentators for so ignorant when even *Ṭabarī* (XIII 50 ff.) says on the subject: اختلف أهل التأويل في البيان عن تأويل ذلك "on the interpretation of this (expression) the commentators are of various opinions." Among the forty opinions listed by *Ṭabarī* (*bad, trifling, low-grade, inaccessible goods; clarified butter and wool; inferior, insufficient money*) only one of them comes close to the actual Biblical sense to which this expression alludes. It is the interpretation attributed to *Abū Ṣāliḥ* (*op. cit.* 51) according to which it means الصنوبر والحبة الخضراء (*aṣ-ṣanawbar wa-l-ḥabba al-ḫaḍrā'*) "*pine seeds and terebinths* (*turpentine pistachios*)."

This opinion is not at all as outlandish as it appears at first glance. Rather, one must assume that this *Abū Ṣāliḥ* was aware of the corresponding passage in the Bible (Genesis 43: 11). Namely, there it is said that Israel (Jacob), before the second journey of his sons to Egypt with Benjamin, instructs each of them, in addition to the double amount of money, to take something with them of the best fruits in the land as a present. These fruits are enumerated (*op. cit.*) as follows (according to the *Pšiṭṭā*):

> "Pine seeds (or balsam), honey, resin, pistachios, terebinths (turpentine pistachios) and almonds."[127]

This hint could have contributed to the clarification of the familiarly *obscure* expression مزجية (supposedly *muzǧāt*) if our Koran translators had taken a closer look at the corresponding passage in the Bible and not been satisfied with repeating the wavering opinions of the commentators.[128] If *Ṭabarī*, however, has taken the trouble to list up to forty *hadith*, he surely must have imagined that one or the other interpretation was correct. In the process, this again confirms that occasionally the Arabic exegesis of the Koran has preserved a correct interpretation of an expression that was considered to be unclear. The task of Koran research should have then been, on the basis of philological and objective criteria, to identify this one interpretation.

In the present case, the above-mentioned Bible passage gives us an objective indication concerning the identity of the Syro-Aramaic root of the spelling misread as مزجية (*muzǧāh* / *muzǧāt*). For in reality (a) the dot over the ز / *z* has been falsely placed and this letter should be read as ر / *r* and (b) the next to the last peak should not be read as long *ā* but as ـيـ / *y* / *ī*. This results in the reading مرجية = Syro-Aramaic ܡܪܓܝܬܐ (*m-raggaytā*). As the active or passive feminine attributive participle of ܪܓܝ (*raggī*) (*to moisten, to wet, to refresh*) the *Thes.* (II 3806) gives us

127 The Jerusalemer Bibel [Jerusalem Bible] renders this passage as follows: "some balsam, a little honey, gum, ladanum, pistachios and almonds."

128 R. Paret, for example, says in his *Kommentar* [*Commentary*] (253) on this passage (12:88): "The interpretation of *biḍāʿa muzǧāt* is not certain." In his *Koranübersetzung* [*Koran translation*] (198) he renders the expression with "Ware von geringen Wert [goods of little value] (?)." R. Blachère (268) translates in a corresponding manner: "une marchandise de peu de prix [low-priced merchandise]"; and R. Bell (225): "we have brought transported goods."

under “poma ܪ̈ܓܝܐ (*rḡayyā*) *recentia*” the meaning “*fresh fruits,*” which would fit our context. Moreover, under ܪܓܐ (*rḡā*) (3805, l. 43805) the *Thes.* gives the following as synonyms for ܪܓܝ (*raggī*): ܐܪܛܒ (*arṭeḇ*), ܪܛܒ (*raṭṭeḇ*), (in Arabic) يرطب (*yuraṭṭib*) (*to wet, to moisten, to refresh*).

Now, although the Syro-Aramaic participial form ܡܪܓܝܬܐ (*m-raggaytā*) can be understood actively or passively, it would be more likely to be understood as active here since in Syro-Aramaic usually the passive participle of *Pʿal* ܪܓܐ (*rḡā*) is used for the passive meaning.[129] In the case of the synonymous ܪܛܒ (*rṭeḇ*) we would have by analogy the Arabic رطب (*raṭib*) for the latter and مرطب (*muraṭṭib*) for the former case.

Thus the most obvious thing to do would be to read the Koranic transcription مرجية , for which there is no root in Arabic in this sense, actively as *muraǧǧiya.* The expression جئنا ببضعة مرجية (*ǧiʾnā bi-biḍāʿa^{tin} muraǧǧiya^{tin}*) (Syro-Aramaic: ܐܝܬܝܢܢ ܬܐܓܘܪܬܐ ܡܪܓܝܬܐ *aytīnan tēḡurtā m-raggaytā*) would then be in Arabic understandable today:

جئنا ببضاعة مرطّبة (*ǧiʾnā bi-biḍāʿa^{tin} muraṭṭiba*)
“We have brought along <u>refreshing</u>[130] fruits.“

Hence, according to the Biblical account, Joseph's brothers have brought along with them the present for the host that is still in part customary according to Oriental practice today.

---

129 Cf. *Thes.* (II 3805 f.), under ܪܓܐ (*rḡā*): ܩܝܣܐ ܪܓܝܐ (*qaysā raḡyā*) ξύλον χλωρόν (*fresh wood*), ܣܘܟܐ ܪ̈ܓܝܬܐ (*sawkē raḡyāṯā*) κλάδοι απαλοί (*tender, young, fresh twigs*).

130 Supporting this meaning, moreover, is the synonymous expression given by the *Thes.* (II 3893) ܡܝܐ ܡܪܛܒܝܢ (*mayyā m-raṭṭḇīn*) (*refreshing water*), as well as the explanation cited from the Syrian lexicographers on the *Afel* ܐܪܛܒ (*arṭeḇ*): ܘܡܬܐܡܪܐ ܥܠ ܡܝܐ ܘܕܒܫܐ ܘܡܫܚܐ ܘܚܡܪܐ ܘܡܐ ܕܕܡܐ (*w-meṯamrā ʿal mayyā w-ḏeḇšā w-mešḥā w-ḥamrā w-mā d-dāmē*) (*arṭeḇ* “*to refresh*”: *said of water, <u>honey</u>, oil, wine and the like*).

Sura 9:1 and Sura 54:43
Example 7: براءة *(barāʾa) = Hebrew* ברית *(brīṯ)*

The hypothesis of the seemingly early abandonment of the little peak ـيـ also used in the first generation of Koranic orthography to designate a word-medial long *ā* and its replacement by an *alif* ا in a second or third phase can be partially proven on the basis of extant manuscripts of the Koran of the second and third generation. The suspicion that many a word was misread and distorted in the course of this orthographic reform may, for example, be confirmed by the spelling براءة (*barāʾa*). This word occurs twice in the Koran (Suras 9:1 and 54:43). In the context of Sura 9:1, for instance, one reads:

<u>براة</u> من الله ورسوله الى الذين عهدتم من المشركين

The expression, in keeping with *Ṭabarī* (X 58 ff.), is understood by our Koran translators as follows:

> (Bell I 173): "<u>Renunciation</u> by Allah and His messenger of the polytheists with whom ye have made covenants;..."
>
> (Paret 150): "Eine <u>Aufkündigung</u> (des bisherigen Rechtsverhältnisses und Friedenszustandes) [Note: Oder: Eine Schutzerklärung] von seiten Gottes und seines Gesandten an diejenigen von den Heiden, mit denen ihr eine bindende Abmachung eingegangen habt [Note: Oder (nach F. Buhl): (gerichtet an die heidnische Welt, jedoch nicht) an diejenigen von den Heiden, mit denen ihr eine bindende Abmachung eingegangen habt.]"
>
> (Blachère 212): "<u>Immunité</u> d'Allah et de Son Apôtre, pour ceux des Associateurs avec qui vous avez conclu un pacte."

In his note on this expression, R. Blachère rightfully questions whether براءة (*barāʾa*) really signifies a "*renunciation*" [Bell] or "*termination*" [Paret's *Aufkündigung*]. What was meant by this was the termination of the agreement of *Ḥu-daybīya* after the taking of Mecca in the year 630, which would clearly contradict Verse 2.

The occasion for R. Paret's proposal of contradictory alternatives for براءة (*barāʾa*), "*termination* [*Aufkündigung*]" (of an agreement) or "(*declaration of*) *immunity* [*Schutzerklärung*]," must have been the distortion, by the insertion of the *alif*, of the original spelling برية (*barīya*). Namely, on the basis of the context, this spelling can only be the transliteration of the Hebrew ברית (*brīṯ*) (*agreement*). Among the definitions listed by W. Gesenius (*Hebräisches und aramäisches Handwörterbuch* [*Concise Dictionary of Hebrew and Aramaic*] 116) for this well-known Biblical expression, the following should suffice:

> "1. An agreement which receives through a solemn ceremony an especially forceful and obligatory character.... Such a solemn obligation occurred in various cases, for example (a) when a *covenant* was concluded between persons, nations or tribes; (b) in the case of treaties, or contracts, referring to specific obligations or performance; (c) in the case of agreements between winners and losers..."

The meaning of براءة (*barāʾa*) = برية (*barīya*)[131] would thus be established as a rendering of the Hebrew ברית (*brīṯ*) (*agreement, covenant*). The same applies for Sura 54:43: ام لكم براة في الزبر "or have you, say, a <u>covenant</u> (with God) in the Scripture?"[132] Here, too, it is probably not براءة (*baraʾa*) that should be read but برية (*barīya*). The corresponding Syro-Aramaic expression in the *Pšiṭṭā* is ܩܝܡܐ (*qyāmā*). This is also what must be meant in Sura 5:97: جعل الله الكعبة البيت للناس قيما الحرام "God has made the Kaʿba, the Sacred House, a <u>covenant</u> for mankind."

131 This word, pronounced *"brīya,"* is very current in actual spoken Algerian Arabic in the meaning *"letter"* (= *written document*).

132 Properly considered, "*Book of Psalms*," which (being part of the *Scripture*) *Ṭabarī* (XXVII 108) also explains with "*Scripture*."

The determination that the little peak not only serves as the carrier of five letters ـبـتـثـنـيـ (*b*, *t*, *ṯ*, *n*, *ī* / *y*), but occasionally (except for the endings of verbs *tertiae yāʾ* before suffixes) can also designate long *ā*, provides a solution to many a phenomenon considered inexplicable in the Koran until now. As W. Diem comments under (e) طيب / *ṭāba* and the like (op. cit., §60, 250 f .):

> "For the spellings 4:3 طاب / *ṭāba* 'it was good,' 2:228 وللرجال *wa-li-r-riǧāl* 'and to the men,' as well as for جا / *ǧā* "he came" and جات / *ǧāt* 'she came' ad-Dānī reports [*Muqniʿ* 71. See also Jeffery-Mendelson: 'Samarquand Qu'ran Codex' 186] as variants the spellings جيات , جيا , وللرجيل , طيب . The spellings with *yāʾ* are explained by Nöldeke [*GdQ* [1]1860, 255], Vollers [*Volkssprache und Schriftsprache* 102] and Bergsträsser-Pretzl [*GdQ* III 40, 92] by *imāla*; Brockelmann [*GvG* I 608, Note 1] also assumes an *imāla* in the case of جيا , which he sees as being derived from forms containing an *ī* such as *ǧīt*. The explanation with *imāla* is made too ad hoc to be convincing, and would also be surprising in the case of *ṭāb*, in emphatic surroundings. Not to mention the fact that I consider it impossible that a phonologically irrelevant variant could have caused a change in the orthography. There is still no explanation for this: at best, for جات , جيا , طيب [sic! for جيات] one could imagine the possibility that the *yāʾ* of spellings of other derivations (*yaṭību; ǧīt* etc.) had infiltrated by association, as was also considered for the *wāw* in الربوا (§ 47). However, للرجيل cannot be explained in this way."

The determination presented above now makes it clear that what is meant by the spelling طيب is طاب (*ṭāb*), what is meant by the spelling جيا is جاء (*ǧāʾ*), and what is meant by the spelling جيات is جاءت (*gāʾat*). The same applies for the clarification above of the spelling ابرهيم = ابرهام (*Abrāhām*), which W. Diem (*op. cit.* §30, 227) considers equally puzzling, and for the examples cited by Th. Nöldeke (Bergsträßer-Pretzl, *GdQ* III 49): بايید = بأياد (*bi-ayād*^{in}) (Sura 51:47), بأييم = بأيام (*bi-ayyām*)

(Sura 14:5), جياتهم = جاءتهم (*ǧāʾathum*) (92). Further examples would be the variants from Sura 7:40 الخياط (*al-ḫiyāṭ*) (< Syro-Aramaic ܚܝܛܐ *ḥyāṭā* or *ḥayyāṭā*) and المخيط (< ܡܚܛܐ *m-ḥāṭā*) (*sewing needle*) (*op. cit.* 67), no matter how hard the *Lisān* (VII 298 f.) tries to explain these Syro-Aramaic forms as Arabic. This also renders superfluous the concluding remarks on the corresponding orthography in the Lewis palimpsests (*op. cit.* 57).

In this way, too, many a Koranic spelling قيل (*qīl*) will turn out to be قال (*qāl*) (perhaps even the Syro-Aramaic ܩܠܐ / *qālā* "*word, speech*"). As to the later use of the peak as the carrier of the *hamza* in the Koran, it should finally be noted that in the early Koran manuscripts the peaks were conceived of exclusively as carriers of the above-mentioned sounds, but never as carriers of the *hamza*. A later analysis will show that many a distortion has resulted from the subsequent incorrect provision of a traditional peak with an unforeseen *hamza*.

On the Morphology and Etymology of Syro-Aramaic ܣܛܢܐ (*sāṭānā*) and Koranic شيطن (*šayṭān*)

Concerning the thesis that the medial peak ـيـ (*y*) in the Koranic spelling of شيطن (*šayṭān*) is a *mater lectionis* for the vowel *ā* corresponding to the transliteration of Syro-Aramaic ܣܛܢܐ (*sāṭānā* / *sāṭān*) a preliminary remark is to be made about the Koranic orthography of this word. For while, for example, the spelling of ابرهيم (*Ibrāhīm* = *Abrāhām*) occurs in the Cairo Koran edition fifteen times (in Sura 2) as ابرهم (*Abrāhām*), without the facultative *mater lectionis* ـيـ / *y* (= *ā*), as has been noticed by Th. Nöldeke (Bergsträßer-Pretzl) in *GdQ* [*History of the Qur'ān*] III, 17, n. 1 (see above p. 93), this is not the case for the regular spelling of شيطن (*šayṭān*), whose pronunciation is moreover very common in vernacular Arabic. It is therefore unjustified to maintain that the Koranic orthography simply reproduces the phonetic spelling of Syro-Aramaic ܣܛܢܐ (*sāṭānā*).

This thesis has been recently rejected by M. Kropp, who tries to demonstrate the correlation between the Arabic and the Ethiopic origin of *šayṭān.*[133] It is here not the place to discuss the conclusions of this instructive contribution which foreshadows the complexity of this momentous term for cultural, religious and linguistic history. However, apart from the detailed examples of the usage of this word in Arabic and Ethiopic, no explanation is given as to his original meaning. Thus further details will be briefly provided here to point out that شيطن (*šayṭān*) is originally neither Arabic nor Ethiopic, but that the two spellings, ܣܛܢܐ (*sāṭānā*) as well as شيطن (*šayṭān*), are morphologically and etymologically two secondary Eastern (Babylonian) Aramaic dialectal variants of one and the same Syro-Aramaic verbal root.

This root is still conserved in Classical Syro-Aramaic with the medial ܥ / *ʿayn* in its unaltered form ܣܥܛ / *sʿaṭ* (or *sʿeṭ*). The original meaning is given by C. Brockelmann (*Lexicon Syriacum*, 487b f.) as follows: "*taeduit eum, abhorruit* " (*to loath, abhor, abominate*). From this root two verbal adjectives were derived:

1. a) A first adjective was derived from an early passive participle of the first stem of regular three-consonant verbs according to the

---

133 A more extensive version of this chapter has appeared in the meantime in the anthology ed. by Christoph Burgmer: *Streit um den Koran. Die Luxenberg-Debatte. Standpunkte und Hintergründe* [*Dispute about the Koran. The Luxenberg-Debate. Standpoints and Backgrounds*], 3rd ed., Berlin 2006, p. 72–82; on the etymology of Koranic ܨܡܕ /*ṣamad* (Sura 112:2) see p. 76, note 1; further contributions by the author see there: a) p. 62-68: *Weihnachten im Koran* [*Christmas in the Koran*] (Sura 97); b) p. 83-89: *Der Koran zum „islamischen Kopftuch*" [*The Koran on the „Islamic Veil*"] (Sura 24:31). The two latter contributions have appeared in French as follows: a) Anne-Marie Delcambre, Joseph Bosshard et alii, *Enquêtes sur l'islam. En hommage à Antoine Moussali* [*Inquiries about Islam. In Homage to Antoine Moussali*], Paris (Desclée de Brouwer), 2004, p. 117-134 : *Noël dans le Coran* [*Christmas in the Koran*] ; b) Yves Charles Zarka, Sylvie Taussig, Cynthia Fleury (ed.), *L'Islam en France* [*Islam in France*], in: Cités (Revue) Hors Série, Paris (Presses Universitaires de France), 2004, p. 661-665: *Quelle est la langue du Coran*? [*Which is the Language of the Koran?*], p. 665-668: *Le voile islamique* [*The Islamic Veil*]. Cf. Manfred Kropp, *Der äthiopische Satan = šayṭān und seine koranischen Ausläufer; mit einer Bemerkung über verbales Steinigen* [*The Ethiopic Satan = šayṭān and his Koranic ramifications; with a notice about verbal stoning*], in: *Oriens Christianus*, Band [vol.] 89, 2005, p. 93-102.

form *paʿlā*[134] = ܣܥܛܐ /*saʿṭā* + the suffix *ān* + the suffix of *status emphaticus ā* = *ܣܥܛܢܐ /*saʿṭānā*. The suffix *ān* has among other things the same function as the Latin suffix *-abilis* (English *-able*) and confers on the participle the meaning of a gerund. Thus *ܣܥܛܢܐ / *saʿṭānā* means *"worthy to be abominated = abominable."* This is the *classical* form of the original Syro-Aramaic root.

b) From this *classical* form the medial ܥ / *ʿayn* was dropped early on in the vernacular Eastern Syro-Aramaic. The phonetical consequence of this dropping is the *compensative lengthening* (*Ersatzdehnung*) of the initial *ā*. So *ܣܥܛܢܐ / *saʿṭānā* became > ܣܛܢܐ / *sāṭānā* as it is attested in the Hebrew Bible (> שטן /*sāṭān*) as well as in the New Testament, and, since then, in many modern European languages. Because this word came with this (dialectal) spelling into Syriac through the translation of the Old and New Testament, the Syrian lexicographers were no longer able to recognize its actual Syro-Aramaic etymology (with the medial ܥ / *ʿayn*). Even Ephraem the Syrian derived it falsely from the root ܣܛܐ /*sṭā* which means *"deviate, lose the way,"* for which rea-

134 In the classical Syriac grammar this form is limited to verbs *tertiae ā* or *y* (with final *ā* or *y*), as e.g. (for masculine singular in *status emphaticus*): ܡܠܝܐ /*malyā* (*full*), ܫܢܝܐ / *šanyā* (*mad*), ܣܡܝܐ / *samyā* (*blind, a blind man*) (see C. Brockelmann, *Syrische Grammatik* [*Syriac Grammar*], *Paradigma* p. 140. Yet, that this form had also existed in early Syriac in regular verbs is attested in some still conserved adjectives as e.g.: ܥܣܩܐ / *ʿasqā* (*difficult*), ܛܢܦܐ / *ṭanpā*, ܨܥܠܐ / *ṣaʿlā* (*impure*), ܫܠܡܐ / *šalmā* (*sound, wholesome*), etc. Interesting is this earlier form in the Syro-Aramaic adjective ܚܢܦܐ / *ḥanpā* (*heathen*) beside the regular, in Syro-Aramaic unused but in the Koran transmitted form *ܚܢܝܦܐ > Arabic حنيفا / *ḥanīfā* = حنيف / *ḥanīf*. The same is to be found in the substantivied (i.e. used as a noun) Syro-Aramaic ܚܠܦܐ / *ḥalpā* (secondary *ḥelpā* > Arabic خلف / *ḫalaf*) and the Arabic, from Eastern Syro-Aramaic *ܚܠܝܦܐ (with the vernacular pronounciation of *ḥ* > *ḫ*) borrowed form خليفة /*ḫalīfa* (*substitute*). A further example we have in the Syro-Aramaic substantive ܚܠܒܐ /*ḥalḇā* and Arabic حليب /*ḥalīb* (*milk*). Both participial forms occur finaly in a few number of substantivied participle adjectives in Classical Syriac, as e.g.: ܟܪܟܐ / *karḵā* (*a fortified town, fortress, citadel*) = ܟܪܝܟܐ / *krīḵā* (*surrounded, encircled*).

son, he explains, the devil was called ܣܛܢܐ / *sāṭānā* (cf. *Thes.* II 2601, Ephr. ii. 474 D).

However, before *Satan* became a name of the devil, its actual meaning was "*abominable.*" Therefore, when Jesus rebuked Peter with the words: "Get thee behind me, *satan!* " (Mt 16:23), the latter word was not to be understood as a proper name, but verbatim: "Get thee behind me, *abominable!*" The same meaning is to be assumed in Mt 4:10, when Jesus repulsed the devil just once with the same epithet: ܣܛܢܐ / *sāṭānā* (= *abominable!*), whereas in this passage in the *Pešiṭṭā* the devil is called four times ܐܟܠܩܪܨܐ / *ʾākel-qarṣā* (*calumniator, accusator* = *adversary*) (Mt 4:1–11).

2. a) The second adjective derived from the root ܣܥܛ / *sʿaṭ* (according to the pattern of the passive participle *paʿīlā* / *pʿīlā* of the first stem of regular verbs) runs in Classical Syro-Aramaic *ܣܥܝܛܐ / *saʿīṭā* > *sʿīṭā*. After the dropping of the medial ܥ / *ʿayn* in the vernacular Eastern Syro-Aramaic, the spelling and the pronunciation become ܣܝܛܐ / *sayṭā*, as attested in Mandaic. C. Brockelmann (*Lexicon Syriacum*) gives on the one hand the Classical Syro-Aramaic form as ܣܥܝܛܐ / *sʿīṭā* (488a 4), and on the other hand the Mandaic form as סאיטא / *sayṭā* (487b -3), both with the same meaning: "*repudiandus*" (*abominable*). But Brockelmann did not notice that he just needed to add to this word the suffix *ān* / *ānā*[135] to have the vernacular Eastern Syro-Aramaic form סאיטאנא / *sayṭānā* from which (after changing the *s* > *š* and omission of the final *ā*) the Koranic Arabic شيطن / *šayṭān* is derived.[136]

---

135 Cf. Th. Nöldeke, *Syrische Grammatik* [*Syriac Grammar*], § 128, § 129: "To form adjectives, *ān* is added to very various words…" See further *ibid.*, *Mandäische Grammatik* [*Mandaic Grammar*], § 114 e): "Nouns formed with suffixes: With *ân* and its variants. The suffix אן , *ân*, that can be substituted in some cases by ין (§ 20), is likewise very common in Mandaic, namely, both for abstract nouns and for adjectives…."

136 Concerning the alternation of س / *s* and ش / *š* in Syro-Aramaic and Arabic see S. Fraenkel, *Die aramäischen Fremdwörter im Arabischen* [*The Aramaic Foreign Words in Arabic*], p. XII f., XXI.

As one can see, though the determination that the little peak ـيـ as occasional *mater lectionis* for medial long *ā* may be of some importance for Koranic research, however, it can not be considered as a key to solve such intricate riddles as the Koranic شيطن / *šayṭān*. Moreover, the erudite investigation of M. Kropp as to the use of this cultural word in Ethiopic confirms once more the view of Th. Nöldeke with regard to some Ethiopic words borrowed from Aramaic (cf. *Mandäische Grammatik / Mandaic Grammar*, p. 134, note 4 explaining the Syro-Aramaic word ܐܘܪܝܬܐ / *Ōraytā*): "Auch ins Aethiop(ische) ist dies Wort mit anderen durch die aram(äischen) Missionäre als ôrît hineingetragen [This word has with others also been introduced into Ethiopic as *ôrît* by the Aramean missionaries]."

Qurʾān < Qəryān: Lectionary

If *Koran*, however, really means *lectionary*, then one can assume that the Koran intended itself first of all to be understood as nothing more than a liturgical book with selected texts from the *Scriptures* (the Old and New Testament) and not at all as a substitute for the *Scripture*s themselves, i.e. as an independent *Scripture*. Whence the numerous allusions to the *Scriptures*, without a knowledge of which the Koran may often seem to be a sealed book to the reader. The reference to the Scriptures, however, is not only apparent from the individual allusions; rather, in more than one passage the Koran refers explicitly to the *Scriptures*, of which it conceives itself to be a *part*. So, for example, we read in Sura 12:1–2:

Sura 12:1–2

تلك ايات الكتاب المبين / إنا انزلناه قرانا عربيا لعلكم تعقلون

(Bell I 218): 1. "These are the signs of the Book that is clear. 2. Verily We have sent it down as an Arabic Qurʾān; mayhap ye will understand."

(Paret 190): 1. „Dies sind die Verse der deutlichen Schrift. 2. Wir haben sie als einen arabischen Koran hinabgesandt. Vielleicht würdet ihr verständig sein."

(Blachère 258): 1. "Ce sont les *aya* de l'Ecriture explicite.2. Nous l'avons fait descendre en une Prédication arabe [*afin que*] peut-être vous raisonniez."

The proposed translation according to the Syro-Aramaic understanding:

1. "These are the (*scriptural*) signs (i.e. the *letters* = the *written copy, script*) of the *elucidated*[137] Scripture: 2. We have sent them

137 Borrowed from Syro-Aramaic, the Arabic verbal root بان (*bāna*), second stem بين (*bayyana*), is identical with the Syro-Aramaic ܒܘܢ / ܒܵܢ (*bwan / bān*, undocumented in Peal), Pael ܒܝܢ (*bayyen*). Thus, in this context the Syro-Aramaic (as well as Arabic) meaning *to elucidate, to explain* (*Thes*. I 468: *intelligere, discernere fecit*) gives the more exact sense. It is to this extent to be understood as a synonym of فصل (*faṣṣala*) (as a loan translation from Syro-Aramaic ܦܪܫ / *praš* / *parreš*, see below). As a passive participle of the second stem it ought to have been *mu-bayyan* (corresponding to Syro-Aramaic ܡܒܝܢ *m-bayyan*), as the active participle of the fourth stem *mubān*. The active participle of the fourth Arabic stem *mubīn* (*elucidating, explaining*), as the Koran now reads, would only be justifiable here from the necessity to rhyme, since the fourth stem أبان (*abāna*) does not occur elsewhere in the Koran. The participial form مبين (*mubīn*) monotonously derived from it without any consideration for the semantic context should therefore have been read or understood, depending on the context, either passively *mubayyan* (thus, for example, in Sura 19:38 في ضلال مبين *fī ḍalāl^{in} mubayyan* "*in apparent error*"), or actively *mubayyin* (as, for example, in Sura 46: 9 ما أنا إلا نذير مبين *mā anā illā naḏīr^{un} mubayyin* "*I am only an elucidating, explaining warner*" [Paret: "*a clear warner*"]).

down as an Arabic lectionary (= Koran) (or in an Arabic reading[138]) so that[139] you may understand (it).“

The Koran makes even more explicit, with further expressions borrowed from Syro-Aramaic and explained below, that what is meant by *“elucidated”* Scripture is the *“translated”* Scripture.

With the Syro-Aramaism أم الكتب (*umm al-kitāb*)[140] (*umm al-kitab*) (“*mother of the scripture*” = *main scripture or proto-scripture*) the Koran names the *Scriptures* as its actual source in Suras 3:7, 13:39, and 43:4. This emerges most clearly from Sura 3:7:

Sura 3:7

هو الذى انزل عليك الكتب منه
ايت محكمت هن ام الكتب واخر متشبهت

By the Koran translators, this verse segment has been understood as follows:

(Bell I 44): 5. “He it is who hath sent down to thee the Book; in it are clearly formulated verses; these are the essence [Lit. “mother”] of the Book; other (verses) are ambiguous.“

(Paret 44): “Er ist es, der die Schrift auf dich herabgesandt hat. Darin gibt es (eindeutig) bestimmte Verse (*āyāt muḥkamāt*) – sie

138 See further below.

139 As a rule Arabic لعل (*laʿalla*) (*perhaps*) expresses a supposition. However, in the Koran, as the equivalent of Syro-Aramaic ܟܒܪ (*kḇar*), for which the Syrian lexicographers give, among other things, ليت (*layta*), it can also express a longed-for desire, a hope (cf. *Thes.* I 1673).

140 For the meaning of ܐܡ ܐܡܐ (*em, emmā*) appropriate here, cf. *Thes*. I 222, 2) *caput, fons, origo* (*head, source, origin*). The Koran provides a parallel expression in Sura 6: 92 und 42: 7 with ام القرى (*umm al-qurā*) (*metropolis, capital*), whose Syro-Aramaic equivalent the *Thes.* (*ibid.*) documents, among other things, as follows: ܐܡܗܬܐ ܕܡܕܝܢܬܐ (*emhāṯā ḏa-mḏīnāṯā*), *matres urbium* (*metropolis*), ܢܝܢܘܐ ܐܡܐ ܕܐܬܘܪ (*Nīnwē emmā ḏ-Āṯūr*), *Nineve Assyriae metropolis* (*Nineveh, capital of Assyria*).

sind die Urschrift (*umm al-kitāb*) – und andere, mehrdeutige (*mutašābihāt*)."

(Blachère 76): 5/7 "C'est Lui qui a fait descendre sur toi l'Ecriture. En celle-ci sont des *aya* confirmées (?) qui sont l'essence de l'Ecriture, tandis que d'autres sont équivoques."

On the basis of both Arabic and Syro-Aramaic, this verse segment is to be understood as follows:

"He it is who has sent the Book[141] down to you. *Of it*[142] (a part consists of) *precise* (or *well-known*) writings (i.e. *texts*),[143] which (are) (quasi) the *Proto-Scripture* (*itself*),[144] and (a part of) other (writings), which (are) *alike in meaning* (to these)."

Only if one analyzes each term according to its equivalent Aramaic semantic contents does one do justice to the real meaning of this verse. In connection with the *"elucidated"* scripture, there is, behind the Arabic participial adjective محكمات (*muḥkamāt*) (here "*precise*" or "*well-known*"), the Syro-Aramaic ܚܬܝܬܐ (*ḥattīṯā*) or ܚܟܝܡܐ (*ḥḵīmā*). The first adjective is used precisely in connection with "*exact*" *translations*. The latter can refer to the knowledge of the content.[145] Behind متشبهت (*mutašābihāt*) (*similar*) is the Syro-Aramaic ܕܡܝܬܐ (*dāmyāṯā*) (*similar, comparable*).[146]

---

141 In this case what is meant by this is evidently the Koran.

142 As an expression of the *partitivum*, منه (*minhu*) in this case actually means "(*a part*) *of it*," i.e. of the Koran.

143 With Koranic ايت (*āyāt*) are meant Syro-Aramaic ܐܬܘܬܐ (*āṯwāṯā*): "*signs*" (of *script* or *Scriptures*), i.e. the *written* words of God.

144 What is meant by this is the "*faithful rendering*" of the parts of the Koran taken from the "*Proto-Scripture*."

145 Cf. *Thes*. I 1407, 1) exactus, accuratus; ܡܦܫܩܢܐ ܚܬܝܬܐ (*m-pašqānē ḥattīṯē*) interpretes fidi (*faithful, exact translators*);. ܦܘܫܩܐ ܚܬܝܬܐ (*puššāqē ḥattīṯē*) (*exact translations*), ܡܦܩܬܐ ܚܬܝܬܬܐ (*ma-ppaqtā ḥattittā*) (*exact, faithful translation*). The alternative *"well-known"* results from the meanings proposed by *Mannā*, 237a, under ܚܟܡ (*ḥḵam*): حكم. فهم. عرف. أدرك (*ḥakama, fahima, ʿarafa, adraka*) (*to comprehend, understand, to know*).

146 Cf. *Thes*. I 912: Part. act. ܕܡܐ (*dāmē*) similis; ܕܡܝܬ ܒܦܘܫܩܐ (*damyāṯ ba-*

With these two terms the Koran defines the *origin* of its content. It therefore consists, on the one hand, of *"faithful"* (or well-known) excerpts from the "*Proto-Scripture,*" i.e. the "*canonical Scriptures,*" and, on the other hand, of parts taken, say, from *apocryphal* or other scriptures "*comparable*" to the *Proto-Scripture*. The content of the Koran we have before us also confirms this brief "table of contents." With *comparable* verses, the Koran is at the same time making it clear that for it the standard to which it persistently refers is the "*Proto-Scripture,*" i.e. the *Scriptures* considered to be *canonical*.

Now, notwithstanding the assertion in the Koran itself (in Suras 16:103 and 26:195) that the Prophet had proclaimed the Koranic message in "*clear Arabic speech,*" لسان عربي مبين, all Arab, as well as all non-Arab commentators on the Koran have since time immemorial racked their brains over the interpretation of this language. Generations of renowned Koran scholars have devoted their lives to the meritorious exercise of clarifying the text of the Koran grammatically and semantically, word for word. In spite of all these efforts one would not be far from the truth if one were to estimate the proportion of the Koran that is still considered unexplained today at about a quarter of the text. But the actual proportion is probably much higher insofar as it will be shown that a considerable number of passages that were thought to be certain have in reality been misunderstood, to say nothing of the imprecise rendering of numerous Koranic expressions.

---

mnawwāṯā) ὁμοιομερής, partibus aequalibus constans, متشبّه الاجزاء . The meaning "*comparable*" results from ܕܡܝ (*dammī*), 1) assimilavit, comparavit, pro similis habuit.

11. The Historical Error

We are now in the year 1428 of the *Hiǧra/Hegira*, the emigration of the Prophet from Mecca to Medina in 622 A.D. that marks the beginning of the Islamic calendar. Considering the variety of Arabic dialects spoken at the time of Prophet, it was a legitimate question to ask in what dialect the Koran was sent down. To this end, *Ṭabarī* cites Sura 14:41:

وما أرسلنا من رسول إلا بلسان قومه ليبين لهم

> "We have never sent an apostle except in the language of his people, that he may explain (the message) to them."

This results in the Koran's having being composed in the Arabic dialect of the Qurayš, the Prophet's clan in Mecca.[147]

Thus, when the Koran emphasizes in ten passages that it has been composed in the *Arabic language*, it does so to stress the particularity that differentiates it from the *Proto-Scripture* of the Old and the New Testaments, which had been composed in a foreign language. This reference becomes quite plain in Sura 41:44:

Sura 41:44

ولو جعلناه قرانا أعجميا لقالوا لولا فصلت اياته
اعجمي وعربي قل هو للذين امنوا هدى وشفا

By our Koran translators, this verse has been understood as follows:

> (Bell II 481): "If We had made it a foreign Qurʾān, they would have said: 'Why are not its signs made distinct? Foreign and Arabic?' Say: 'To those who have believed it is guidance and healing'…"

147 *Ṭabarī* I 29. On the morphology and etymology of قريش (*Qurayš*) see below p. 236.

(Paret 399 f.): "Wenn wir ihn (d.h. den Koran) zu einem nichtarabischen Koran gemacht hätten, würden sie sagen: 'Warum sind seine Verse (wörtl.: Zeichen) nicht (im einzelnen) auseinandergesetzt (so daß jedermann sie verstehen kann)? (Was soll das:) ein nichtarabischer (Koran) und ein arabischer (Verkünder)?' Sag: Für diejenigen, die glauben, ist er eine Rechtleitung und ein Quell des Trostes (wörtl.: Heilung)…"

(Blachère 509): "Si nous avions fait de [cette Révélation] une prédication en *langue* barbare, ils auraient dit: 'Pourquoi ces *aya* n'ont-elles pas été rendues intelligibles? Pourquoi [*sont-elles en langue*] barbare alors que [*notre idiome*] est arabe?' – Réponds: '[Cette Édification], pour ceux qui croient, est Direction et Guérison…'"

In connection with the composition of a book, the Syro-Aramaic ܣܡ (*sām*) "*to compose*"[148] is to be assumed to be behind the Arabic جعل (*ǧaʿal*^{a}).

Inasmuch as Arabic فصل (*faṣṣal*^{a}) here lexically renders the Syro-Aramaic ܦܪܫ (*praš* /*parreš*), it should not be understood in its original meaning of "*to separate*" (Paret: *to place asunder in individual parts*), but in its broader sense of "*to explain, to interpret*" (cf. *Thes*. II 3302 ult.: ܠܡܦܪܫܘ / *la-m-parrāšū: interpretari* scriptionem). Moreover, if one considers that in many languages today the earlier expression for "*to explain, to interpret*" is used to mean "*to translate*" (as attested by the modern Arabic ترجم / *tarǧam*^{a} "*to translate*" from the Syro-Aramaic ܬܪܓܡ / *targem* "*to explain, to interpret*" as well as by the French "*interpréter, interprète*"), the meaning of "*to translate*" or "*to render*" becomes virtually unavoidable here. In his commentary on Sura 41:3, 44 *Ṭabarī* also understands فصل (*faṣṣal*^{a}) as a synonym of بين (*bayyan*^{a}) "*to clarify, to explain.*"[149] The Koran verse cited above is therefore to be understood as follows:

---

148 *Thes*. II 2557 (2) *composuit* librum (*to compose* a book). *Mannā* 483b (5) . ألّف أنشأ (*allafa, anšaʾa*).

149 *Ṭabarī* XXIV 90 and 126.

"If we had *composed* it as a *lectionary* in a foreign language, they would say: '*One ought then*[150] *to have translated* its scripts'!"

In the case of the noun clause that follows أعجمي وعربي *"foreign and Arabic,"* *Ṭabarī* without question sides with the majority of the Arab commentators who read an interrogatory particle ء (*hamza*) that was obviously added subsequently in front of أعجمي (ءأعجمي / *ʾa-aʿǧamī*). Though this means an unjustified intervention in the text, the translations given above reproduce the corresponding interpretation by *Ṭabarī*. Only Bell suspects an omission, which he illustrates in his translation by leaving a section of the line blank. Yet this noun clause can be more reasonably explained without an interrogative particle if one follows the minority reading, whose interpretation *Ṭabarī* briefly mentions. This is how the *Qurayš* must have understood the clause: "But this Koran had been sent down foreign (i.e. in a foreign language) and (in) Arabic," so that both foreigners and Arabs could understand it. Whereupon God, according to this verse, had sent down all manner of foreign words, of which *Ṭabarī* cites, as an example, حجارة من سجيل (*ḥiǧāra*^{tin} *min siǧǧīl*) (with) *stones of clay* (Suras 11:82; 15:74; and 105:41), in which case the word *siǧǧīl* is explained as being a Persian loan-word.[151] If one accordingly takes أعجمي وعربي *foreign and Arabic* to refer to the language of the Koran – and not *foreign* to refer to the Koran and *Arabic* to the Prophet – then this part of the verse should be understood as follows:

---

150 Later the question will be dealt with as to why the Arabic لولا (*law-lā*) has been falsely interpreted here and in other passages as an interrogative particle.

151 *Ṭabarī* XXV 126 f. (cf. A. Jeffery 164). But actually سجيل /*siǧǧīl* is a misreading of the Syro-Aramaic passive participle *ܫܚܝܠܐ /*šaḥīlā* >*šḥīlā* = ܫܚܠܐ / *šaḥlā* >*šeḥlā* (cf. *Mannā* 782a (3) وحل. طين /*waḥl, ṭīn* [*mud, clay, argil*]) and is to be read in Arabic سحيل /*saḥīl* (from which is derived Arabic and Koranic [Sura 20:39] ساحل /*sāḥil* [*coast, shore, littoral* – as "muddy"]). That with حجاره من سحيل /*ḥiǧāra min saḥīl* not necessarily "stones of *baked* clay" are meant, as R. Bell translates (according to the allegedly Persian *"sang"* [*stone*] and *"gel"* [*clay*]), but rather "stones of (*dried*) clay", makes Sura 51:33 clear, where the Koran uses as a synonym حجاره من طين /*ḥiǧāra min ṭīn* "stones of *clay*".

"(Now whether it be) foreign or Arabic, say then: It is for those who believe (right) guidance and <u>*pure*</u> (belief)." [152]

In Sura 16:103 there is also talk of a foreign language and Arabic:

Sura 16:103

ولقد نعلم أنهم يقولون إنما يعلمه بشر
لسان الذي يلحدون إليه أعجمي وهذا لسان عربي مبين

(Bell I 258 f.): "We know pretty well that they say: 'It is only a human being who teaches him'; the speech of him they <u>hint</u> at is foreign, but this is Arabic speech clear."

(Paret 225): "Wir wissen wohl, daß sie sagen: ‚Es lehrt ihn (ja) ein Mensch (*bašar*) (was er als göttliche Offenbarung vorträgt).' (Doch) die Sprache dessen, auf den sie <u>anspielen</u> (*?yulḥidūna*), ist nichtarabisch (*aʿǧamī*). Dies hingegen ist deutliche arabische Sprache."

(Blachère 302): "Certes nous savons que [les infidèles] disent: "Cet homme a seulement pour maître un mortel!" [Mais] la

---

152 The translations that have been cited, "*healing, Quell des Trostes/Heilung* [*source of consolation/healing*], *guérison* [*recovery, cure, healing*]," as well as *Ṭabarī's* interpretation, "healing from ignorance" (جهل / *ǧahl*) or from paganism" may well make sense as they stand. But here the Arabic شفاء (*šifā*ʾ) appears to have been borrowed from the Syro-Aramaic ܫܦܝܐ (*šefyā* or *špāyā*). For this the *Thes.* (II 4261) gives: ܫܦܝܐ ܕܫܒܝܠܐ (*špāyā da-šbīlā*) complanatio, defaecatio (*evenness, purity of the way*); metaphorically, puritas, sinceritas (*purity, sincerity*) ܫܦܝܐ ܘܨܠܠܐ ܕܚܘܫܒܐ (*špāyā w-ṣullālā d-ḥūšābē*) (*purity and integrity of thought*). The same is given under ܫܦܝܘܬܐ (*šapyūtā*): ܫܦܝܘܬ ܗܝܡܢܘܬܐ (*šapyūt haymānūtā*) puritas, simplicitas fidei (*purity, integrity of belief*). In connection with هدى (*hudaⁿ*) (< Syro-Aramaic ܗܕܝܐ / *hdāyā, hedyā*, ܗܘܕܝܐ / *huddāyā*) (*right guidance*), the Syro-Aramaic synonymous meaning of "*integrity*" (of doctrine, of belief) should be adopted for شفاء (*šifā*ʾ, actually *šifā*).

langue de celui auquel ils pensent est [*une langue*] barbare, alors que cette prédication est [*en*] claire langue arabe."

Here, the "*speech of him they hint at*" makes reference to the human being that is supposedly teaching the Prophet. In the rejection of this insinuation the Koran employs a heretofore unexplained verb, يلحدون (*?yulḥidūna*), which Paret places in parentheses with a question mark, and which *Ṭabarī* nonsensically reinterprets[153] as "*to be fond of, drawn to, attracted to, inclined towards, lean towards somebody,*" a suggestion that Bell, Paret and Blachère, however, do not follow. Instead, based on the context, they have preferred to "guess" its probable meaning. Yet this meaning is not at all derivable from the Arabic verbal root لحد (*laḥada*) (*to dig, to bury; to deviate from; to incline toward?*),[154] and thus we would seem to be justified in asking whether it is not a question here of a foreign root, the identification of which may lead to a more plausible sense.

With this suspicious verb, يلحدون (*yulḥidūna*), we are in fact dealing with a typical example of the erroneous Arabic transcription of a Syro-Aramaic script, the cause of many misreadings in the Koran. In the present case, it is a question of the Syro-Aramaic spelling of the verbal root ܠܓܙ (*lḡez*), where the ح / *ḥ* in the Koran stands for the Syro-Aramaic ܓ / *g* (= Arabic غ / *ġ*), and the د / *d* either for a misread Syro-Aramaic ܙ or for Arabic ز / *z*. One can assume, that is, with seeming certainty that the original spelling was يلحزون. But because the later Arabic readers, after considering every possible configuration [لحز (*laḥaza*), لخر (*laḫara*), لخز (*laḫaza*), لجر (*lağara*), لجز (*lağaza*)], could not identify the infinitive لحر (*laḥara*) (in *Garshuni/Karshuni* ܠܓܙ / *lḡez* = Arabic لغز / *laġaza*, with any Arabic root, the most obvious possibility for them was to interpret the final ر / *r* as a final د / *d*, and then to read it as لحد (*laḥada*)—which

---

153 *Ṭabarī* XIV 179 f.

154 In the last meaning solely on the basis of this passage in the Koran, and in accordance with *Ṭabarī*, here, as in a large number of other passages, falsely taken up by Arabic lexicography (cf. Hans Wehr, *Arabisches Wörterbuch für die Schriftsprache der Gegenwart* [*Arabic Dictionary for the Written Language of the Present Day*] [Wiesbaden, ^{5}1985]).

is, in fact, an Arabic root, but whose real meaning, "*to fall away from the faith,*" does not fit here at all. However, if one falls away from the faith, one could obviously also say that one *turns away from it*. But if one *turns away* from something, one can also reinterpret this to mean that one *turns toward* something else. Only by means of a train of thought such as this can one arrive at the scarcely convincing interpretation that *Ṭabarī*, without any further details or explanations, wants to suggest.

In reality, there is no evidence in Arabic linguistic usage for this meaning of ألحد (*alḥada*) adopted by *Ṭabarī*. The Arabic lexicons cannot substantiate this meaning – except on the basis of this misread and misunderstood passage. What is in the meantime striking, however, is that the Syro-Aramaic ܠܓܙ (*lḡez*): *aenigmatice locutus est* (*Thes*. II 1891), appears to be a late borrowing from the Arabic لغز (*laġaza*).[155] For this expression, namely, the *Thes.* does not cite any evidence at all from Syro-Aramaic literature, but refers only to the Eastern Syrian lexicographers. More recent native lexicons[156] cite the *paᶜᶜel, eṯpᶜel* and *eṯpaᶜᶜal* forms (*laggez, eṯlḡez, eṯlaggaz*), while Brockelmann does not mention this verbal root at all. The reason for this is that the etymologically correct equivalent of the Arabic لغز (*laġaza*) (with the secondary dot above the *ġ*) is the Syro-Aramaic ܠܥܙ (*lᶜez*).[157]

155 With the same meaning (*to speak enigmatically, allegorically*), whereby the Syro-Aramaic ܓ / *g*, phonetically corresponding to the Arabic غ / *ġ* , is to be pronounced as *ḡ*. In this regard, it is worth mentioning that in the early Hedjazi and Kufic Koran manuscripts the original form of the Arabic letter ـحـ (without the dot) renders quite exactly the Syriac letter ܓ / *g*. This is not the only graphical detail that will prove that the Koranic text was originally written in *Garshuni*, i.e. Arabic with Syriac letters.

156 Cf. *Mannā* 369a/b.

157 Cf. *Thes*. II 1961 f., ܠܥܙ (*lᶜez*): *indistincte locutus est* (*to speak indistinctly, unclearly*) (with further meanings and examples); Brockelmann, *Lexicon Syriacum*, 368b f. The *Lisān* (V 405b) gives under لغز (*laġaza*) the same definition: ألغز الكلام وألغز فيه: عمّى مراده وأضمره على خلاف ما أظهره (In reference to speech *alġaza* means: *to conceal and disguise one's purpose, as opposed to what one actually says*).

Thus, in rendering the verse segment لسان الذى يلحدون اليه as "*the speech of him they hint at*" and "*die Sprache dessen, auf den sie anspielen* [*the language of him to whom they allude*]," Bell and Paret have correctly guessed the meaning of لحد (*laḥada* = *laġaza*) from the context, even though they were unable to recognize its etymology. In particular in the case of the preposition إلى (*ilā*), the Syro-Aramaic ܠܓܙ (*lḡez*)—pronounced لغز (*laġaza*) in Arabic – is to be understood as a synonym for رمز إلى (*ramaza ilā*), لمّح إلى (*lammaḥa ilā*) (*to allude to, refer to something*). Transferred into modern Arabic, this passage would accordingly read:

> لسان الذى يرمزون ، يلمّحون إليه (*lisānu l-laḏī yarmuzūna, yulammiḥūna ilayhi*) (*the language of the one to whom they are alluding*).

Now, although this root is common in Arabic, it is worth noting that the Koran here reproduces the obviously dialectal Syro-Aramaic written form, which was probably created only later under Arabic influence and which turns out to be the phonetic transcription of the Arabic verb. The fact that in the Koran words common to Arabic and Aramaic are occasionally used in the foreign pronunciation has already been established elsewhere.[158] This detail is all the more interesting in that it reinforces other details in the Koran that point to the Eastern Syrian-Mesopotamian region.

The same phenomenon can be observed in two more passages where the root لحد (*laḥada*) appears in the Koran in similar graphic form, but in a different sense. Thus we find in Sura 7:180:

---

158 Cf. Anton Schall, *Coranica*, in Orientalia Suecana XXXII-XXXV (1984-1986) 371. See also Nöldeke's comment on Arabic لجنة (*luǧna*) and Syro-Aramaic ܠܓܝܢܐ. (*lḡīnā*) (*oil drum, wine cask*) in Siegmund Fraenkel's *aramäische Fremdwörter im Arabischen* [*Aramaic Foreign Words in Arabic*] 130: "This is probably an Aramaic-Arabic word that the Fellâḥen of Aramaic origin employ, as is so much in Bar Alî and Bar Bahlûl (whom the *Thesaurus Syriacus* usually cites as local lexicographers)."

Sura 7:180

وذروا الذين يلحدون في أسمئه

(Bell I 155): 179. "… and pay no attention to those who make covert hints in regard to His names."

(Paret 140): "… und laßt diejenigen, die hinsichtlich seiner Namen eine abwegige Haltung einnehmen (?) (Oder: die seine Namen in Verruf bringen (?)."

(Blachère 198): "… et laissez ceux qui blasphèment au sujet de Ses noms."

In the light of the following explanation, this verse from Sura 7:180 will be understood to mean:

"Leave off from those who *scoff* at his names."

Paret repeatedly remarks on this verse in his Commentary (179): "It is not clear what the expression *yulḥidūna fī asmāʾihī* is exactly supposed to mean." In doing so, he refers to the divergent translations by Bell and Blachère. With *Ṭabarī's* comment on the expression, قوله اختلف يلحدون أهل التأويل في تأويل (*the commentators disagree on the meaning of the word* [*of God*] "*yulḥidūna*")[159] and the subsequent hunches (*to deny God, to attribute other gods to Him*, up to and including the interpretations attributed to al-Kisāʾī), one is hardly any nearer to being able to make up one's mind. Although on the basis of his solid feel for the language Bell, with his translation "*make covert hints*," comes closest to the correct sense, this meaning cannot be derived from the root لحد (*laḥada*). However, before going into the etymological and semantic meaning of this expression, Sura 41:40 should be cited as well:

159 *Ṭabarī* IX 133 f.

Sura 41:40

إن الذين يلحدون في ايتنا لا يخفون علينا

(Bell II 480): "Verily those who decry Our signs are not hid from Us."

(Paret 399): "Diejenigen, die hinsichtlich unserer Zeichen eine abwegige Haltung einnehmen (?), sind uns wohl bekannt [gleiche Anmerkung wie oben]."

(Blachère 509): "Ceux qui méconnaissent Nos signes ne Nous sont pas cachés."

Here, too, Bell captures the sense best, but not on the basis of the Arabic meaning of لحد (*laḥada*) or ألحد (*alḥada*). Here, as above, the real meaning of the expression – in itself Arabic – can only be determined with the help of the Syro-Aramaic reading ܠܓܙ (*lḡez*) and its semantic contents. Then, even if يلحدون اليه (*yulḥidūna ilayhi*) (= يلغزون اليه *yalġuzūna / ilayhi*) means "*to whom they allude*" in Sura 16:103, this verb, as Bell correctly supposes, does not have the same meaning in the context of the last two verses. The ensuing analysis will show that the verse cited above from Sura 41:40 is to be understood as follows:

"Those who *scoff* at our signs (i.e. *scriptures*) do not remain concealed from us."

Starting from the original meaning *aenigmatice locutus est* (*to speak enigmatically, in a veiled way, concealing the truth*), the *Thes.* (I 1891) refers to Bar Bahlūl, who explains ܠܓܙ (*lḡez*) with the Syro-Aramaic synonym ܐܡܬܠ (*amṯel*). The additional meanings of this verb prove to be the key to understanding the last two Koran passages. For example, for ܐܡܬܠ (*amṯel*) the *Thes.* II 2250 gives (*a*) *parabolice dixit;* (*b*) *fabulatus est, stulte locutus est* (*to talk a lot of nonsense, to babble stupidly*), and as another synonym for it ܒܕܢ (*bāḏēn*) (*to talk drivel, to blather*). Finally, under ܒܕܐ (*bḏā*) the *Thes.* (I 449 f.) lists, among other things, *finxit, falso, inepte dixit*; under ܐܒܕܝ (*aḇdī*), *nugavit, falso dixit,* خدع . هذى . زور (*ḫadaʿa, haḏā, zawwara*) (*to humbug, to talk twaddle, to feign*); and under ܒܕܘܝܐ (*bāḏōyā*), *qui vana, inepta loquitur, nugax* (a babbler talking nonsense).

An insight into the understanding of لحد = لغز (*laġaza*) in the sense of هذى (*haḏā*) (*to drivel, to talk nonsense*) is provided to us by parallel passages from the Koran. Namely, not in the same, but in a similar context the Koran employs the expressions سخر (*saḫira*), هزأ (*hazaʾa*), and occasionally also لعب (*laʿiba*), the last-named in corresponding passages to be understood as a synonym for the two preceding expressions, and indeed as a loan-translation of the Syro-Aramaic ܫܥܐ (*šʿā*), whose Arabic meaning the Eastern Syrian lexicographers render as follows: لعب مزح. هزل . ازدرى . تكلّم كلاما باطلا (*Mannā* 805b). On the other hand, the Koran uses this ܫܥܐ (*šʿā*), transliterated in the third person plural as سعو (*saʿaw*), in the sense of لعب (*laʿiba*) = هزأ (*hazaʾa*) (*laugh at, scoff at*) in the following context:

Sura 34:5

والذين سعو في ايتنا معجزين أولئك لهم عذاب من رجز أليم

(Bell II 421): "But those who busy themselves with Our signs, seeking to make them of no effect - for them is a punishment of wrath painful."

(Paret 352): "Diejenigen aber, die sich hinsichtlich unserer Zeichen ereifern, indem sie sich (unserem Zugriff ?) zu entziehen suchen (?) (Oder: in der Absicht, (sie) unwirksam zu machen (*? muʿāǧizīna*), haben ein schmerzhaftes Strafgericht (*ʿaḏābun min riǧzin alīmun*) zu erwarten."

(Blachère 455): "Ceux qui [*au contraire*] se seront évertués contre les *aya* d'Allah, déclarant Son Impuissance, [*ceux-là*] auront un tourment cruel."

In this context the Arabic اعجز (*aʿǧaza*) (*to make incapable*) is to be understood as a synonym of ابطل (*abṭala*) or بطل (*baṭṭala*) (< ܒܛܠ *baṭṭel*) in the meaning of "*to dispute*" (a truth, *to contest* its existence), for which the Koran usually employs كذب (*kaḏḏaba*) (< ܟܕܒ / *kaddeḇ*) (*to deny*).

That which is meant by رجز (*riğz*, actually *ruğz*) (< ܪܘܓܙܐ *rugzā*) is (God's) "*wrath*."[160] This then results in the following understanding of Sura 34:5:

> "And those who *contentiously*[161] *scoffed* at our signs (will be meted out) a severe punishment by the (divine) *wrath*."

With the identification of the root, misread in Arabic as لحد (*laḥada*), via the Syro-Aramaic spelling (ܠܓܙ / *lḡez*), as the Arabic لغز (*laġaza*), we would clarify, via the nuances of the Syro-Aramaic semantics, three Koranic passages that had been previously acknowledged to be obscure. At the same time, we have discovered that the synonymous Syro-Aramaic verb ܫܥܐ (*šʿā*) (*to play, to laugh at, to make fun of, to mock*) must be distinguished, depending on the context, from its homonymous Arabic root سعى (*saʿā*) (*to strive after, to make an effort, to run*). The Syro-Aramaic meaning of "*to make fun of*" or "*to amuse oneself, to enjoy oneself*" should therefore be adopted in additional passages of the Koran (such as in Suras 79:22, 2:205, and 5:33).[162]

Linking this again to Sura 16:103, we can gather that the suspicion raised against the Prophet in that verse, i.e. that he had been taught by a human being, is met by the Koran with the argument that the man they meant spoke a foreign language, whereas the Koran itself is (composed) in clearly comprehensible Arabic. However, that a direct connection exists between the Koran and the Scriptures of the Jews and Christians,

---

160 Cf. *Thes.* II 3808, ܪܘܓܙܐ ܕܡܪܝܐ (*rugzā ḏ-māryā*), 2 Reg. xxiii, 26…; *ira* divina (divine *wrath*). It is astonishing that Paret and Blachère have overlooked this meaning, whereas Bell at least renders the word literally.

161 I.e. by denying the existence of God or the Afterworld.

162 Namely, if we trace the Koranic expression سعى في الارض فسادا (*saʿā fī l-arḍⁱ fasādaⁿ*), which as a familiar quotation has become a part of Arabic linguistic usage, back to its suspected Syro-Aramaic origin ܫܥܐ ܒܐܪܥܐ ܥܘܠܐܝܬ (*šʿā ḇ-arʿā ʿawwālāīṯ*), then the Syro-Aramaic meaning "*to have* (*oneself*) *a devilishly good time on earth*" would make more sense than, for example, the translation proposed by Paret for Sura 2:205 "*eifrig darauf bedacht sein, auf der Erde Unheil anzurichten* [*to be eagerly intent upon wreaking havoc, causing mischief on earth*]." Cf. also H. Wehr: "*to be detrimental, to develop a detrimental effectiveness*;" (Engl. Wehr): "to spread evil, cause universal harm and damage."

characterized as كتاب (*kitāb*) (*Book, Scripture*) and as being written in a foreign language, is furthermore admitted by the Koran in the following verse:

Sura 41:3

كتاب فصلت اياته قرانا عربيا

(Bell II 477): 2. "A Book whose signs [or "verses"] have been made distinct as an Arabic Qurʾān ..."

(Paret 396): "... eine Schrift, deren Verse (im einzelnen) auseinandergesetzt sind, (herabgesandt) als ein arabischer Koran."

(Blachère 505): «Ecriture dont les *aya* ont été rendues intelligibles, en une révélation arabe...».

As previously expounded, however, what is meant by فصل (*faṣṣal^a*), as the lexical equivalent of the Syro-Aramaic ܦܪܫ (*parreš*), is in this context, here as well as above, "*to translate, to transfer.*" Therefore the verse is to be understood as:

"A *scripture* that we have *translated* as an Arabic *lectionary* (or into an Arabic *version*) ..."

Insofar as the Arabic قران (*qurʾān*) is, as expounded before, a loan word from Syro-Aramaic ܩܪܝܢܐ (*qəryānā*) (*reading, pericope, selection for reading*),[163] it is not to be understood everywhere in the Koran as a

163 Cf. *Thes.* II 3716. The meaning of ܩܪܝܢܐ /*qeryānā* as a *pericope* (a selection from the *Scriptures* for reading in the ecclesiastical Service) is attested in the Koran in Sura 17:78, where قران الفجر /*qur'ān al-fağr* means the (selected) *reading* (from the Bible = the *Scriptures-reading*) in the matutinal Service (*Hora matutina*). This ecclesiastical technical term corresponds to the Syriac term ܩܪܝܢܐ ܕܥܕܢ ܨܦܪܐ /*qeryānā ḏʿeddān ṣap̄rā* "the (*Scriptures*) *reading of the morning Service*" (cf. *Thes. ibid.*). That with this *reading* not the *Koran* is meant but a *reading* from the Bible, is attested in the Koran itself. In the Mary Sura, namely, it is said five times واذكر في الكتب /*wa-ḏkur fī l-Kitāb* "*Remember in the Book* (= *Scriptures*)" (Sura 19: 16, 41, 51, 54, 56). Furthermore, the

proper name. Rather, in each case it is the context that determines the meaning, which *Mannā* (699a) gives in Arabic as follows: (1) قراءة . درس . علم (*reading matter, study, teaching/learning*), (2) فصل . امثولة يتعلمه الدارس (*unit, lesson*), (3) كتاب القراءات البيعية (*ecclesiastical lectionary*). Sura 75: 17-18 may serve as a test case; there it is said:

Sura 75:17-18

إن علينا جمعه وقرانه / فاذا قراناه فاتبع قرانه

(Bell II 621): 17: "Ours is it to put it together, and recite it; 18: When We recite it follow thou the recitation;"

(Paret 491): 17: „Es ist unsere (und nicht deine) Aufgabe, ihn zusammenzubringen und zu rezitieren. 18: Und (erst) wenn wir ihn dir (vor)rezitiert haben, dann folge seiner Rezitierung!"

(Blachère 626): 17: «A nous de le rassembler et de le prêcher! 18: Quand nous le prêchons, suis-en la prédication.»

Deserving of a preliminary remark here is the verb جمع (*ğamaʿa*) (*to bring together, to collect*), which has a specific meaning in this context with reference to the Koran. Insofar as the Syro-Aramaic ܩܪܝܢܐ (*qəryānā*) (*lectionary*) designates a church book with excerpts (readings) from the *Scriptures* for liturgical use,[164] the Arabic جمع (*ğamaʿa*), as the lexical rendering of the Syro-Aramaic ܟܢܫ (*kanneš*) (*to collect*), has to do directly with the *collecting of these excerpts from the Scriptures*, and indeed specifically in the meaning of "*compilavit* librum" (cf. *Thes.* I 1771, under 1).

If we look further among the meanings cited by *Mannā* for قران (*qur-*

Koran, as a *liturgical Book*, seems to use here this term in the sense of *liturgical Service* (*Officium*), so that قران الفجر /*qur'ān al-fağr* "*the dawn-Reading*" corresponds as a synonym to صلوة الفجر /*ṣalāt al-fağr* "*the dawn-Prayer = the dawn-Service*" (*Officium matutinum*) (Sura 24:58).

164 Cf. Erwin Gräf, "*Zu den christlichen Einflüssen im Koran* [*On the Christian Influences in the Koran*]," in *ZDMG* 111, new series 37 (1962) 396-398; in the collection *Der Koran,* ed. Rudi Paret (Darmstadt, 1975) 188.

ʾān / qəryān) to find ourselves a meaning that fits this context, the result for the previously cited double verse is the following sense:

> "It is incumbent upon us to compile it (the *Koran/Lectionary*) (by means of excerpts from the Scriptures) and to recite it (*instructively*). When We recite (*instructively*), then follow its *recitation* (i.e. the way it has been *taught* you)."

This may be the basis of the above-mentioned remark (p. 111) in Sura 16:103 that it was a man who *has taught* him.[165] Moreover, this meaning emerges clearly from the following verse:

Sura 87:6

سنقريك فلا تنسى

> "We will *teach* you (in such a way) that you will not forget."

That a corresponding expenditure of time is required for the *compiling* of the Koran is made clear in Sura 20:114; there it says:[166]

Sura 20:114

ولا تعجل بالقران من قبل ان يقضى اليك وحيه

165 On this subject, cf. Claude Gilliot, "*Informants*", in: *EQ* II, p. 512-518 (*Encyclopaedia of the Qur'ān*, I-IV, Leiden 2001-2004). Id. "*Les "informateurs" juifs et chrétiens de Muḥammad". Reprise d'un problème traité par Aloys Sprenger et Theodor Nöldeke* [*The Jewish and Christian "Informants" of Muḥammad. Re-examination of a Problem Treated by Aloys Sprenger and Theodor Nöldeke*]", in: *JSAI*, 22 (1998), p. 84-126.
Id. (in German): "*Zur Herkunft der Gewährsmänner des Propheten* [*On the Origin of the Informants of the Prophet*]", in: *Die dunklen Anfänge* [*The Obscure Beginnings*] (*op. cit.*), 1st ed., Berlin 2005, p. 148-178.

166 In the Syrian tradition, the man who teaches the liturgical reading is called ܡܩܪܝܢܐ /maqryānā (cf. *Thes.* II 3717): *qui artem legendi docet* (*who teaches the art of reading*).

"Be not hasty with (the recitation of) the Koran (i.e. *Lectionary*) before it be *taught* you completely."

But because the *Scriptures* are written in a *foreign language*, a translation into Arabic is necessary. This, too, the Koran demonstrates, even more clearly than before, in the following verse from the Mary Sura:

Sura 19:97

فإنما يسرناه بلسانك لتبشر به المتقين

(Bell I 291): "We have made it easy in thy tongue in order that thou mayest thereby give good tidings to those who show piety …"

(Paret 253): "Wir haben ihn (den Koran) (indem wir ihn) eigens in deiner Sprache (eingegeben haben) dir leicht gemacht, damit du den Gottesfürchtigen mit[167] ihm frohe Botschaft bringst…"

(Blachère 336): "Nous l'avons simplement facilité par ta voix pour que tu en fasses l'heureuse annonce…"

Arabic يسر (*yassara*) does in fact mean "*to facilitate, to make easy.*" The corresponding Syro-Aramaic verb on which it is lexically based is ܦܫܩ (*paššeq*), which has the following meanings: 1. *To make easy, facilitate;* 2. *to explain, to annotate;* 3. *to transfer, to translate*; in the last meaning, of all things, in connection with "*language*," documented, among others, by the following example:

ܦܫܩ ܟܬܒܐ ܗܢܐ ܡܢ ܠܫܢܐ ܝܘܢܝܐ ܠܣܘܪܝܝܐ (*paššeq kṯāḇā hānā men leššānā yawnāyā l-suryāyā*) ("*he translated this book from the Greek into the Syriac language*") (*Thes.* II 3326, with further examples).

167 Paret and Bell have here overlooked the fact that in connection with the verb بشر (*baššara*) the preposition بـ / *bi* governs the indirect object of the direct object: بشره بـ (*baššarahu bi-*) = *to proclaim something to someone.*

The verse cited above from Sura 19:97 is then to be understood as follows:

> "We have <u>*translated*</u> it (the Koran or the Scripture) into your language so that you may proclaim it (the Koran or the *Scripture*) to the (god-)fearing ...".

All of the other verses in which يسر (*yassara*) is used in connection with the Koran are to be understood accordingly; these are:

Sura 44:58

فإنما يسرناه بلسانك لعلهم يتذكرون

> "We have <u>*translated*</u> it (the Koran) into your language so that they may allow themselves to be reminded."[168]

In addition to this there is the recurring verse in Sura 54:17,22,32, and 40:

ولقد يسرنا القرءان للذكر فهل من مذكر

> "We have <u>*translated*</u> the *Koran* (= *the Lectionary*) as a reminder; are there then those that may (also) allow themselves to be reminded?"

In these passages, as a *technical term*, يسر (*yassara*) cannot be paraphrased in such a way as to say that God has "*made it easy*" for the Prophet insofar as He has "<u>*prompted*</u>" the Koran to him *"specifically in his own language,"* as Paret, for example, says. Instead, the term clearly states that this occurs indirectly by way of a *translation* from the *Scriptures*.

---

168 In this meaning, Arabic ذكر (*ḏakar*[a]) and its derivatives do not come from Syro-Aramaic ܕܟܪ (*dḵar*) (*to recall, to remember*), but from the synonymous ܥܗܕ (*ʿhaḏ*) in the *Ap̄ʿel* form, ܐܥܗܕ (*aʿheḏ*). For this *Mannā* cites, at 530b under (3), the following Arabic equivalents: نصح . وعظ . نبه (*naṣaḥ*[a], *waʿaẓ*[a], *nabbah*[a]) (*to advise, to preach / admonish, to warn*).

The fact that the Koran to this extent does not claim that it is a direct revelation is underscored by the Koran itself in the following verse:

Sura 42:51

وما كان لبشر ان يكلمه الله الا وحيا او من وراى حجاب
او يرسل رسولا فيوحي باذنه ما يشاء

(Bell 489): "It belonged not to any human being that Allah should speak to him except by suggestion or from behind a veil, or by sending a messenger to suggest by His permission what He pleaseth;"

(Paret 406): "Und es steht keinem Menschen (*bašar*) an, daß Gott mit ihm spricht, es sei denn (mittelbar) durch Eingebung (*waḥyan*), oder hinter einem Vorhang, oder indem er einen Boten sendet, der (ihm) dann mit seiner Erlaubnis eingibt, was er will."

(Blachère 517): "Il n'a pas été donné à un mortel (*bašar*) qu'Allah lui parle, sinon par révélation, ou de derrière un voile, ou en envoyant un messager tel que celui-ci révèle ce qu'Il veut [*à l'Homme*], avec Sa permission."

The Arabic root وحى (*waḥā*) (with its denominative-like fourth verbal stem أوحى *awḥā*) is restricted in Arabic usage to the meaning of *to give, to inspire, to reveal.* Speaking in favor of its being a borrowing (with metathesis) from the Syro-Aramaic root ܚܘܝ (*ḥawwī*) is the fact that one can also find in the Koran the further meanings deriving from the Syro-Aramaic verb – "*to show, to indicate, to present, to announce, to communicate, to teach*"[169] – although only a part of these have been guessed

169 Cf. *Thes.* I 1208 f. *Mannā* (223) quotes the following Arabic meanings: (1) أرى (*to allow to be seen, to show*), (2) أبان . اوضح . اظهر (*to demonstrate, to make clear, to expound*), (3) دل . اخبر . حكى (*to indicate, to inform, to tell*), (4) علم (*to teach*). C. Brockelmann, *Lexicon Syriacum* 220a, had already noticed the etymological relation between Syro-Aramaic ܚܘܝ / *ḥawwī* and Arabic وحى / *waḥā*.

by the Koran translators on the basis of the context. This is why all of the Koranic passages in which this expression occurs need to be examined in terms of the corresponding Syro-Aramaic meaning in each instance.

If one furthermore does not automatically understand رسول (*rasūl*) as an angel, but as a man (sent by God) (*apostle, missionary*), which is also what the Koran usually calls the Prophet of Islam, then the verse cited above ought to be understood as follows:

> "With no man has God ever (directly) spoken except through inspiration or behind a curtain or in that he sends a messenger (*apostle*) who, with His permission, teaches (him or communicates to him) what He wants."

With this linguistically clear and sober statement the Koran gives us an unambiguous indication of the language it acknowledges as the language of the *Scriptures* and which is essential for its *conception of itself*. With this language, which it for the first time calls "*Arabic*," the Koran surely did not intend that language whose norms were established two hundred years later in part by non-Arab grammarians no longer capable of properly understanding the Koranic language. This is the reason for the present attempt to decipher the previous mystery of this language by means of that language, the key to which the *Koran* delivers us in its clear reference to the original, unadulterated Syro-Aramaic term "*Qəryān*".

12. Analysis of Individual Sura Verses

The now following philological analysis of individual expressions recognized in part by Koran scholarship as *obscure* is intended to serve as an illustration of the working method that was discussed at the outset.

Concerning case (a) and (c) (p. 22 f.): There is no agreement among the Arab commentators on the Koran about the real meaning of the expression occurring in two variants تحت (*taḥta*) as well as of سريا (*sarīyā*) in the following verse of the Mary Sura:

Sura 19:24

فناداها من تحتها الا تحزني قد جعل ربك تحتك سريا

In keeping with the majority of the Arab commentators, the Western Koran translators render this verse as follows:

> (Bell I 286): 24. "Then he (probably 'the child') called to her from beneath her: 'Grieve not; thy Lord hath placed beneath thee a streamlet';...".
>
> (Paret 249): 24: "Da rief er (d.h. der Jesusknabe) ihr von unten her zu: ‚Sei nicht traurig! Dein Herr hat unter dir (d.h. zu deinen Füßen?) ein Rinnsal (*sarī*) (voll Wasser) gemacht'."
>
> (Blachère 331): 24 "[Mais] l'enfant qui était à ses pieds lui parla: 'Ne t'attriste pas! Ton Seigneur a mis à tes pieds un ruisseau'."

For Arabic تحت (*taḥta*), which is understood as the preposition *under* by all of the commentators cited in *Ṭabarī*, Jeffery in *The Foreign Vocabulary* (32 f.) makes a reference to as-Suyūṭī (1445-1505), who reports that Abū l-Qāsim in his work *Lughāt al-Qur'ān* [(*Foreign*) *Expressions in the Koran*] and al-Kirmānī in his *al-'Ajā'ib* [*The Miracles*] had both thought that this was a Nabatean (i.e. an Aramaic) word and meant as much as بطن (*baṭn*), (which Jeffery renders in English, on the basis of the Arabic understanding, as *womb*, although here, based on the Syro-

Aramaic ܒܛܢܐ (*baṭnā*), *foetus*[170] is more likely what should be understood), a view that is not held by anyone in *Ṭabarī.* But Jeffery rejects the notion, saying that there is nothing in Nabatean that would confirm this assumption since, even in Aramaic, Hebrew, Syriac and Ethiopic, the homophonic expressions have exactly the same meaning as the Arabic expression تحت (*taḥta*) (namely *under*).

Yet had Jeffery considered that in the Semitic languages precisely the triliteral prepositions and adverbs were originally nouns and could at times even appear as subjects and objects,[171] he would have perhaps come to another conclusion. The above-mentioned tradition, according to which تحت (*taḥta*) was in this case to be understood as a noun, confirms the supposition that the Arabic tradition has occasionally preserved a memory of the original Aramaic form. Namely, the lack of a verbal root in Arabic suggests a borrowing from Syro-Aramaic ܢܚܬ (*nḥeṯ*), of which the preposition ܬܚܬ (*taḥt*) (> Arabic تحت / *taḥt*) / ܬܚܝܬ (*tḥēṯ*) is only a secondary form. Let's first of all examine this clue in a little more detail.

Although the corresponding Syro-Aramaic nominal form ܢܚܬܐ (*nḥāṯā*) (as well as ܢܘܚܚܬܐ *nuḥḥāṯā*, ܢܚܬܘܬܐ *naḥtūṯā*, ܡܚܬܬܐ *maḥattā* and further derivatives) does not exactly mean *foetus*, it does have something to do with it insofar as, among other meanings, by way of the meaning *descent, origin*, what is meant here is *delivery.*[172] Therefore, the meaning of تحتها (*min*) *taḥtihā* would not be "*under her*," but "*her delivery.*"

This Syro-Aramaic reading, however, first has the coherence of the context in its favor to the extent that we have interpreted the preposition من (*min*) before تحتها (*taḥtihā*) not *locally* (*from beneath her*), but *temporally* in the Syro-Aramaic sense of "*from* (*that point in time*), i.e.: *in-*

---

170 Cf. *Thes* I 514: Improprie de *foetu*, ܒܛܢܗ (*baṭnāh*): *id quod conceperat.*

171 Cf., e.g., C. Brockelmann, *Arabische Grammatik* [*Arabic Grammar*] § 85; *Syrische Grammatik* [*Syriac Grammar*] § 201.

172 Cf. *Thes*. II on ܢܚܬ (*nḥeṯ*) 2344, (γ) *ortus est, genus duxit;* further in C. Brockelmann, Lexicon Syriacum 424a, under 10: *oriundus fuit* (*to spring from, to be descended from, to be born*).

stantly, immediately after her delivery."[173] This temporal use of من (*min*), though not attested in Classical Arabic,[174] is nonetheless quite common in modern Arabic dialects of the Near East as a Syro-Aramaic substratum, for example, in: من وصولي قلت له = حال وصولي قلت له (*instantly, immediately after my arrival I said to him*).

The memory of an earlier nominal use of تحت (*taḥt*) has, moreover, been retained by the *Lisān* (II 17b f.): تحت: تكون مرة ظرفا ، ومرة اسما (*taḥt sometimes occurs as an adverb, sometimes as a noun*). Even the adjectival use قوم تحوت : أرذال سفلة (*qawmun tuḥūtun: lowly people*) (*Lisān, op. cit.*) can be traced back to Syro-Aramaic ܬܚܬܝ̈ܐ (*taḥtāyē*) (*Thes.* II 4425: *infimi hominum*).

Now that the *Lisān* has confirmed the nominal usage of تحت (*taḥtu*), there would be nothing to criticize about the traditional Koranic reading were it not that the reading من نحتها (*min naḥtihā* or *nuḥātihā*) based on Syro-Aramaic ܢܚܬܐ / *nḥāṯā* or ܢܘܚܬܐ / *nuḥḥāṯā* is better. Namely, under the root نحت / *naḥata* the *Lisān* gives a series of phases indicating the Syro-Aramaic origin of this root. For example, among others, it gives the following verse by the poet الخرنق / *al-Ḫirniq*, the sister of the Old Arabic poet طرفة / *Ṭarafa* (c. 538-564 A.D.):

الخالطين نحيتهم بنضارهم

"who brought the lowly among them together with their nobles"

وذوي الغنى منهم بذي الفقر

"and the wealthy among them with the needy."

As a conjecture the *Lisān* explains the expression نحيت (*naḥīt* as دخيل (*daḫīl*) (*stranger*). Yet the opposites of *lowly*[175] and *noble*, *poor* and *rich* in both parts of the verse clearly refer to members of one and the same community. The ignorance of Aramaic prompts the Arab lexicographers to guess the meaning of borrowed expressions from the context. That the error rate in the process is relatively high is evidenced by the countless

---

173 Cf. *Thes.* II 2155: Valet etiam ܡܢ ܕ (*men d-*): *postquam* (*after*). *Mannā*, 407a: ܡܢ ܕܩܪܝܗܝ (*men da-qrāy*) : حالما دعاه (*as soon as he called him*).

174 Not to be confused with the temporal من in the sense of مذ ، منذ (cf., e.g., *Lisān* XIII 421 b): من سنة = مذ سنة (*min sana*^{tin}: *for a year*).

175 Discovered with the help of Syro-Aramaic.

unrecognized Aramaic roots in the *Lisān*, the encyclopedic dictionary of the Classical Arabic language. In our case, نحيت (*naḥīt*) is a clear borrowing from Syro-Aramaic ܢܚܝܬ (*naḥīṯ* or *naḥḥīṯ*), documented by the Thesaurus with ܢܚܝܬ ܓܢܣܐ (*naḥīṯ* /*naḥḥīṯ gensā*) *vir infimus, e plebe oriundus*: (*a man*) *of lowly origin*, and, citing the Syrian lexicographers, with the corresponding Arabic translation: لئيم الحسب و النسب و الجنس , *ignobilis, humilis genere et conditione,* وضيع . وطيّ الاصل . قليل الحسب و النسب as well as further ܢܚܝܬ (*naḥīṯ*: *descendens,* نازل هابط (*Thes*. II 2345). As in opposition to نحيت (*naḥīt*) is also how the *Lisān* explains النضار (*an-nuḍār* – actually النصار / *an-nuṣār*):الخالص النسب[176] (*al-ḫāliṣu n-nasab*) (*a man*) *of noble descent*, which clearly confirms the antonymous Syro-Aramaic meaning of نحيت (*naḥīt*).

The situation is similar for the other expressions connected with this root, all of which the *Lisān* tries to explain through popular etymology, but whose real meaning is to be determined through Syro-Aramaic. Rich pickings are guaranteed to anyone willing to devote himself or herself to the deserving task of studying the Aramaisms in the *Lisān*. Such would reveal the extent of the Aramaic influence on the Arabic language[177] and

---

176 *Lisān* II 98a. The reading النصار / *an-nuṣār* results from the lexical equivalent of Syro-Aramaic ܢܨܝܚܐ / *naṣīḥā*, the meanings of which *Mannā* (461b) gives as follows: (4) مظفر . قاهر . فائز (*successful, victorious, triumphant*), and under (7) شريف. جليل. نبيل. فاضل (*noble, honorable, highborn, illustrious*). The Arabic expression النصار /*an-nuṣār* renders the Syriac meaning under (4), presupposing that the semantic nuance under (7) is included. Thus here النصار /*an-nuṣār* means الأشراف / *al-ašrāf* (the *notables*).

177 Theodor Nöldeke writes about this influence in a work that he labels a *sketch*: *Die semitischen Sprachen* [*The Semitic Languages*] (Leipzig, ^{2}1899) 52:
"During the entire dominance of Aramaic this language had at least a great influence on the vocabulary of Arabic. The more meticulous one's examination, the more one recognizes how many Arabic words signifying concepts or objects of a certain culture have been borrowed from the Arameans [Reference to the aforementioned work by Siegmund Fraenkel, *Die aramäischen Fremdwörter* (*Aramaic Foreign Words*)]. The northern cultural influence expressed in these borrowings contributed considerably to preparing the Arabs for their powerful intervention in world history."
Nöldeke correctly traces the richness of the Arabic vocabulary partially to the arbitrarily devised expressions of Arabic poetry and partially to words that were

smooth the way for a yet non-existent etymological dictionary of Classical Arabic.

Still, the above-mentioned evidence merely confirms the Syro-Aramaic meaning "*to be low*(*ly*)." For the meaning "*to be hereditary, innate,*" the *Lisān* cites والنحيتة : الطبيعة التي نحت عليها الانسان أي قطع (*wa-n-naḥīta: aṭ-ṭabīʿatu l-latī nuḥita ʿalayhā l-insānu, ay quṭiʿa*): (*an-naḥīta is the nature that is hereditary to a person = that is innate to him*). In the definition of the loan term from Syro-Aramaic *naḥīta* (possibly in Syro-Aramaic *nḥāṯā*), the *Lisān* uses the loan verb from Syro-Aramaic *nuḥita* (in the passive voice) (*to be descended from, to come away from, to be delivered of* in the sense of *to be born*), which it takes to be the possibly homonymous root نحت (*naḥata*), but which was probably first borrowed from Syro-Aramaic and only understood in later Arabic in the sense of *to chisel* (actually *to knock off, to chop off, to knock down*), and correspondingly explains it as (the nature according to which one) "*was hewn, cut, cut to fit,*" i.e. in its sense as "*shaped.*" There is then a citation from *al-Liḥyānī*, which somewhat correctly explains the expression in question: هي الطبيعة و الأصل (*hiya ṭ-ṭabīʿatu wa-l-aṣl*) (*it is nature and origin*, i.e. *the innate*).

The other examples in the *Lisān*, الكرم من نحته (*noble-mindedness is innate to him*), إنه لكريم الطبيعة و النحيتة (*he is of a noble-minded nature and birth*), وقد نحت على الكرم وطبع عليه (*noble-mindedness is his by birth and nature*),[178] furnish evidence of the earlier use of the root نحت

---

common only to individual tribes. His concluding opinion on the subject (58) is all the more surprising:

"But still the abundance of words is exceedingly large, and the Arabic dictionary will always remain the principal aid in the search for instruction on obscure expressions in other Semitic languages [where just the opposite seems to be the case, though he then adds the qualifier]: only if this occurs with the requisite amount of level-headedness; then it's quite all right."

178 *Lisān* II 98b; through the conjectural explanation of Arabic نحت (*naḥata*) (97b) – النحت (*an-naḥtᵘ*) with النشر و القشر (*an-našrᵘ wa-l-qašr*) (*to saw, to peel*) – the *Lisān* testifies to its ignorance of the original meaning of this root originally borrowed from Aramaic, when, for example, it explains النحاتة / *an-nuḥātā* with ما نحت من الخشب (*mā nuḥita min al-ḫašab*) (*what has been planed from wood*). At the same time, this nominal form already exhibits a direct borrowing

(*naḥata*) (or *naḥita*) in Arabic as a borrowing from Syro-Aramaic ܢܚܬ (*nḥeṯ*) in the meaning "*to come down from, to give birth to, to be descended from.*"

Now, whether one were to read من تحتها (*min taḥtihā*), من نحتها (*naḥtihā*), or (on the basis of the customary defective spelling in the Koran) *nuḥātihā*,[179] would, to be sure, change nothing in terms of the sense,

---

from Syro-Aramaic ܢܚܬܐ (*nḥāṯā*) or ܢܘܚܚܬܐ (*nūḥḥāṯā*) with the correspondent meaning here, "*what has fallen off.*" Also, نحت الجبل (*naḥata l-ǧabal*) does not actually mean قطعه (*qaṭaʿahu*) "*to cut*", but according to the original Syro-Aramaic meaning "*to chop off, to strike down*" (the mountain); the same is true for النحائت (*an-naḥāʾit*) (98a): آبار معروفة (*ābār maʿrūfa*) (*well-known wells*), whose original meaning the *Lisān* again derives from "*to cut.*" The figurative sense "*to degrade,*" on the other hand, derives from the following expressions (98b): نحته بلسانه : لامه وشتمه (*naḥatahū bi-lisānihi: lāmahū wa-šatamahū*) (*to "degrade" somebody with the tongue: to rebuke, revile him*); النحيت (*an-naḥīt*) (< Syro-Aramaic ܢܚܝܬ / *naḥīt*) means primarily that which is *inferior, bad, reprehensible*; نحته بالعصا : ضربه بها (*naḥatahū bi-l-ʿaṣā : ḍarabahu bihā*) (*to hit somebody with a stick*, actually in this way "*to degrade*" him, "*to knock*" him "*down*" with it); the same is true when one is said نحت المرأة : نكحها (*naḥata l-marʾa^ta: nakaḥahā*) (*to "degrade = to dishonor" a woman*: *to lie with her*).

On the other hand, in his *Lexicon Syriacum* 424b, C. Brockelmann categorizes the Syro-Aramaic ܢܚܬ (*nḥeṯ*) etymologically with the Arabic حت (*ḥatta*), and that its first radical ܢ / ن (*nūn*) has fallen off suggests, in turn, according to the expressions cited in the *Lisān* (II 22a ff.), a borrowing from this very Syro-Aramaic root with the original meaning "*to fall off.*" That this root was unknown to the Arabs is shown not least by its reduction in colloquial modern Arabic to a verbal form with the meaning "*to rub off, to scratch off*" (see, for example, Hans Wehr) as well as "*to become worn through use*" (said of pieces of clothing and carpets, actually "*to be worn out, run down*") .

179 Cf. *Lisān* II 98a where النحاتة (*an-nuḥāta*) is explained with the help of البراية (*al-burāya*) (*shavings*). For this unidentified Syro-Aramaic root in the *Lisān* the derivation of the Arabic نحاتة (*nuḥāta*) from Syro-Aramaic ܢܚܬܐ (*nḥāṯā*) or ܢܘܚܚܬܐ (*nuḥḥāṯā*) would nevertheless be obvious, whereby the Arabic feminine ending is to be viewed occasionally as a purely phonetic rendering of the Syro-Aramaic emphatic ending of the masculine nominal form. This, however, does not rule out the possibility that an Arabic feminine ending may be derived from such an ending in Syro-Aramaic. Concerning this nominal form Nöldeke writes in his *Beiträgen zur semitischen Sprachwissenschaft* [*Essays on Semitic Lin-*

in any event what does speak for the last reading is the fact that both in Syro-Aramaic and in the *Lisān* this root corresponds more closely to the meaning "*delivery*," which the *Lisān* also documents with further derivatives. Since the Koran elsewhere uses the root ولد (*walada*) for the general sense of *to give birth* and *to procreate*, but specifically uses the root وضع (*waḍaʿa*) (*to lay, to lay down*) (cf. Suras 3:36; 22:2; 35:11; 41:47; 46:15; and 65:4,6) for *to be delivered of, to give birth to*, the latter appears to correspond lexically to the Syro-Aramaic ܢܚܬ[180] (*naḥḥeṯ*). Accordingly, من نحتها (*min nuḥḥātihā*), expressed otherwise in Koranic Arabic, would be من وضعها (*min waḍʿihā*) in the sense of حال وضعها (*ḥāla waḍʿihā*), which in turn could be rendered in modern Arabic as

---

guistics] (Strasbourg, 1904) 30, under *Nomina of the Form Fuʿāl* : "In Arabic, then, the *femininum* فعالة (*fuʿāla*) is still quite alive as the form of refuse, of shavings. This is shown, among other things, by the fact that it can even be formed from recently borrowed words."

That Nöldeke, in the case of the examples named here نشارة (*nušāra*) (*wood shavings*) and كناسة (*kunāsa*) (*sweepings*), does not already recognize a borrowing from the Syro-Aramaic equivalents that he has also cited, ܢܣܪܬܐ (*nsārtā*) and ܟܢܫܬܐ (*knāštā*), may be because he views his presentation from the sole perspective of a neutral study in comparative Semitistics. The same applies for the Arabic form فعال (*fuʿāl*), which Nöldeke would like to see as separate from the preceding form, but which seems merely to be the Arabic pausal form or the reproduction of the *status absolutus* of the Syro-Aramaic nominal form ܦܥܠܐ (*pʿālā*), as several of the examples he cites also attest. Thus سعال (*suʿāl*) (*coughing*) can most likely be derived from ܫܥܠܐ (*šʿālā*), عطاس (*ʿuṭās*) (*sneezing*) from ܛܥܫܐ (*ṭʿāšā*), خناق (*ḫunāq*) (*angina*) from ܚܢܩܐ (*ḥnāqā*). Other forms derived from Arabic roots would be merely analogous formations. From a purely philological perspective, comparative Semitics may be useful, but it leads one all too easily to blur the reciprocal influences, relevant to cultural history, of its individual languages.

180 Although not specifically in the meaning *to be delivered of, to give birth to*, but in the general meaning *to send down, to drop, to lower*, the Eastern Syrian lexicographers include among the various derivations the following Arabic equivalents: أنزل (*anzala*), أخفض (*aḫfaḍa*), حط (*ḥaṭṭa*), واضع (*wāḍaʿa*). (Cf. *Thes.* II 2344 f.; *Mannā* 442b f.). Since the *Thes.* does not provide any examples for ܢܚܬ (*naḥḥeṯ*) in the meaning *to be delivered of, to give birth to*, it would be interesting to document this usage in other Aramaic dialects.

حال توليدها (*ḥāla tawlīdihā*) or حال ولادتها (*ḥāla wilādatihā*) (*immediately upon her giving birth*).

The fact that the Koran here uses as a *hapax legomenon* borrowed from Syro-Aramaic this verbal root نحت (*naḥḥata*) (in the sense of نزل /*nazzala*, أنزل /*anzala: to make descend, to bring down = to give birth*), instead of the otherwise customary Arabic root وضع (*waḍaʿa*) (*to lay, to lay down, to give birth to*), raises the question, relevant both theologically and in terms of the history of religions, as to whether the Koran does not want deliberately, by this unusual expression, to connect and emphasize in a special way the extraordinary *delivery* of Mary with the supernatural *descent* of her son. This question imposes itself all the more since the basic stem ܢܚܬ (*nḥeṯ*) *"to come down"* (said, for example, of Christ, who came down from heaven) and the causative stems ܢܚܬ (*naḥḥeṯ*) / ܐܚܬ (*aḥḥeṯ*) *"to cause to descend, to send down"* (said, for example, of God, who sent down his son) have in fact been documented in this sense in Syro-Aramaic, though not in the specific meaning of *"to give birth, to be born"* in the sense of a natural birth.

The search for an equivalent usage in Aramaic finds its confirmation in a synonymous expression that Gesenius[181] gives under the Aramaic root נפל (*np̄al*) "*to fall*" in the meaning of "*to be born*" and explains as "*actually an extra term for a birth standing in opposition to regular natural processes.*" This usage, attested nowhere else in Arabic, of نحت (*naḥata*) or (*naḥḥata*) < Syro-Aramaic ܢܚܬ (*nḥeṯ* or *naḥḥeṯ*) in the meaning of "*to give birth, to be born*" (actually "*to cause to descend* [*from above*]")[182] would imply, at least in the case of this segment of the Mary Sura, an earlier period in the editing of the Koran than the second Meccan period estimated by Nöldeke-Schwally.[183] In it one can recognize

181 Wilhelm Gesenius, *Hebräisches und aramäisches Handwörterbuch* [*Concise Dictionary of Hebrew and Aramaic*], 1915, unrev. reprint (Berlin, Göttingen, Stuttgart, [17]1959) 512b, under (b).

182 What is striking here is that, regarding the *"sent-down Scriptures"* in the sense of revelations, the Koran usually employs the Arabic أنزل (*anzala*) (*to have come down, to send down*) in addition to آتى (*ātā*) (< Syro-Aramaic ܐܝܬܝ / *aytī*) (*to have come, to bring, to deliver*).

183 Cf. *GdQ* I 117-143; but on page 130 (line 3) it is conceded: "The Sura is the

with certainty a central element of the Christian components of the Koran.

According to the Syro-Aramaic reading, the first verse segment of Sura 19:24 should therefore be understood as follows:

> "Then he called to her *immediately after her giving birth*: Be not sad!"

Based on this understanding, the concerns expressed by Paret in his Koran commentary to this passage (324) as to whether the caller is *the newborn infant Jesus or the infant Jesus still located in the womb*, as well as the reference to the text from Pseudo-Matthew cited below, are unnecessary.

It follows from the preceding remarks that in the second part of the verse قد جعل ربك تحتك سريا (according to the previous understanding) "Your lord has made a rivulet beneath you," the repeatedly occurring تحتك (*taḥtaki*) does not mean "*beneath you,*" but "*your giving birth.*" Still to be explained, however, is the expression سريا (*sarīya*), misinterpreted as "*rivulet,*" with which we would have an example of case (c) (see page 24).

Ṭabarī (XVI 69 ff.) prefaces the explanation of the word سري (*sarī*) with the stereotypical remark that the commentators are of different opinions about its meaning. The majority (over nineteen traditionary chains) favor the meaning *river, little river, a river named Sarī, designation of the ʿĪsā river* (= *Jesus river*), *stream, rivulet*. In particular, *Muǧāhid* and *aḍ-Ḍaḥḥāk* believe it is *river* or *stream* in Syriac, whereas *Saʿīd b. Ǧubayr* is of the opinion that it is a *stream, rivulet* in Nabatean. On the other hand, two traditionaries object and advocate the view that Jesus himself is meant by the designation *sarī*. Probably on the basis of the conjectured Persian meaning *noble, honorable,*[184] *Ibn Zayd* asks: "But who, after all, could be أسرى منه (*asrā minhu*) *nobler* than Jesus!" Con-

---

oldest, or at least one of the oldest, in which holy persons from the New Testament such as Mary, Zachary, John the Baptist and Jesus are mentioned."

184 Cf. *Lisān* XIV 377b: السرو : المروءة والشرف (*as-sarwᵘ: al-murūʾa wa-š-šaraf*) (*manfulness, noblemindedness*); 378a: additional remarks on سريّ (*sarī*) in the meaning of شريف (*šarīf*) (*noble, nobleminded*).

cerning the erroneous opinions of those who see a river in this term, he makes use of his good common sense and argues: "If this is a river, then it ought to be *beside her* and not, of all places, *beneath her*!"[185]

But *Ṭabarī* does not follow him. Like an arbitrator, on democratic principles he agrees with the majority that sees in it a stream, from which – in his opinion – God has, according to Sura 19:26, expressly ordered Mary to drink: فكلي واشربي "*So eat and drink*."

Among our selected Western translators of the Koran, only Paret (by placing *sarī* in parentheses) suggests that the meaning of this expression is unclear. Blachère and Bell seem for the most part to approve of the explanation *Ṭabarī* gives. Blachère only observes concerning من تحتها (*min taḥtihā*) that in accordance with Koranic usage this expression means "*at her feet*," and not, as so often translated, "*from beneath her*."[186] Bell, on the other hand, refers to *Ṭabarī* (XVI 67 f.) and the controversial issue among the Arab commentators as to whether it was the Angel Gabriel or the Infant Jesus that called to Mary "*from beneath her*," concerning which he rightly supposes: "*probably 'the child*.'"[187] As to the word *sarī*, in his commentary (I 504 f., v. 24) he considers "*stream*" to be the most likely meaning, but points to the opinion held

---

185 The compiler of the *Lisān* nevertheless saw no reason not to include the unrecognized Syro-Aramaic expression سري (*sarī*) in the supposed meaning of نهر (*nahr*) (*river*) and جدول (*ǧadwal*) (*brook*) and to cite in connection with it the corresponding misinterpretation by the Koran commentators: النهر الصغير كالجدول يجري إلى النخل (*a small or a stream-like river that flows to the palms*) (*Lisān* XIV 380a). As we shall see, this is not an isolated case of misread and misunderstood Koranic expressions that have been accepted into the Arabic lexicography without being contested up to the present day. But also other expressions cited by the *Lisān* under the root شري (*šariya*) and سري (*sariya*) and explained by means of folk etymology provide ample proof of their Aramaic origins. To point these out here, however, would be to exceed the scope of this study. It would therefore be of eminent importance not only from the standpoint of cultural history, but also from that of philology, to scrutinize the Arabic lexicon for the countless Aramaisms that have until now been overlooked or falsely taken to be "*Old Arabic*."

186 Blachère, *loc. cit.* 331, notes 23-32.

187 Bell, *loc. cit.* I 286, note 2.

by several commentators that it could also mean *"chief, head"* (referring to Jesus) in accordance with the (probably Persian) meaning "*to be manly, noble*," which is listed in the *Lisān* (XIV 377b) under سرا (*srw*) and with a reference to سيبويه / *Sībawayh* and اللحياني / *al-Liḥyānī.*

In examining the corresponding passage more closely, Paret refers in his Koran commentary (323, on Sura 19:23-26) to W. Rudolph,[188] who says about the *attendant circumstances* of the birth of Jesus described therein: "The most likely explanation is that Muhammed is here influenced by a scene the so-called Pseudo-Matthew reports of the flight to Egypt in chapter 20 and transfers this to the birth":

> „*tunc infantulus Jesus laeto vultu in sinu matris suae residens ait ad palmam: flectere, arbor, et de fructibus tuis refice matrem meam ... aperi autem ex radicibus tuis venam, quae absconsa est in terra, et fluant ex ea aquae ad satietatem nostra*m."

(Translation of the Latin text):

> "Thereupon spoke the Infant Jesus, of joyful countenance sitting in his mother's lap, to the palm tree: Bend over, tree, and refresh my mother from your fruits ... further open out of your roots a vein that lies hidden in the earth, and let waters stream out upon us to quench our thirst."

Blachère, too, sees a parallel to our Koranic verse and an explanation for *the stream at Mary's feet* in this description from Pseudo-Matthew.[189] Bell argues along similar lines in his commentary (*loc. cit.*). By citing the quoted passage from Pseudo-Matthew the Western Koran scholars had their proof that in the case of the expression سري (*sarī*) it must indeed be a question of a *watercourse, a stream*, just as the Arab exegetes had also finally assumed after all.

The commentators in the East and the West will be shown, however,

188 Wilhelm Rudolph, *Die Abhängigkeit des Qorans von Judentum und Christentum* [*The Dependence of the Koran on Judaism and Christianity*] (Stuttgart, 1922) 79.

189 Blachère 331, notes 23-32.

that in the interpretation of this Koran passage they have succumbed in the first case to a linguistic error and in the second to fallacious reasoning.

Careful attention to the Koranic context is the fundamental prerequisite for a linguistically coherent understanding. That the Koran transferred the scene depicted by Pseudo-Matthew of the flight to Egypt to the birth of Christ is in no way proven by the passage cited above. The sole parallel is the palm that is spoken of in both passages. The other circumstances, however, are completely different.

Namely, when according to Pseudo-Matthew the infant Jesus directs the palm to cause water to flow forth, the logical reason may lie in the fact that for mother and son there was otherwise no water in the surrounding desert. Hence the command that water bubble forth to slake their thirst.

Not so in the Koran. Namely, when Mary according to Sura 19:23 calls out in despair, يليتني مت قبل هذا وكنت نسيا منسيا "*If only I had died beforehand* (i.e. before the birth) *and been totally forgotten!*" it is clearly not because she was *dying of thirst*! What depressed her so much was much more the outrageous insinuations of her family that she was *illegitimately* pregnant, something which is clearly implied by the scolding she receives in Verse 28: يأخت هرون ما كان ابوك امرأ سوء وما كانت أمك بغيا "Sister of Aaron, your father was after all no miscreant and your mother no strumpet!" (Paret: "Sister of Aaron! Your father was after all not a bad guy [note: man] and your mother not a prostitute!"). Most likely for the same reason it is also said, after she became pregnant, in Verse 22, فانتبذت به مكانا قصيا "whereupon she *was cast out* with him to a remote place" (Paret: "And she withdrew with him to a distant place").

What is crucial here is the Arabic verb فانتبذت (*fa-ntabaḏat*), which our Koran translators have incorrectly rendered with "*she withdrew*" (Bell), "*sie zog sich zurück*" (Paret), and "*elle se retira*" (Blachère). Despite the original meaning of Arabic نبذ (*nabaḏa*), namely, "*to send back, to reject, to cast out,*" this expression is actually explained in *Ṭabarī* with فاعتزلت (*fa-ʿtazalat*) and وتنحت (*wa-tanaḥḥat*) (*she with-*

drew).[190] The reflexive eighth Arabic verbal stem may have also led the Koran translators to make this grammatically equivalent, but nonetheless nonsensical assumption. When one considers, namely, that the Koran, following Syro-Aramaic usage, also uses reflexive stems with a passive meaning,[191] the result is the better fitting sense for this verse, "*she was cast out*," which indeed also represents a continuation of the introductory statement of Verse 16:

واذكر في الكتب مريم اذ انتبذت من اهلها مكانا شرقيا

"Make mention further in the scripture of Mary when she was *cast out by* her family to an *empty* (= a *waste*)[192] place." (Paret: "Und gedenke in der Schrift der Maria (Maryam)! (Damals) als sie *sich vor* ihren Angehörigen an einen *östlichen* Ort *zurückzog*!" ["And make mention in the scripture of Mary (Maryam)! (that time) when she *withdrew* from her family to a place in the *East*"]). The passive usage is additionally confirmed here by the preposition من (*min*) (*by*), which again corresponds to Syro-Aramaic practice,[193] but is totally impossible according to Ara-

190 *Ṭabarī* XVI 63.

191 Cf. C. Brockelmann, Syrische Grammatik [Syriac Grammar] § 167.

192 The Koranic spelling سرقيا is to be read *sarqīyā* according to Syro-Aramaic ܣܪܩܝܐ /*sarqāyā* (*empty* = *waste*) and not as Arabic شرقيا / *šarqīyā* (to a place,) "*eastward*" (Bell). The Syro-Aramaic reading is logically confirmed by the parallel verse 22, where it is said that Mary, after having become pregnant, was expelled with her child to a place "*far away*" (*makānan qaṣīyā*):

فحملته فانتبذت به مكانا قصيا

193 Cf., e.g., Lk. 2:18: ܘܟܠܗܘܢ ܕܫܡܥܘ: ܐܬܕܡܪܘ ܥܠ ܐܝܠܝܢ ܕܐܬܡܠܠ ܠܗܘܢ ܡܢ ܪܥܘܬܐ (*w-kullhōn da-šmaʿ(ū) eddammar(ū) ʿal aylēn d-etmallal(ī) l-hōn men rāʿawwāṯā*) "And all they that heard (it) wondered at those (things) which *were told* them *by* the shepherds" (from the Syriac Bible 63DC, United Bible Societies [London, 1979] 77a). The Koran, moreover, has the same passive construction in Sura 21:43, where it is said of the *idols*:

لا يستطيعون نصر انفسهم ولا هم منا يصحبون

"they are not (even) capable of helping themselves nor are they (as idols) accompanied by us (as helpers)" (i.e. nor are we *put with* them as god).

This construction, which is indefensible from the point of view of Arabic syntax, also confuses our Koran translators. Paret, for instance, translates (265): "(–Götter) die weder sich selber Hilfe zu leisten vermögen noch (irgendwo) gegen

bic grammar. There is namely no reason for the Koran to submit, as classical Arabic grammar would have it, to the prohibition imposed by later Arabic (or Persian) grammarians against naming the active subject in a passive sentence by means of the preposition من *min* (*by*).[194] Therefore, seen in this light, the classical Arabic grammar proves rather to be a hindrance in determining the proper understanding of particular passages in the Koran, while attention to Syro-Aramaic grammar assists in opening up insights into heretofore unimagined aspects of the Koranic language. This basic Syro-Aramaic structure of the Koranic language must be gone into in more detail.

Thus Verse 22 – correctly understood – indicates that Mary is cast out by her family because she is suspected of illegitimate conception, especially considering that the Koran does not place any fiancé or *sham husband* at her side to protect her from malicious tongues. As a result it is understandable that Mary in Verse 23, immediately before giving birth, longs desperately for her own death. The initial words of consolation from her newborn child would naturally need to be directed first of all to removing the reason for her desperation. But this could surely not occur by attempting to console her with the simple reference to a *stream* allegedly located beneath her. The idea assumed by *Ṭabarī* that God according to Verse 26 had commanded Mary to drink from it (فكلي واشربي / *so eat and drink*), therefore misses the mark. For it is not, say, the lack of food and drink that keeps Mary from eating and drinking, but much more her depressive mental state. That is why the consoling words of her child had to have such a content, so that she would no longer have any reason to be depressed and would therefore regain her desire to eat and drink.

---

uns Beistand finden [(– gods) who neither are capable of rendering themselves assistance nor find assistance against us (anywhere)] (*?wa-lā hum minnā yuṣḥabūna*)." Similarly Blachère (351): "et il ne leur est pas donné de compagnon contre nous [and they are not given a companion against us]" Only Bell translates correctly in terms of the meaning (I 308b 44): "and from Us they will have no company."

194 Cf. C. Brockelmann, *Arabische Grammatik* [*Arabic Grammar*] § 96.

The Western Koran scholars' reference to the above-mentioned passage from Pseudo-Matthew is also fallacious because the expression سريا (read *sarīyā* in today's Koran), which the Arab Koran commentators had already argued about and falsely interpreted as a *watercourse*, was thereby just as unphilologically and conjecturally confirmed and provided, once and for all, with a seal of approval.

Namely, in the case of this spelling سـريا it is not a question of an Arabic, but of a Syro-Aramaic root. The problem is also already solved if it is presented in its original Syro-Aramaic form as ܫܪܝܐ (*šaryā*). For what one expects in the Koranic context is a countering expression to the reproach of her illegitimate pregnancy that would suffice to free her of this stigma. Now if one understands *unmarried* in the sense of *unlawful, illegitimate*, then its countering expression *married* would accordingly be *lawful, legitimate*. And so it is in modern Arabic usage that an *illegitimate son* (especially as a swearword) is إبن حرام (*ibn ḥarām*), which is countered by its opposite إبن حلال (*ibn ḥalāl*) (*a legitimate, legally born = an upright, honest person*).

In this context the Syro-Aramaic expression ܫܪܝܐ (*šaryā*) has exactly this meaning, however, here it is not to be understood as a substantive (*stream, rivulet*), but as a verbal adjective in the sense of "*legitimate.*"[195]

The twenty-fourth verse of the Mary Sura, which has previously been misunderstood as follows by all of the Koran commentators we know of,

> "Then he (probably "the child") called to her from beneath her: 'Grieve not; thy Lord hath placed beneath thee a streamlet.'" (Bell)

is now, after this elucidation of its original meaning, to be understood as summarized in the following way:

---

195 See *Thes.* II 4308: ܫܪܐ (*šārē*) *absolvens; solvit, liberavit.* Further, *Mannā* 816b (among the 27 different meanings of ܫܪܐ *šrā*) (21): اذن . حلّل . ضد حرّم (*to allow, to declare legitimate*; *opposite of to forbid, to declare illegitimate*), and under ܫܪܝܐ *šaryā* (7): حلال. مباح. خلاف ممنوع ومحرّم (*legitimate, allowed, opposite of forbidden and illegitimate*). C. Brockelmann, *Lexicon Syriacum* [*Syriac Lexicon*] 804a: 6. ܫܪܝܐ (*šaryā*): *licet* (it is *allowed, legitimate*).

“Then he called to her *immediately after her delivery*: ‘Do not be sad, your Lord has made your *delivery legitimate’*.”

Only after the infant Jesus has consoled this hitherto despairing mother with the *acknowledgment of his legitimacy* does he direct to her the encouraging words (from Verse 26) that she is therefore (and not because she is dying of thirst) “*to eat and drink and be happy*.”[196] Just as logically does Mary (according to Verse 27) then take heart and return with her newborn child to her family. Confronted with the family’s initial indignation (Verse 28), she follows the instructions of her newborn and allows her child to respond (Verses 30-33) and in so doing to reveal his miraculous birth.

Thus, in contrast to the hitherto distortedly rendered Arabic reading of this passage, the Koranic presentation of the birth of Christ now for the first time acquires its original meaning through the bringing in of Syro-Aramaic.

Misreadings of Identical Spellings

The Arabic misreading of سريا (*sarīyā*) for Syro-Aramaic ܫܪܝܐ (*šaryā*) henceforth opens our eyes to insights into other misread, but originally identical spellings in the Koran. So, for instance, in the Koranic version of the Tale of Alexander (in which Moses has taken the place of Alexander) about the dead fish which upon contact with aqua vita comes back to life and escapes into the ocean:[197]

196 For the Koranic expression وقري عينا (*wa-qarrī ʿayna*^{n}), Mannā gives (698a) as the Syro-Aramaic equivalent ܩܘܪܬ ܥܝܢܐ *qurraṯ ʿaynā*), ܩܘܪܬ ܠܒܐ ܪܘܚܐ (*qurraṯ lebbā, rūḥā*): قرّة العين . فرح . تعزية (*qurrat*^{u} *l-ʿayn, faraḥ, taʿziya*) (*cheerfulness, joy, consolation*); see also *Thes.* II 3711: ܩܘܪܬ ܪܘܚܐ (*qurraṯ rūḥā*): *consolatio* (*consolation*).

197 Cf. R. Paret, *Kommentar* [*Commentary*] 316 ff.

Sura 18:61

فاتخذ سبيله في البحر سـربا

The last expression (*saraba*) is understood by our Koran translators as follows:

> (Bell I 280): 60. "(They forgot their fish,) and it took its way in the sea freely (*saraban*)."
>
> (Paret 243): "Der nahm seinen Weg in das große Wasser (*baḥr*) (und schwamm) auf und davon."
>
> (Blachère 324): "(Ils oublièrent leur poisson) qui reprit son chemin dans la mer, en frétillant."

After remarking (اختلف أهل العلم) that the scholars disagree about the meaning of this expression (*saraba^n*), *Ṭabarī* enumerates the following opinions: (a) the way the fish took, so to speak, *turned to stone* after it; (b) rather the water was *frozen* after its passage; (c) whatever the fish touched in the ocean was *solidified* into a *rock*, and (d) the fish made its way to the water not in the ocean, but on *land*. *Ṭabarī* lets all of these explanations stand. However, he considers as most plausible the interpretation, attributed to the Prophet, according to which the water divided itself as if into a *passageway* in front of the fish.[198]

Paret disapproves of this last explanation by *Ṭabarī* and the corresponding translation by Friedländer, according to which the fish "had made its way through a *subterranean passage* into the ocean." He himself takes the expression to be an adverbial infinitive of Arabic *sariba* "to flow," which would mean as much as "(and it swam) *away*." To this extent he concedes the correctness of Bell's translation, "and it took its way in the sea *freely*," whereas Blachère – perhaps inspired by the *shimmering* of a *mirage* (in Arabic سراب / *sarāb*) – translates the expression with "*en frétillant*" (*wriggling*).[199]

In fact, only Bell, with "*freely*," has correctly *guessed* the expression

---

198 *Ṭabarī* XV 273 f.

199 R. Paret, *Kommentar* [*Commentary*] 318.

from the context, though without justifying it philologically. For it has nothing to do with Arabic *sariba* (*to flow*); otherwise the Arabic commentators would have probably also figured it out. The fact, however, that they had arrived, so to speak, *at the limits of their Arabic* simply suggests that here it is not a question of an Arabic root. It is surely as a result of the preceding and the following rhyme that the Arabic readers have here read سربا (*saraba*^{n}), especially since there is an equivalent Arabic root. From this root, however, the Arabic commentators were justifiably incapable of wresting any reasonable meaning.

However, one of the meanings of the Syro-Aramaic participial adjective discussed above, ܫܪܝܐ (*šaryā*), which in this case of course cannot mean "*legitimately*," exactly fits the correct meaning here, "*freely*." Thus *Mannā* (*loc. cit.*) lists under (5): حرّ . مطلق . غير مقيّد (*free, unrestricted, unattached*); and the *Thes.* (II 4307) under the root ܫܪܐ / *šrā*: (d) *solvit* vincula, *liberavit, dimisit*; further C. Brockelmann, *Lexicon Syriacum* [*Syriac Lexicon*] 803b (under ܫܪܝܐ / *šaryā*): 2. *liber* (*free*). And so in this way only the Syro-Aramaic reading سربا = شريا = ܫܪܝܐ (*šaryā*) gives the expression from Sura 18:61 its proper meaning: "*And it* (the fish) *made its way freely into the ocean.*" Or expressed in modern Arabic: فاتخذ سبيله في البحر حرّاً (*fa-ttaḫaḏa sabī-lahu fī l-baḥri ḥurra*).

Sura 78:20

We come across another homonymous and misread spelling in Sura 78:20. There we read: وسيرت الجبال فكانت سرابا (*wa-suyyirat*^{i} *l-ǧibāl*^{u} *fa-kānat sarāba*^{n}). According to the understanding until now:

> (Bell II 630): "The mountains will have been moved and become a mirage."

> (Paret 497): "und die Berge bewegen sich (von der Stelle) und sind (schließlich nur noch) eine Luftspiegelung."

> (Blachère 633): "[où] les montagnes, mises en marche, seront un mirage."

Noteworthy here is that in the cited translations none of the three translators has taken exception to the underlined expressions. Thus they, too, are following *Ṭabarī* (XXX 8), who explains this verse in the following manner: The mountains are blown up out of their foundations and reduced to dust so that like a mirage they only seem to have their original form.

What is conspicuous in the process is that *Ṭabarī* does not understand the verb سيّرت (*suyyirat*) in the original Arabic meaning of the word, "*to be set into movement*," but instead interprets it as "*to be blown up*." In doing so, he may have had other parallel passages in mind, such as, say, Sura 19:90, وتخر الجبال هدا (*and the mountains will fall down in ruins*), or when it is said of mountains in Sura 20:105 that ينسفها ربي نسفا "*my Lord will blow them up*" (according to the Arabic understanding) or "*pulverize them, turn them into dust*" (according to the Syro-Aramaic understanding[200]). The following verse provides us with a further example:

Sura 69:14

وحملت الأرض والجبال فدكتا دكة واحدة

This is how our Koran translators have understood this verse:

> (Bell II 601): "And the earth and the mountains shall be moved, and shattered at a single blow."
>
> (Paret 480): "und [*wenn*] die Erde und die Berge hochgehoben [Note W: aufgeladen] und (auf) einmal (zerstoßen und) zu Staub gemacht werden; ..."

---

200 This last meaning is supported by Syro-Aramaic ܢܫܦ (*nšap̄*), which in the *Thes.* (II 2477) is equated with the synonym ܢܚܠ (*nḥal*) (*to sift through*) and thus "*to turn into powder, into flour*." The Arabic نسف (*nasafa*) seems to be derived from this, according to the explanations provided by the *Lisān* (IX 328b), which correspond exactly to Syro-Aramaic usage, نسف الشيء: غربله (*nasafa š-šay'a: ġarbalahu*) (approximately, *to sift through*), as is sifted flour, نسافة (*nusāfa*) (< Syro-Aramaic ܢܫܦܐ / *nšāp̄ā*).

(Blachère 612): "[*quand*] la terre et les monts, emportés, seront pulvérisés d'un seul coup; …"

Ṭabarī may have Sura 99:1 or Sura 56:4 and 5 in mind insofar as he sees a *simultaneous quaking of the earth and mountains* in this verse. According to a further explanation attributed to *Ibn Zayd,* the earth and mountains are turned *to dust.*[201] Little persuaded by this interpretation, Paret chooses to stick closely to the original meaning of the Arabic حمل (*ḥamala*) (*to carry*) with his "*hochheben* [*to lift up*]" (or "*aufladen* [*to load*]"). On the other hand, Blachère with "*emporter* [*to carry away*]" and Bell with "*to move*" venture solely on the basis of the context to come closer to the actual sense (*to carry away*), here too without justifying it philologically. In fact, this meaning can only be determined via the Syro-Aramaic ܫܩܠ (*šqal*) (original meaning, "*to carry*"). Namely, the meanings that fit this context are listed by C. Brockelmann (*Lex. Syr.* 798b f.) under the numbers 7 and 8, "*abolevit*" as well as "*removit, separavit*" in the sense of "*to remove, to destroy*"; further examples in this sense are cited by the *Thes.* under "*abstulit*" and "*sustulit*"[202]; finally, under (2), *Mannā* (812b) gives the equivalent Arabic as رفع . حمل . نسف (*rafaʿa, ḥamala, nasafa*) (*to lift up, to carry* [*away*], *to pulverize/to remove*).

With the establishment of the meaning of the Arabic حمل (*ḥamala*) that fits this context – "*to carry away, to remove, to destroy*" – via the lexically equivalent Syro-Aramaic expression ܫܩܠ (*šqal*), we would thus have an example of case (f) (see above page 24).

For Arabic دكّ (*dakka*) the meaning given by the *Lisān* (X 424b), "*to destroy, to tear down,*" is actually adequate. A parallel is also furnished by Sura 19:90: وتخر الجبال هدا (*wa-taḫirru l-ğibālu hadda*ⁿ) (*nearly might the earth split open*) "*and the mountains fall to pieces.*" Although

201 *Ṭabarī* XXIX 56.

202 *Thes.* II 4286 (e) *abstulit*; for example, it is said in Ex. 10:19 that Yahweh turned a mighty strong west wind, which *drove away, removed* the locusts: ܘܫܩܠܬܗ ܠܩܡܨܐ (*wa-šqalteh l-qamṣā*); in addition: ܫܩܠ ܢܦܫܗ ܒܣܡܐ (*šqal napšeh b-sammā*) *seipsum veneno sustulit* (literally: "*he carried* (*off*) *his soul with poison*" = *he destroyed himself, he did away with himself with poison*).

Bell has understood the Arabic expression correctly, in accordance with the *Lisān*, the translations proposed by Paret with "*(zerstoßen und) zu Staub gemacht* [*to (crush and) turn to dust*]" and by Blachère with "*pulvérisés* [*pulverized*]" are nevertheless to be taken into account. Namely, among other expressions, the *Thes.* gives as an onomatopoeic equivalent to the Syro-Aramaic ܕܩ (*daq*) (*contudit, contrivit, comminuit: to crush, to grind, to smash to pieces*), Arabic دك (*dakka*), which it presents as a synonym of the Syro-Aramaic ܕܚܝܚܐ (*daḥīḥā*) (as a passive participle: *ground, crushed*; as a noun: *dust, powder*).[203] The last meaning would be the more logical consequence of *removal*, *destruction*, namely their being *reduced to dust* or *powder*.

According to this clarification and on the basis of the meaning of the Arabic expression حمل (*ḥamala*) (*to carry = to carry away, to remove*) established via the semantics of its Syro-Aramaic lexical equivalent, the verse under discussion (69:14) is thus to be understood as follows:

> "and [when] the earth and the mountains <u>are</u> <u>destroyed</u> (removed) and at the same time <u>reduced</u> (to dust)."

The Koranic conception, according to which the mountains *are crushed* or *turned to dust* on Judgment Day, may now explain why *Ṭabarī* interprets the verb سيرت (*suyyirat*) in Sura 78:20 accordingly and does not understand it, as our Koran translators do, on the basis of the Arabic sense of "*to set in motion*." This makes one wonder whether it is not much more likely that *Ṭabarī* had read the Arabic transcription of Syro-

---

203 *Thes.* I 936 f. connects Syro-Aramaic ܕܩ (*daq*) (referring to K.) with ܡܕܟܬܐ (*mḏākṯā*) (*mortar*) as a synonym for ܡܕܩܬܐ (*mḏaqqṯā*). This would to this extent suggest a secondary formation of the Syro-Aramaic root ܡܕܟ *mḏaḵ* / *maddeḵ*) (*to mix*) from ܕܩ (*daq*) (in the meaning of *to crush* > ܕܟ *daḵ*). Arabic دمك (*damaka*) has most likely been borrowed from Syro-Aramaic ܡܕܟ (*mḏaḵ*) (*Lisān* X 428b) as a metathesis understood in the meaning of "*to grind*": دمك الشيء : طحنه (*damaka š-šayʾa*: *ṭaḥanahu*), to which the "*grinding millstone*" رحى دموك (*rahaⁿ damūk*), as an obvious borrowing from Syro-Aramaic ܪܚܝܐ ܡܕܘܟܐ (*raḥyā mad-dōḵā*), clearly points, whereby the *Lisān* interprets the general sense of the Syro-Aramaic *nomen agentis* ܡܕܘܟܐ (*maddōḵā*) (> Arabic دموك *damūk*) as سريعة الطحن (*sarīʿa^tu ṭ-ṭaḥn*), a "*fast*" *grinding* (but actually a "*thoroughly*" *grinding*) millstone.

Aramaic ܣܬܪ (*s̱ṯar / sattar*) سترت (*sutirat / suttirat*), since only the Syro-Aramaic root produces, besides the Arabic meaning of ستر (*satara*), "*to protect, to wrap, to veil*," the further meaning of "*to destroy*."[204]

In fact, it is also only through this Syro-Aramaic interpretation that the further reading and the respective understanding of the subsequent obscure expression سرابا (*sarāban*) is cleared up. It is hard to imagine that this expression is supposed to mean, according to the Arabic understanding, a *mirage* which the *mountains set in motion* would eventually become. In comparison, the Syro-Aramaic rectification of the misread Arabic spelling شريا = سرابا (since the medial ا is probably a later insertion) = Syro-Aramaic ܫܪܝܐ (*šaryā*) or in plural (referring to mountains) ܫܪ̈ܝܐ (*šrayyā*) produces a meaning in harmony with the verb ستر (*satara*) = ܣܬܪ (*sṯar / sattar*) "*to destroy*." This we find namely in *Mannā* under the root ܫܪܐ (*šrā*) (816a), be it under (10) in the meaning هدم نقض البناء وغيره (*to destroy or tear down something or other such as a building*),[205] or under (11) in the meaning أبطل . ألغى . أزال (*to wipe out, to annul, to cancel, to remove*).[206] The latter meaning gives, to be sure, the more logical sense to the extent that, as a result of their destruction, the mountains "*are wiped out, removed, destroyed, disintegrated.*" Accordingly, if we understand the misread Arabic spelling سرابا (*sarāban*) not as a noun (*mirage*), but as a Syro-Aramaic masculine plural participial adjective ܫܪ̈ܝܐ (*šrayyā*) (*destroyed, disintegrated* [*mountains*]), Sura 78:20 produces the following Syro-Aramaic reading:

ܘܡܣܬܬܪܝܢ ܛܘ̈ܪܐ ܘܗܘܝܢ ܫܪ̈ܝܐ

(*w-me-stattrīn ṭūrē w-hāwēn šrayyā*)

---

204 Cf. *Thes.* II 2756: (2) *destruxit* (*to destroy*); further (2757), with a reference to the Syrian lexicographers: (1) *evertit, destruxit, diruit,* هدم . نقض . خرب (*hadama, naqaḍa, ḫarraba*) "*to destroy, to tear down.*" The same explanation is given in *Mannā* (519b) under (3).

205 For this meaning, cf. *Thes.* II 4309 (Mk. 15:29): ܐܘܢ ܫܪܐ ܗܝܟܠܐ ܘܒܢܐ ܠܗ ܠܬܠܬܐ ܝܘܡܝܢ (*ʾūn šārē hayklā w-ḇānē leh la-ṯlāṯā yawmīn*): (*Ah, thou that destroyest the temple, and buildest* (*it*) *in three days!*).

206 Cf. C. Brockelmann, *Lexicon Syriacum* [*Syriac Lexicon*] 803b: (k) *delevit, destruxit*; (l) *abolevit* (*to destroy, to annihilate; to extinguish, to eradicate*).

Accordingly this verse ought to be read:

وسترت الجبال فكانت شرايا

(*wa-suttirat*^{i} *l-ğibāl*^{u} *fa-kānat šarāyā*)

In other words, in Koranic Arabic in the style of Suras 19:90 and 56:6:

وهدت الجبال فكانت هباء (= تلاشت)

(*wa-huddat*^{i} *l-ğibāl*^{u} *fa-kānat habāʾa*^{n}) (*ᶜtalāšat*)

The verse that has heretofore been misunderstood on the basis of the Arabic misreading as

> "and the mountains move (from their place) and are (eventually just) a mirage" (Paret)

is now to be understood according to the Syro-Aramaic reading as:

> "and [then] the mountains *collapse* and *disintegrate*."

First of all, the identification would thus be attested of three Syro-Aramaic spellings in the Koran which, though originally homonymous in terms of orthography, were later misread in Arabic due to the incorrect placement of points (or vowels):

a) سريا (*sarīya*^{n}) (Mary Sura 19:24) ("*rivulet*") as the Syro-Aramaic ܫܪܝܐ (*šaryā*) in the sense of "*legitimately*" (*born*);

b) سربا (*saraba*^{n}) (Sura 18:61) (said of the fish, Ṭabarī: "*escaped through a channel*"; Bell – guessed from the context: "*freely*", Paret: "*away*"; Blachère: "*wriggling*") as the Syro-Aramaic ܫܪܝܐ (*šaryā*) in the sense of (*swam*) "*freely*" (*into the ocean*);

c) سرابا (*sarāba*^{n}) (Sura 78:20) ("*mirage*") as the Syro-Aramaic plural ܫܪ̈ܝܐ (*šrayyā*) (in reference to the mountains) in the sense of "*disintegrated, dispersed.*"

Secondly, in connection with this we would at the same time have identified the Arabic spelling سيرت (*suyyirat*) – which has been misread, subject to no challenge by previous Koran scholars and misinterpreted in the sense of "*to be set in motion, to be moved*" – as the Syro-Aramaic root ܣܬܪ (*sṯar*) (*to destroy, to tear down*) in the passive form ܐܣܬܬܪ

(*estattar*) = read in Arabic: سترت (*suttirat*) (*to be torn down, to be destroyed*).

Sura 13:31

This last root in turn clears the way for us to identify other homonymous and likewise misread spellings, three more of which are given to us by the Koran concordance in Suras 13:31; 18:47 and 81:3. Thus, for instance, we read in Sura 13:31:

ولو أن قرانا سيرت به الجبال أو قطعت به الارض

(Bell I 232, 30): "Though / If only by a qurʾān the mountains had been moved, or the earth been cleft, …".

(Paret 204): "Und wenn durch einen (Offenbarungs)text (*qurʾān*) bewirkt würde, daß Berge sich (von der Stelle) bewegen oder die Erde in Stücke zerreißt (Note: oder sich spaltet)…"

(Blachère 276): "Si une incantation par laquelle les montagnes seraient mises en marche, ou par laquelle la terre serait mise en pièces…"

Here, too, it is not سيرت (*suyyirat*) that should be read, but following the Syro-Aramaic form, as above, سترت / *suttirat* (*to be torn down, to be destroyed*). As for the other Arabic verb قطعت (*quṭṭiʿat*) (literally: *to be torn to pieces*), Paret with the meaning "*had been split*" in the note and Bell with "*had been cleft*" have correctly suspected, though without justifying this, that it is a synonym of شق (*šaqqa*), which is usually used in this context in the Koran, for example in Suras 19:90 and 80:26. In this respect, it is lexically equivalent to Syro-Aramaic ܨܪܐ (*ṣrā*), which can mean both.[207]

207 Cf., e.g., *Mannā* (647b): ܨܪܐ (*ṣrā*): (1) قطع (*qaṭaʿa*) (*to cut off, to detach*), (2) شق (*šaqqa*) (*to split*). This meaning occurs in Sura 2:260: فخذ اربعة من الطير فصرهن اليك (Bell I 39, 262): "Then take four of the birds and incline them to thyself [[1] Sense uncertain.]." The latter can be only understood in the meaning of the Syro-Aramaic loan-word quoted above as follows: "Then take four of the

We thus would have another instance of case (f) (p. 24) where frequently the Koran will employ a genuine Arabic expression that renders only *one* of the meanings of the lexically equivalent Syro-Aramaic expression on the assumption that the Arabic equivalent must have had the identical semantic content. Thus in countless cases the actual and precise meaning of an Arabic expression that does not harmonize perfectly with the Koranic context can usually be established by way of the semantics of the lexically equivalent Syro-Aramaic expression. The following verse offers us a further example:

Sura 18:47

ويوم نسير الجبال وترى الأرض بارزة
وحشرنهم فلم نغادر منهم أحدا

(Bell I 278, 45): "On the day when We shall cause the mountains to move, and one will see the earth stepping forward, And We shall round them up and leave of them not one;"

(Paret 242): "Und am Tag (des Gerichts), da wir die Berge (von der Stelle) bewegen und du die Erde (darunter?) herauskommen siehst und wir sie (d.h. die Menschen) (schließlich alle zu uns) versammeln und nicht einen von ihnen auslassen!"

(Blachère 323): "au jour où Nous mettrons les montagnes en marche, où tu verras la terre [rasée] comme une plaine, où Nous rassemblerons les [les Humains] sans laisser personne parmi eux."

After the lexical and syntactic analysis that follows, this is how this verse will be understood:

"On the day when the mountains *collapse* and the earth *appears*

---

birds and cut them (in two)." The prepositional reflexive pronoun اليك (*ilayka*), unusual in Classical Arabic, is known in the Syro-Aramaic grammar as *dativus ethicus* (cf. Th. Nöldeke, *Syrische Grammatik* [*Syriac Grammar*], § 224: "The preposition ܠ (*l*-) with a reflexive personal pronoun often follows a verb without essentially changing its sense."

to be split open, we will gather them (the people) together and none of them will be *overlooked*."

First of all, here, too, it is not نسير (*nusayyir*[u]) (we move from the spot), but نستر الجبال (*nusattir*[u] *l-ğibāl*[a]) (when we shall tear down the mountains) or the passive تستر الجبال (*tusattar*[u] *l-ğibāl*[u]) (when the mountains will be torn down). The next problem case occurs in وترى الأرض بارزة (*wa-tarā l-arḍ*[a] *bāriza*[tan]) and concerns the participial adjective بارزة (*bāriza*), which has been variously interpreted by our Koran translators:

(Bell): "the earth stepping forward."

(Paret): "und du die Erde (darunter?) herauskommen siehst (*and you will see the earth coming out* [*underneath them?*])."

(Blachère): "la terre [*rasée*] comme une plaine" (*the earth* [*shaved*] *like a plain*).

Blachère to some extent follows *Ṭabarī*, who explains this passage as follows: On the day when we shall set the mountains in motion and they will be removed from the earth, it will appear to the observer to have been stripped of every object whatsoever.[208] Paret and Bell both attempt in their own ways to interpret logically the Arabic root برز (*baraza*) (*to stand out*), one in the sense of "*to step forward*," the other in the sense of "*to stand out*."

The divergence in these attempts at interpretation is understandable, considering that in the case of the misread Arabic spelling بارزة (*bāriza*) (with the secondarily inserted ا) it is not a question of the Arabic برز (*baraza*), but of the Syro-Aramaic ܬܪܙ (=ترز) (*traz*), the meaning of which *Mannā* (849a) renders in Arabic as انشق (*inšaqqa*) (*to rip open, to split*).[209] In Syro-Aramaic this clause would read ܐܪܥܐ ܬܪܝܙܐ

---

208 *Ṭabarī* XV 257.

209 Cf. further *Thes.* II 4498, ܬܪܙ (*traz* / *tarrez*): *dirupit* (*to tear, to tear open*); ܐܬܬܪܙ (*ettrez* / *ettarraz*), ܐܬܬܬܪܙ (*ettaṯraz*): *diruptus, scissus fuit* (*to be torn open, split open*).

ܘܬܬܚܙܐ (*w-teṯḥzē arʿā ṯrīzā*), "and (when) the earth *appears to be split open*," and would be translated into Arabic وترى الأرض منشقة (*wa-tarā l-arḍ^a*) or in the passive voice (*wa-turā l-arḍ^u munšaqqa*), whereby we would have an example of case (e) (see page 24, above).

Finally, what is striking about the genuinely Arabic expression نغادر (*nuġādir*) is that its actual sense (*to abandon*) does not quite match the usage expected here and approximately presumed by our translators with "*to leave*," "*auslassen* [*to leave out*]," and "*laisser* [*to leave*]." However, if we bring in the lexically equivalent Syro-Aramaic verb ܫܒܩ (*šḇaq*), we notice that *Mannā* (765a) cites among the eight different meanings: (1) ترك . غادر (*to leave, to abandon*); (2) اهمل . اغفل (*to neglect, to fail to do, to overlook*). From the last meaning it becomes clear that the Koranic expression is meant in this way, and that only this meaning lends the Koranic expression its precise nuance.

The same is true of Sura 18:49, where the identical expression appears once more:

Sura 18:49

مال هذا الكتب لا يغادر كبيرة ولا صغيرة الا احصاها

> "What is it with this register that it *overlooks* neither a large nor a small (deed) without taking it into account! (Roughly: What kind of register is that, that does not fail to take into account the smallest thing!)"

Thus we would have a further example of case (f) (see p. 24).

In other words, in Koranic Arabic the verse under discussion from Sura 18:47 would accordingly read:

ويوم نهد الجبال وترى الأرض منشقة وحشرنهم فلم نغفل منهم احدا

> "On the day when we shall tear down the mountains and you will see the earth split open and we will gather them (the people), without overlooking even a single one of them."

Read this way, however, the sentence does not have a very harmonious ring to it. But if we read the first part of the verse passively, “On the day when the mountains are destroyed and the earth appears (literally: is to be seen) split open,” this reading would produce a more plausible sense.

The main problem, however, is of a syntactical nature and can be found in the second part of the verse, which, as a coordinate clause, is combined with the first by means of the conjunction و / *wa* (*and*) with a simultaneous shift in tense and subject, which here emerges as God in the first person plural. Our Koran translators have noticed that the temporal clause introduced by the adverb يوم (*yawm*[a]) (*on the day when*) lacks the expected apodosis. As a result, each has tried in his own way to deal with the problem. Whereas Paret makes it into an exclamatory clause that requires no apodosis, Blachère links it with the preceding verse and sees in it a simple succession of individual statements. Bell, on the other hand, reproduces the Koranic sentence faithfully, but sees that the clause hangs “in the air” and therefore suspects a gap, which he illustrates in his translation by starting a new paragraph with the second part of the verse and by leaving the line before it empty.

For this kind of sentence structure, the ܦܫܝܛܬܐ / *Pšiṭṭā*, the Syro-Aramaic translation of the Bible, offers us several typical examples. There is the following passage, for example, from the story of Joseph (Genesis 39:10-11):

ܟܕ ܐܡܪܐ ܗܘܬ ܠܗ ܟܠܝܘܡ. ܘܠܐ ܫܡܥ ܗܘܐ ܠܗ̇ : ܠܡܕܡܟ
ܠܘܬܗ̇ ܘܠܡܗܘܐ ܥܡܗ̇ : ܘܗܘܐ ܒܚܕ ܡܢ ܝܘܡܬܐ... ܘ

(*w-ḵaḏ āmrā (h)wāṯ leh kullyōm , w-lā šāmaʿ (h)wā lāh , l-meḏmaḵ l-wāṯāh wa-l-mehwē ʿammāh , wa-hwā ḇ-ḥaḏ men yawmāṯā*...):

“When she spoke to him day by day, but he harkened not to her (insofar as) to lie by her and to be with her, [*and*] it happened one day …”.[210]

In the case of this temporal sentence introduced by ܟܕ (*kaḏ*) (*as, when*)

210 The *Jerusalemer Bibel* [*Jerusalem Bible*] (15th edition, Freiburg, 1979) makes a new sentence out of the apodosis of the *Pšiṭṭā* (Verse 11).

the apodosis begins with the conjunction ܘ / *w* (*and*): "When she spoke to him ..., and it happened ...". Just as in the English (and German) construction, however, this *and* in both the Syro-Aramaic and the Arabic temporal sentence is not only superfluous to introduce the apodosis, but above all confusing. It appears, if only sporadically, to have slipped into Syro-Aramaic as a Hebraism via the translation of the Bible. In most cases, however, it is left out in the *Pšiṭṭā*. The same applies for the Koran.

To this extent the observation about Ancient Hebrew that Theodor Nöldeke had already made in his above-mentioned sketch *Die semitischen Sprachen* [*The Semitic Languages*] (26) comes into play:

> "The character of Ancient Hebrew is in essential parts of it, in particular in sentence construction, very old-fashioned. The coordination of sentences predominates over subordination more than in another Semitic written language more exactly known to us. The sentences are preferably joined together only with an "and." Even subclauses and adverbial modifiers, especially of a temporal nature, are commonly combined to form a whole with a mere "and it was," "and it will be," and then the main clause is loosely linked to that with an "and."[211] Naturally, it is thus for us often

211 Note (1) "For example, 'And it was when he had made an end to offer the present, and he sent away the people,' Judg. 3:18 (= 'And when he had made an end..., he sent away the people'). 'And it came to pass that Isaac became old, and his eyes became weak to see, and he called Esau his eldest son,' Gen. 27:1. 'And it was at her coming, and she moved him,' Judg. 1:14. 'And it came to pass in the evening, and he took Leah his daughter,' Gen. 29:23 – 'And it shall be if the wicked man (be) worthy to be beaten, and the judge shall cause him to lie down and to be beaten...,' Deut. 25:2. 'And it will come to pass on that day, and I will break...,' Hos. 1:5. Similarly in countless cases."
In the case of all of these passages the "*and*" before the apodosis is left out in the *Pšiṭṭā*. The passage cited from Judges 1:14, however, reads according to the *Pšiṭṭā* version: ܘܟܕ ܥܐܠܐ. ܐܬܪܓܪܓܬ ܠܡܫܐܠ ܡܢ ܐܒܘܗ ܚܩܠܐ (*w-kad ʿāy-lā, eṯraḡrḡaṯ l-mešal men aḇūh ḥaqlā*) "And when she came in (to her husband, i.e. when she was led to him), she was moved (by him) to ask of her father a field."

doubtful where, according to the sense, the apodosis begins.[212] What are so lacking are particles that could clearly express the finer concatenation of thoughts. To a large extent fantasy determines the usage of the verb tenses, sometimes seeing what has not been completed as completed, at other times what has been completed as still taking place."

This observation of Nöldeke's on the syntax of Ancient Hebrew fits the sentence from Sura 18:47 being discussed here exactly, because:

(a) as a result of the "*superfluous*" و / *w* (*and*), the apodosis beginning with وحشرنهم (*wa-ḥašarnāhum*) has not been identified as such by our Koran translators, even though the tense change it introduces (perfect as opposed to the imperfect in the protasis) particularly emphasizes this and clearly distinguishes the two parts of the sentence from each other;

(b) Nöldeke's comment, according to which something future (*not completed*) is presented as having already happened whereas the protasis is in the imperfect (or future) tense, is further true here of the apodosis in the perfect tense وحشرنهم فلم نغادر منهم أحدا (literally, "and we have gathered them and overlooked none of them" instead of "and we shall gather them and overlook none of them"). According to the modern-day understanding just the opposite relationship would be correct: "On the day when = when one day the mountains have collapsed and the earth has split open, we shall gather them together and overlook none of them." In this respect, Nöldeke's previously cited comment on Ancient Hebrew is also true of this unusual sentence construction: "To a great extent fantasy determines the usage of the verb tenses,

212 Indeed, Nöldeke's comment (18) in his *Neue Beiträge zur semitischen Sprachwissenschaft* [*New Essays on Semitic Linguistics*] in the chapter on "Stylistic and Syntactic Peculiarities of the Language of the Koran," (paragraph four), bears witness to this: "Frequently a protasis in the Koran lacks the apodosis or the main clause." At the same time, Nöldeke apparently did not notice that his observations about Ancient Hebrew can also in part be carried over to the Koran.

> sometimes seeing what has not been completed as completed, at other times what has been completed as still taking place."

The lexically as well as syntactically misunderstood and distortedly rendered sentence from Sura 18:47,

> "And on the day (of the Last Judgment), when we move the mountains (from their places) and you see the earth (under them?) come out and we (finally) gather (all of) them (i.e. the people) (to us) and do not leave out one of them! [Und am Tage (des Gerichts), da wir die Berge (von der Stelle) bewegen und du die Erde (darunter?) herauskommen siehst und wir sie (d.h. die Menschen) (schließlich alle zu uns) versammeln und nicht einen von ihnen auslassen!]" (Paret)

should be understood, on the basis of the lexically more reasonable Syro-Aramaic reading, but syntactically on the basis of a sentence construction that is also attested in part in the Syro-Aramaic translation of the Bible under the influence of Biblical Hebrew, as follows:

> "On the day when the mountains *collapse* and the earth appears *to be ripped open*, we *shall* gather them together and *overlook* none of them."

Sura 37:78-79

Insofar as for Arabic غادر (*ġādara*) (*to leave, to abandon*) the Koran also uses ترك (*taraka*) as a synonym, reference will be made in the case of the latter to the following spellings misread in four passages as تركنا (*taraknā*) (*we have left, to be left over*) instead of ركنا (= باركنا < ܒܪܟ / *barrek*) (*bāraknā*) (*we have blessed*). These are the following verse refrains in Sura 37 to the memory, respectively, of the prophets Noah, Abraham, Moses and Aaron, and Elias: 78, 108, 119, and 129. Verses 78, 108 and 129 each run: وتركنا عليه في الاخرين (*wa-taraknā ʿalayhi fī l-ʾāḫirīn*); Verse 119, referring to Moses and Aaron, says in the dual:

وتركنا عليهما في الاخرين (*wa-taraknā ʿalayhimā fī l-ʾāḫirīn*). By our Koran translators this verse refrain (78) has been rendered as follows:

> (Bell II 445): 76. "We have left upon him among those of later times (the saying)…"
>
> (Paret 371): "Und wir hinterließen (als ein Vermächtnis) unter den späteren (Generationen den Segenswunsch) für ihn…"
>
> (Blachère 477): "et Nous le perpétuâmes parmi les Modernes."

Thus our Koran translators follow *Ṭabarī* (XXIII), who essentially interprets verses 78 (68) and 108 (88) in the following way: We have preserved a good memory of him (Noah or Abraham, respectively) among the generations after him until doomsday. Thus may he be assured of the blessing: "Peace be (respectively) upon Noah, upon Abraham!"

What is surprising, however, is that the same spelling in Verse 113 وبركنا عليه وعلى اسحق (*wa-bāraknā ʿalayhi wa-ʿalā Isḥāq*) "and we *blessed* him and Isaac," has here been read correctly, in contrast to the four misread passages. For particularly in connection with the preposition على / *ʿalā* this spelling scarcely allows any other reading than برك (*bāraka*) (*to bless*). In the sense of "*to leave a legacy,*" as Paret understands it, ترك (*taraka*) ought to be followed positively by the preposition لـ / *li-* (*in favor of*) and not by على (*ʿalā*), which would have the negative meaning of "*to leave (something) to someone as a burden.*"

Undoubtedly responsible for this incorrect reading is the misinterpretation of the expression في الاخرين (*fī l-ʾāḫirīn*), which can have two meanings, depending on which substantive one infers with it: (a) the "later (*generations*)," as *Ṭabarī* interprets it, or (b) the "later (*times*)" = the *future world*, the *hereafter*. In the singular feminine form the latter meaning is common in Arabic (الآخرة / *al-ʾāḫira* / الأخرى / *al-ʾuḫrā* < Syro-Aramaic ܐܚܪܝܬܐ / *(a)ḥraytā*).[213] The plural form that appears in

213 Cf. *Lisān* IV 14b: والأخرى والآخرة : دار البقاء (*al-ʾuḫrā* and *al-ʾāḫira* : the *perpetual place of residence*, the *hereafter*). With regard to its being a borrowing from Syro-Aramaic ܐܚܪܝܬܐ / *(a)ḥraytā* cf., e.g., *Mannā* (14a): (2) آخرة (*ʾāḫira*), نهاية (*nihāya*) (*end = last days, hereafter*).

the Koran الاخرين (*al-ʾāḫirīn*) here refers either to Syro-Aramaic ܙܒܢܐ (*zabnē*) (*times*)[214] or ܥܠܡܐ (*ʿālmē*) (*worlds*).[215] Precisely the latter meaning is referred to in the verse immediately following Verse 78, i.e. Verse 79, سلم على نوح في العلمين , which has been misunderstood by our Koran translators as follows:

(Bell II 445, 77): "Peace be upon Noah in (all) the worlds."

(Paret 371): "Heil (*salām*) sei über Noah unter den Menschen in aller Welt (*al-ʿālamūn*)!"[216]

(Blachère 477): "Salut sur Noé dans l'Univers!"

Yet what is to be understood in this context under العلمين (*al-ʿālamīn*) is, as a transliteration of the Syro-Aramaic ܥܠܡܝܢ (*ʿālmīn*), "*both worlds*": *this world, the secular world*, and *the next world, the hereafter*. What is intended here by the Syro-Aramaic plural suffix ܝܢ / *-īn* would be the Arabic dual suffix ين / *-ayn*. Namely, this understanding follows from the Koranic context insofar as God (a) rescued Noah and his family from the Flood (Verse 76) and kept his descendants alive (Verse 77) and (b) in addition to this, he has praised him in the *hereafter* (Verse 78); from which results (c) (Verse 79): "Peace be upon Noah in *both worlds*!" In other words, God's blessing applies to Noah in *this* and the *next world*. Also corresponding to this sense is the summarizing conclusion in Verse 80: "Thus (namely) do we reward the righteous!" The previously cited Verses 78 and 79 are therefore to be understood as follows:

"And we *blessed* him (in addition to this) in the *hereafter*: Peace be upon Noah in *both worlds*!"

---

214 Cf., e.g., *Thes.* I 127: ܒܙܒܢܐ ܐܚܪܝܐ (*b-zabnē* [*a*]*ḥrāyē*) "*novissimis temporibus*."

215 Cf. *Thes.* II 3009: ܥܠܡܐ ܕܩܝܡܝܢ ܘܕܥܬܝܕܝܢ (*ʿālmē ḏ-qāymīn w-ḏa-ʿṯīḏīn*) *saecula praesentia et futura* (*present and future* "*worlds*"); in addition, 2899 under (2): ܗܢܐ ܥܠܡܐ (*hānā ʿālmā*) *haec vita* (*this* [earthly] *life, this world*), in opposition to: ܥܠܡܐ ܕܥܬܝܕ (*ʿālmā ḏa-ʿṯīḏ*) (*future world*); hence the "*two worlds*": ܬܪܝܢ ܥܠܡܐ (*trēn ʿālmē*) (Ephr. II 338A,...).

216 The plural form (*al-ʿālamūn*) that Paret puts in parentheses and gives in the Arabic *status rectus* should therefore be viewed as hypothetical.

The other verse refrains 108, 119 and 129 are to be understood accordingly. Furthermore, in Sura 26:84 what is meant by the term الاخرين (*al-ʾāḫirīn*) is also not the "*later* (generations)" (Paret), but the "*last* (times)" = the "*hereafter*."

Sura 26:90-91

In order to return to the spelling برز (*baraza*), the verses 90-91 from Sura 26 may be cited in this context:

وازلفت الجنة للمتقين وبرزت الجحيم للغاوين

Without further ado following the laconic interpretation by *Ṭabarī* (XIX 87), our Koran translators render the underlined expressions as follows:

> (Bell II 357): 90. "The Garden shall be brought nigh to those who show piety, 91. And the Hot Place advanced to those who are beguiled,..."
>
> (Paret 304): (90) "Und das Paradies wird (an jenem Tag) an die Gottesfürchtigen nahe herangebracht. (91): Und der Höllenbrand wird denen, die abgeirrt sind, vor Augen gestellt (*burrizat*)."
>
> (Blachère 397): 90 "[*au jour où*] le Jardin sera avancé pour les Pieux 91 et la Fournaise sortie pour les Errants...".

It remains to be seen whether in Arabic the root زلف (*zalafa*) really does mean دنا (*danā*) (< Syro-Aramaic ܕܢܐ / *dnā*) or قرب / *qaruba* (< ܩܪܒ / *qreḇ*) "*to be near, to come closer*," as the *Lisān* (IX 138a ff.) conjecturally explains it in referring to two dubious Arabic verses. On the other hand, if we base it on the Syro-Aramaic root ܙܠܦ (*zlap̄*), what results in the first place is the figurative sense "*to shine, to gleam, to adorn*."[217] Whence the reflection on whether the spelling ازلفت should be read, not

217 Thus the *Thes.* I 1130 cites: ܙܘܠܦܐ (*zūlāp̄ā*) *ornatio, politio,* ܙܘܠܦܐ ܕܡܐܢܐ (*zūlāp̄ā ḏ-mānē*) *elegantia vestium,* (in Arabic): صقل الثياب وبروقها (*ornament and shine of clothing*); further 1131, under ܡܙܠܦܐ (*m-zalp̄ā*), also as applied figuratively to "*elegant and brilliant discourse.*"

"*uzlifat*," but ازلقت "*azlaqat*" or "*uzliqat*." In fact, only the Syro-Aramaic root ܙܠܩ (*zlaq*) yields the original meaning of "*to radiate, to shine*," which the *Thes.* (I 1131) assigns to its more common variant form ܙܠܓ (*zlag̱*). This is, in turn, used most of the time in the *Ap̄ʿel* form.[218] Therefore the reading ازلقت (*azlaqat*) would be justified. Accordingly, Paradise would not be "brought near unto the god-fearing" (Paret), but would, more reasonably, "*shine forth for* the god-fearing."

This reading is confirmed by a number of expressions that the *Lisān* (X 144b) cites under the root زلق (*zaliqa*), whereby it, in turn, is also not always able to distinguish here between the Arabic original meaning "*to slide*" and the homonymous Syro-Aramaic root with the original meaning "*to shine*." What is in any case revealing is the meaning "*to adorn oneself*" used to explain (with reference to *Abū Turāb*) the reflexive stem تزلّق (*tazallaqa*): تزلّق فلان وتزيّق إذا تزيّن (it is said of someone *tazallaqa* and *tazayyaqa* when he smartens himself up). This meaning is also confirmed by the ensuing *ḥadīṯ* according to which *ʿAlī* characterized two men coming out of the baths متزلّقين (*mutazalliqayn*) "*all spruced up*" as من المفاخرين (*min^a l-mufāḫirīn*) "belonging to *those who strut*." The closing explanation is equally clear: تزلّق الرجل إذا تنعم حتى يكون للونه بريق وبصيص (one says of someone *tazallaqa* when he looks after himself in such a way that his [skin]color receives a *glow* and a *shimmer* [a *shimmering glow*]). On the other hand, the *Lisān* (IX 138a ff.) cites several expressions under the root زلف (*zalafa*) that probably belonged under the root زلق (*zaliqa*), for instance, when it describes the *mirror* as الزلفة (*az-zalafa^tu*) (139b) although it points rather to the Syro-Aramaic ܙܠܩ (*zlaq*) (*to shine*).

Now that the *Lisān* has also confirmed the Syro-Aramaic reading, the first part of Verse 90 cited above is accordingly to be understood as follows:

> "(on the day when ... ,) and Paradise will shine forth (or adorn itself) for the god-fearing ..."

218 Cf. *Thes.* I 1126, under aph. ܐܙܠܓ (*azleg̱*) *affulsit, effulsit, splenduit;* and with reference to the Syrian lexicographers: اشرق انار لمع . سطع . اضاء .

The spellings that were misread (as ازلفت / *uzlifat*) in Suras 50:31 and 81:13, but which are in reality homonyms (ازلقت / *azlaqat* / *uzliqat*), are to be corrected in the same way.

As for the misread spelling برزت (*burrizat*) in the second verse segment, what was already said above about the Syro-Aramaic root ܬܪܙ (*traz*) (*to split, to split open*) in Sura 18:47 can be applied, so that here Hell will *split* itself *open* (in the sense of *to open up suddenly*) in order to "devour"[219] the damned. Summarizing, the double verse from Sura 26: 90-91 would thus read:

> "(On the day when … ,) (90) Paradise will *shine forth* (or *adorn itself*) (91) for the god-fearing and Hell will *split itself open* for the damned."[220]

Sura 68:51

Picking up from the root زلق (*zaliqa* / *zalaqa* (< ܙܠܩ / *zlaq*), reference will be made to a passage in Sura 68:51 that, though read correctly, has nevertheless been misinterpreted:

وان يكاد الذين كفروا ليزلقونك بابصرهم لما سمعوا
الذكر ويقولون انه لمجنون

219 Compared to this, immediately after Christ's death on the cross, according to the Christian idea, *Sheol* is "*split open*" to free the souls imprisoned therein as a result of the work of salvation; this is documented by the *Thes.* (II 4498) with the following citation from Jacob of Sarug (d. 521 A.D.): ܐܬܬܪܙܬ ܫܝܘܠ ܘܢܦܩ ܣܕܪܐ ܕܚܒܝܫܝܢ ܒܗ (*ettarzat šyōl wa-npaq sedrē da-ḥbīšīn bāh*) (*Sheol split itself open, and the rows* [*of people*] *imprisoned therein came out*).

220 Namely, the lexical basis of the Arabic word غاوين (*ġāwīn*) is the Syro-Aramaic ܛܥܐ (*ṭʿā*), which *Mannā* (289b) defines in Arabic as follows: (1) غوي (*ġawiya*) (*to lose one's way, to go astray*), (4) هلك . باد (*bāda, halaka*) (*to be lost, to be damned*). It is also likely that it was from the latter meaning that the Arabic هلاك (*halāk*) "*eternal damnation*" (cf. H. Wehr) originated as a religious *technical term*. Here, too, as so often, the Koran uses the first lexical meaning of the Syro-Aramaic expression in the assumption that the further meanings will emerge from it as a matter of course.

Our Koran translators render the underlined expression as follows:

> (Bell II 599): 51. "Lo, those who have disbelieved almost cause thee to stumble with their looks, when they hear the Reminder, and they say: 'Surely, he is mad'."

> (Paret 479): 51: "Diejenigen, die ungläubig sind, würden dich, wenn sie die Mahnung [d.h. den Koran] hören, mit ihren (bösen) Blicken beinahe zum Straucheln bringen. Und sie sagen: ‚Er ist (ja) besessen'."

> (Blachère 611): 51 "En vérité, ceux qui sont incrédules, ayant entendu cette Édification, te perceront[221] certes de leurs regards et diront: 'Certes, il est possédé!'."

Thus they partially follow the interpretations enumerated in *Ṭabarī* (XXIX 46) for the expression ليزلقونك (*la-yuzliqūnaka*). In doing so, however, they pay no attention to the one that comes closest to the Syro-Aramaic sense, namely: ليصرعونك (*la-yaṣraʿūnaka*) (they would almost "*knock*" you "*down*" with their looks). In connection with this, *Ṭabarī* makes reference to a saying of the *Arabs:* كاد فلان يصرعني بشدة نظره إليّ (so-and-so nearly "*knocked*" me "*down*," "*floored*" me with his penetrating glance). The *Lisān* (X 144b) cites the expression أزلقه / زلقه ببصره (*azlaqahu /zalaqahu bi-baṣarihi*), though without quite knowing how to interpret the verb أزلق (*azlaqa*). As a conjecture it gives the explanation "*to force someone from his spot* or *position*" as well as the above-mentioned saying with the meaning "*to knock down, to dash to the ground,*" to which it adds the following: نظر فلان إلي نظرا كاد يأكلني وكاد يصرعني ("so-and-so cast me such a look as to almost *devour* me or *knock* me *down*").

In fact, however, the root زلق (*zaliqa* / *zalaqa*) is connected with the Syro-Aramaic ܙܠܩ (*zlaq*) to the extent that the latter can mean not only "*to be radiant, to shine, to gleam,*" but also – under the *Ap̄ʿel* form

---

221 Here Blachère adds the following note: "*yuzliqûna-ka* '*they will pierce you.*' Literally: *they will make you slide*. The sense seems to be: Considering the Prophet to be possessed, they try to exorcise him and resort to hypnotism."

ܐܙܠܩ (*azleq*) – "*to flash, to cause to flash,*"[222] and thus in a general sense: "*to kill by lightning, to dash to the ground, to strike down.*"[223]

However, the findings made in the meantime as to the confusion of specific Syro-Aramaic letters in the process of transcription from *Garshuni* / *Karshuni* into the Arabic writing system[224] make it more likely that the Arabic letter ـلـ /*L* in يزلقونك / *yuzliqūnaka* is a mistranscription of the Syriac letter ܥ / *ʿayn*. Read *Garshuni* /*Karshuni* ܝܙܥܩܘܢܟ = Arabic يزعقونك / *yuzʿiqūnaka* (< Syro-Aramaic √ ܙܥܩ /*zʿaq*, 1. *to cry*, *yell*, 2. *to peal*, *rumble* [thunder], Afʿel ܐܙܥܩ /*azʿeq* – cf. *Mannā* 205b), this verb means as a variant of Arabic صعق /*ṣaʿaqa* (1. originally: *to cry* < Old Aramaic / Hebrew צעק /*ṣʿaq*): 2. *to strike down with lightning* – the latter meaning Arabic rather أصعق /*aṣʿaqa* (cf. *Lisān* X 198a: إذا أصابته : أصعقته الصاعقة /*aṣʿaqat-hu ṣ-ṣāʿiqa* : *is said of someone struck by lightning*). This meaning is to be assumed figuratively, in the causative / transitive stem in the sense of "*to strike suddenly down*", as in the verse discussed above, and in the intransitive stem in the sense of "*to collapse suddenly*", as attested in Sura 7:143: وخر موسى صعقا "*and Moses fell* (suddenly) *down thunderstruck.*"[225]

---

222 Cf., e.g., C. Brockelmann, *Lexicon Syriacum* 198b: ܙܠܝܩܐ (*zalīqā*) 1. *Fulgor, radius* (*lightning, ray*); *Af. Fulgere fecit* (*to cause to flash*).

223 Cf. *Thes.* I 1131: ܙܠܩܐ (*zalqā*) *fulgur*, ܙܠܩܐ ܕܡܚܐ (*zalqā d-māḥē*) ("*lightning strike*" = "*flash of lightning*") κεραυνός.

224 Cf. the contribution of the author "*Relics of Syro-Aramaic letters in Early Koran Codices in Ḥiǧāzī and Kūfī Style* " in the anthology "*Der frühe Islam* [*The Early Islam*]" cited above, p. 377–414.

225 Morphologically, the Koranic spelling صعقا (traditional pronunciation *ṣaʿiqan* – Syro-Aramaic *ṣaʿqā*) renders accurately the Syro-Aramaic *status emphaticus* as attributive form of the passive participle *ܙܥܩܐ /*zaʿqā*, Old Aramaic * צעקא /*ṣaʿqā*, as discussed above in the chapter on *Satan* (p. 98). In the vernacular of the Near East the word زاعقة /*zāʿiqa* > *zāʿqa* in the sense of *lightning, thunderbolt* (< Syro-Aramaic ܙܥܩܬܐ / *zʿaqtā* [*cry*], ܙܥܘܩܬܐ /*zāʿoqtā* [*lightning*] – cf. *Mannā* 205b) is quite common.

Sinse it appears now clear that the meaning *lightning*, *thunderbolt* is a metaphorical sense derived from the original meaning *cry*, none of our Koran translators seems to have noticed that the Koran employs the synonymous Arabic substantive صيحة /*ṣayḥa* in the same sense (*cry* = *lightning*, *thunderbolt*). This meaning can be inferred from the context of the following ten Koran passages:

The philological discussion of Sura 68:51 leads us henceforth to the following understanding:

> "Truly, those who are unbelieving would with their scowls have almost *struck you down* (= *looked daggers at you*) when they heard the admonition, saying: 'He is indeed a possessed one!'."

So understood, the verse being discussed from Sura 68:51 would thus be:

> „Truly, those who are unbelieving would with their scowls have almost *dashed you to the ground* (as if with a bolt of lightning) when they heard the admonition and (at the same time) said: 'He is indeed one possessed!'."[226]

Suras **11**: 67,94; **15**: 73,83; **23**: 41; **29**: 40; **36**: 29,49; **38**:15; **54**:31. Although *Ṭabarī* (XIV 44) explains this word in Sura 15:73 (الصيحة / *aṣ-ṣayḥa* = the *cry*) as صاعقة العذاب / *ṣāʿiqat al-ʿaḏāb* (the *lightning* of pain = punishment), all our three Koran translators understand it literaly as *cry* (Bell: the *Shout*; Blachère: le *Cri*; Paret: der *Schrei*). On the other hand, the word صيحة / *ṣayḥa* (*cry*) in eschatological connexion has the sense of the (trumpet)-*blast* on the Judgement Day. This understanding can be derived from the following passages: Suras **36**:53; **50**:42 (cf. following Suras, where *it will be blast upon the trompet*: **6**:73; **18**:99; **20**:102; **23**:101; **27**:87; **36**:51; **39**:68; **50**:20; **69**:13; **74**:8; **78**:18). The word صيحة / *ṣayḥa* (*cry* / *lightning* / *trump of doom*), that occurs thirteen times correctly in the Koran, is once misread in Sura 80:33. The Koranic seeming *hapax legomenon* with the spelling الصاخة (allegedly *aṣ-ṣāḫḫa*), from a nonexistent Arabic root صخ / *ṣaḫḫa*, is nevertheless correctly explained in the *Lisān* (III 33a) as الصيحة / *aṣ-ṣayḥa* (the *cry* = *crack of doom*). The medial ـا / *alif* in the misread الصاخة is, as seen above (p. 72-96), an alternative writing of medial ـيـ / *y* as in براة (falsely براءة / *barāʾa*) = برية / *barīya* > *brīya* (Suras 9:1 and 54:43; see above p. 97 ff.). That this uncommon spelling has its origin in an occasional Syro-Aramaic orthographical peculiarity will be shown elsewhere.

226 From the different renderings of the verb tenses one can see that our Koran translators are having trouble coming to terms with the syntactic cohesion of this sentence. What determines the tense in this case is the main clause in the past tense لما سمعوا (*lammā samiʿū*) "when they heard." The imperfect subordinate clause, ويقولون (*wa-yaqūlūn*) (literally) "in that they *speak*" describes an action occurring in the past and is therefore to be rendered in the perfect tense

Additional examples in the Koran of apodoses introduced by و / wa (and)

Sura 37:103-104

The further apodoses exceptionally introduced by the conjunction و / *wa* (*and*) will demonstrate that Nöldeke's remark – that in the case of many a protasis in the Koran the apodosis is lacking – is for the most part not true. Among other places, we encounter such a temporal clause in Sura 37:103-104:

فلما أسلما وتله للجبين / وندينه ان يابراهيم

Here, despite the و / *w* (*and*) preceding it, the apodosis has been cor-

---

with "in that they *spoke*." The same applies for the modal and main verbs that are likewise dependent on the main clause and in the imperfect tense at the beginning, يكاد . ليزلقونك / *yakād*[u] , *la-yuzliqūnaka*, which for the same reason should be rendered in the perfect tense with "they *were* almost *able to dash* you *to the ground*" or subjunctively "they *would* almost have *dashed* you *to the ground*." In this regard, cf. C. Brockelmann, *Arabische Grammatik* [*Arabic Grammar*], § 92 (*a*): "The *imperfectum* (indicative) describes an event or state of affairs as taking place or existing before the eyes of the speaker; it can thus refer to all three time levels."

This last comment thus justifies not only the perfect, but also the subjunctive understanding of يكاد . ليزلقونك (*yakād*[u] , *la-yuzliqūnaka*), here, however, with reference to the past and not to the present or future, as all three of our Koran translators have it, without exception. This in turn finds its justification in § 92 (e): "By means of an imperfect subordinated to a perfect, an action is expressed that accompanies another action, and indeed a past action."

If necessary, one could also see in this imperfect tense a case following § 92 (b): "As *praesens historicum* it can also vividly describe the past."

Accordingly, the syntactical relationship of these connected clauses ought to be seemingly clear. Paret, however, rips apart this structural harmony by making the adverbial complement ويقولون (whereas what وهم يقولون *wa-hum yaqūlūn* really means is "*whereby they said*") into an independent clause in the present ("And they say"). As one can see, it is not the fault of the Koran if it is even misunderstood in places in which *in Arabic* it is seemingly مبين (*mubīn*) "*clear*."

rectly identified, already by Nöldeke,[227] and by our Koran translators.[228] Because of other misreadings, however, their translations will be given in the following:

(Bell II 446): "When they had resigned themselves, and he had laid him down upon his face (literally, 'to the forehead'), (104) We called to him: 'O Abraham!'..."

(Paret 372): "Als nun die beiden sich (in Gottes Willen) ergeben hatten und Abraham seinen Sohn (W.: er ihn) auf die Stirn niedergeworfen hatte (um ihn zu schlachten), (104) riefen wir ihn an: ‚Abraham!'..."

(Blachère 479): "Or quand ils eurent prononcé le *salâm* et qu'il eut placé l'enfant front contre terre, (104) Nous lui criâmes: 'Abraham!'..."

The following Syro-Aramaic reading will result from the philological analysis of this connected double verse:

(103) "Now when the two of them *were finished* (arranging the pyre) and he (Abraham) had (laid) him (his son) *bound upon the fire(wood)*, (104) we called to him: Abraham! ..."

The first thing to be said about the verb اسلم (*aslama*) (< Syro-Aramaic ܐܫܠܡ *ašlem*) is that according to its Syro-Aramaic transitive usage it is *a priori* not to be viewed as reflexive in this passage, as Paret and Bell

227 Th. Nöldeke, *ibid.* 18 (penultimate paragraph).

228 Nevertheless, Paret remarks in his *Commentary* (417) in this regard: "The apodosis seems to be missing. For this reason an equivalent supplement must be inserted at the end of Verse 103 (according to Zamaḫšarī and Baiḍāwī after *qad ṣaddaqta r-ruʾyā* in Verse 105). Or it is to be assumed that the apodosis is exceptionally introduced by *wa-* (as *Ṭabarī* says concerning this passage;...)." In fact, *Ṭabarī* (XXIII 80) maintains that the "*Arabs*" sometimes set the واو / *wāw* (*and*) in front of the apodosis of فلما وحتى وإذا (*fa-lammā, ḥattā, iḏā*) (*as, until, when*) (i.e., of temporal clauses beginning with these three words). Still apparently nobody has noticed that this usage, limited to the Koran, is to a certain extend indirectly a Syro-Aramaism, but is more frequently a Hebraism.

have done, in part following *Ṭabarī*.[229] In his *Commentary* Paret refers to Helmer Ringgren, *Islam, ᵓaslama and muslim* (Uppsala, 1949) 26 f. The Künstlinger translation reproduced there, "When they were finished" (27), should not be dismissed just because *ᵓaslama* in this meaning is not attested in Arabic and because Künstlinger had taken this from Hebrew. To be more exact, it has been taken from Syro-Aramaic. Both meanings, (a) *to submit* (oneself) and (b) *to finish* (something), would in themselves be acceptable according to the Syro-Aramaic ܐܫܠܡ (*ašlem*), depending on which object one is imagining with it.[230] For the understanding of the Koranic context, however, Genesis 22:9 ought to be quoted:

> "And they came to the place which God had told him of; and Abraham built an (or the) altar there, and laid the (fire)wood in order (upon it); then he bound his son Isaac, and laid him on the altar upon the (fire)wood."[231]

In contrast to this, the Koranic report skips the details relating to the arranging of the altar and the firewood, but summarizes it in the outcome with فلمآ اسلما (*fa-lammā aslamā*): "*Now when they were finished* (with the arranging of the pyre)." This interpretation is supported by the traditional reading according to *Ibn Masᶜūd, Ibn ᶜAbbās* and *Muǧāhid* upon which Blachère (479, note 103) bases his translation: *fa-lammâ sallamâ* (misunderstood by Blachère as follows): "Quand ils eurent prononcé le *salâm*" (when they had spoken the *salaam*). Yet precisely this variant reading, which in the Arabic transcription is to be pronounced

229 *Ṭabarī* (XXIII 79) gives three interpretations for the verb: (a) *to agree, to be of the same opinion* (both Abraham and his son agreed…); (b) *to submit* (to the divine will); (c) the son *surrendered himself* to God, whereas Abraham *surrendered* his son to God. All three interpretations correspond to the Syro-Aramaic ܐܫܠܡ (*ašlem*) (*Thes.* II 4186f.): *concordavit; se dedivit; tradidit.*

230 Cf. *Thes.* II 4186: ܐܫܠܡ (*ašlem*) (1) *complevit, perfecit* (*to bring to an end, to complete*); (4187): Cum ܢܦܫܐ (nap̄šā): *se dedidit* (*to devote oneself, to submit*).

231 Translation according to the *Syriac Bible 63DC*, United Bible Societies (London, 1979) 15b.

سلما / *salimā* and not *sallamā*, is equivalent to the Syro-Aramaic ܫܠܡܘ *šlem(ū)*: "(when they) *were finished*.[232]

Against Ringgren's opinion that the most natural explanation here would be that Abraham and his son had submitted to God's will, one can point to Verse 102 from which this already follows. Namely, in response to Abraham's question concerning the sacrifice of his son, which God had demanded of him in a dream, the son consents and declares that he is willing to submit to God's command.[233] That the two then set out on their way, as well as the other unmentioned details from Genesis 22:3-9, is presupposed by the Koran as already known. As a result it is more likely that فلما اسلما (*fa-lammā aslamā*) ("*now when they were finished*") is to be understood as the conclusion of the prior preparations. The related وتله للجبين / *wa-tallahu li-l-ǧabīn* (according to the previous reading): "(after they were finished, and he) had *thrown* (him) *down on his forehead*" (Paret), fits just as logically as the last act before the burnt offering. The following analysis concerns itself with this last detail.

Of all the previous scholars of the Koran, none appears to have become suspicious about the detail just cited, although neither in the Biblical account nor in the Apocrypha, nor in any other literature is there any indication that Abraham had specifically *laid* (Speyer)[234] or *thrown* his son *down on his forehead* (Paret). The Western Koran scholars must have seen in this a Koranic variation.

But even linguistically nobody has raised any objections, although the conjectural explanations on this point by the Arabic Koran commen-

---

232 See *Thes.* II 4183: ܫܠܡ (*šlem*), Ar. سلم (*salima*), *finitus, completus, absolutus est*; and with a reference to the Syrian lexicographers (4184): ܫܠܡܢܢ (*šlemnan*): فرغنا (*faraġnā* / *fariġnā*): ("*we are finished*"). The expression mentioned by the *Lisān* (XII 291a) سلم من الأمر (*salima min al-amr*) is accordingly not to be understood, as interpreted by the *Lisān* in Arabic, as نجا (*naǧā*) (*to escape from, to successfully elude* an affair), but in the Syro-Aramaic sense as فرغ منه (*faraġa* / *fariġa minhu*) (*to be finished* with it).

233 The reference in the Haggadah to the devotion of Abraham and his son, mentioned by Heinrich Speyer, may also refer to this (*Die biblischen Erzählungen im Qoran* [*The Biblical Stories in the Koran*] 165).

234 Cf. H. Speyer, *loc. cit.* 164.

tators are scarcely convincing. Thus, for example, *Ṭabarī* (XXIII 80) offers the following interpretations for this passage: (a) *He threw him to the ground on his* (*temple?*) (here *Ṭabarī* explains the dual الجبينان [*al-ǧabīnān*] as that which is located *to the left and right of the forehead*, and furthermore that the face has *two* [*temples*?] جبينان [*ǧabinān*] between which is the forehead); (b) *he laid him down with his face to the ground;* (c) *he threw him down on his mouth;* (d) *he threw him down on his forehead;* (e) *he held him by the forehead to slaughter him.*

Jeffery (101), uncontested and without any further justification, adopts the interpretation given by *Ṭabarī* under (a) with the definition: "The temple, or side of the forehead." But his subsequent explanation is indecisive:

> "The exegetes got the meaning right, but neither they nor the Lexicons have any satisfactory explanation of the origin of the word from the root جبن."

Citing Barth, he nonetheless considers an early borrowing from Aramaic גבינא (*gḇīnā*) (*brow* or *eyebrow*) or Syro-Aramaic ܓܒܝܢܐ (*gḇīnā*) (*eyebrow*) to be possible. What is lacking here, however, is any indication of the usage of جبين (*ǧabīn*) (*forehead*) in modern written Arabic,[235] as well as in the contemporary Arabic dialects of the Near East.

But actually the above-mentioned clarification of the expression by *Ṭabarī* does suggest the meaning of the Syro-Aramaic ܓܒܝܢܐ / *gḇīnā* (*eyebrows*). When *Ṭabarī* explains that there are جبينان (*ǧabīnān*) to the *left* and the *right* of the *forehead*, he with certainty means by that the Syro-Aramaic ܓܒܝܢܐ / *gḇīnē*, namely the two "*eyebrows*," and not, as this came to be misunderstood by the Arabic lexicographers, the two "*sides of the forehead*."[236] But if the forehead lies "*between the two eye-*

---

235 See, for example, Hans Wehr *Arabisches Wörterbuch für die Schriftsprache der Gegenwart* [*Arabic Dictionary for the Written Language of the Present Day*] (Wiesbaden, ^{5}1985), in which the meaning given there besides "forehead," "side of the forehead," must have stemmed from this misinterpretation by *Ṭabarī*.

236 The *Lisān* (XIII 85a) explains this as follows: والجبين: فوق الصدغ ، وهما جبينان عن يمين الجبهة وشمالها (*al-ǧabīn is the upper part of the temple; of*

brows," this absolutely corresponds to the Syro-Aramaic expression ܒܝܬ ܓܒܝܢܐ / *bēṯ gḇīnē*), namely that which lies "*between the eye-brows*" (or *in the area of the eyebrows*), i.e. precisely: the "*forehead*."[237] Arabic جبين (*ǧabīn*) in the meaning of "*forehead*" probably originated etymologically from the Syro-Aramaic by omitting the Syro-Aramaic ܒܝܬ *bēṯ*) (*between*) and adopting the singular or pausal form of ܓܒܝܢܐ / *gḇīnā*).

But the real problem does not lie in the etymologically correct explanation of this expression, but in its misreading. In fact, the concrete guidelines of the Biblical account (Gen. 22:9) provide us with an indication of the real sense of this passage. There it says namely that Abraham has "*bound* (his son) *and laid* (him) *over the* (*fire*)*wood.* Upon closer examination, the Koranic passage proves to be absolutely adequate.

Namely, unsubjected to further justification by Arab commentators on the Koran and just as seldom subject to examination by Western Koran scholars, the meaning of the verbal root تلّ (*talla*) in the sense of

---

these there are two جبينان / *ǧabīnān to the right and to the left of the forehead*); and according to ابن سيده / *Ibn Sayyidih*: والجبينان حرفان مكتنفا الجبهة من جانبيها فيما بين الحاجبين مصعدا إلى قصاص الشعر (*the ǧabīnān are two margins surrounding the forehead on both sides in the area above the eyebrows up to where the hair begins*); وقيل: هما ما بين القصاص إلى الحجاجين (*others say: these are each located between where the hair begins and the rim of the eye socket*); وقيل حروف الجبهة ما بين الصدغين متصلا عدا الناصية ، كل ذلك جبين واحد (*on the other hand, others say: the edges of the forehead in the area between the two temples through to the forehead hair, all this is a ǧabīn = a forehead*); وبعض يقول هما جبينان (*some say however that there are "two"* جبينان *ǧabīnān*—by which probably only Syro-Aramaic ܓܒܝܢܐ / *gḇīnē* "eyebrows" can be meant) قال الأزهري : وعلى هذا كلام العرب . والجبهتان : الجبينان (*al-Azharī said: the linguistic usage of the "Arabs" corresponds to this; al-ǧabhatān "the two foreheads" = al-ǧabīnān "the two eyebrows"* (?). As Jeffery has remarked above, one scarcely knows, in fact, what to do with such interpretation attempts. This, however, is a typical example of Arabic lexicography whenever it is a question of the etymological explanation of borrowed expressions. Especially striking here is the constant appeal to the linguistic usage of the "*Arabs*," even when it is not infrequently a question of Aramaisms.

237 Cf. *Thes*. I 643: BH, cf. Philos. Syr. 12: ܒܝܬ ܓܒܝܢܐ (*bēṯ gḇīnē*) *frons*, جبهة (*ǧabha*); *Mannā* (89a): جبين (*ǧabīn*), جبهة (*ǧabha*) (*forehead*).

صرع (*ṣaraʿa*) (*to throw to the ground*) has become accepted. And this although this root has never been accepted in this meaning in the Arabic language (in H. Wehr it is not even cited once). Even if the *Lisān* (XI 77b) can explain تلّه (*tallahu*) with صرعه (*ṣaraʿahu*), in doing so it is relying on this misinterpretation by the Koran commentators. That it furthermore cites as evidence for it, among other things, a verse by the poet الكميت / *al-Kumayt* (*al-Asadī*) (680-744 A.D.), illustrates precisely that often clumsy method of the Arabic lexicographers, who, in order to explain obscure Koranic expressions, invoke, as false evidence of them, their misunderstood use in later Arabic literature.

In reality the Koranic spelling تله / *t-l-h* is in turn based on the Syro-Aramaic root ܬܠܐ (*tlā*), which the *Thes.* (II 4440) links etymologically with the Arabic تلا (*talā*) (*to follow*), but whose lexical meaning it gives with the Arabic علّق (*ʿallaqa*) (*to hang, to hang up*).[238] That Syro-Ara-

238 C. Brockelmann, *Lex. Syr.* 824b, instead cites the Arab. تلّ (*talla*) *demisit funem* (*to let down a rope*), which he may have taken from the *Lisān* (XI 79b). However, the verse that the *Lisān* quotes as evidence for this interpretation (*to let a rope down when drawing water in a well*) is seeemingly unclear and does not, to be sure, permit this assumption. What suggests itself more would be, in imitation of the Syro-Aramaic root, the meaning "*to hang, to hang up*" or "*to tie up*," say, on a hanger or a roller (cf. the Arabic explanation given in *Mannā* [149b] for the Syro-Aramaic term ܕܘܠܝܬܐ (*dōlītā*): دعامتان تنصبان على البير وعليهما عجلة لاستقاء الماء "*two suppports affixed above a well on which a wheel is attached for the drawing of water*"). Namely, the meaning "*to attach, to tie* (*to*)*, to tie up*" for the Syro-Aramaic ܬܠܐ (*tlā*) is rendered by *Mannā* (838b) in Arabic under (3) as follows: علّق (*ʿallaqa*), أناط (*anāṭa*), ربط (*rabaṭa*). Similarly, in reference to a female camel (spoken of in a *ḥadīṯ*) with فتلّها (*fa-tallahā*) (*Lisān* XI 78a), it is not "*he had her kneel*," as presumed by the *Lisān*, but rather "*he tied her up*" that is meant. In general, the *Lisān* here confuses the roots تلّ (*talla*) and تلا (*talā*) because of the defective Arabic spelling. Only with the help of the cited expressions can a given meaning sometimes be determined on the basis of the context from the equivalent Syro-Aramaic root. As concerns the further *ḥadīṯ* أتيت بمفاتيح خزائن الأرض فتلّت في يدي (*Lisān* XI 78a f.) (*the keys to the treasures of the earth were brought to me and hung on, tied to my hand*), this last meaning from Syro-Aramaic ܬܠܐ (*tlā*) would fit better than the interpretation presumed by the *Lisān*, "*thrown down into my hand*." The same is true of the Syro-Aramaic root ܬܠ (*tal*) to which the *Thes.* (II 4437)

maic ܬܠܐ (*tlā*) can at the same time mean "*to hang, to hang up*" and "*to tie* (*to*)*, to bind*" is illustrated by the *Thes.* (II 442) under (3) with the following citations:

> ܬܠܐܘܗܝ ܒܙܩܝܦܐ (*tlāwū(h)y ba-zqīpā*) (*they hung him on* = *bound him to the cross*); ܬܠܐ ܥܠ ܩܝܣܐ (*tlē ʿal qaysā*): in *cruce pendens* (*hanging on the cross* = *bound to the cross*).

But the *Thes.* (II 4441) presents us with a further instance that could have virtually be taken from our Koran passage. Namely, in speaking of Abraham it is said: ܬܠܐ ܒܪܗ ܥܠ ܥܠܬܐ (*tlā breh ʿal ʿlāṯā*) "*he bound his son* (*and placed him high*) *upon the pyre*" (i.e: *he placed his son bound upon the pyre*). The Syro-Aramaic expression ܥܠܬܐ (*ʿlāṯā*) (here to be understood as *altar, pyre*)[239] in turn helps us to decipher the misread expression للجبين (*li-l-ǧabīn*) (previously understood as: to be thrown down *upon one's forehead*). Namely, read differently, this should yield a synonym of ܥܠܬܐ (*ʿlāṯā*) (*altar, pyre*). For that, we only need to imagine the point under the ـجـ / *ǧ* as not being there, which results in the reading للحبين (*li-l-ḥabīn* or *li-l-ḥābbīn*). However, read in Arabic the root حبن (*ḥabana*), after a search through the *Lisān*, produces no meaning. Yet here, too, as in the case of the two preceding expressions, an identical Syro-Aramaic root should help us further.

First of all the Koranic spelling للحبين suggests the triliteral Syro-Aramaic root ܚܒܢ (*ḥḇan*). With the original meaning of "*to be lazy, sluggish,*" this proves, however, after a check of the *Thesaurus* and Brockelmann's *Lexicon Syriacum*, to be unsuitable. The next root to be considered is the *mediae geminatae* ܚܒ (*ḥaḇ*) whose original meaning "*to burn*"[240] appears to fit our passage. The suffix ين / *-īn* would correspond

---

assigns the Arabic تلّ (*talla*). Here, too, the explanations provided by the *Lisān* (79b) are not always convincing.

239 Cf. *Thes*. II 2891 (2) *excelsum, altare, ara*.

240 *Thes*. I, 1168: ܚܒ (*ḥaḇ*), *exarsit, accensus est*. *Mannā* (213b): اتقد (*ittaqada*), التهب (*iltahaba*), اضطرم (*iṭṭarama*). Arguing in favor of a borrowing from Syro-Aramaic is the Arabic root حبّ (*ḥabba*), which is still common usage only in the meaning "*to love, to like,*" which derived originally from "*to be inflamed in love for*."

to the Syro-Aramaic masculine plural suffix ـܝܢ -*īn*. The Syro-Aramaic transcription ܚܒܝܢ (*ḥābbīn*)[241] would accordingly be an active masculine plural participle, congruent with the reference – implicit in the Koran but explicitly named in Genesis 22:9 – to ܩܝܣܐ (*qaysē*) (*pieces of wood*), which would yield the meaning "*the* (pieces of wood) (for) *burning.*" The originally attributive active participle (the *burning*), referring to the implicit noun (*pieces of wood*), would substitute for it as the substantive. Accordingly, under حبين (*ḥābbīn*) = ܚܒܝܢ (*ḥābbīn*), in analogy with the Koranic plural وقود (*waqūd*) (Suras 2:24; 3:10; 66:6; 85:5), one would understand "*burning*" (materials / pieces of wood) = "*burning materials*" / "*pieces of wood for burning*" (or collectively: *firewood*).[242]

Still to be explained in the case of للحبين (*li-l-ḥābbīn*) is the function of the prefixed preposition لِـ / *li-*. On the basis of the examples cited above from the *Thesaurus*, one would here expect the equivalent of the Syro-Aramaic ܥܠ (*ʿal*) (*on, above*), i.e. the Arabic على (*ʿalā*). It is not documented in Classical Arabic that the preposition ل / *l-* is used in this meaning.[243] The *Thesaurus* also gives no example for this usage in

241 On the *verba mediae geminatae*, cf. Nöldeke, *Syrische Grammatik* [*Syriac Grammar*], § 178 B.

242 On the attributive use of the active participle, see Nöldeke, *Syr. Gramm*, § 282, par. 2: ܢܘܪܐ ܝܩܕܬܐ (*nūrā yāqettā*) "*a burning fire*," several times in Daniel 3; on the nominal use of the participles: §§ 281, 282; the *Thes.* (I, 1621) provides a further example in this regard with ܝܩܕܐ (*yāqdā*) (1) *fomes, ligna quibus ignis accenditur,* الحطب (*al-ḥaṭab*) (*firewood*), for which *Mannā* (315a) additionally cites the Koranic وقود (*wuqūd*) (*firewood, fuel*). The *Thes.* documents ܚܒ / *ḥaḇ* as a verb (I 1168): ܓܘܡܪܐ ܚܒܝܢ ܡܢܗ (*gumrē ḥaḇēn meneh*) *carbones succensi sunt ab eo* (*coals blazed up out of him*), 2 Sam. 22:9, Ps. 13:9; and additionally as a substantive (1170): ܚܒܘܒܐ (*ḥabbūḇā*) *quidcunque facile accenditur, quisquiliae, sarmentum* (*anything easily inflammable, hay, brushwood*), accompanied by further examples.

243 Yet what Carl Brockelmann calls "the direction-pointing *la*," as discussed in his *Grundriss der vergleichenden Grammatik der semitischen Sprachen* [*Outline of the Comparative Grammar of the Semitic Languages*] II, Berlin, 1913 (rpt. Hildesheim, 1961), 377, § 242, has in reality the same function. This appears clearly from the example quoted there: *inkabba liuağhihi* meaning (he) "fell on his face." That this *la-* is a reduced form of على / *ʿalā* > إلى / *ilā* > لـ / *la* (not *li-*)will be explained in a forthcoming publication.

Syro-Aramaic. *Mannā*, however, out of a total of 31 functions of the ܠ / *l-* , mentions under the twenty-fifth the meaning على (*ʿalā*) (*on*) with the following example (364 a):

ܠܐ ܐܝܬ ܠܗܘܢ ܕܘܡܣܐ ܒܐܪܥܐ ܘܫܬܐܣܬܐ ܣܝܡܐ ܠܫܘܥܐ

(*lā īṯ l-hōn dumsē ḇ-arʿā w-šeṯesṯā sīmā ḻ-šōʿā*)

لا بناء لهم في الأرض ولا إسّا موضوعا <u>على</u> صخرة .

> "They have neither bases (anchored) in the ground nor foundation based <u>on</u> rock."

Further Utilization of لـ / *li- instead of* على (*ʿalā*)

Sura 7:143

We further encounter this function of لـ / *li-* in the meaning of على (*ʿalā*) (*on*) in Sura 7:143: فلما تجلى ربه للجبل (*fa-lammā tağallā rabbuhu <u>li</u>-l-ğabal*). The preposition لـ / <u>*li-*</u> (actually *la-*), here as dative, has been misunderstood by our Koran translators as follows:

> (Bell I 150, 139): "but when his Lord unveiled His glory <u>to</u> the mountain, …"
>
> (Paret 135): "Als nun sein Herr <u>dem</u> Berg erschien, …"
>
> (Blachère 191): "[*Mais*] quand son Seigneur se manifesta <u>à</u> la montagne, …"

However, what is probably meant here is that God appeared <u>*on*</u> the mountain, as is confirmed by Exodus 24:16. This function of the preposition لـ / *li-* (*la-*) in the sense of على (*ʿalā*) (*on, above*), a function that is documented by the Eastern Syrian lexicographers, is one of the hitherto unappreciated Eastern Syriac details in the Koran.

Thus, according to the Syro-Aramaic reading, the double verse 103-104 from Sura 37 is to be understood as follows:

> „Now when the two of them <u>*were finished*</u> (with the arranging of the altar for the burnt offering) and he (Abraham) had (laid) him (his son) <u>*bound upon the fire(wood)*</u>, we called to him: Abraham!"

Another reading of the spelling للحبين (*la-l-ḥābbīn*) would be conceivable since, unlike the *Thesaurus* and Brockelmann's *Lexicon Syriacum*, *Mannā* (216a) also quotes the Syro-Aramaic verbal root ܚܒܢ (*ḥḇan*), parallel to ܚܒ (*ḥāḇ*), in the meaning اضطرم (*iṭṭarama*), اشتعل (*išta*ʿ*ala*), تأجّج (*ta*ʾ*ağğağa*) (*to burn, to flare up, to blaze up*) and with it the extended verbal stems ܚܒܢ (*ḥabben*), ܐܬܚܒܢ (*eṯḥabban*), ܐܚܒܢ (*aḥben*), and ܐܬܬܚܒܢ (*ettaḥban*). The absence of this root with this meaning in the other lexicons, however, gives rise to the suspicion that this might only be a secondary formation from ܚܒ (*ḥaḇ*).[244] However, if this variant was in fact in use among the Eastern Syrians, two things would be conceivable:

(a) as a singular passive participle ܚܒܝܢܐ (*ḥḇīnā*) (in the Arabic pausal form حبين / *ḥabīn*) it could be included among the substantives as a synonym for ܝܩܕܐ (*yāqdā*) (*firewood*), something which would change nothing in the proposed interpretation;

(b) however, if by it one understands, in reference to Isaac, the "*burnt offering*," it would then be permissible to understand the preposition ـل / *li-* (*la-*), not in the meaning على (ʿ*alā*) (*on, above*), but as a particle of determination in the sense of *as, to* (respectively, to do or to become something). Even though Nöldeke considers this function in Syro-Aramaic to be a Hebraism from the translation of the Bible (*Syrische Grammatik* [*Syriac Grammar*] § 247, e.g., Gen. 2:7), *Mannā* (363a) cites it under عاشراً (ʿ*āšira*ⁿ) (*tenth*) للصيرورة (*li-ṣ-ṣayrūra*) (*as an expression of becoming*) with the example: ܐܗܘܐ ܠܟܘܢ ܠܐܒܐ (*ehwē l-ḵōn l-aḇā*) أكون لكم أبا (*akūnu la-kum aba*ⁿ) (*I will become as a father to you*). In this meaning, the verse فلما اسلما (سلما) وتله لِلحبين (*falammā aslamā / salimā wa-tallahu / talāhu la-lḥabīn*) (Syro-Aramaic: ܟܕ ܕܝܢ ܫܠܡܘ ܘܬܠܝܗܝ ܠܚܒܝܢܐ (*kaḏ dēn šlem(ū) wa-ṯlāy(hī) la-ḥḇīnā*) would be understood as follows:

"Now after the two of them were finished (with the arranging of

244 Perhaps falsely derived from the unrecognized suffix of the 3rd person perfect feminine plural of ܚܒ̈ܝܢ (*ḥaḇēn*) or the 3rd person masculine plural of the active participle ܚܒܝܢ (*ḥābbīn*), or of the feminine plural ܚܒܢ (*ḥābbān*).

the altar for the burnt offering) and he (Abraham) *had* bound him (his son) *to become (as) a burnt offering*, (we called to him: Abraham!) ...".

Yet as reasonable as this reading may appear, it has two arguments against it: (a) the prototype of the Biblical account (Gen 22:9), according to which Abraham bound his son and laid him *on* the firewood, and (b) the circumstance that, at least until now, the Syro-Aramaic root ܚܒܢ (*ḥḇan*), except in *Mannā*, does not appear to have occurred anywhere else in Syro-Aramaic literature. Thus, as things stand, preference must be given to the first reading.

Finally, a point should be made about a further detail in the last verse. The borrowed Arabic particle أن / *an* (properly *ēn* > *ən*, from Old Aramaic הן / *hēn* > אן / *ēn*, originally, among other things, a demonstrative pronoun) used so frequently in the Koran to introduce direct speech (أن يابرهيم / *an yā Ibrāhīm*) is nothing other than the rough translation of the corresponding Syro-Aramaic particle ܕ / *d*, which also has this function.[245] As a Syriacism, this use of the particle أن / *an* proper to the Koran has never really been absorbed into the Arabic language, even though it was employed in later classical Arabic literature in imitation of the Koran, and this, probably also for the reason that, because unusual, it was considered particularly *classical*.[246]

Sura 12:15

Moreover, another apodosis introduced by the conjunction و / *wa* (*and*) occurs in the following temporal sentence from Sura 12:15:

فلما ذهبوا به واجمعوا ان يجعلوه في غيبت الجب
واوحينا اليه لتنبئنهم بامرهم هذا وهم لا يشعرون

245 Cf. Th. Nöldeke, *Syrische Grammatik* [*Syriac Grammar*] §§ 341, 367, 372.

246 Cf. C. Brockelmann, *Arabische Grammatik* [*Arabic Grammar*] § 147, note 2 (184). However, Brockelmann refers, in the case of the function of أن / *an* to introduce the direct question in classical Arabic, to no dependence whatsoever on Syro-Aramaic.

Confused by the و / *wa* (*and*), our Koran translators are unable to comprehend the syntactical scheme of this temporal sentence made up of a protasis and an apodosis and try in different ways to find a solution:

> Bell (I 219) fails to see the apodosis and suspects a gap in the text: "So when they had taken him away, and agreed to place him in the bottom of the cistern … … . and We suggested to him the thought: 'Thou wilt certainly tell them of this affair of theirs, when they are not aware'."

> Paret (191) comes up with the apodosis and puts it in parentheses: "Als sie ihn dann mitgenommen hatten und übereingekommen waren, ihn auf den Grund der Zisterne zu tun (war es um ihn geschehen). Und wir gaben ihm ein[247]: ‚Du wirst ihnen (später) über das, was sie da getan haben (W: über diese ihre Angelegenheit) Kunde geben, ohne daß sie (es) merken (daß du selber zu ihnen sprichst)'."

> Blachère (260) shifts the apodosis to Verse 16 and reads three protases in front of it: "Quand ils eurent emmené Joseph et furent tombés d'accord pour le jeter dans les profondeurs d'un certain puits, [*quand*] Nous eûmes révélé [à Joseph *pour le consoler*]: ‚Tu leur rediras, sans qu'ils le pressentent, leur actuel méfait!', 16 [*quand*] ils furent revenus le soir à leur père, en pleurant, ils s'écrièrent:.."

Here our Koran translators seem to have overlooked *Ṭabarī*, since he has recognized that in this temporal sentence a و / *wa* introduces the apodosis, although he places the latter too early. In his opinion the sentence should be read:

> "Now when they had taken him with them, they *came* to an agreement to let him down into the depths of the cistern. *And* we

247 However, under note 11a Paret makes a correct assumption: "Or, 'to put him onto the bottom of the cistern, we gave him in.'"

> gave in him: ‚Truly, you will, without their noticing it, proclaim them this, their affair'."[248]

One could accept this reading if the verse had not been cut unnecessarily into two sentences as a result. Yet the unity of the sentence is preserved if one places, as follows, the apodosis in the last part of the sentence (which Nöldeke,[249] however, overlooked):

> "Now when they had taken him with them and together decided to let him down into the depths (or into the darkness) of the cistern, we *gave* in him: 'You'll see, you will, without their noticing it, proclaim them this their *conspiracy*'."

The Arabic expression اجمع (*aǧmaʿa*) in the meaning "*to agree, to agree on something*" has become so common in Arabic that no one would think of questioning its Arabic origin. If one compares it, however, with the lexically equivalent Syro-Aramaic expression ܟܢܫ (*kanneš*) (*to meet*) in its reflexive form ܐܬܟܢܫ (*eṯkannaš*), it becomes clear from the meaning documented in the *Thes.* (I 1171) under (1) *convenit* (*to come together; to come to an agreement; to decide together*) and under (2) *conclusus est* (*to be decided, to come to the conclusion*)[250] that Arabic اجمع (*aǧmaʿa*) in this specific sense is a *loan formation* from the lexically equivalent Syro-Aramaic expression. This would be a further example of our case (f) (see page 24 above).

An interpretation of the expression غيبت (*ġayābaᵗ*) is lacking in *Ṭabarī* (XII 160). The meaning assumed by Bell and Paret, "*bottom*" (of the cistern), corresponds to that advocated – without any further explanation – by the *Lisān* (I 655b). The meaning "*profondeurs*" (*depths*), as Blachère has in part correctly conjectured (but without justifying this philologically), corresponds to the Syro-Aramaic ܥܘܒܐ (*ʿubbā*), evi-

---

248 Cf. *Ṭabarī* XII 160.

249 Th. Nöldeke, *Neue Beiträge* [*New Essays*] 18 (penultimate paragraph). It is astonishing that Nöldeke here saw no connection with his remark, cited above, on the function of the conjunction و / *wa* (*and*) to introduce the apodosis in Ancient Hebrew.

250 The same in C. Brockelmann, *Lexicon Syr.* 336a (under 7): *conclusum est.*

dence for which we find in the following examples cited in the *Thes.* (II 2823) under (2): ܥܘܒܐ ܬܚܬܝܐ ܕܐܪܥܐ (*ʿubbē taḥtāyē d̲-arʿā*) (*the lower depths of the earth*); ܥܘܒܐ ܥܡܝܩܐ (*ʿubbē ʿamīqē*) (*the deep abysses*); ܥܘܒܗ ܕܫܝܘܠ (*ʿubbāh da-šyōl*) *abyssus inferorum* (*the* immeasurable *depths of Hell*). However, because of the Koranic defective spelling, probably the Koranic as well as the variant reading of *Ubayy* في غيبة الجب (*fī ġayba^{ti} l-ğubb^{i}*) given by the *Lisān* (I 655b, ult.) correspond to the Syro-Aramaic ܥܘܝܒܐ (*ʿūyāḇā*) (*Thes.* II 2824): *obscuratio* (*darkening, darkness*), which would justify the pronunciation عيبة (*ʿuyyāba* / *ʿuyāba*). Also coming close to this sense is the additional nominal form ܥܝܒܐ (*ʿaybā*),[251] for which the *Thes.* under (2) gives the

---

251 A probable derivative of this is Arabic عيبة (*ʿayba*) which the *Thes.* (II 2824) associates with it in the meaning of *large basket, trunk, closet*. Cf. the *Lisān* I 634a: والعيبة: وعاء من أدم ، يكون فيه المتاع (*ʿayba: is a container made of leather in which tools/baggage are kept*); والعيبة أيضا: زبيل من أدم ينقل فيه الزرع المحصود (*ʿayba: is in addition a basket made of leather,* زبيل / *zabbīl* < Syro-Aramaic ܙܒܝܠܐ / *zabbīlā* < Persian زنبيل / *zanbīl* / *zambīl* [S. Fraenkel, *Aramäische Fremdwörter* (*Aramaic Foreign Words*) 78], *in which the harvested grain is transported*); والعيبة: ما يجعل فيه الثياب (*ʿayba: is furthermore that in which clothing is kept*). What the *Lisān* then cites is interesting here, the *Ḥadīṯ* (a saying of the Prophet) on the occasion of the peace treaty with the Meccans in *Ḥudaybīya:* لا إغلال ولا إسلال ، وبيننا وبينهم عيبة مكفوفة *Abū ʿUbayd* is said according to *al-Azharī* to have explained الإغلال والإسلال (*al-iġlāl wa-l-islāl*), but to have refrained from the interpretation of عيبة مكفوفة (*ʿayba makfūfa*). Then the *Lisān* explains the expression عيبة (*ʿayba*), with reference to the "*Arabs*," who are said to designate that which is concealed in the heart with عياب (*ʿiyāb*) (probably < Syro-Aramaic ܥܘܝܒܐ / *ʿūyyāḇā:* the *dark, concealed*), just as one would keep his clothes in an عيبة (*ʿayba*) (*closet*) (< Syro-Aramaic ܥܝܒܐ / *ʿaybā*). Yet the oscillating explanation in the *Lisān* (XI 500 f.) of إغلال (*iġlāl*) between "*theft, plunder*" and "*betrayal*" points rather to a borrowed variant from Syro-Aramaic ܡܥܠܬܐ (*ma-ʿaltā*) (*Mannā* 542a/b, under [4]: غزوة [*ġazwa*], زحفة [*zaḥfa*] *marauding, military expedition*). إسلال (*islāl*) then proves to be a parallel expression as a further variant based on Syro-Aramaic ܫܠܠܐ (*šlēlā*) (*Mannā* 790b: نهيبة / *nahība*, غنيمة الحرب / *ġanima^{tu} l-ḥarb: spoils of war;* [2] اشتباك القتال / *ištibāk al-qitāl: thick of battle*). Among others, the *Lisān* (XI 342a) lists the following approximative conjectures: (a) السرقة الخفية (*as-sariqa l-ḫafīya*) (*secret purloining*); (b) الغارة الظاهرة (*al-ġāra ẓ-ẓāhira*) (*open attack*). In the case of the helplessness of the *Lisān* to explain

following example from *Bar Bahlūl*: ܥܝܒܐ غيم غليظ اسود (*ʿaybā* : *thick, dark clouds*). Based on this and in view of the homonymous Koranic orthography (though probably with a plural ending), the meaning *darkness* (of the cistern) seems to fit best in our passage.

As far as the spelling غيبت is concerned, it should be noted that this orthography, whose final ت / *-t* could be explained as a feminine singular *status constructus*, suggests rather a plural ending in the style of the intensifying Syro-Aramaic plural form ܥܘܒܐ (*ʿubbē*) (*depths* or *darknesses*). The current canonical pronunciation *gayābat*[i] (sing.) should accordingly be changed to *ġayābāt*[i] (plur.). This is significant because it

---

the expression عيبة مكفوفة (*ʿayba makfūfa*), the Syro-Aramaic can once more be of assistance. This is because عيبة (*ʿayba*) as a borrowing from Syro-Aramaic ܥܝܒܐ (*ʿaybā*) is etymologically related to ܥܘܒܐ (*ʿubbā*) ("*abyss*," etc.). As to the participial adjective مكفوفة (*makfūfa*), it should be noted that the Arabic sound ك / *k* can correspond to the Syro-Aramaic ܓ / *g* (cf. S. Fraenkel, *Aramäische Fremdwörter* [*Aramaic Foreign Words*], xix: "Only in isolated cases does one find a ك for hard G ...."). The etymological equivalent of the Arabic root كف (*kaffa*) would accordingly be the Syro-Aramaic ܓܦܦ (*gp̄ap̄*) (although the *Thes.* cites the variants ܓܦܝܦܐ [*gp̄īp̄ā*] and ܟܦܝܦܐ [*kp̄īp̄ā*] in the same meaning *gibbus, gibbosus*). Interesting here is the Arabic equivalent that the *Thes.* (II 765, penult.) gives for ܓܦܦ (*gp̄ap̄*): "Ar. كف (*kaffa*) *clausit* (*to close*), cf. مكفوف (*makfūf*)" (*Lisān* IX 303b, designation for a blind person whose eyes are *closed*). Finally, under the variant ܓܦ (*gāp̄*), *Mannā* (99a) lists as an Arabic equivalent (2): اوصد . اغلق . سكر الباب (*awṣada, aġlaqa, sakkara l-bāb*) (*to close the door*), and C. Brockelmann, *Lexicon Syriacum* 110a, under Etpa. ܐܬܓܝܦ (*etgayyap̄*) *clausus est* (*to be closed*), the Arabic equivalent: "ut ar. أجاف (*aǧāfa*)" (*to close*), which documents the borrowing of this no longer common Arabic expression from Syro-Aramaic (cf. *Lisān* IX 35b, according to a *Ḥadīṯ* of the *Ḥaǧǧ*, the *pilgrimage:* أجاف الباب [*aǧāfa l-bāb*] [< ܐܓܝܦ / *agīp̄*] "he *closed* the door"; أجيفوا أبوابكم [*aǧīfū abwābakum*] ["*close* your doors"]). It follows from this that كف (*kaffa*) and جاف (*ǧāfa*) in this meaning were in all probability originally dialectally caused variants of one and the same Syro-Aramaic root, wherein the Syro-Aramaic sound ܓ / *g* was sometimes rendered in Arabic by a ك / *k*, thus explaining the origin of both variants in Arabic. According to this, the previously cited *Ḥadīṯ* لا إغلال ولا إسلال ، وبيننا وبينهم عيبة مكفوفة would, with the help of Syro-Aramaic, have the following sense: "*No raiding and no fighting* (*any more*)*;* (*from now on*) *the rift between you and us is closed*."

here rules out the meaning قعر (*qaʿr*) "*bottom*" that was falsely conjectured by the *Lisān* and that in this context is only possible in the singular. On these grounds it seems justified, as proposed above, to translate في غيبت الجب (*ġayābāt*^{i} *l-ǧubb*^{i}) with the intensifying plural: *into the* "*depths*" (*into the abyss*) or *into the* "*darkenesses*" (*into the dark*) *of the cistern*.

In this connection in the case of the Syro-Aramaic root ܥܒ (*ʿāḇ*) (in the first stem, *to be ridiculous*; *to go under, to disappear* no longer common) one should note the following Arabic equivalents that *Mannā* (531b) cites under ܥܝܒ (*ʿayyeḇ*) (and in part under ܐܥܝܒ / *aʿīḇ*): عيب (*ʿayyaba*), سخر (*saḫira*) (*to ridicule, to make fun of*); (2) غيب (*ġayyaba*), وارى (*wārā*), عتم (*ʿattama*) (*to make invisible, to cause to disappear, to darken*); (3) غيم (*ġayyama*) (*to cover with clouds, to cloud over*).

From this Syro-Aramaic root two main variants, which were in all likelihood originally created dialectally, then developed in Arabic with each of them being assigned one of the two original meanings of the Syro-Aramaic expression: (a) one variant faithful to the original عاب (*ʿāba*) / عيب (*ʿayyaba*) in the meaning of "*to bear a stigma; to find fault with, to revile* due to a stigma," and (b) a second Arabicized variant غاب (*ġāba*) / غيب (*ġayyaba*) in the meaning of (I) "*to go under, to disappear, to not be seen*" and (II) "*to cause to disappear, to make invisible*," from which was derived an extended Arabic secondary variant: عيهب (*ʿayhab*) and غيهب (*ġayhab*) (which the *Lisān* [I 632b f. / 653b] gives, respectively, as an additional root: عهب or غهب). That these last are secondary variants is evidenced by the nominal form cited in the *Lisān* with the meaning "*dark* of night, *darkness*," غيهب (*ġayhab*), whose plural form غياهب (*ġayāhib*) (*darknesses, obscurities*) corresponds exactly to the Koranic غيبت الجب (*ġayābāt*^{i} *l-ǧubb*) (*darknesses of the cistern*). In the same way, the *Lisān* (I 633ff., 654a ff.) quotes under each of the earlier main variants expressions that indicate their Syro-Aramaic origin. As a result of the pronunciation-based splitting of this originally single root, it was practically inevitable that the later Arabic lexicography would in part mix up the interpretation of these two variants.

An expression from the Koranic reworking of the story of Alexander (Sura 18:60-82)[252] in which Moses takes the place of Alexander offers is a typical example of such a misunderstanding. In Verse 71 it is said that Moses and his companion get into a boat. Moses abruptly knocks a hole (Arabic خرق / *ḫaraqa* < Syro-Aramaic ܚܪܩ / *ḥraq*) in the boat. Indignant, his companion shouts at him asking whether his intention in doing so was to cause those sitting in the boat to drown; this indeed would have been absolutely "unheard-of"![253] In Sura 18:79 Moses later represents to

---

252 Cf. Paret, *Kommentar* [*Commentary*] 316.

253 On the expression امرا (*imra^n*) (in the context: لقد جئت شيا امرا "There you have done something terrible," Paret's translation [244]), Paret remarks in his *Commentary* on the passage (318) that its interpretation is uncertain. Yet the context suggests a borrowing from the Syro-Aramaic root ܡܪ / *mar* : (original meaning) "*to be bitter*," (of persons) "*to feel pain*," (impersonal) "*to pain*" (cf. Brockelmann, *Lexicon Syriacum* 400b : *1. acerbus fuit; 2.* ܠܝ (ܠܗ) ܡܪܬ [*meraṯ* (*lāh*) *lī*] *dolui*). In terms of its form, امرا is an unrecognized Arabic elative (an absolute superlative, a comparative form of the adjective) and accordingly to be read *amarr^a* (and not *imra^n*) in the sense of ممرا (*mumirra^n*) (*extremely upsetting = extremely shocking, scandalizing*). Moreover, a homonymous elative امر (*amarr^u*) occurs in Sura 54: 46, where the final hour is characterized as "*very painful*" (only correspondingly translated by Blachère [566] with "*très* amère"). Under aph. ܐܡܪ (*amar*) and palp. ܡܪܡܪ (*marmar*), the *Thes.* (II 2200) gives a whole series of equivalents in this figurative sense: مرمر ، آلم ، كدّر ، أغاظ ، أسخط etc. For the expression ما أمرّ فلان وما أحلى the *Lisān* (V 167b) explains أمرّ (*amarra*) verbally (*what that one has said is neither bitter nor sweet*). Moreover, here too the *Lisān* is not always able to distinguish the root borrowed from Syro-Aramaic مرّ (*marra*) (*to be bitter* or *to feel pain*) from the homonymous Arabic root مرّ (*marra*) (*to go past, to pass by*). An example of this is provided by the expression مرت (*marrat*) in Sura 7:189 when it is used in reference to a woman at the beginning of her pregnancy: فلما تغشاها حملت حملا خفيفا فمرت به Bell (I 156 f.): "[S]he bore a light burden and passed on with it." Paret (140 f.) translates: "Als er ihr dann beigewohnt hatte, war sie auf eine leichte Weise schwanger. Dieser Zustand dauerte bei ihr eine Zeitlang an." Finally, Blachère (199) "...elle porta [*d'abord*] un fardeau léger et alla sans peine." In this, our translators follow the interpretation by *Ṭabarī* (IX 143 f.), advocated among others by the *Lisān* (V 165b), for the expression مرّت (*marrat*): "*she*

bore it (in this easy state) *for a time without complaining*." Here it suffices to read *murrat* (passively) in the sense of تمرمرت (*tamarmarat*) to arrive at the meaning cited above in Brockelmann of ܒܗ (ܠܗ̇) ܡܪܛ / *meraṭ* (*lāh*) *beh* = مرت به (*murrat bihi*) "*she had trouble with it*," where exactly the opposite is meant, namely the complaints at the beginning of pregnancy. In the case of the spelling امرا the made-up misreading (*imra*^{n}) is in the same way responsible for its misinterpretation. Here the identical expression in Sura 54:46 should have suggested the reading *amarr*^{a}. A conceivable explanation for this might be that the Arabic readers, confused by the final End-ا / *ā*, did not want to see in the spelling امرا an elative of their familiar adjective مر (*murr*) because, according to the rules of the later Arabic grammar, the elative is considered to be *diptotic* and to that extent cannot take a final ا / *ā* in the accusative case. They seem never to have hit upon the idea that the latter could be justified due to the rhyme. That may be why they considered it preferable to devise an expression with this vocalization that did not exist in Arabic than to assume that the Koran had (in their opinion) committed a grammatical *error*. In the process, the fact that *Ṭabarī* (XV 284) refers to the linguistic usage of the "*Arabs*" and to a verse by *al-Rāǧiz* does not mean at all that the expression إمرا (*imrā*) has not been misread or that it has not been used further in this misread form. The explanation that الإمر (*al-imr*) is a nominal form of أمّروا (*ummirū*), that according to بعض أهل العلم بكلام العرب, that is, *certain persons knowledgeable in the linguistic usage of the Arabs*, it is said of people إذا كثروا واشتدّ أمرهم *when they get out of hand and grow stronger*, shows precisely that this has no connection whatsoever with our Koranic context (to say nothing of the doubtful interpretation). On the other hand, the remaining explanations لقد جئت شيئا منكرا و فعلت فعلا عظيما "*you have done something monstrous and committed a reprehensible deed*" as well as نكرا (*nukra*^{n}) (Sura 18:74 جئت شيا نكر / *ǧiʾta šayʾa*^{n} <u>*nukrā*</u> < Syro-Aramaic ܢܘܟܪܝܐ / <u>*nukrāyā*</u> "*you have done something repugnant*") come closer to the suspected sense. Nevertheless, it remains astonishing that the Arabic commentators have not hit upon the idea of the elative of أمرّ (*amarr*) still quite common today in expressions like ذاق الأمرّ (*ḏāqa l-amarr*) (*he experienced, suffered something bitter*), usually in the intensifying dual form الأمرّين (*al-amarrayn*) (*something doubly bitter*, cf., e.g., H. Wehr under امر / *ʾamarr*). Thus the expression امرا (*amarrā*) with the Arabic elative and the Syro-Aramaic semantic content (*shocking, scandalous*) offers us a typical example of the combination of two linguistic components in terms of form and content. In passing, it should also be noted that the Koranic use of جئت شيئا (*ǧiʾta šayʾa*^{n}) (as well as elsewhere أتى / *atā*, with and without ب / *bi-*, e.g. Sura 4:15,19,25; 60:12; 65:1) in the meaning of "*to commit*" is obviously derived from the Syro-Aramaic ܐܬܐ ܠ (*etā l-*) (cf. *Mannā* 45: ܐܬܐ ܠܣܟܠܘܬܐ

his companion the true sense of his – at first glance – shocking action: The boat belonged to poor boatmen; a king who was seizing every boat in the surrounding area had been pursuing them. For this reason, he explains, اردت ان اعيبها (*arattu an a'ībahā*) "I wished [according to the previous understanding:] *to damage* it." The underlined Arabic expression is in fact understood in this way by our Koran translators without having any doubts about the explanation given by *Ṭabarī*.

[*eṯā la-ḥṭāhā*] [literally: *to come to the sin*]: ارتكب خطيّة [*irtakaba ḫaṭīya*[tan]] "*to commit a sin*"). Thus, likewise, in the Mary Sura 19:27: لقد جئت شيا فريا (*la-qad ği'ti šay'a*[n] *farīyā*) "*truly you have done something abominable*" (according to Paret, *Kommentar* [*Commentary*] 324, the meaning of *farī(yan)* – "*something unheard-of,*" *Übersetzung* [*Translation*] 249 – is disputed). The Arabic spelling فريا (*farīyā*), however, corresponds to the Syro-Aramaic ܦܪܝܐ (*paryā* or *pāryā*), depending on whether a passive or an active participle of the root ܦܪܝ (*prī*) or ܦܪܐ (*prā*) is to be read here (although the comparative form *parrāyā* would also be possible). Taking into account the fact that the Arabic meaning that *Mannā* 605a gives under ܦܪܐ (*prā*) (2) بعج (*ba'ağa*), شق (*šaqqa*) (*to rip open, to tear to pieces*) is the Arabic meaning with the greatest likelihood of being correct here, the most reasonable reading appears to be ܦܪܝܐ (*pāryā*) in the figurative sense of "*heart-rending*." Following this sense the *mediae geminatae* ܦܪ (*par*) – under whose *palpel* ܦܪܦܪ (*parpar*) *Mannā* (604b) lists precisely the meanings (6): سلب قلبه من شدة الوجع (*suliba qalbuhu min šiddat*[i] *l-wağa'*) (*his heart passes away, is torn to pieces from all the pain*), (8): عذب (*'aḏaba*), مزّق (*mazzaqa*) (*to torture, to tear to pieces*) – appears to be a variation of the root ܦܪܝ (*prī*) and ܦܪܐ (*prā*). A fourth variety still to be named is the *mediae* ܘ / *w* ܦܪ (*pār*), whose Arabic meanings *Mannā* (580) gives as follows: (1) فار . غلا (*fāra, ġalā*) (*to cook, to overcook*); (2) غضب . إغتاظ (*ġaḍiba, iġtāẓā*) (*to be angry, to become furious*); (3) نفر . إشمأزّ (*nafara, išma'azza*) (*to experience an aversion to, to detest*). It is not impossible that the Koran means the last root based on the meaning, but based on the rhyme employs the *tertiae* ܐ / *ālap̄*. This all the more so since the latter meaning ("*scandalous, repugnant, disgusting*") seems best to fit the previously named parallel expressions امرا (*amarrā*) (*irritating, outrageous*) and نكرا (*nukrā*) (*disturbing, repugnant*). The expression from Sura 19:27 لقد جئت شيا فريا (*la-qad ği'ti šay'a*[n] *farīyā*) (= Syro-Aramaic ܐܬܝܬܝ ܠܡܕܡ ܦܪܝܐ / *eṯayt(ī) l-meddem pāryā /parrāyā*) would accordingly have the following meaning, equivalent to the Syro-Aramaic participial adjective ܦܪܝܐ (*pāryā* or *parrāyā*): "You have truly done something *disgusting*!"

(Bell I 281,78): "… I wished to damage it …"

(Paret 245): "… Ich wollte es nun schadhaft machen …"

(Blachère 326): "… j'ai voulu l'endommager …"

For his part, *Ṭabarī* (XVI 1 f.) refers to *Muǧāhid*, who explains the (general) sense of the expression with the verb occurring in Verse 71, خرق (*ḫaraqa*): "*to damage* (something) *by ripping a hole* (in it)." The sceptical question, what the use of this would have been, since in the Koran it is said of this king after all that he was taking *every* boat whether damaged or not, is met with the answer: This king was seizing every *intact* boat (كلّ سفينة صحيحة) as certain readings show. At the same time *Ṭabarī* refers to the alleged reading of *Ibn Mas'ūd* وكان وراءهم ملك يأخذ كلّ سفينة صالحة غصبا , whom, without further ado, Blachère also follows and translates: "… un roi qui, derrière eux, s'arrogeait tout bon vaisseau, comme prise [a king who, behind them, was seizing every good vessel as booty]." The fact that this dubious addition has in reality had to take the rap for the misinterpreted reading اعيبها (*a'ībahā*) will be shown in the following.

The explanation provided by *Ṭabarī* to interpret the statement فأردت أن أعيبها (*I wished to "damage" it*), فأبان بذلك أنه إنما عابها (*by that he made it clear that he also "damaged" it*), testifies namely to an uncustomary transitive use in Arabic of the basic stem عاب (*'āba*), even though the Arabic lexicons, probably on the basis of this misinterpreted Koranic passage, in addition to the customary intransitive use (*faulty, to have defects*) also falsely list this transitive use (*to make faulty*)[254]. This is just one among other examples of misunderstood and distorted Koranic expressions that have been accepted into the Arabic lexicography.

The actual basis for this misunderstanding, however, is that the traditional Koranic reading اعيبها (*a'ībahā*) leaves absolutely no room for

254 See, for example, Hans Wehr's *Arabisches Wörterbuch* [*Arabic Dictionary*], under (عيب) عاب (*'āba*). Information on the transitive use, exclusively, of the 2nd stem عيّب (*'ayyaba*) (*to find fault with, to criticize for having a flaw*, etc.) is given to us by the linguistic usage of modern Arabic dialects, particularly in the Near East.

doubt in this context about the transitive use of the root عاب (*ʿāba*), understood in Arabic. But if one imagines under it the Syro-Aramaic causative stems ܥܝܒ (*ʿayyeḇ*) and ܐܥܝܒ (*aʿīḇ*), it becomes clear that what is meant by the traditional Arabic reading اعيبها (*aʿībahā*) is nothing other than the Syro-Aramaic ܐܥܝܒܗ (*aʿīḇāh*) (ܨܒܝܬ ܕܐܥܝܒܗ *ṣḇīṯ d-aʿīḇāh* "*I wanted to camouflage it*"). Namely, under both of the causative stems *Mannā* (531b) gives the Arabic equivalent as, among other things, غيّب . وارى (*ġayyaba, wārā*) (*to cause to disappear, to make invisible*). Thus, to this extent, the only thing that would have been needed to obtain the equivalent correct Arabic reading in the second causative stem, أغيّبها (*uġayyibahā*), was a dot over the ع/ *ʿayn*. Read in this way, فاردت ان اغيبها (*fa-arattu an uġayyibahā*), the verse segment therefore acquires its real sense for the first time: "…I wanted in this way to make it (the boat) invisible = to camouflage it." As a result, the interpretation according to which Moses wanted "*to make*" the boat "*defective*" is not only linguistically and grammatically, but also objectively false.

In other words, if one asks oneself to what extent Moses wanted only *to make* the boat *invisible* or *camouflage* it, against the reproach that he wanted instead to allow those sitting in it to drown, this is made fairly clear to the extent that he wanted to make the boat virtually *invisible* from a distance for the greedily prowling king. Namely, speaking of the latter, the Koran says he was seizing *every* boat. The attempt to evade him by "*making* the boat *defective*" would accordingly have been in vain. From his companion's reproach one can thus infer instead that he wanted only to sink the boat *partially* as camouflage so that from a distance it could no longer be identified as such. Moreover, that the boat has not been completely sunk is proven not least by the circumstance that Moses was only able to make this statement to his companion after the apparently successful weathering of this adventure.

A final comment on this verse will be accorded to the expression غصبا (*ġaṣba^n*) (*violent*), referring to the king who *was forcing entry* to every ship. Conspicuously, the Arabic root غصب (*ġaṣaba*) (*to force*) or the corresponding reading occurs only in this passage in the Koran. All of the other comparable spellings (with personal suffixes) are based on the roots غضب (*ġaḍiba*) (*to anger*) or عصى (*ʿaṣā*) (< Syro-Aramaic

ܥܨܐ / *ʿṣā*) (*to be unruly, disobedient*). However, a look at the other meanings of the Syro-Aramaic verb ܥܨܐ (*ʿṣā*) yields in addition the transitive meanings "*to force, to capture*," which *Mannā* (557b) renders in Arabic under (2) as follows: الزم . اجبر . قسر . قهر . غلب (*alzama, aǧbara, qasara, qahara, ġalaba*). The *Thes.* (II 2952) also cites equivalent expressions and other Arabic expressions from the Eastern Syrian lexicographers, with the exception of غصب (*ġaṣaba*). This suggests that the spelling غصبا is not to be read as *ġaṣba^n*, but – corresponding to the Syro-Aramaic expression – as عصيا / *ʿaṣya^n*, although in the end this changes nothing in the sense. Namely, compared with the Arabic terms attested to by the Eastern Syrian lexicographers, the reading *ġaṣba^n* appears to be a more recent secondary form which, though common in modern Arabic, first arose etymologically from the root عصب (*ʿaṣaba*) < Syro-Aramaic ܥܨܒ (*ʿṣaḇ*) (*to wind, to tie, to wrap*). The root عصا (*ʿaṣā*) has also been misread in the following case:

Sura 21:87

An additional, similarly misread spelling based on the Syro-Aramaic root ܥܨܐ (*ʿṣā*) (*to be disobedient, unruly*) occurs in Sura 21:87: وذا النون اذ ذهب مغضبا (*wa-ḏā n-nūn iḏ ḏahaba muġāḍiba^n*). The expression has been understood by our Koran translators as follows:

> (Bell I 311): "And him of the fish – when he went off at cross purposes…"
>
> (Paret 268): "Und (weiter) dem mit dem Fisch [d.h. Jonas]. (Damals) als er zornig wegging…"
>
> (Blachère 354): "Et [*fais mention de*] l'Homme au Poisson quand il s'en fut courroucé…"

The fact that Jonah did not exactly go off "*in rage*," but in *rebellion* against Yahweh's command, Bell may have correctly assumed from the corresponding Bible passage (Jonah 1:3), but not from the Arabic misreading مغضبا (*muġāḍiba^n*) (*enraged*). This he seems to have trusted just as little as the interpretation *Ṭabarī* (XVII 76 ff.) gives of it according to which Jonah was not *incensed* at God, but rather at his own people, because it ill befit a prophet to bear his Lord a grudge. But Bell could have justified his legitimate suspicion by the adequate Syro-Aramaic reading ܡܥܣܝܐ (*m-ᶜaṣyā*), which results in the like-meaning Arabic معاصيا (*muᶜāṣiyaⁿ*) "*refusing to comply with, disliking, rebellious.*"

This relatively simple example precisely illustrates the inhibitions of Western Koran scholars to question in any way, let alone to correct, the traditional canonical reading of the Koran, even if they occasionally see themselves forced, out of objective considerations, to interpret the Koranic expression tacitly in a way that deviates from its actual Arabic meaning.

The following may serve to exemplify the nuances or shades of meaning of a term in general usage.

Sura 12:15

واجمعوا ان يجعلوه في غيبت الجب

What we are looking for is the appropriate *nuance* for the Arabic expression جعل (*ǧaᶜala*) (here: *to do, to place or put somewhere*) with regard to the cistern whose *abyss* (or *gloom*) Joseph has been "*done*" into by his brothers (Paret). Once more this can be established via the lexically equivalent Syro-Aramaic expression. If we assume, among other possibilities, that this is ܣܡ (*sām*), *Mannā* (483b) then gives for this as the Arabic original meaning جعل (*ǧaᶜala*) (*to do, to place or put somewhere*), وضع (*wa-ḍaᶜa*) (*to lay, to place somewhere*), and under (11): قبر (*qabara*), دفن (*dafana*) (*to bury, to inter*), where what is actually meant is "*to lay, to lower into the grave.*"[255] In light of the Biblical account according to which the majority of his brothers are of a mind to kill Joseph, it appears more reasonable to carry over precisely this meaning to the cistern Joseph was "*let down*" or "*deposited*" into (as into a grave).[256]

---

255 Similarly in the *Thes.* II 2557 under (1): terrae *mandavit* cadaver, *sepelivit.*

256 The comparison is not unfounded when one considers the other meanings of ܓܘܒܐ (*gubbā*), which *Mannā* (87a) gives in Arabic as follows: (2) قبر (*qabr*)

Finally, in this context a more meaningful sense is expected for the expression امرهم (*amrihim*) (according to the Arabic understanding, *their* "*affair*") than Paret, for example, gives it. Although Blachère with "*méfait*" (*monstrous crime, outrage*) is closest, he again does not provide a more detailed justification for his choice. Now, although in modern Arabic the original Arabic stem أمر (*amara*) is restricted solely to the meaning "*to command*," whereas its nominal form أمر (*amr*) can mean both "*command*" and analogous derivatives like "*matter, affair*," its extended verbal stems, such as the sixth تآمر (*ta'āmara*) "*to talk something out, to arrange something together* (*conspiratively*)," recall the Aramaic origin אמר or the Syro-Aramaic ܐܡܪ (*emar*) "*to say, to speak*." That the Koran, however, with the nominal form أمر (*amr*) can mean not only "*command*" or "*matter, affair*," but also "*conspiracy, plot*," in the sense of the modern Arabic nominal form مؤامرة (*mu'āmara*) is documented by the following sentence from Verse 102 of our Sura: وما كنت لديهم اذ اجمعوا امرهم وهم يمكرون , roughly paraphrased, but more or less correctly, by Paret (199): "And you were not with them (i.e., Joseph's brothers) when they put together and hatched plots."

However, understood exactly it reads: "For you were not there (literally: with them) when they *agreed on* their *plot* (اجمعوا امرهم) and in so doing *behaved in an underhanded manner* (وهم يمكرون)." To this extent امر (*amr*) in the sense of مؤامرة (*mu'āmara*) (*conspiracy, plot*) corresponds to the Syro-Aramaic synonym ܡܠܬܐ (*mellṯā*), which the *Thes.* (II 2111) documents among other things with the meaning *conspiratio* (4): *collusion, plot*. Thus, in order to do justice to each of the meanings of the Koranic terms امر (*amr*) (Arabic: *command, affair*), كلمة (*kalima*) (*word*), and even قول (*qawl*) (*speaking*, or its contents: *words*) and their derivatives, the different semantic contents of the Syro-Aramaic synonyms ܡܐܡܪܐ (*memrā*) (the infinitive or nominal form of the verbal root ܐܡܪ *emar*, "*to say, to speak*"), ܡܠܬܐ (*mellṯā*) (original meaning: *word*, substantive of the root ܡܠܠ / *mallel*, "*to speak*") and ܩܠܐ (*qālā*) (*voice, words*) must absolutely be taken into account.

(*grave*), (3) سجن تحت الأرض (*siğn taḥt al-arḍ*) (*dungeon*). Corresponding examples are provided by the *Thes.* (I 670).

It is astonishing that all three Koran translators miss the direct reference in this verse to Verse 15, even though Verse 102 with its اجمعوا امرهم (*ağmaʿū amrahum*) (*they resolved together, they agreed upon their plot*) again takes up exactly the same expressions occurring in Verse 15. Thus the grounds are provided for rendering the expression لتبئنهم بامرهم هذا with "you'll see, you will proclaim to them this their *conspiracy*."

Additional Apodoses Introduced by و / *wa* (*and*)

Sura 2:259

Beyond this syntactical particularity this verse segment offers a series of lexically interesting expressions, which, though neither questioned by *Ṭabarī* nor by our Koran translators in any way, should nonetheless be rethought. In terms of content, it is a question of a man who does not believe in resurrection. To prove its existence to him, God has him die. After a hundred years have passed, He awakens him again and asks him how long he thinks he has been dead. "One day or just a fraction of a day," the man answers. "It was all of a hundred years," God replies, and continues:

فانظر الى طعامك وشرابك لم يتسنه وانظر الى حمارك
ولنجعلك اية للناس وانظر الى العظام كيف ننشزها ثم نكسوها لحما

This verse segment has been understood by our Koran translators as follows:

(Bell I 38, 261): "[L]ook at thy food and drink; it has not become stale; and look at thy ass – in order that We may make thee a sign to the people – and look at the bones how we shall make them stand up and clothe them with flesh."

(Paret 38): "Sieh auf dein Essen und dein Getränk (das du vor dem Einschlafen bei dir hattest)! Es ist (trotz der hundert Jahre) nicht verdorben [Note: W: alt (und schlecht) geworden]. Und sieh auf deinen Esel! (Auch er hat sich nicht verändert.) (Wir haben dieses Wunder) auch (deshalb bewirkt) um dich zu einem Zeichen für die Menschen zu machen. Sieh nun auf die Gebeine (dieser verödeten Stadt?), wie wir sie sich erheben lassen und sie hierauf mit Fleisch bekleiden!"

(Blachère 70): "Regarde ta nourriture et ta boisson! Elles ne sont point gâtées. Regarde ton âne! Nous allons faire certes de toi un signe pour les hommes. Regarde ces ossements comment Nous les ressuscitons et les revêtons de chair!"

This lexically and syntactically misunderstood verse segment will be examined in further detail in the following.

1. Arabic طعام (*ṭaʿām*) (*nourishment, food*) is etymologically identical with Syro-Aramaic ܛܥܡܐ (*ṭʿāmā*). The original meaning of the equivalent verbal root ܛܥܡ (*ṭʿem*) (*to eat, to taste*) is not in common use (in the first verbal stem) in modern Arabic, but occurs four times in the Koran in the former meaning (*to eat*) (Sura 5:93; 6:138,145; 33:53), and once in the latter (*to taste, to sip*, said of *water*) (Sura 2:249).

One cannot see, however, why God first of all points out to the man who has been restored to life that his *food* and *drink* have not *gone bad*, even though Blachère sees in this a parallel to the legend he cites. Namely, one must pay attention to the essential difference between ʿAbed-Melek, who in said legend has only been asleep, and the man restored to life who is spoken of in our Koran passage. This particular circumstance makes it seem difficult to comprehend the connection with *eating* and *drinking*, as well as with the *donkey*. Now, although from the point of view of Arabic such elementary terms as *eating*, *drinking* and the *donkey* allow no leeway at all for alternative interpretations, which is also why our Koran translators have not doubted them in the least, we should still try with the help of a Syro-Aramaic reading to arrive at a more plausible sense.

In fact, according to the *Thes.* (I 1497), Syro-Aramaic ܛܥܡܐ (*ṭaʿmā*) also has the meaning (*γ*) *mens* (*understanding*).[257] Nearer to

257 The same can be found in W. Gesenius, *Hebräisches und aramäisches Handwörterbuch* [*Concise Hebrew and Aramaic Dictionary*] (Berlin, Göttingen, Heidelberg, 1959^7) 278a: "טעם (*ṭaʿam*) – 2. Feeling and accordingly intelligence,

hand here, however, is the variant ܛܥܡܬܐ (*ṭʿamṯā*), for which the *Thes.* (I 1497) gives the meaning (3) *qualitas* (*condition*), and *Mannā* (291a) (7)شان . امر . حال . خاصّة (*ša'n, amr, ḥāl, ḫāṣṣa*) (*condition, matter, state, property*).

2. This latter meaning is fitting as a synonym for the next expression شرابك (*šarābika*), which, transcribed in Syro-Aramaic without the secondary ا / *ā*, reads ܫܪܒܟ (*šarbāḵ*) and according to the *Thes.* (II 4322) results in the following meanings: (1) *res, negotium, causa, quod attinet ad* (*state of affairs, circumstance, relationship, that which affects one*). *Mannā* (819a) gives for ܫܪܒܐ (*šarbā*) under (3) the same Arabic synonyms as above: امر . شان (*amr, ša'n*) (*matter, condition, that which affects one*).

3. That we are dealing in the case of these two synonyms with one and the same term is confirmed by the subsequent *singular* verb لم يتسنه (*lam yatasanna*). The fact that this verb is derived from Syro-Aramaic ܫܢܐ (*šnā*), ܐܫܬܢܝ (*eštnī*) (*to change, to alter*),[258] explains the uncertainty of the Arabic commentators in interpreting it. For instance, in *Ṭabarī* (III 37 ult.) it is said that during the editing of the Koran, in answer to a question by *Zayd ibn Ṯābit* as to whether one should write the verb لم يتسنن (*lam yatasannan*) or لم يتسنه (*lam yatasannah*), *ʿUṯmān* had ordered the latter spelling with the final ـه / *h*. Whence the folk-etymological explanation that this is a denominative of سنة (*sana*) (*year*) (> أسنه / *asnaha*) which would mean as much as "*to alter over the years*."[259] With the former spelling the verb is explained with لم ينتن (*lam yuntin*) (*it is not rotted*) (*loc. cit.* 38 f.). Instead of "Look at your food and drink! It has (despite the hundred years) not gone bad [literally: has not become old (and bad)]" (Paret), the following understanding results for this part of the verse according to the Syro-Aramaic reading:

---

understanding." The expression حكي بلا طعمه (*ḥakī balā ṭaʿme*) (*meaningless talk*) is common, as a Syro-Aramaic substrate, in modern dialects of the Near East.

258 Cf. *Thes.* II 4233, 4236: *mutatus est. Mannā* (802b): تغيّر . تبدّل (*taġayyara, tabadalla*).

259 Here, however, according to the Aramaic orthography, the final *h* simply marks the short vowel *a*.

"Look at your *condition* (i.e.: *how* you are *constituted*) and your (overall) *state*: it has not changed!"

4. As for the spelling حمارك (*ḥimārika*), it must first be noted that it could not be read by Arabic readers as anything but "*donkey*" since (except for a denominative from the elative احمر / *aḥmar* "*red*") that is the only verbal root in Arabic. In Syro-Aramaic, on the other hand, there is the root ܓܡܪ (*gmar*) with the original meaning "*to be perfect, to be complete*" and further derivatives. The only word borrowed from this in Arabic is the noun جمر ، جمرة (*ğamr, ğamra*) "*glow*," probably insofar as this denotes *perfectly* or *completely glowing coal*. In the Koranic context, however, the reading جمارك (*ğamār*^{i}*-k*^{a}) offers itself as the transliteration of Syro-Aramaic ܓܡܪܟ (*gmārāḵ*) "*your perfection* or *completeness*" (referring to the man who has been restored to life), particularly since there is absolutely no explanation here for this abruptly appearing *donkey*. It is simply astounding that in the previous research on the Koran nobody has ever wondered about this *donkey*.

The explanation for it in *Ṭabarī* (III 40) is that God said to the man: Look at your dead donkey whose bones were rotted and behold how we have stood it up again and covered it with flesh. Then God caused a wind to come up and collect the donkey's bones, which had been carried away by birds and animals of prey and were lying scattered about. The man then beheld how the bones fitted themselves together piece by piece and assembled themselves into a donkey skeleton. Then this was provided by God with flesh and blood so that a living donkey was standing there with flesh and blood, but still without a soul. An angel then came along and blew into the donkey's nostrils. And, behold, the donkey began to bray. Amazed, the man exclaimed: "Truly, God is capable of everything!"

Concerning this passage (56), Paret has already referred in his *Kommentar* [*Commentary*] to the allusion to Ezekiel 37 (1-10). For his part, Blachère refers (69 f.) to a widespread legend especially popular in Jewish-Christian literature, and which is reminiscent of the Seven Sleepers. According to the Ethiopic version of the *Book of Baruch*, ʿAbed-Melek had slept for 66 years and, upon awakening after the Captivity, had found Jerusalem rebuilt. Moreover, through a miracle his bread and his figs were as fresh as they had been the day before he fell asleep.

Meanwhile, the legend told about the donkey in *Ṭabarī* is in contradiction with the Koranic context insofar as there it is said explicitly: ولنجعلك اية للناس "to make you an example for the people," not the *donkey*. From this it follows that the subsequent description of the resurrection in the Koranic text refers unequivocally to the man. This is all the more so the case because there is no talk anywhere in the Bible about animals also being resurrected. The following analysis may thus serve to provide us with another understanding of this passage.

Therefore, the subsequent وانظر الى حمارك does not say, "And look at your donkey!" (Paret), but logically:

> "Behold your perfection (or completeness) (i.e.: how perfect, how complete you are)!"

To instruct the other people who will one day be resurrected, it is graphically depicted to the resurrected man *in retrospect*, on his example, how God will proceed in the restoration of the resurrected people. Hence this description does not refer to the abruptly appearing *donkey*, of which it cannot at all be a question here. In the process, the subsequent sentence is composed syntactically of a protasis and an apodosis that is introduced by a (*superfluous*) و / *wa* (*and*):

> "And therewith we make you an example for the people, [*and*] behold how we *restore* your bones and cover them *anew* with flesh."

5. In reading ننشزو (*nanšuzu*) the dot of the ز / *z* has been falsely placed, which is all the more surprising since the verb نشر (*našara*) occurs several times in the Koran in connection with resurrection (for example, in Suras 21:21; 25:3,40; 35:9; 44:35; 67:15; 80:22). The reason must be that the verb here refers explicitly to the bones. Whence, also, the misinterpretation ascribed to it: "*to cause to rise up*."[260] This circumstance

260 This misinterpretation has made its way into the Arabic lexicography. Thus, H. Wehr, for example (*loc. cit.*) explains both أنشز (*anšaza*) and أنشر (*anšara*) with

speaks in favor of a loan translation from Syro-Aramaic ܦܫܛ (*pšaṭ*), whose original meaning *Mannā* (618a) gives in Arabic as بسط . فرش . نشر (*basaṭa, faraša, našara*) (*to unfold, to reach out, to spread out*), as well as the following figurative senses under (4): سوّى . عدّل . قوّم . اصلح (*sawwā, ʿaddala, qawwama, aṣlaḥa*) (*to make straight, to rectify, to straighten, to restore*). From the Koranic context it is now clear that the last meaning is what is meant.

What is interesting in this connection are the synonyms سوى (*sawwā*), which the Koran uses several times, in addition to خلق (*ḫalaqa*) (*to create*), in the sense of "*to make*," and عدّل (*ʿaddala*) (*to make straight*), which occurs in Sura 82:7 (الذي خلقك فسواك فعدلك) (*who created you, formed you and made you straight*). It is now clear from the loan translation that what is meant by the Koranic expression نشر (*našara*) is not *per se* "*to raise from the dead*," but, with reference to Syro-Aramaic ܦܫܛ (*pšaṭ*), "*to restore*." Also corresponding to this idea of the *renewed creation* of man on the day of resurrection is the Koranic formula, repeated in different variations, as for example in Sura 10:4, انه يبدوا الخلق ثم يعيده "He created a first time and repeated it anew."

It becomes clear from this example of case (f) (page 24),

(a) that a genuinely Arabic expression has been misread because the Arabic philologists were unable to recognize its meaning in the Koranic context;

(b) that its rectification is only possible after identifying, on the basis of the context, the Syro-Aramaic expression of which it is apparently a loan translation;

(c) that its more exact meaning can be subsequently determined thanks to the semantics of the lexically equivalent Syro-Aramaic expression.

6. Finally, the Arabic adverb ثم (*ṯumma*) is not to be understood here in the normal sense of "*thereupon, afterwards*." Following Syro-Aramaic ܬܘܒ (*tūḇ*),[261] the meaning "*anew*" is more appropriate to the context.

---

the same meaning, respectively, "*to bring back to life*" and "*to raise from the dead*."

261 Cf., e.g., C. Brockelmann, *Lexicon Syriacum* [*Syriac Lexicon*] (817b), 1. Iterum

From this philological discussion the following syntactic and lexical understanding results according to the Syro-Aramaic reading for the verse segment from Sura 2:259 cited above:

> "Yet behold your condition (i.e.: how you are *constituted*) and your (overall) state: it has not changed. Behold your perfection (i.e.: *how complete* you are)! And therewith we make you an example[262] for the people, [*and*] *behold* how we restore your bones and cover them anew with flesh!"

Period Construction

Sura 11:116-117

(116) فلولا كان من القرون من قبلكم اولو بقية ينهون عن الفساد في الارض الا قليلا ممن انجينا منهم واتبع الذين ظلموا ما اترفوا فيه وكانوا مجرمين
(117) وما كان ربك ليهلك القرى بظلم واهلها مصلحون

Not alone the failure to appreciate the true function of the extrinsically "*superfluous*" conjunction و / *wa* (*and*) has had as a result that the subsequent apodosis has been overlooked and that the syntactical structure of these two connected verses, Verses 116 and 117 of Sura 11, has been thus totally distorted by our Koran translators and, as a consequence, nonsensically rendered as follows:

(again). Mannā (831b): ثمّ . ايضاً . ثانية (*tumma, ayḍan, ṯāniyatan*) (*afterwards, also, once more / again*). That the Koranic ثمّ (misread as *ṯumma*) is not Arabic at all, but a defective spelling of the secondary Eastern Syriac dialectal form ܬܘܡ (*tūm* < Syro-Aramaic *tūḇ*), as is attested in Mandaic (cf. E.S. Drower, R. Macuch, *A Mandaic Dictionary*, Oxford 1963, p. 483a: "tum 1 [Talm תוּ, Syr. ܬܘܒ, Ar. ثمّ], then, after that, MG xxxiii n. 1, 49:ult., 204:13, 429:9-15"), will be discussed (with other Koranic particles) in a forthcoming study.

262 In the case of the Koranic اية (*āya*), as a loan word from Syro-Aramaic ܐܬܐ (*āṯā*), the Syro-Aramaic meaning should regularly be taken into account, depending on the context. In this case, *Mannā* (46a) gives it under (8) in Arabic: عبرة (*ʿibra*) (*example, instance, model*).

(Bell I 216b): 118. "If only there had been of the generations before you men of perseverance restraining from corruption in the land – except a few of those whom We rescued from amongst them – ; but those who have done wrong have followed that in which they luxuriated, and have become sinners. 119. Thy Lord was not one to destroy the towns wrongously, their peoples being upright livers."

(Paret 189): 116: "Warum gab es denn unter den Generationen vor euch nicht Leute (begabt) mit (moralischer) Stärke (?) [Note: Oder: mit einem trefflichen Charakter (*ʔulū baqīyatin*)], die dem Unheil auf der Erde Einhalt geboten, – abgesehen von (einigen) wenigen von ihnen, die wir erretteten [Note: Oder: abgesehen von (einigen) wenigen, (Leuten) die wir vor ihnen (d.h. ihren sündigen Zeitgenossen) erretteten(?)]? Diejenigen, die frevelten (– und das war die überwiegende Mehrzahl –) folgten dem Wohlleben, das ihnen zugefallen war (*mā utrifū fīhi*), und waren sündig. 117: Dein Herr konnte die Städte unmöglich zu Unrecht zugrunde gehen lassen, während ihre Bewohner taten, was recht ist (*wa-ahluhā muṣliḥūna*)."

(Blachère 257): 118/116 "Parmi les générations qui furent avant vous, pourquoi les gens de piété qui interdirent le scandale sur la terre et que Nous sauvâmes, ne furent-ils que peu nombreux, alors que les Injustes suivirent le luxe où ils vivaient et furent coupables? 119/117 Ton Seigneur n'était pas capable de faire injustement périr ces cités alors que leurs habitants pratiquaient la sainteté."

The following discussion will show in the case of the double verse cited above that we are dealing with a previously unrecognized *hypothetical conditional sentence*, the first part of which (Verse 116) forms the protasis and the second part (Verse 117) the apodosis. Two elements have essentially led our Koran translators to tear apart the syntactical unity of this sentence by carving it up into either two (Blachère) or three sentences (Bell and Paret):

(a) The determining factor is the misinterpretation of the Arabic particle لولا (*law-lā*), which Paret and Blachère see as an interrogative particle, whereas Bell sees in it an optative particle and, in so doing, is following *Ṭabarī* (XII 138), who indeed explains لولا (*law-lā*) with هلا (*hallā*) (*oh, if only*). Right from the start, however, in both cases, this erroneous assumption excludes an apodosis. As to the former case, it is astonishing first of all that one could take لولا (*law-lā*) to be an interrogative particle at all. Bergsträsser's view[263] that, insofar as it does not have the meaning "if not" it corresponds to the German "warum nicht" (English "why not") in a rhetorical question, is misleading to the extent that thus only an optative clause introduced by لولا (*law-lā*) (e.g., لولا جاء / *law-lā ǧāʾa* "if he had only come!") can also be formulated as a rhetorical question ("Why in the world didn't he come?"). What is needed for this, however, is not the optative particle لولا (*law-lā*), but only the interrogative particle لما (*li-mā*) or لماذا (*li-māḏā*). That it is even possible according to *ibn Hišām* to consider لولا (*law-lā*) as a genuine interrogative particle must be based on a misinterpretation of the Koranic use of this particle. This is confirmed, moreover, by Bergsträsser's remark that such a use is unknown in the non-Koranic language, which is why one substituted *hallā* for it in the exegesis of the Koran. With this exclamation particle, however, the intention was precisely to make clear the meaning of لولا (*law-lā*) as an *optative particle* and not as an *interrogative particle*. From this it becomes clear that all of the Koran passages in which لولا (*law-lā*) was taken to be an interrogative particle,[264] and in which the meaning was thus partially distorted, should be revised.

---

263 Gotthelf Bergsträsser, *Verneinungs- und Fragepartikeln und Verwandtes im Kurʾān.* Ein Beitrag zur historischen Grammatik des Arabischen [*Negative and Interrogative Particles and Related Elements in the Koran. A Contribution on the Historical Grammar of Arabic*] (Leipzig, 1914) 81, ch.12, § 59.

264 On the basis of a preliminary examination, these are for Paret the following 38 Sura passages: 2:118; 4:77; 5:63; 6: 8,37,43; 7:203; 9:122; 10:20,98; 11:12, 116; 13:7,27; 18:15,39; 20:133,134; 24:12,16; 25:7,21; 27:46; 28:47,48; 29:50;

41:44; 43:31,53; 46:28; 47:20; 56:57,62,70,83,86; 58:8; 68:28; plus one occurrence of لوما (*law-mā*) (15:7) (the use of which besides that of لولا / *law-lā*, as a hypothetical optative particle has been documented in modern Arabic dialects of the Near East). Moreover, Nöldeke had in a way acknowledged this use at least in the case of لو (*law*) in his *Neue Beiträge zur semitischen Sprachwissenschaft* [*New Essays on Semitic Linguistics*] (last paragraph of page 18):

In the case of لو (*law*) the omission of the final clause is, to be sure, at times effective or at least permissible. Indeed, لو occasionally passes over into the meaning of ليت (*layta*) somewhat or introduces a modest (perhaps ironically modest) question; in such cases, no main clause is expected.

Nöldeke's understanding of the particle لو (*law*) in the case of the lacking apodosis in the sense of ليت (*layta*) (*if only, were it just*) is correct. Its interpretation as a question, however, is only to be understood in a general sense and as an alternative; لو (*law*) in itself can never be an interrogative particle. Nöldeke's interpretation of the particle لولا (*law-lā*), which, probably trusting the Arabic philologists, he understands, like Bergsträsser, as a negative interrogative particle (*loc. cit.* 21), is, however, incorrect: Much affected in the Koran is لولا (*law-lā*) "whether…not?", "ought not?", for our "why not"; otherwise هلا (*hallā*) is usually used for that. I can still remember a use of لولا (*law-lā*) in a verse by Ǧarīr: تعدون عقر النيب أفضل مجدكم بني ضوطرى لولا الكمي المقنعا

"You cover yourselves in magnificent glory for butchering the old camels, you scoundrels; why not the heavily-armed warriors?"

As a conjecture, Nöldeke attributes the uncommon use of لولا (*law-lā*) in this verse to either the Koran or the language of Mecca and Medina. In fact, however, this لولا (*law-lā*) had already been misunderstood by the Arabic editor of the divan in question in the sense of the exclamation particle هلا (*hallā*) (cf. the presumably homonymous Hebrew הַלְאָה) and misinterpreted as an interrogative particle. In reality this لولا is made up, separately (*law lā*), of a hypothetical and a negative particle with the meaning "*if not*" (nominally) or "*were not*" (verbally). Thus it is a question in this verse of a hypothetical conditional sentence with reversed protasis and apodosis in which for emphasis the apodosis is placed in front, as described by Nöldeke himself in his *Syrischen Grammatik* [*Syriac Grammar*], § 379:

"For stronger emphasis the governed clause is sometimes positioned far in front of the governing clause."

Accordingly, the introductory verb تعدّون (*taʿuddūna*) is not to be understood as indicative "*you cover*," but as subjunctive: "you *would* cover… *if* there were *not* = *were* there *not* the heavily-armed warrior." This is, in turn, explained in Nöldeke's *Syrische Grammatik* [*Syriac Grammar*], § 375 (300, second paragraph):

Sometimes there is no other indication of the unreal at all besides the ܐܠܘ (*ellū*

However, the lack of this meaning in both post-Koranic Arabic literature and vernacular Arabic suggests that the explanation quoted in the *Lisān* is actually made up. Thus, the assumption is more likely that the later points set on both ر /*r* are superfluous and that the original spelling was استفرر / *istafrir* : "*put to flight*" (i.e. *avert, turn away from me*).

(b) In contrast to Bergsträsser, Bell initially grasps لولا (*law-lā*) correctly as an optative particle in the meaning of "if only." In the process, this Koranic usage also corresponds to that of current Arabic dialects of the Near East where the attached particle لا (*lā*), which is unstressed in its pronunciation, is perceived as a pure filler particle without further meaning. To this extent an optative clause introduced by the particle لولا (*law-lā*) (actually *láw-la*) makes an apodosis superfluous. Bell also translates Verse 116 accordingly.

But the following exception particle connected with it الا (*illā*) ("*except*" or after a negation "*only*") suggests here a negative use of لولا (*law-lā*), even if Bergsträsser in considering this passage (*loc. cit.*, note 2) thinks that this may have been "invented" because of the *illā* or may perhaps even be based on the "misunderstanding" that the sentence would for that reason have a negative sense. This is because the Arabic philologists that Bergsträsser cites certainly did not have in mind the equivalent Syro-Aramaic usage of ܐܠܘ ܠܐ (*ellū lā*) ("*if not*").[265] However, if we take this Syro-Aramaic understanding as a basis, Arabic لو لا is to be read separately as *law lā* and understood as a *hypothetical conditional particle* with negation. From that point of view لو لا كان (*law lā*

= Arabic لو / *law*), which is clear in itself, and that is followed by a clause with the imperfect, the participle or a noun clause…."

As one can see, in interpreting the verse in question Nöldeke has thus allowed himself to be misled by the Arabic philologists.

265 Cf. *Thes*. I 198: ܐܠܘ ܠܐ (*ellū lā*) (also written together), *si non, nisi*, which is compared, citing the Syrian lexicographers, with the Arabic لولا (*law-lā*) or لولا أن (*law-lā an*). For the expression of a *condition presented as impossible* by ܐܠܘ (*ellū*) or ܐܠܘ ܠܐ (*ellū lā*), see further Nöldeke, *Syrische Grammatik* [*Syriac Grammar*] § 375.

kānā) should be understood to mean لو لم يكن (*law lam yakun*) (*had there not been*). From this it becomes clear that what is being introduced with it is in fact a *hypothetical conditional clause* which by definition requires an *apodosis*.

(c) This apodosis in Verse 117 is perhaps not accidentally introduced by the particle و / *wa* ("*and*"). Namely, this is to be distinguished from the *superfluous* particle before the apodosis of a temporal sentence insofar as *Mannā* (182b) cites as the eighth function of the equivalent Syro-Aramaic conjunction ܘ / *w* لتقوية المعنى (*li-taqwiyat al-maʿnā*) "*for meaning intensification, emphasis*." It would to this extent correspond to the Arabic intensification particle لـ / *la-* , which among other things serves to introduce the apodosis of a hypothetical conditional sentence. Thus the <u>و</u>ما كان (<u>*wa*</u>*-mā kāna*) introducing the apodosis in Verse 117 is to be understood in Arabic in the meaning لما كان (<u>*la*</u>*-mā kāna*) (<u>*then*</u> [would have …] *not*).

Once one has stopped to think about the Syro-Aramaic meaning of the two introductory particles, لولا (= *law lā*) (*if not*) in the protasis and وما (*wa-mā*) in the sense of لما (*la-mā*) (*then…not*) in the apodosis, one can, as follows, reconstruct the aforementioned double verse as a *hypothetical conditional sentence*:

116: "<u>If</u> among the generations before you there had <u>not only</u> been few <u>virtuous</u> (people) – some of whom we saved – to stand up to the evil on the earth, <u>so that</u>[266] those who committed wicked deeds continued in their <u>excesses</u>[267] and remained[268] sinners, 117:

---

266 The consecutive meaning of the Syro-Aramaic conjunction ܘ *w* (*and*) in the sense of "*so that*" is documented by *Mannā* (182b) under سادسا (*sādisa*ⁿ) as follows: ܗܘܐ ܝܘܩܪܢܐ ܗܟܢܐ ܘܣܥܘ ܐܢܫܐ ܘܥܠܘ (*hwā yuqrānā hā*<u>*k*</u>*ānā* <u>*wa*</u>*-sʿaw* (*a*)*nāšā w-ʿal*(*ū*)) هكذا اشتد الغلاء حتى انّ الناس تجرّأوا فدخلوا (*the rise in prices was such* <u>*that*</u> *the people became bold and entered*).

267 Literally: "to follow up on that wherein they were committing excesses."

268 In this context the Arabic verb كان /*kāna* (*to be*) is to be understood with the meaning of its Syro-Aramaic equivalent ܗܘܐ /*hwā* (*to be*), that among other things means (as in English) *to remain, to stay* (cf. C. Brockelmann, *Lexicon Syriacum*, 173a: 1. *fuit* (*to be*), 2. *duravit* (*to remain, stay, persist*); cf. also

so[269] your lord would not have come to destroy the cities (had) their inhabitants (been) righteous."[270]

Through the syntactical elucidation of this double verse the allusion becomes clear to the Biblical account in which it ensues from a dialogue between Yahweh and an Abraham begging for mercy that there were not even ten righteous people to be found in Sodom (Gen. 18:23-32), which is why Yahweh let brimstone and fire rain upon Sodom and Gomorrah and destroyed these cities (Gen. 19:24-25), but spared Lot and his family (Gen. 19:16,29).

Mannā 170b: ܗܘܐ ܠܘܬ ܦܠܢ (*hwā l-wāṯ plān*) أقام عند فلان . مكث (*makaṯa, aqāma ʿinda fulān*) (*to remain, to stay with someone*).

269 On the function of the Syro-Aramaic ܘ / w (*and*) before the apodosis, Nöldeke explains in his *Syrischen Grammatik* [*Syriac Grammar*] § 339:
The conjunction ܘ does not serve to introduce the apodosis (like the German "so," etc.). Wherever it seems like that in the Old Testament, it is a literal translation of the Hebrew ו ; in other passages it has occurred as a result of textual corruption. Now, however, ܘ has seemingly acquired the entire scope of meaning of the Greek *καί* and is often "also," where it then alternates with ܐܦ or ܘܐܦ; such a ܘ "also" can appear in all positions of the sentence, therefore also at the beginning of the apodosis.
In addition to this, the Koranic usage of و / *wa* to introduce the apodosis can be explained in particular as an intensifying particle in connection with the negative particle ما / *mā* (وما كان ربك / *wa-mā kāna rabbuka*), although not exactly in an exclusive meaning, as Nöldeke then explains it in cases like ܘܠܐ ܚܕ (*w-lā ḥaḏ*) (> Arabic ولا أحد / *wa-lā aḥad*) "not even one" and ܘܠܐ ܡܕܡ (*w-lā meddem*) (Arabic ولا شيء / *wa-lā šay*ʾ) "nothing at all."

270 As a participial clause this subordinate final clause is not defined in more detail in terms of time; literally it reads "*and* (= while) their inhabitants *righteous*." Paret and Blachère nonsensically translate it in the indicative since they have not grasped the hypothetical context of the entire sentence construction. To this extent, however, it should accordingly be understood as subjunctive. What Nöldeke said *loc. cit.* § 375 (300, second paragraph) about ܐܠܘ (*ellū*) also applies here:
"Sometimes beyond the ܐܠܘ , which is in itself clear, there is no other indication of the unreal at all and that is followed by a clause with the imperfect, the participle or a nominal clause…."

With this distortedly rendered *hypothetical conditional sentence* previously unrecognized by Western Koran scholars, the Koran offers us at the same time a perfect example of a syntactically demanding sentence composition like those Nöldeke sketches in his *Syrischen Grammatik* [*Syriac Grammar*] under the chapter heading "*Period Construction: Crossing Clauses and Other Irregularities*" in § 378:

> "Grounded in the make-up of their language, the Syrians' tendency to construct longer *periods* is in no small way encouraged by the model of the Greek style. Such periods arise through the coordination and subordination of clauses of the discussed types or of types quite similar to them. Here there is an unlimited abundance of possible ways in which to combine the familiar elements in individual cases. § 379. The freedom of the word order in the clause is in part also carried over into the arrangement of the clauses serving as the component parts of the period. For stronger emphasis the governed clause is sometimes placed far before the governing clause, and not infrequently veritable *crossing clauses* occur."

With this in mind, the underlined expressions in the previously cited double verse still need to be individually examined.

On the Meaning of بقية *(baqīya)*

Koran scholars have puzzled a great deal over the Koranic expression اولوا بقية (*ūlū baqīya*) (*virtuous* [people]). *Ṭabarī* (XII 138), starting from the Arabic meaning of بقية (*baqīya*) (*rest, what is left*), explains the expression succinctly with, ذو بقية من الفهم و العقل , "such as have (so much) insight and understanding *left over* [to spare, i.e. they have more than they need]" that they recognize what an advantage they have as believers in God, and what a disadvantage they have as nonbelievers. In his *Kommentar* [*Commentary*] on this passage Paret refers to his note on Sura 2:248, and there to *baqīya* in Sura 11:86 and 116 (53):

"Thus in both cases *baqīya* appears to mean a quality or power that in some way works against disaster."

Looking more closely at Verse 2:248, in which it is said of the Ark of the Covenant that it is equipped with "*sakīna*" and "*baqīya*" (not translated in Paret's *Übersetzung* [*Translation*] 36), he continues:

> "Accordingly one can also interpret the expression in the present verse as such a quality possessed, together with *sakīna*, by the Ark of the Covenant. But the subsequent *mimmā taraka*...("of which something ... has been left") does not specifically refer to *baqīya*, but generally to the Ark and its contents. See R. Paret, "Die Bedeutung des Wortes *baqīya* im Koran [The Meaning of the Word *baqīya* in the Koran]" (*Alttestamentliche Studien*, Friedrich Nötscher zum sechzigsten Geburtstag [*Old Testament Studies*, Festschrift for Friedrich Nötscher on His Sixtieth Birthday], Bonn 1950, pp. 168-171); A. Spitaler, "Was bedeutet *baqīya* im Koran? [What Does *baqīya* Mean in the Koran?]" (*Westöstliche Abhandlungen*, Rudolf Tschudi zum siebzigsten Geburtstag [*West-to-East Monographs*, Festschrift for Rudolf Tschudi on his Seventieth Birthday], Wiesbaden 1954, pp. 137-146). Spitaler translates *baqīya* in 2:248, depending on one's interpretation of the passage, either with "favor," "goodness" or simply with "remains or relics"."

The guessing game over the explanation of this expression can in the meantime be put to an end by the Syro-Aramaic. Following our proven method we need only look for the Syro-Aramaic lexical equivalent. This we find in the erbal root ܝܬܪ (*iṯar*), whose original meaning the Eastern Syrian lexicographer *Mannā* (320b) gives in Arabic as follows: . فضل . بقي (*faḍula*, baqiya) (*to be left, to remain as* rest). With that, however, the Arabic expression بقية (*baqīya*) is still not explained. To determine the real sense, the further semantic meanings of the Syro-Aramaic verbal root must then be examined. Among these *Mannā* gives us under (4) the following Arabic meaning: فضل . كان فاضلا (*faḍula, kāna fāḍilaⁿ*) (*virtuous, to be excellent*). And corresponding to these *Mannā*

(321a) gives us further under (2) the Arabic meaning of the Syro-Aramaic nominal forms ܡܝܬܪܬܐ (*m-yattartā*) and ܡܝܬܪܘܬܐ (*m-yattrūṯā*): فضيلة . حسنة (*faḍīla, ḥasana*) (*virtue, excellence*). In Arabic, the expression فضيلة (*faḍīla*), a lexical borrowing from Syro-Aramaic, has been taken up into the language in the figurative sense of "*virtue, excellence*," but not the synonymous expression, بقية (*baqīya*), which is only understood in its concrete sense of "*rest*."[271] It is clear from the Koranic context, however, that with بقية (*baqīya*) ("*rest*") the Koran, following the Syro-Aramaic semantics, really means فضيلة (*faḍīla*) (*virtue*). As a result, our Koranic expression اولو بقية (*ūlū*[272] *baqīya*) (= اولوا فضيلة / *ūlū faḍīla*) would be explained as "[people] with *virtue* = *virtuous* [*people*]."

On the Meaning of اترفوا (*utrifū*)

Our Koran translators have for the most part correctly translated the verb اترفوا (*utrifū*) (from Verse 116). Referring to the linguistic usage of

---

271 To be sure, in many an Arabic dialect in the Near East the variant بقوة (*baqwa*) (pronounced: *baʾwe*) is still in use today, say, in the following expression, انسان بلا بقوة (*insān ba-lā baqwe*) (*a man without "rest" = without morals, without moral backbone*), where again a loan translation from the lexically equivalent Syro-Aramaic expression has also been additionally confirmed in the vernacular.

272 The pronunciation *ulū* (with a short first *u*), as the canonical version of the Koran reads it, is implausible. It contradicts the Koranic orthography to the extent that this generally omits the و / *u* in a closed first syllable as a *mater lectionis* for short *u*. This is evidenced by the Arabic transcription of numerous Syro-Aramaic loan words in the Koran, such as فرقان / *furqān* (< ܦܘܪܩܢܐ / *purqānā*), طغيان / *ṭuġyān* (< ܛܘܥܝܢܐ / *ṭuʿyānā*), سلطان / *sulṭān* (< ܫܘܠܛܢܐ / *šulṭānā*), جبّ / *ǧubb* (< ܓܘܒܐ / *gubbā*), جناح / *ǧunāḥ* (< ܓܘܢܚܐ / *gunḥā* / *gūnnāḥā*), نطفة *nuṭfa* (< ܢܘܛܦܬܐ / *nuṭpṯā*), قدس / *quds* / *qudus* (< ܩܘܕܫܐ / *quḏšā*), etc. The complete spelling اولوا, if it was originally not to be pronounced with a diphthong *awlū* (in imitation of the demonstrative pronoun هولا – in all likelihood pronounced *hawlā* or *hawlē* – of which it appears to be a secondary formation with a hypercorrect plural ending in the nominative case), at any rate suggests rather a monophthongization to *ō* than to *ū* (and thus in many a dialect today in the Near East هولا is pronounced *hōlē*). Arbitrary, in any case, is therefore the pronunciation *ulū* (with a short first *u*).

the *Arabs* and a *Rāğiz* verse, *Ṭabarī* (XII 140) explains the expression مترف (*mutraf*) as "*one who enjoys the pleasures of life to the full.*" But, that a reference to the linguistic usage of the "*Arabs*" offers no guarantee that the expression is also genuinely *Arabic*, is proven in this case by the circumstance that the actual Syro-Aramaic verbal root ܪܦܐ (*rpā*) (*to be soft, limp, flabby, slack, loose*) was not recognized by the Arab philologists. Instead, the Arabic verbal form أترف (*utrifa*), which had been borrowed from the Syro-Aramaic extended verbal stem ܐܬܪܦܝ (*eṯrappī*) (*to live a dissolute life, a life of licentious indulgence*),[273] has been falsely incorporated into the Arab lexicography as the root ترف (*tarafa*). In doing so, the Arabic philologists have not recognized the prefix تـ / *t-* as such and have taken it to be the first radical. From this, there then arose in Arabic such logically false derivatives as the noun ترف (*taraf*) (*luxurious, dissolute life*) (to which the Syro-Aramaic ܪܦܝܘܬܐ / *rappyūṯā* actually corresponds) or the corresponding adjective ترف (*tarif*), both of which are still in use today.[274] Thus we have an example of a Koranic expression, borrowed from Syro-Aramaic, whose general sense the Arabic philologists have understood correctly, although they have categorized it falsely in terms of etymology.

This is all the more surprising since with the root رفه (*rafuha*) (whose final ه / *h* was probably originally conceived of as a *mater lectionis* for the final ا / *ā*) and its quite common derivatives,[275] modern Arabic has preserved an authentic variant of the Syro-Aramaic form ܪܦܐ / *rpā*). On the basis of the partially identical examples cited in the *Lisān* under each of these forms, the further varieties رفأ (*rafaʾa*), رأف (*raʾafa*), راف / روف (*rawafa* /*rāfa*) and رفا (*rafā*), also suggest a common Aramaic root, of which the variations preserved in Arabic are apparently dialectal. Even

---

273 C. Brockelmann, *Lexicon Syriacum* [*Syriac Lexicon*], 741a, Etpa. 3. *luxuriatus est*. The *Thes*. II 3960 cites: ܥܝܕܐ ܪܦܝܐ (*ʿyāḏē rpayyā*) *mores dissoluti* (*loose morals*).

274 Cf., e.g., H. Wehr, *Arabisches Wörterbuch* [*Arabic Dictionary*], under ترف / *tarifa*.

275 E.g., in H. Wehr, *loc. cit.*: رفاهة / *rafāha*, رفاهية / *rafāhiya* / *rafāhīya: easy life, comfort, well-being,* etc., as well as ترفيه / *tarfīh* (verbal noun of the 2nd stem): providing oneself or others an easy life.

though the *Lisān* continually refers to the linguistic usage of the "*Arabs*," its occasionally clumsy explanation of it demonstrates precisely that it is unfamiliar with the expression in question, for example, when it cites the still commonly used congratulations for newlyweds, بالرفاء والبنين (*bi-r-rifāʾi wa-l-banīn*), under both رفأ (*rafaʾa*) (I 87b) and رفا (*rafā*) (XIV 331a) and falsely explains the expression رفاء (*rifāʾ*) with "*harmony*." H. Wehr (*loc. cit.*) even translates it accordingly: "*Live in harmony and have sons!*" Yet according to one *ḥadīṯ* the Prophet is said to have forbidden the use of this congratulatory formula. This indicates that under رفاء (*rifāʾ*) he did not exactly understand "*harmony*," but instead must have understood the more negative Syro-Aramaic meaning of ܪܦܝܐ (*rpāyā*) or ܪܦܝܘܬܐ (*rappyūṯā*) ("*softness*" = *exuberant, dissolute life*). Positively, however, the borrowed رفاء (*rifāʾ*) is equivalent to the expression, probably created in Arabic via a loan translation, رخاء (*raḫāʾ*) ("*softness*" = *carefree life, prosperity, luck*). In this way the above-mentioned congratulations also become comprehensible: "*The best of luck and many children!*"

Just as suspicious is the meaning "*to bring on shore*" for رفأ (*rafaʾa*) (see H. Wehr, *loc. cit.*), from which مرفأ (*marfaʾ*) "*harbor*" is derived. Namely, it is contradicted by the *ḥadīṯ* of *Abū Hurayra* about the Day of Judgment, which the *Lisān* (I 87a) cites as evidence of its use: فتكون الأرض كالسفينة المرفأة في البحر تضربها الأمواج (*the earth will then become like a* (*violently*) *shaken ship on the ocean that is thrown to and fro by the waves*). In terms of the meaning, the expression المرفأة (*al-murfaʾa*) is based on the *mediae geminatae* root رفّ (*raffa*) (< Syro-Aramaic ܪܦ / *rap̄*), so that المرفأة (*al-murfaʾa*) should actually be pronounced المرفّة (*al-muraffa*) (Syro-Aramaic ܕܡܪܦܐ / *da-m-rappā*). For only this reading produces the expected sense here, "*to be shaken, to be shocked*," corresponding to تضربها الأمواج (*taḍribuhā l-amwāǧ*) "*to be thrown to and fro*" (< Syro-Aramaic ܛܪܦ / *ṭrap̄*)[276] by the waves.

---

276 On the rendering of the Syro-Aramaic ܦ / *p* by the Arabic ب / *b* see S. Fraenkel, *Die aramäischen Fremdwörter im Arabischen* [*The Aramaic Foreign Words in Arabic*] xxii: "Occasionally ب occurs for Aramaic ܦ פ (Φ) ...." Here it must be pointed out that ܦ/ *p* in the oral tradition of the East Syrians is always pronounced as a hard (*p*), which is also still evidenced today by the New

Namely, the sense of the Arabic verb ضرب (*ḍaraba*) (*schlagen*) expected in this context could only be discovered via the semantics of the Syro-Aramaic verb ܛܪܦ / *ṭrap̄* – as reproduced above. Whence the suspicion that ضرب (*ḍaraba*) is only a phonetically Arabicized form of the Syro-Aramaic ܛܪܦ (*ṭrap̄*) (or the East Syriac *ṭrap*).

Excursus on the Etymology and Semantics of Arabic ضرب (*ḍaraba*) (*to strike*)

If this assumption is correct, then this finding should open up new perspectives for a potentially different understanding of each use of the verb ضرب (*ḍaraba*) in the Koran. For this, a comparison must be made with the semantic contents of the Syro-Aramaic verb ܛܪܦ (*ṭrap̄*) to determine first of all to what extent Arabic ضرب (*ḍaraba*) stands for Syro-Aramaic ܛܪܦ (*ṭrap̄*). For in the process one must not lose sight of the fact that (a) another Syro-Aramaic synonym may stand behind it, and that (b) ضرب (*ḍaraba*) has perhaps slipped into Arabic and became

---

East Syriac dialects. The presumption that Arabic ضرب (*ḍaraba*) is a secondary dialectal formation derived from Syro-Aramaic ܛܪܦ (*ṭrap̄*) (or East Syriac *ṭrap*) is supported by the semantic contents of the Syro-Aramaic root. In this regard, see *Thes.* I 1523 ff., which lists among the Arabic expressions quoted by the Eastern Syrian lexicographers يضرب (*yaḍrib*) (1524), اضطراب (*iṭṭirāb*), الضرب and ضرب (*ḍarb*) (1525 f.).

Insofar is Fraenkel, who sees in ضرب (*ḍaraba* / *ḍarb*) a *genuine Arabic expression for striking coins* (*loc. cit.* 195), to be contradicted. Here one must consider whether it is not more likely that behind this stands the Syro-Aramaic ܨܪܦ (*ṣrap̄*) (East Syriac *ṣrap*), which among other things can mean both "*to cast, to smelt, to purify*" (especially with regard to precious metals) and "*to press, to punch*" and "*to hurt*" (cf. *Thes.* II 3446 ff.; Brockelmann, *Lexicon Syriacum* 638). In any case, the Arabic expressions Fraenkel discusses and whose origins he questions, are traceable back to this Syro-Aramaic root: (a) صرف (*ṣirf*) "*the pure wine*" (172), (b) the same in the meaning "*pure* red" (185), further صراف (*ṣarrāf*) (probably originally "*caster of coins*," then "*changer of coins*") as well as صرف (*ṣarafa*) "*to creak, to crunch*," which in Fraenkel's opinion does not appear to belong here at all (see *Mannā*, ܨܪܦ / *ṣrap̄*, 650a, under (4): صرّ اسنانه / *ṣarra asnānahu* "*to press* one's teeth *together*, *to grind* one's teeth").

semantically independent long before the Koran. We find a first example in an expression that confirms the former assumption. In Sura 24:31 certain rules are listed concerning the behavior of women; among them we find:

Sura 24:31

و لا يَضرِبنَ بِارجلهن ليعلم ما يخفين من زينتهن

Until now this verse segment has been understood, in accordance with *Ṭabarī* (XVIII 124), in the following way:

> (Bell I 339): 2.“… and let them not <u>beat with their feet</u> so as to let the <u>ornaments</u> which they conceal be known.”

> (Paret 289): “Und sie sollen nicht <u>mit ihren Beinen (aneinander)</u> <u>schlagen</u> und damit auf den <u>Schmuck</u> aufmerksam machen, den sie (durch die Kleidung) verborgen (an ihnen) <u>tragen</u> [Note: W.: damit man merkt, was sie von ihrem <u>Schmuck geheimhalten</u>].”

> (Blachère 379): “Que [les Croyantes] ne <u>frappent</u> point [*le sol*] <u>de</u> <u>leurs pieds</u> pour montrer les <u>atours</u> qu'elles cachent.”

According to this understanding, women are indeed allowed to wear jewelry, but not to show it on the outside or to draw attention to it by slapping their legs together or stamping on the ground with their feet. From this conjectural and unsuccessful interpretation one sees that the Arabic commentators did not know what to do with this, to their ears, foreign-sounding expression: يضربن بارجلهن (*yaḍribna bi-arǧulihinna*) (speaking of women, "*they strike with their feet*"). However, the sense becomes clear as soon as one imagines the equivalent Syro-Aramaic expression that stands behind it, and which the *Thes.* (I, 1524) cites as follows: "ܡܛܪ̈ܦܢ ܒܪ̈ܓܠܝܗܝܢ (*m-ṭarrp̄ān b-reġlayhēn*) *pedibus suis tripudiantes*, incessu artificiali utentes ("*striking*" with their feet, "*stamping*" their feet = hopping, skipping, in that they walk about in an artificial way), Isa. 3:16." What is interesting here is that the Koran paraphrases this Bible passage with the Syro-Aramaic expression of the

Pšiṭṭā more accurately than, say, the *Jerusalem Bible*.[277] However, in Syro-Aramaic the expression actually means "*to hop on one's feet = to skip*." Furthermore, if one were to compare the Arabic زينة (*zīna*) (*jewelry*) with the Syro-Aramaic ܨܒܬܐ (*ṣeḇtā*), for the latter the Syrian lexicographers also give the figurative sense بهاء . حسن . جمال (*bahā', ḥusn, ǧamāl*) (*magic, grace, beauty*) (*Thes.* II 3360, *decus*). Thus, roughly translated, the verse cited above from Sura 24:31 should instead be understood as follows:

„They should not (walk around) with their *feet hopping* (=*skipping*) so that their concealed <u>*charms*</u> stand out."[278]

---

277 In other words, there (*loc. cit.* 1036b) this passage from Isa 3:16 is rendered as follows: "and *jingling* their *ankle bracelets*." Here the Hebrew וברגליהם תעכסנה (*wu-ḇraḡlēhem t'akkasna*), contrary to the explanation given in Gesenius (585a), "*to adorn oneself with ankle bracelets, or to jingle them to cause a stir*" with the indication "(a coquetry also disapproved of in the Korân [Sur. 24:32], cf. Doughty 1:149)," probably has less to do with *jingling ankle bracelets* than with the Hebrew variant עקש (*'qaš*) and the Arabic (عقص / *'aqaṣa*, عقس / *'aqasa*) as well as Syro-Aramaic (ܥܩܣ / *'qas*) equivalents that Gesenius (614a) etymologically associates with it with the meaning "*to spin, to wriggle*." Interesting in this respect is the expression that is cited by the *Lisān* (VI 145a) for عكس (*'akasa*): تعكّس الرجل: مشى مشي الأفعى (*ta'akkasa r-raǧul : mašā mašya l-af'ā*) (*said of someone ta'akkasa means: to walk like a snake = to wriggle, to weave*), وربما مشى السكران كذلك (*this is also by analogy said of one who is drunk*). Accordingly, the Hebrew expression would mean (*to skip, so that while walking one*) "(*artificially*) <u>*twists*</u> *or* <u>*turns*</u> *one's feet*," whereas the Koranic or Syro-Aramaic variant means (*to skip, so that while walking one*) "(*artificially*) <u>*hops*</u> *on one's feet*." The fundamentally seductive intent in this is documented by the *Thes.* (II 2967a) in the figurative sense of *stimulatio, incitatio* (*stimulation, seduction*) with, among other things, the following Hebrew-related Syro-Aramaic expression ܫܘܦܪܝܗܘܢ ܘܥܘܩܣܝܗܘܢ (*šup̄rayhōn w-<u>'uqsayhōn</u>*) (*her charms and <u>enticements</u>*) (*Ephr.* ed. Lamy i. 489. 5).

278 Literally: "They ought not "*to stamp*" with their *feet* (= "*to hop*") in such a way that what they conceal of their *charm* becomes *known* (= *revealed*)." By that what is meant is: in that they *display* their concealed charms in a seductive way. The meaning "*to reveal, to display*" for Arabic اعلم (*a'lama*) (*to cause to be known*) results from the lexically equivalent Syro-Aramaic expression ܐܘܕܥ

Another Meaning of بقية (*baqīya*)

Sura 11:86

بقيت الله خير لكم ان كنتم مومنين

(Bell I 213): 87. "The abiding (portion) [*i.e.* the eternal reward] of Allah will be better for you, if ye be believers."

(Paret 186): "Die Kraft (?) [note: Oder: Güte (*? baqīya*)] Gottes ist besser für euch, wenn (anders) ihr gläubig seid. "

(Blachère 254): 87/86 "Ce qui reste auprès d'Allah [note 87. Text.: le reste d'Allah] est un bien pour vous si vous êtes croyants."

In this verse the expression بقيت الله (*baqīya^{tu} llāh*) has a different meaning than اولوا بقية (*ūlū baqīya*) in Sura 11:116. In the verse which precedes it, Verse 85, *Šuʿayb* (*Shu'aib*) warns the Midianites against dishonest profit through the falsification of weights and measures. The expression بقيت (*baqīya^{t}*) is directly connected with this unlawful enrichment. Blachère and Bell do in fact approximate the sense, but without being able to explain the term properly.

That is because here, too, the real meaning is to be determined via the semantics of the same Syro-Aramaic lexical equivalent ܝܘܬܪܢܐ (*yutrānā*) (*profit*). Under the root ܝܬܪ (*iṯar*) *Mannā* (320a), besides the original meaning بقي (*baqiya*) (*to remain*), lists under (6) the following Arabic meaning: اكتسب . ربح (*rabiḥa, iktasaba*) (*to win, to acquire*). Under the aforementioned nominal form (321b) he accordingly lists under (2): مكسب . ربح (*ribḥ, maksab*) (*profit, acquisition*). As a synonym for ܬܐܓܘܪܬܐ (*tēgurtā*) (*trade, profit*)[279] the *Thes.* (II 4389) cites the fol-

---

(*awdaʿ*) (*Thes.* I 1557): *scire fecit, ostendit, indicavit* (*to cause to be known, to reveal, to indicate*).

279 The Koranically borrowed تجارة (*tiǧāra*) in Sura 35:29 (يرجون تجارة لن تبور *they expect a profit that will not become worthless*, i.e. *a profit of lasting value*) and Sura 61:10 is meant in this Syro-Aramaic sense of "*acquisition, profit.*" So, too, البقيت الصلحت (*al-bāqiyāt^{u} ṣ-ṣāliḥāt*) (probably for ܡܝܬܪܬܐ ܛܒܬܐ / *myattrāṯā ṭāḇāṯā*, *Thes.* I 1653, *egregia facta, gesta praeclara*) "*good, excellent works*" in Sura 18:46 and 19:76.

lowing expressions: "*de mercatura spirituali* ܬܐܓܘܪܬܐ ܕܕܝܪܝܘܬܐ (*tēḡurtā d-dayrāyūṯā*) (*spiritual acquisition through a monastic way of life*); (2) *labor, opus,* ܬܐܓܘܪܬܗ ܕܒܥܠܕܒܒܐ (*tēḡurteh da-ḇʿeldḇāḇā*) (*the work of the adversary, of Satan*). That could be contrasted with بقيت الله (*baqīya*^{tu} *llāh*) as the "*work of God,*" here in the sense of "*acquisition well pleasing to God.*" From this the following sense results for this expression in the context of Sura 11:86:

> "The acquisition (pleasing to) God is of greater advantage to you if you are believers!"

A Third Meaning for بقية (*baqīya*)

Sura 2:248

ان اية ملكه ان ياتيكم التابوت فيه سكينة من ربكم
وبقية مما ترك ال موسى وال هرون

In his translation (36) Paret leaves the expressions *sakīna* and *baqīya* untranslated as special Koranic terms, although in his *Kommentar* [*Commentary*] (52) he suggests for *baqīyatun* the meaning "rest" (= "relic"?). The latter seems to be the best fit here inasmuch as *Mannā* (821b) gives for the Syro-Aramaic synonym ܫܪܟܢܐ (*šarkānā*), in addition to the original meaning بقية (*baqīya*) (*rest*), under (2) ذخيرة (*ḏaḫīra*) (*relic*). There is accordingly in the Ark of the Covenant a "*relic*" that Moses' and Aaron's clans have left behind.

13. On Many a Syro-Aramaic Basic Structure in the Language of the Koran

To return once more to the above-mentioned grammatical basic structures of the language of the Koran, we want to take a closer look from this perspective at the previously cited (p. 95) Verse 23 of the Mary Sura: يليتني مت قبل هذا وكنت نسيا منسيا *"If only I had died beforehand and been totally forgotten!"*

There is nothing to quibble about concerning the sense. What interests us here is the component part of the sentence وكنت نسيا منسيا (*wa-kuntu nasya^{n} mansīyā*) "(*had*) *been totally forgotten.*" This well-known Koranic expression, which has entered the Arabic language and the Arabic lexicography as a *familiar quotation,*[280] is an example of a syntactical figure characterized in Arabic grammar as مفعول مطلق (*maf'ūl muṭlaq*) (in English: *accusative of the inner* [*verbal*] *content*, or *of the absolute* or *inner object*).[281] Reduced to a simple formula, this object consists of the infinitive or a noun derived from the employed verb, which stands in place of a lacking adverb or to reinforce the homonymous verb as that verb's object in the accusative.

A familiar example of this is provided by the sentence: *He slept the sleep of the righteous* (i.e., he slept *like* one who is righteous). The key here, however, is that in Arabic (as in English) this object regularly stands *after* the verb and as a noun naturally remains unchanged, whereas the verb itself can assume any form whatsoever.

In our Koranic clause, however, what stands out is that the infinitive object نسيا (*nasya^{n}*) (*forgetting*) stands *before* the verbal form, in other words, that the order prescribed according to the rules of Arabic grammar is reversed. Were one to assert that this is caused by the need to rhyme, one could reply that the final syllables of the two words are ho-

---

280 See, for example, Hans Wehr, *Arabisches Wörterbuch* [*Arabic Dictionary*], under نسي / *nasy* : أصبح نسيا منسيا / *'aṣbaḥa nasyan mansīyan* "*to fall into oblivion.*"

281 Cf. C. Brockelmann, *Arabische Grammatik* [*Arabic Grammar*] § 112.

monymous. That according to the current reading of the Koran منسيا (as a transcription of Syro-Aramaic ܡܢܫܝܐ actually to be read *m-našyā*) is to be pronounced *mansīyā* with a doubling of the *ī* and for this reason should stand at the end of the verse, is not a convincing argument since إنسيا (in Verse 26), which as an unequivocal transliteration of Syro-Aramaic ܐܢܫܝܐ should not be pronounced *insīyā*, but (*a*)*nāšāyā* (*a human being*), is also, according to the modern reading of the Koran because of the rhyme, to be pronounced in exactly the same way with a reinforced *ī*.

Even presupposing that this reading in light of the purely Aramaic prototype is not arbitrary, نسيا (*nasya*^{n}) could have been in the correct word order according to the rules of Arabic sentence construction and could have nevertheless been pronounced for the sake of the rhyme in the same way *nasīyā*. The purely formal, superficial argument used to justify this sequence of clauses running counter to the strict rule of Arabic grammar is therefore not convincing.

For this obvious irregularity from the point of view of Arabic, the Arabic commentators have tried to give another interpretation. What is meant by the masculine verbal noun نسيا (*nasya*^{n}) is allegedly a "*forgotten memory*" or a "*forgotten object*," which as the predicate of كنت (*kuntu*) according to the rules of Arabic grammar is correctly in the accusative, which would in turn be why the منسيا (*mansīya*^{n}) following it is logically understood as its corresponding masculine attributive participial adjective. Accordingly, Mary would be thinking: "*Oh, were I only a forgotten object!*" or "*were my memory forgotten*!"[282]

The deeper cause, however, actually lies in the fact that we are dealing here with a typical Syro-Aramaic sentence construction. Theodor Nöldeke accurately outlines this as follows:

> "It is a characteristic of Aramaic that it has a much greater capacity for linking clauses than Hebrew and Arabic. It possesses many

282 *Ṭabarī* XVI 66 f.

conjunctions and lightly modifying adverbs. In addition to this it has considerable freedom in terms of word order."[283]

Such a word order occurs in the Koranic verse under discussion: In contrast to Arabic, the verb comes *after* the noun. Accordingly, the word order وكنت نسيا منسيا (*wa-kuntu* nasya^{n} *mansīyā*) exactly corresponds to, and has the same meaning as, the Syro-Aramaic ܘܗܘܝܬ ܢܫܝܐ ܡܢܫܝܐ (*wa-hwīṯ* *nšāyā m-našyā*).

Once we have become conscious of the Syro-Aramaic form of this verse, we are then be able to perceive another detail: not only the word order, but also the congruence of the subject and the participal adjective does not correspond to the rules of Arabic grammar. That is to say, if one asks an educated Arab well-versed in grammar how he accounts for this sentence construction, he will at first be taken aback because this sentence in this form is so familiar that he has never thought about it. Its problematic nature is only brought home to him by a series of elementary questions:

a) What is the subject here of كنت (*kuntu*) (*were I*)?
   – Answer: Mary .
b) What is its corresponding predicate participial adjective?
   – Answer: منسيا (*mansīya*^{n}) (*forgotten*).
c) Is the ending here masculine or feminine?
   – Answer: Masculine.
d) To what then does this predicate refer?
   – Answer: Obviously to the masculine نسيا (*nasya*^{n}) (a *forgetting*).
e) Conclusion: نسيا منسيا (*nasya*^{n} *mansīyā*) would accordingly be: *a "forgotten forgetting.*" Hence, not Mary should be forgotten, but *the forgetting* itself should be *forgotten*.
f) What would be correct here, referring to Mary, according to the rules of Arabic grammar?
   – Answer: وكنت منسية نسيا (*wa-kuntu mansīya*^{tan} *nasya*^{n}).

283 Th. Nöldeke, *Die semitischen Sprachen* [*The Semitic Languages*] (Leipzig, ^{2}1899) 46.

This is in fact how the sentence should read in correct Arabic.

Such deviations from the norms of Arabic grammar are habitually explained as peculiarities of the language of the Koran. Yet, to anyone who would conclude from this that the Koran was composed in faulty Arabic, it should be replied: This is not incorrect Arabic, but perfectly correct Aramaic. Namely, in the participial form, منسيا (*mansīyā*) (*forgotten*), what looks like an Arabic masculine accusative ending is, in reality, if one imagines the transliterated Syro-Aramaic spelling ܡܢܫܝܐ (*m-našyā*), a Syro-Aramaic feminine predicate ending. According to the rules of Syro-Aramaic grammar the predicate participle and adjective are namely in the so-called *status absolutus*. In the case of the feminine this means that the ܬ / *t* of the emphatic feminine ending ܬܐ / *tā* drops away leaving only the final ܐ / *ā* behind.[284]

Arabic has no such rule. No distinction is made between attributive and predicate adjective and participial adjective in written Arabic, so that in the case of the feminine the final ة / *t* is always retained. It is therefore from an Arabic perspective impossible to see a feminine ending in a form like منسيا (*mansīya*^{n}) unless one sees it through Syro-Aramaic glasses.

We encounter this Syro-Aramaic feminine predicate ending in additional passages of the Koran. There is, for example, بغيا (*baġīyā*) in Verse 20, ولم اك بغيا (*since I am no prostitute*) and in Verse 28, وما كانت امك بغيا (*and yet your mother was no prostitute*), is a faithful rendering of Syro-Aramaic ܒܥܝܐ (*bāʿyā*). One tries to justify the fact that بغية (*baġīya*^{t}) does not have an Arabic feminine ending here, not just on account of the rhyme, but in particular with the argument that certain adjectives referring exclusively to women formally take a masculine ending.

This explanation, however, is not valid because we encounter other cases in the Koran that cannot be justified by it. Thus, for example, in Sura 33:63 it says: وما يدريك لعل الساعة تكون قريبا "*What do you know? The* (*final*) *hour may be near.*" The fact that قريبا (*qarībā*) as a predicate for الساعة (*as-sāʿa*) (*the hour*) here has the Syro-Aramaic feminine end-

284 Cf. C. Brockelmann, *Syrische Grammatik* [*Syriac Grammar*] §§ 90, 91 (paradigm).

ing in *status absolutus*, one would like to explain according to Arabic grammar as an adverbial ending in the sense of عن قريب (*ʿan qarīb*) (*in the near future, soon*). But that would be contradicted by Sura 42:17, وما يدريك لعل الساعة قريب (with the same meaning). That here قريب (*qarīb*), although a predicate of الساعة (*as-sāʿa*) (*the hour*), does not have the expected feminine, but instead (also according to Syro-Aramaic grammar) a masculine ending, will again be explained here by the evident need to rhyme.

There is still Sura 7:56: إن رحمت الله قريب من المحسنين (*The goodness of God is near to those who are righteous*). Here there is no excuse for the fact that the predicate قريب (*qarīb*[un]) (*near*), referring to the feminine رحمة (*raḥma*[ta]) (*goodness*), has a masculine ending. The real reason for this, however, is that when masculine Aramaic words are taken over into Arabic they customarily pass over into Arabic in the *status absolutus*, i.e. with the omission of their originally determining emphatic ending ܐ / *ā* (in other words: in the so-called *pausal form* in Arabic). Examples: Syro-Aramaic ܐܠܗܐ (*allāhā*) = Arabic الله (*allāh*) (*God*); ܩܪܝܒܐ (*qarīḇā*) = قريب (*qarīb*) (*near*).

In the present case, we must keep the Syro-Aramaic equivalent of إن رحمت الله قريب (*the goodness of God is near*) in mind as follows: ܪܚܡܬ ܐܠܗܐ ܩܪܝܒܐ (*reḥmaṯ allāhā qarīḇā*). According to this, the original Arabic form must have been قريبا (*qarībā*) (*near*). Arguing in favor of a primary Arabic transcription into قريب (*qarīb*) would be the explanation that an early copyist has taken the Syro-Aramaic predicate feminine ending in *status absolutus* ܩܪܝܒܐ (*qarīḇā*), which is formally indistinguishable from an attributive emphatic masculine ending, for such a masculine form and has, *mutatis mutandis*, *Arabicized* it, that is, by dropping the Syro-Aramaic emphatic *ā* ending, has converted it into the masculine Arabic pausal form.

The explanation of a secondary conjecture could be that a later copyist saw in the ending قريبا (*qarība*[n]) an Arabic accusative, which is here in obvious contradiction with the subsequently established Arabic grammar. This prescribes, namely, that in a noun clause introduced by the particle إنّ *inna* the subject is to be in the accusative, but the predicate in the nominative case. As such, however, قريبا (*qarība*[n]) has, according to

Arabic orthography, a masculine accusative ending. Instead of replacing it with the appropriate feminine ending, the final ا / *ā* was dropped without replacement. This is, to be sure, a mere supposition, the correctness of which could only be proven by corresponding examples from earlier Koran manuscripts.

In any case, the former explanation is confirmed by a further instance in Sura 3:40 : رب أنى يكون لي غلم وقد بلغني الكبر وامرأتي عاقر ("Lord, how shall I have a son when old age has now overtaken me and my wife [is] barren?"). Here, too, عاقر (*ʿāqir*) (*barren*) is a predicate of امراتي (*my wife*) and has, from the point of view of Arabic, a masculine ending. As discussed above, however, this is based upon an *optical illusion*, since the Syro-Aramaic *status absolutus* feminine ܥܩܪܐ (*ʿaqrā*) is formally indistinguishable from the *status emphaticus* masculine ܥܩܪܐ (*ʿaqrā*). Whence the conversion by analogy into the Arabic masculine pausal form.

Finally, the two instances in Sura 19:5 and 8, where it is repeated, وكانت امراتي عاقرا (*wa-kānat imraʾatī ʿāqiraⁿ*) ("in that my wife is *barren*"), are not to be explained by the need to rhyme. Here the Syro-Aramaic spelling of the *status absolutus* feminine ܥܩܪܐ (> عاقرا) (*ʿaqrā*) is faithfully reproduced.

Omission of the Feminine Ending of the Adjective in Classical Arabic

This rule of Syro-Aramaic grammar according to which the *status absolutus* feminine in the predicate adjective and participle, through the dropping of the ܬ / *t* and the retention of the final ܐ / *ā*, does not differ formally from the *status emphaticus* of the corresponding attributive masculine form, now opens our eyes to a phenomenon of classical Arabic grammar that has until now been considered a mystery. Carl Brockelmann (*Arabische Grammatik* [*Arabic Grammar*] § 65) summarizes this phenomenon as follows:

Note 1. "Thus the adjectives that refer to the sexual life of a

woman or a female also do not require the feminine ending, such as مرضع (*murḍiʿun*) 'suckling,' عاقر (*ʿāqirun*) 'barren.'.
2. The adjectives فعول (*faʿūlun*) in the active and فعيل (*faʿīlun*) in the passive sense as well as كذوب (*kaḏūbun*) "lying" and جريح (*ǧarīḥun*) "wounded" also take no a feminine ending as predicate and attribute."

Brockelmann derives this analogy from those Semitic words that are also feminine in gender without a feminine ending. He makes no mention of the Aramaic background, although the first group is documented in the Koran and the adjectives named in the second group فعول (*faʿūl*) and فعيل (*faʿīl*) clearly point the way to the equivalent Aramaic (or Syro-Aramaic) prototypes.

But even before him Theodor Nöldeke drew attention to the problem. In his study *Zur Grammatik des classischen Arabisch* [*On the Grammar of Classical Arabic*] (Vienna, 1897; reprint Darmstadt, 1963), he remarks in this connection (20 §19):

> "In the case of adjectives, the use or omission of the feminine ending ة merits a more comprehensive examination. What the ancient and modern grammarians have given[285] does not exhaust the subject. In Sura 22:2, تذهل كل مرضعة عما أرضعت, one would expect مرضع; the feminine form is explained very artificially."

Nöldeke would surely have been able to recognize the quite simple reason for this phenomenon, if only his view had not been obstructed by his respect for the exaggerated antiquity of the so-called old Arabic poetry. As already discussed with regard to the example from Sura 22:2 cited above, there is no reason to leave off the feminine ending of مرضعة

285 Note 1: "See, among others, Sib. 2, 222 f.; Ibn Qotaiba, "Adab alkâtîb," 104 ff.; Mufassal 83; contribution at 268 f.; Reckendorf 18. The reason for the phenomenon that the feminine ending is lacking in the case of so many feminine adjectives is still fully obscure. It is true though that in the case of words of feminine sexual meaning this could be connected with the fact that the Semitic substantives that exclusively designate what is by nature feminine, all seem to have originally been without a feminine ending… .".

(*murḍiʿaᵗ*) (*one giving suck*) according to Syro-Aramaic grammar since this word does not assume a predicate position in the sentence. That is also why it appears correctly in the *status emphaticus* with the feminine ending.

It's a different story for the other examples, ويا جارتا بيني فإنك طالقه "Oh, neighbor woman (= wife), go forth, you are dismissed" (line 8) and وراءك عني طالقا "retire from me as dismissed" (line 9), where the underlined expressions appear as predicates in the *status absolutus* feminine and thus have the corresponding (Syro-Aramaic) *ā* (not the Arabic ة / *t*) ending, insofar as one can regard the vowel less final ه / *h* in طالقه as a variant for the emphatic final ا (*ṭāliqā*).

Thus, the phenomenon of the lacking feminine ending in certain adjectives and participles originally appearing in a predicate position in the Koran and in classical Arabic is explained as an Aramaic (or Syro-Aramaic) substratum.

Misinterpretation or Mistaking of Syro-Aramaic Roots

Sura 16:79 provides us with two examples of the mistaking or misinterpretation of Syro-Aramaic roots; there we read:

الم يروا الى الطير مسخرت في جو السما ما يمسكهن الا الله

Our Koran translators have understood this verse as follows:

> (Bell I 256): 81. "Have they not seen the birds, performing their service in the midst of the heaven, no one holding them but Allah?"

> (Paret 222): "Haben sie denn nicht gesehen, wie die Vögel in der Luft des Himmels in den Dienst (Gottes) gestellt sind? Gott allein hält sie (oben, so daß sie nicht herunterfallen)."

> (Blachère 299): "N'avez-vous pas vu les oiseaux soumis [*au Seigneur*] dans l'espace du ciel où nul ne les soutient hormis Allah?"

1. For the expression في جو السما (*fī ǧaww^i s-samā*ʾ) Bell, with his translation "in the midst of the heaven," was the only one who correctly recognized from the context the equivalent Syro-Aramaic root expression ܒܓܘ ܫܡܝܐ (*b-ḡaw šmayyā*ʾ) (cf. *Thes.* I 665: ܒܓܘ (*b-ḡaw*) *intra, in medio* ("*inside, in the midst of*"). As a Syro-Aramaic substratum the expression جوّا (*ǧawwā* / *ǧəwwā*ʾ) (*inside*), as the opposite of برّا (*barrā*ʾ) (< Syro-Aramaic ܒܪܐ / *barrā* "*outside*"), is quite common in contemporary Arabic dialects of the Near East, both adverbially and as a preposition (as in جوّاة البيت *ǧəwwāt əl-bēt* "*inside the house*"), yet not in classical or modern written Arabic. It is very likely that in today's Arabic the common expressions البريد الجوي (*al-barīd al-ǧawwī*ʾ) (*airmail*), السلاح الجوي (*as-silāḥ al-ǧawwī*) (*airforce*), الخطوط الجوية (*al-ḫuṭūṭ al-ǧawwīya*) (*air routes, airlines*), النشرة الجوية (*an-našra l-ǧawwīya*) (*weather report*), etc. are traceable back to the unrecognized Syro-Aramaic prepositional expression ܒܓܘ (*b-ḡaw*) = Arabic في جوّ (*fī ǧaww*) (*inside, in the midst of*) in Sura 16:79 and its misinterpretation as a noun (*air*, *atmosphere*).

Now, even if جوّ (*ǧaww*) in the mentioned Sura has been read correctly, it has nonetheless been misunderstood. On the other hand, the spelling الحوايا (allegedly *al-ḥawāyā*) (< Syro-Aramaic ܓܘܝܐ / *gwāyē*) (the *innards*) in Sura 6:146 has been correctly understood, but uncorrectly read. That is also why it has not been recognized that both expressions stem from one and the same Syro-Aramaic root.

2. In the Koranic usage of the verb سخر (*saḫḫara*) it has until now apparently not been noticed by Koran scholars that two Syro-Aramaic roots must here be distinguished from one another:

a) ܫܚܪ (*šaḥḥar*), which corresponds to the Arabic سخّر (*saxxara*) (cf. *Mannā*, 784a: 1. فحّم. سوّد / *faḥḥamaṭ sawwada* / *to blacken, to make black* [this meaning has been retained with the unchanged pronunciation شحّر / *šaḥḥara* in Arabic]; 2. فضح. هتك / *faḍaḥa, hataka* / *to disgrace, to expose*; 3. سخّر. شغّل / *saxxara, šaǧǧala* / *to exploit, to make someone work without pay*). Without exception our Koran translators have based their translations on this last meaning, which has entered into Arabic with the Arabicized pronunciation سخر (*saḫḫara*).

b) What has been overseen in the process, however, is that with the spelling سخر (*saḫḫara*) the Koran is also reproducing the Syro-Aramaic causative stem (*šafʿel*) ܫܘܚܪ (*šawḥar*). This, however, is cognate with the root ܐܚܪ (*eḥar*) and is a variant of the causative stem (*afʿel*) ܐܘܚܪ (*awḥar*), which corresponds to the Arabic أخّر (*aḫḫara*). For example, for this the *Thes.* (I 125f.) gives in Arabic the (transitive as well as intransitive or reflexive) أخّر (*aḫḫara*) (*to hold back, to detain*), تأخّر (*taʾaḫḫara*) (*to be late, to stay*); and for ܫܘܚܪ (*šawḥar*): *retardavit, retinuit* (*to hold back, to hold onto*). Although the last meaning emerges clearly from the context of Sura 16:79, and in particular from the subsequent Arabic verb ما يمسكهن الا الله (*only God holds onto them*), none of our Koran translators have noticed that here مسخرت (*musaḫḫarāt*) cannot mean "*to be in the service of*". Read as the Syro-Aramaic ܡܫܘܚܪܬܐ (*m-šawḥrātā*) (*held back, held onto*), the verse has the following meaning:

"For have they not seen how the birds stay in the middle of the sky (whereby) only God is holding onto them?"

Depending on the context it will accordingly be necessary to examine whether in a given passage the Koran means with the Arabic سخر (*saḫḫara*) (a) the Syro-Aramaic ܫܚܪ (*šaḥḥar*) (*to subject, to make subservient*) or (b) ܫܘܚܪ (*šawḥar*) in the Arabic sense of اخر (*aḫḫara*) (*to detain, to hold back*).

This idea that God holds the birds *suspended* in the sky and *prevents* them from falling to the earth is also based on the verbal form مواخر (*mawāḫir*) in Sura 16:14 and 35:12. There it is said of ships on the sea وترى الفلك مواخر فيه / فيه مواخر that they are "*ploughing through it*" (Bell I 250). Paret translates "Und du siehst die Schiffe darauf (ihre) *Furchen ziehen*" (216, 359), and Blachère *"voguer"* (293).

Yet the Arabic plural form مواخر (*mawāḫir*) is not, as until now wrongly assumed, based on the imaginary Arabic root مخر (*maḫara*), which has falsely entered into the Arabic lexicography with the likewise imaginary meaning of "*to plow, to plow furrows*" (see, for example, H. Wehr, *Arabisches Wörterbuch*, where ماخر / *māḫir* supposedly means "*cutting through the water, a ship setting to sea*" and ماخرة / *māḫira* (plural مواخر / *mawāḫir*) supposedly even means "*ship*"). Instead, what we have here is a Syro-Aramaic masculine plural present participle ܡܘܚܪܝܢ (*m-awḥrīn*) (the feminine plural being ܡܘܚܪ̈ܢ / *m-awḥrān*) of the causative stem ܐܘܚܪ (*awḥar*) (*to hesitate, to linger, to stay*). This means that ships *linger* on the sea (on the *surface of the water*) (i.e., that God *prevents* them from *sinking*).

This again shows how Western Koran scholars have allowed themselves to be led astray by Arabic philologists who, in ignorance of Syro-Aramaic, have once more taken the prefix *m-* (from ܡܘܚܪ / *m̲-awḥar*) for a radical. This has also led A. Jeffrey to place مواخر (*mawākhir*) in the corresponding alphabetical order (*m-*). He explains the expression as follows:

> "Plu. of ماخرة (*māḫira* ^{tun}), that which ploughs the waves with a clashing noise, i.e. a ship. Zimmern, *Akkad. Fremdw*, suggests that it was derived from Akk. *elippu māḫirtu*, a ship making its way out into a storm. If this is so it would have been an early borrowing direct from Mesopotamia."

Although the expression may stem directly from Mesopotamia, in any case not from the Akkadian *māḫirtu*, but from the *af'el* form of the Syro-Aramaic root ܐܚܪ (*eḥar*) (which is not common in *p'al*), namely ܐܘܚܪ (*awḥar*), whose masculine singular and plural present participles are, respectively, ܡܘܚܪ (*m-awḥar*) and ܡܘܚܪܝܢ (*m-awḥrīn*, the feminine being ܡܘܚܪ̈ܢ *m-awḥrān*) (cf. *Thes.* I 125 f.: act. part. ܡܘܚܪ [*m-awḥar*] *moratur, cunctatur, tardat* [*he is hesitating, lingering, staying*]). The Koran gives the last form with the Arabic plural of nouns مواخر (according to the modern reading, *ma-wāḫir*),[286] where here too the middle *alif* ا / *ā* is

286 The lack of the earlier Syro-Aramaic feminine ending plural (*-ān*) of the participle in Arabic is substituted in the Koran mostly by the suffix *–āt* of the regular feminine plural (*pluralis sanus* / *sound plural*) of *verbal adjectives* (as substantives), but also sporadically (in contradiction to the *classical Arabic*) by the irregular plural form (*pluralis fractus* / *broken plural*) of some nouns derived from participles (e.g. باخرة /*bāḫira* [*steamboat*], plural بواخر / *bawāḫir*) as in this case (مواخر /*mawāḫir*(*a*) instead of classical Arabic مؤخّرة /*mu'aḫḫara*). A fur-

possibly secondary. However, because this form is foreign to Arabic, one can see in it a transliteration of the Syro-Aramaic participle adapted to the Arabic plural. Karl Vollers (*Volkssprache und Schriftsprache* 90) had considered it difficult to say whether مواخر (*mawāḫir*) should be viewed as an offshoot of أخر (*aḫara*). It is thus scarcely necessary to consider his further remarks on the root مخر (*maḫara*) (189 f.) and the corresponding references (namely to the later use of ماخر / *māḫir* in Arabic poetry in the sense of "*ship, sailing vessel*" according to *ZDMG* 40, 575).

The idea that God is maintaining ships (*letting them linger*) on the water's surface also underlies the verb سخر (*saḫḫara*) (<ܫܘܚܪ / *šawḥar*) in Sura 14:32 and the synonymous verb يرجئ (*yurǧi*^{ʾu}) (= يسخر / *yusaḫ-ḫir*^{u}) (*he maintains = he causes to linger*) in Sura 17:66, which has been misread (and just as falsely included in the Arabic lexicography) as يزجي (*yuzǧī*, allegedly "*to drive along*"). The same is true of the sun, moon and stars, which "*linger*" in heaven at God's command (مسخرات / *musaḫḫarāt*. = ܡܫܘܚܪܢ / *m-šawḥrān*) (Sura 7:54; 16:12), as well as of the clouds (السحاب / *as-saḥāb*) that are "*maintained*" (مسخر / *musaḫḫar* = ܡܫܘܚܪ / *m-šawḥar*) (and not, as in Bell, "*performing their service*," or Paret "*in Dienst gestellt sind,*" and Blachère "*soumis*") between heaven and earth (Sura 2:162/164).

Georg Hoffmann, in a review of two University of Göttingen dissertations published in "Bibliographische Anzeigen [Bibliographical Reports]" (*ZDMG* 32, 1878, 738-63), has already drawn attention to the phenomenon of the occasional disappearance of و / *w* in the diphthong *aw* and the concomitant compensatory lengthening of the preceding vowel *a* in many an Eastern Aramaic dialect. Following the Eastern Syrian lexicographers *Bar Bahlūl* he reports that among the Aramean of Ḥarrān as well as in Ṭrīhān, the region from Ḥaṭra on the Tigris downstream to Teg^{h}rît^{h} (Teḡrīṯ / Takrīt) and Samarra, m<u>āše</u> was said for *mauše*, in Arabic *mauš* (with a reference to *Bar ʿAlī* 5588). Thus *ā* would have emerged here from *au* by way of the Nestorian (i.e. Eastern Syrian) $\bar{a}^{u}$.

ther example may be found in Sura 42:33, where it is said of the ships رواكد / *rawākid*(*a*) (*still, stagnant*) instead of classical Arabic راكدة / *rākida*).

This is probably also why one pronounced ררב *rāreḇ* (instead of ܪܘܪܒ / *rawreḇ*)[287] (op. cit. 756).

The localization of this phenomenon in the East Syrian-Mesopotamian region may give us an interesting clue concerning the orthography of many a word in the Koran. In this regard the Koranic spelling of سخر (*saḫḫara*) for the Syro-Aramaic ܫܘܚܪ (*šawḥar*) seems to provide a parallel, though here too, at any rate according to the traditional reading, instead of the compensatory lengthening of the preceding vowel *a*, a doubling of the following consonant occurs. However, one must not overlook the fact that the Syro-Aramaic verbal stem under discussion, *šafʿel* , is unknown in Arabic and for this reason a distinction could not be made between سخر (*saḫḫara*) for ܫܚܪ (*šaḥḥar*) and ܫܘܚܪ (*šawḥar*), which is why, in the last instance, analogy is to be assumed to the verbal stem which has made its way into Arabic. سخر (*saḫḫara*), This example precisely illustrates the problem, that not only different verbal classes are identifiable behind the *scriptio defectiva* (defective spelling) of the Koran, but also verbal roots that have to be distinguished from one another.

On the Etymology of the Koranic Word صراط (*ṣirāṭ*)

Regarding the etymology of the word صراط (*ṣirāṭ*), Jeffery (p. 195 f.) refers to the early Arab philologists, who had taken it to be a borrowing from Greek. He concedes that they are right, but he points out that the Greek word is in fact a Hellenized form of the Latin *strata*. However, all the Western authorities cited by Jeffery (*Fraenkel, Kremer, Dvořák, Vollers*) seem to have overlooked the fact that the Koranic orthography is merely the phonetic transcription of the Syro-Aramaic ܣܪܛܐ (*serṭā* and *srāṭā*ʾ) or ܣܘܪܛܐ (*surṭā*ʾ). Jeffery also cites the variants سراط / *sirāṭ* and زراط / *zirāṭ*, whereby the latter variant also corresponds to the Syro-Aramaic ܙܪܛܐ / *zerṭā* (as recorded in *Thes*. II 2739). Under the verbal root ܣܪܛ (*sraṭ*) the *Thes.* (II 2738 f.) gives the following corre-

287 This would explain the creation of the Arabic interrogative particle أ / *ʾa* from the Syro-Aramaic ܐܘ / *aw* (see below, p. 245, note 300).

sponding Arabic words: (a) شرط (*šaraṭa*), (2) *scalpsit* (*to score, to striate*) (b) it. *lineas duxit, delineavit, scripsit,* كتب .خط (*ḫaṭṭa* , *kataba*) (*to draw a line ,or write*). Furthermore, the *Thes.* (II 2739) gives under the nouns ܣܪܛܐ (*serṭā*ʾ) and ܣܘܪܛܐ (*surṭā*ʾ) the corresponding Greek *γραμμή* and Latin *linea* (*line*), as well as the Arabic metathesis سطر (*saṭr*) (*line*) that is quite common in today's Arabic. The verbal form سطر (*saṭara*) (*to write*) occurs five times in the Koran (Sura 17:58; 33:6; 52:2; 54:53; 68:1) (Jeffery p. 169 f.).

Consequently, the Koranic expression صراط مستقيم (*ṣirāṭ mustaqīm*) does not mean *"straight path"* but *"straight line."* Therefore, one is justified in asking whether the Latin *strata* does not come from Syro-Aramaic ܣܪܛܐ (*srāṭā*ʾ), with the emphatic phoneme *ṣ* being rendered by *st*. As proof for this thesis one can cite the historically attested Greek and Latin transcription of the name of the North Nabatean town بصره /*Boṣra* as *Βοστρα* and *Bostra* respectively, whereas the first *t* in the Latin word *strata* is not found in the Koranic spellingصراط /*ṣirāṭ*. In one case the emphatic phoneme *ṣ* is rendered in Greek and Latin by *ps* as attested in the name of the town ܡܨܝܨܬܐ (*Maṣṣiṣtā*), which is transcribed as *Mopsuestia* (see *Thes*. II 2195).

Are Latin lexicographers right in deriving *strata* from the verb *sternō* (to sprinkle and, only secondarily. *to flatten, to pave*), or, given the secondary meaning of this verbal root, unless the Latin is a coincidental allophone of the Koranic word, is not this etymology more likely a fiction? The usage of line in the sense of way is, moreover, quite common in modern European languages, as for example in English bus line or in German *Eisenbahnlinie* (*railway line*). It is therefore not contradicted by the Koranic parallel expression سواء السبيل (*sawāʾ as-sabīl*) (< Syro-Aramaic ܫܘܝܘܬ ܫܒܝܠܐ / *šawyūṯ š īlā*, *the straight path*, literally: *the straightness of the path*) (Sura 2:108; 5:12,60,77; 60:1).

On the etymology of the word قصر (*qaṣr*)

A further example of the Greek and Latin transcription of the emphatic phoneme *ṣ* by *st* is the Koranic word قصر (*qaṣr*) (< *castle*) (Suras 7:74; 22:45; 25:10;), borrowed from Eastern Syro-Aramaic "קצרא (*qaṣrā*ʾ) as allophone of Syro-Aramaic ܓܙܪܐ (*gzārā*) / ܓܙܝܪܬܐ (*gzirtā*)[288] and transcribed in Latin as *castrum* and in Greek as *κάστρον* (Jeffery p. 240). All the western specialists quoted by Jeffery (*Guidi*, *Fraenkel*, *Nöldeke*, *Krauss*, *Vollers*) have overlooked this phonetic phenomenon. If Jeffery is right with his assertion that this word has no verbal root in Arabic, it does not automatically follow that the root must be either Greek or Latin. The Arabic form قصر (*qaṣr*ͦ) is a direct borrowing from Eastern Syro-Aramaic קצרא (*qaṣrā*) (morphologically a passive participle like ܣܥܛܐ / *saʿṭā*, ܣܥܛܢܐ / *saʿṭānā* > *sāṭānā* = *Satan* – see above p. 100 ff.), the root of which is a phonetic variant of Syro-Aramaic ܓܙܪ (*gzar*) with the original meaning *"to cut"* (referring to the *crenelated* wall or to *"cut"* trenches or any trench-like defensive measures giving protection from assailants *"cutting"* fortifications).

That according to Nöldeke (ZDMG xxix 423) "קצרא (*qaṣrā*) as used in the Mishnah and Jerusalem Talmud is but a form of קסטרא (*qasṭrā*ͦ), which like (Syriac) ܩܣܛܪܐ (*qasṭrā*ͦ) was derived directly from *κάστρον*" (Jeffery 240, note 6), is get it backwards. Both Aramaic קסטרא (*qasṭrā*) and Syriac ܩܣܛܪܐ (*qasṭrā*) (scarcely used in Syro-Aramaic, though quoted in dictionaries) are nothing but a secondary re-borrowing from Latin *castrum* or Greek *κάστρον*. Hence it follows that Latin *castrum*[289] > (diminutive) *castellum castellum castellum* > English

---

288 See C. Brockelmann. Lexicon Syriacum, 112 b, under ܓܙܝܪܬܐ (*gzirtā*), 5. *pinna muri* (*battlement*); further in *Mannā*, 102 b, (4) حجر منحوت مربع (stine cut square), (9) شرفقزة افريز البناء (battlement), (3) رحبة هيكل او دير مسورة (a courtyard protected by a wall in a temple or monastery). From the battlement of the wall as rampart of en encampment, this word passed on to the whole fortress, citadel. The Syro-Aramaic verbal root ܓܙܪ (*gzar*) (*to cut*) explains the original meaning of Arabic جزيرة (*ǧazīra*) (*island* = *"cut" from the mainland*) as direct borrowing from Syro-Aramaic ܓܙܝܪܬܐ (*gzirtā*).

289 The relation of *castrum* with the Old Aramaic verbal root קצר (*qṣar*) (*to cut*) (cf. S. Segert, *Altaramäische Grammatik* [*Old Aramaic Grammar*], *Glossar* [*glossary*] p. 550: קצר / *qṣar* "*ernten* [*to harvest*] (?)" – properly *"to cut"*, as in New Hebrew – cf. W. Gesenius, *Hebräisches und Aramäisches Handwörterbuch*, 722a) helps us again to elucidate the etymology of the Latin verbal root *castrō* (*to castrate*) in its original meaning according to the semantics of the Syro-Aramaic root. Therewith the proper sense of the derived Latin word *cas-*

castle, German *Kastell*, French *château* (and similar words in other European languages) are a borrowing from Syro-Aramaic via Greek and Latin.

These examples show how the etymology can contribute to reveal us, be it in a small way, a hidden side of a former cultural interchange in the Mediterranean area between East and West. Some of these borrowed Semitic words in Greek and Latin are traceable in the Occident to the Phoenicians, whose language is closely akin to Hebrew and Syro-Aramaic, or to the Hellenes in the Orient since Alexander the Great. This can explain the etymology of some still unexplained (or incorrectly explained) Greek or Latin words as e.g. *taurus* (*bull;Taurus*) < Greek *ταῦρος*, that C. Brockelmann (*Lexicon Syriacum* 819b) compares to Syro-Aramaic ܬܘܪܐ (*tawrā*) and Arabic ثور (*ṯawr*). Yet rather than a common Semitic origin (SEM) assumed by Brockelmann, the original meaning of this word can be concluded from the secondary Syro-Aramaic verbal root ܬܘܪ /*twar* < ܬܒܪ /*tḇar* (*to break*, *to cut up* [the soil, the field] = *to plough*). This meaning makes clear the Koranic passage in Sura 2:71, where the cow that Moses demands from his people as sacrifice is described as follows:

يقول انها بقرة لا ذلول <u>تثير</u> الارض ولا تسقي الحرث مسلمة لا شية فيها

(Bell I 10, 66.): "He says, she is to be a cow not <u>broken</u> in to plough up the land or to <u>irrigate</u> the cultivated ground, but kept sound without a blemish upon her. "

Philological analysis:

a) According to Old Aramaic (whereof in some Syro-Aramaic verbal adjectives still preserved forms) as well as to Hebrew, ذلول / *ḏalūl* is grammatically a passive participle (like رسول / *rasūl*

---

trātus (*castrated* = "*cut*" = *eunuch*) becomes clear. Both Old Aramaic and Syro-Aramaic variants (קצר /*qṣar* with the variant כצר /*kṣar* and ܓܙܪ /*gzar*) continue as substratum in Arabic (as قصر /*qaṣara* [*to restrict*, *restrain*, *confine*], *qaṣura* [*to be* or *to become short*, *to be unable*], كسر /*kasara* [*to break* < *to cut*] and جزر /*ğazara* [*to slaughter* < *to cut*], therefrom جزار /*ğazār* [*butcher*]) with some further semantical variations.

[*messenger*] = مرسل / *mursal* [*dispatched*]) and were to be rendered in classical Arabic accordingly by مذللة / *mu<u>d</u>allala* in the sense of مسخّرة / *musa<u>hh</u>ara* (*subjected, made subservient*). The lack of the feminine ending in ذلول / *<u>d</u>alūl* (instead of ذلولة / *<u>d</u>alūla*) is due to the dropping of the feminine end-*t* of the Syro-Aramaic participle in predicative position (as explained above p. 217 ff.). Thereby the latter form (as *status absolutus*) is orthographically no longer to be distinguished from the masculine participle in attributive position as *status emphaticus* (*ܕܠܘܠܐ / *dalōlā* > *dalūlā* = ܕܠܝܠܐ / *dalīlā*). This explains the analogous transposition of the Syro-Aramaic predicative feminine form into the Arabic masculine form (as in Sura 7:56: ان رحمت اللـــه <u>قريب</u> [*qarīb*] instead of <u>قريبة</u> [*qarība* = Syro-Aramaic ܩܪܝܒܐ / *qarī<u>b</u>ā*] من المحسنين [*assuredly, the mercy of God is near to the benefactors = those who do well, right*]).

b) The following verbal form تثير / *tu<u>t</u>īr*ᵘ, derived from the secondary Syro-Aramaic verbal root ܬܘܪ / *twar* > ܬܪ / *tār*, renders the Afʿel form ܐܬܝܪ / *a<u>t</u>īr* with the meaning quoted by *Mannā* (833b) under (3): حرث. فلح الأرض / *ḥara<u>t</u>a, falaḥa l-arḍ* (*to plough, to till the land*).
This meaning makes clear that the derived noun ܬܘܪܐ / *tawrā* is etymologically the form from which the Arabic, Greek and Latin words ثور / *<u>t</u>awr, ταῦρος* and *taurus* are borrowed and that semantically, according to Syro-Aramaic ܬܘܪܐ / *tawrā*, the proper meaning of this word was originally a *"plough-(animal)"* (and not necessarily a *bull*).

c) The spelling تسقى / *tasqī*, as imperfect of the Arabic root سقى / *saqā* (< Syro-Aramaic ܫܩܐ / *šqā*) means indeed *"to give to drink = to irrigate"*. Yet who has observed the agricultural labor knows that the working order subsequent to the ploughing is not to *irrigate* the cultivated ground, but to *harrow* it. Now, to obtain this sense, we just need to read the *retroflexed* Arabic end-ـى / *ī* (ـے), as it is attested in the Koran codex of Samarqand (CD 0024, l. 2; see p. 348), as a Syriac end-ܢ / *n* (= Arabic ـن / *n*) and to strike out one dot on the ـقـ / *q* to obtain the Arabic reading تسفن /

tasfīn[u] (< Syro-Aramaic ܫܦܢ / *šp̄an*) instead of the false modern Arabic transcription تسقى – misread as *tasqī*. The Syro-Aramaic verbal root ܫܦܢ / *šp̄an* explains *Mannā* (801b) in Arabic as follows: سلف سوّى الأرض بالمسلفة لتزرع / *salafa, sawwā l-arḍ bi-l-mislafa li-tuzraʿ* (*to harrow, to level the field with a harrow for sowing*). The *Lisān* (XIII 209b f.) is not able to understand what the root سفن / *safana* exactly means, since he interprets it approximately by قشر / *qašara* (*to peel*). Consequently, the solely derived and in modern Arabic very common word سفينة / *safīna* (*ship, boat*) is so called, because it *peels* the surface of the water (لأنها تسفن وجه الماء أي تقشره), whereas the Syro-Aramaic verb means *to glide* on the water surface. Hence سفينة / *safīna* means properly a *"glider"*.

d) Since the Arabs have borrowed the agricultural expressions from the Arameans,[290] it is only logical that the Koranic word حرث / *ḥart̲* (a *ploughed* field) is a direct borrowing from Syro-Aramaic ܚܪܬܐ / *ḥart̲ā* < verbal root ܚܪܬ / *ḥrat̲* (*to plough, to cleave*).[291] Yet the latter meaning suggests that the Syro-Aramaic verb is a secondary formation of an original root *mediae geminatae* *ܚܪ / *ḥarr* (>*ḥār*), of which some verbal adjectives are still conserved in Syro-Aramaic, as ܚܪܘܪܐ /*ḥrōrā* (*hole*), ܚܘܪܐ / *ḥurrā* (*hollow, cavern*), ܚܪܘܬܐ /*ḥarrūt̲ā* (*well, cistern*).[292] This original meaning shows that the Syro-Aramaic substantive ܚܪܬܐ / *ḥart̲ā* (= Koranic حرث / *ḥart̲*) is grammatically an early passive participle as attributive adjective (hence in the *status emphaticus*) with feminine ending (according to the feminine Syro-Aramaic ܐܪܥܐ / *arʿā* [*soil, field*]) as explained above on *Satan* (adjective masculine *ܚܪܪܐ / *ḥarrā* , feminine *ܚܪܪܬܐ / *ḥarrᵊt̲ā* > ܚܪܬܐ / *ḥart̲ā* = Koranic حرث / *ḥart̲*).

290 Cf. S. Fraenkel, *Die aramäischen Fremdwörter im Arabischen*, p. 125 ff.

291 Cf. C. Brockelmann, *Lexicon Syriacum*, 260a, 1. *fodit, excavavit* (*to dig, to excavate*); Mannā, 267a: حرث. فلح. شق / *ḥarat̲a, falaḥa, šaqqa* (*to plough, to till, to cleave*).

292 Cf. *Mannā*, 259b.

Thus it appears that the Syro-Aramaic verb ܚܪܬ /*ḥraṯ* (> Arabic حرث /*ḥaraṯa*) is formed by the addition of the feminine ending of the attributive participle to the original verbal root *ܚܪ / *ḥarr* (> *ḥār*). Both Syro Aramaic verbs ܐܬܪ / *aṯīr* (> Arabic أثار / *aṯāra*) < ܬܒܪ / *tḇar* > *ܬܘܪ / *twar* > ܬܪ / *tār* as well as ܚܪܬ / *ḥraṯ* (> Arabic حرث / *ḥaraṯa*) turn out to be synonyms as to their original meaning (*to cleave*, *to break up* [the ground]).

e) The Koranic verbal adjective مسلمة / *musallama* (*perfect*, *faultless*) renders the Syro-Aramaic passive participle of the second stem ܡܫܠܡܐ / *m-šallᵊ mā* > *m-šalmā* and corresponds to the common Arabic form سالمة / *sālima* or سليمة / *salīma*. The end ـه / *-h* in the Koranic spelling is an alternative writing of the Syro-Aramaic end-*ā* that marks the Aramaic feminine *status absolutus* of the predicative participle (without end-*t*). Grammatically, it does not differ from the pausal form ذلول / *ḏalūl*, that in Syro-Aramaic must be written with an end-*h* or an end-*ā* (ذلوله = ذلولا / *ḏalūlā*). From the point of view of the historical Semitistics, the reading of the Cairo version is erroneous as far as the Aramaic end-*h* has been taken for an Arabic ـة / *tāʾ marbūṭa*. Consequently, the Koranic spelling مسلمه, as accurate Aramaic orthography, is to be read without dots on the ـه / *-h* and without hypercorrect classical Arabic inflection (*nunation*): *"mu-sallama"* (and not *mu-sallama-tun*).

f) Presumably, non-Arabs must have read the next spelling شية as *šiyata* – that hardly exists in Arabic. The supposed root وشى / *wašā*, from which the noun شية / *šiya* is supposed to be derived, as explained by *Ṭabarī* (I 351 ff.), is nothing but a conceived secondary form of the root *وشح / *wašaḥa* (used in the IInd, Vth and VIIIth stem) as denominative from the noun وشاح / *wišāḥ* (*ornamented belt*) by dropping of the end-ح / *ḥ* (a phenomenon that occurs in some dialects). It is hence not a mere accident that the imagined root وشى / *wašā* has quite the same derived sense (*to decorate*, *embellish with many colors*). The second meaning attributed to this root, as quoted in the dictionaries (cf. for example H. Wehr: *to slander*, *defame*; *to denounce*, *betray*) is probably due to the mistranscription of the Syro-Aramaic ܪ / *r* of the verbal root ܪܫܐ / *ršā* as an Arabic و /*w* = وشى / *wašā* instead of رشى = رشا / *rašā* (cf. *Mannā* 755b: رشا. برطل / *rašā*, *barṭala* [*to bribe*], 2. لام. عتب. مّذ / *lāma*, *ʿataba*, *ḏamma* [*to blame, censure, dispraise*]; under Afʿel ܐܪܫܝ / *aršī* : قرّف. اتهم / *qarrafa*, *ittahama* [*to charge*, *suspect*, *accuse*]). The general meaning supposed by some commentators relates to the clearness of the colour of the cow, while some others are of the opinion that she has to be without any blemish. The latter sense can be approximately confirmed, if we read instead of شية / *šiyata* : لا شبه فيها / *lā* *šibha* or *šubha* *fīhā* "without [any] *suspicion*" (as to her blamelessness).

After this philological analysis, the discussed passage of Sura 2:71 can henceforth be reconstructed as follows:

يقول انها بقرة لا ذلول تثير الارض ولا تسفن الحرث مسلمه لا شبه فيها

(*yaqūl*(*u*) *innahā baqara*(*tun*) *lā* *ḏalūl*(*a*) *tu-ṯīr*(*u*) *l-arḍ*(*a*) *wa-lā tasfin*(*u*) *l-ḥarṯ*(*a*), *mu-sallama lā šibh*(*a*)/*šubh*(*a*) *fīhā*)

"He says: she is to be neither a cow *subjected* to *plough* the soil nor to *harrow* the *ploughed* [field], [she shall be] faultless, without [any] *suspicion* [as to her blamelessness]."

Further misunderstood identical spellings

The same homonymous root of the latter form, written with the alternative emphatic ص / ṣ in Sura 52:37, المصيطرون (*al-muṣayṭirūn*), and Sura 88:22, مصيطر (*muṣayṭir*), was falsely understood as *"to dominate."* With the stereotypical phrase اختلف أهل التأويل في تأويل ذلك (*the commentators are divided in their opinions of this word*), *Ṭabarī* (XXVII 33 f.) in this regard quotes two meanings: (a) المسلطون / *al-musallaṭūn* (*those who are established as rulers*), (b) المنزلون / *al-munazzilūn* (*those who cause to descend* – in the context of Sura 52:37 [according to Bell] – from the *treasuries of thy Lord*). Although this understanding is nearer to the intended sense, *Ṭabarī* decides in favor of the majority of commentators who conjecture that صيطر / *ṣayṭara*, allegedly according to the *language use of the Arabs* (في كلام العرب), means *to dominate, to command, to be mighty*. This meaning has led to a verbal root that does not exist in any Arabic dialect or any Semitic language. Nonetheless, this fictitious root has persisted in modern Arabic to this day in this sole irregular form (*fay'al*), in a false lexical order and with this false meaning. But actually, the intercalated يـ / *y*, pronounced correctly as the diphthong *ay*, serves here to dissolve the following gemination of the medial radical of the second stem صطر / *ṣaṭṭara* = سطر / *saṭṭara* < Syro-Aramaic ܣܛܪ / *saṭṭar* = Arabic شطر / *šaṭara*, **šaṭṭara* = قسم / *qasama, qassama, "to divide, to distribute"* (cf. *Mannā*, 410b). This phenomenon is known in a small number of verbs of the second stem in some local Arabic dialects of the Near East, as for example in بدل / *baddal* > بيدل /*baydal* (*to change*), بعّد / *baʿʿad* > بيعد / *bayʿad* (*to go far away*), دحش / *daḥḥaš* > ديحش / *dayḥaš* (*to cram, to stuff*), دخل / *daḫḫal* > ديخل / *dayḫal* (*to make enter*), رجّع / *raǧǧaʿ* > ريجع / *rayǧaʿ* (*to give, to send back; to repeat, reiterate*), ضهر / *ḍahhar* > ضيهر / *ḍayhar* (*to bring out*), شلح / *šallaḥ* > شيلح / *šaylaḥ* (*to undress, to plunder*), ملح / *mallaḥ* > ميلح / *maylaḥ* (*to salt* – used in the passive participle مميلح / *m-maylaḥ, salted*), نزل / *nazzal* > نيزل / *nayzal* (*to make descend*), طلع / *ṭallaʿ* > طيلع / *ṭaylaʿ* (*to make ascend, to move out*). Further examples may exist in different individual dialects. In some few cases the inserted يـ / *y* can be substituted by a و / *w*, as e.g.: ركب / *rakkab* > روكب / *rawkab* (*to jam, get jammed / stuck* – Metathesis of ربك / *rabak*, إرتبك / *irtabak* [*to become embarrassed, get entangled, be caught, come to a standstill*]), صفر / *ṣaffar* > صوفر / *ṣawfar* (*to whistle*), عكر / *ʿakkar* > عوكر / *ʿawkar* (*to render turbid, to make cloudy*).[293]

Sometimes the و / *w* can be postponed, as e.g.: زعّط / *zaʿʿaṭ* > زعوط / *zaʿwaṭ*, زعّق / *zaʿʿaq* > زعوق / *zaʿwaq* (both *to scream, to shriek*), قرّش / *qarraš* > قروش / *qarwaš* (*to chatter, to gossip*). This phenomenon con-

293 Cf. Jacob Barth, *Die Nominalbildung in den semitischen Sprachen* [*Nominal Formation in the Semitic Languages*], 2d. ed. Leipzig 1894, reprint Hildesheim 1967, § 38. See also Siegmund Fraenkel, *Die aramäischen Fremdwörter im Arabischen* [*The Aramaic Foreign Words in the Arabic Language*], Leiden 1886, reprint Hildesheim – New York 1982, p. 184.

cern likewise substantives, as the common noun شوبك / *šawbak* (*rolling pin*), a secondary form of the *nomen agentis* *شبّاك / *šabbāk*, derived from شبّك / *šabbak* < Syro-Aramaic ܣܒܶܟ /*sabbek̲* (*to paste, to stick together*). S. Fraenkel and J. Barth had noticed this relatively scarce formation, but without to recognize its secondary character.[294] While namely S. Fraenkel considers the form فيعل / *fayʿal* to be genuine Arabic, adducing as argument the word *šayṭān*, that he takes for Ethiopian (see above p. 100 ff.), J. Barth sees these cases reduced only to substantives in Arabic and means that such forms apparently doe not occur in other (Semitic) languages. But in reality both S. Fraenkel and J. Barth have overlooked a) the above quoted verbal forms in spoken Arabic, b) at least two verbs in Syro-Aramaic, namely: ܗܝܡܢ / *haymen* < Old Aramaic ܗܡܢ* / *hammen* (> Arabic آمن / *'āmana* < أمّن / *'ammana*) (*to believe*) and ܣܝܒܪ / *saybar* < ܣܒܪ* / *sabbar* (> Arabic صبر / *ṣabara*) (*to be patient*, *to endure*, *to persevere*).

Since it is now clear that صيطر / *ṣayṭara* is nothing but a secondary form of the root صطر / *ṣaṭara* = سطر / *saṭara* < Syro-Aramaic ܣܛܪ / *sṭar* (from which the Arabic word ساطور / *sāṭūr*, *cleaver*, is morphologically and etymologically derived), the two Koranic passages are henceforth to be understood as follows:

(Sura 52:37): ام عندهم خزائن ربك ام هم المصيطرون

"Do they have the treasuries of your Lord? Are they the distributors?"

(Sura 88:21-22): فذكر انما انت مذكر / لست عليهم بمصيطر

"So warn, you are just a warner, you are not the distributor[295] (i.e.: the one who allots the retribution) among them."

The subsequent verses 23-26 confirm this meaning, since it is there said that it is God that will punish the unbelievers.

---

294 Cf. Siegmund Fraenkel, *Die aramäischen Fremdwörter im Arabischen* [*The Aramaic Foreign Words in the Arabic Language*], Leiden 1886, reprint Hildesheim – New York 1982, p. 184 f.; Jacob Barth, *Die Nominalbildung in den semitischen Sprachen* [*The Nominal Formation in the Semitic Languages*], 2nd ed. Leipzig 1894, reprint Hildesheim 1967, §§ 38, 135.

295 R. Bell (II 653) translates: "But thou art not over them an overseer" and notes to the last word: "The meaning and derivation of the word is not quite certain."

The same root is finally misread in Sura 2:126 :

ومن كفر امتعه قليلا ثم <u>اضطره</u> الى عذاب النار

> (Bell I 17, 120): "And whosoever disbelieves I shall give enjoyment of life for a little and shall then <u>drive</u> to the punishment of the fire…"

The eighth Arabic stem اضطر / *iṭṭarra* (by the Arab lexicographers falsely attributed to the root ضر / *ḍarra* [*to damage*, *to harm*], whereas the original meaning of Syro-Aramaic ܛܪܐ / *ṭrā* [*to strike*, *to overtake*] shows that the Arabic ض / *ḍ* is the result of a secondary sonorization of the Syro-Aramaic emphatic ܛ / *ṭ* > ض / *ḍ*)is primarily a reflexive (*to force oneself*) with a secondary passive meaning (*uṭṭura – to be forced*). Hence it is paradoxical to use this reflexive stem as a transitive, as if one were to say: *I shall be forced him*. The transitive meaning given in the dictionaries (*to force*, *oblige someone*) is contradictory and refers exclusively to this sole misreading in the Koran. To resolve this grammatical nonsense we only need to eliminate the point from ضـ / *ḍ* and to read: اصطره / *aṣṭuruhu* = اسطره / *asṭuruhu* = اشطره / *ašṭuruhu* – in the modern Arabic sense of افرزه / *afruzuhu: "I shall <u>segregate</u> him"* (to the punishment of the fire).

Excursus:
On the Morphology and Etymology of قريش *(Qurayš)*

The Arabic spelling قريش (Sura 106:1), taken for an Arabic diminutive and falsely pronounced *Qurayš*, corresponds morphologically to the Syro-Aramaic masculine plural of the passive participle ܩܪܝܫܐ / *qarīšē* > *qrīšē* = *gathered together*, i.e.: *foederati*, and hence is to be pronounced in Arabic (without the Syro-Aramaic ending *ē*) *Qarīš*. This meaning is attested in the *Lisān* (VI 335a) in one among other (from Aramaic) transmitted explanations as follows:

وقيل: سميت بذلك <u>لتقرّشها</u> أي <u>تجمّعها</u> إلى مكة من حواليها بعد تفرّقها
في البلاد حين غلب عليها قصيّ بن كلاب ، وبه سمّي قصيّ مجمّعا

"It is said: the name of *Qurayš* is derived from (the verb) *ta-qarraša* i.e. *ta-ǧammaʿa* (= *to meet, come together*) to Mecca from its surroundings after they (i.e. the *Qurayš / Qarīš*) were dispersed in the countries, when *Quṣayy* (atually *Qaṣī* < Syro-Aramaic ܩܨܝܐ /*qaṣyā* = the *Far One* – as far as he is said to be almost a Nabatean originating from Syria) *b. Kilāb* had triumphed over it; for this reason *Quṣayy / Qaṣī* was called *'assembler'*."

From this philological understanding *Qurayš / Qarīš* cannot be the name of a single tribe, particularly of that of the Prophet, as it is assured by the Islamic tradition. What this word designates is rather a *tribal confederation* known as *foederati* in the Eastern Roman Empire. It is hence not excluded that with these *Qurayš / Qarīš* (quoted once in Sura 106:1) the almost Christianized Arabs *foederati* of Syria were meant (to compare with Sura 30:2-5, where it is said that the *Believers* will rejoice about the victory of the Romans with the help of God). This would in return explain that *Quṣayy / Qaṣī*, said to be coming from Syria, was possibly able to occupy Mecca with the help of these *Qurayš / Qarīš* = *foederati* (assuming, however, that this account of the traditional Muslim historiography is authentic.[296]

From the original meaning of the Syro-Aramaic verbal root ܩܪܫ / *qraš* (*to gather* –that C. Brockelmann, *Lexicon Syriacum*, 702a II, takes mistakenly for a borrowing from Arabic قرش /*qaraša*), are further derived figurative meanings as quoted by *Mannā* (710a/b). To these meanings belong in classical Arabic: برد قارس / *bard qāris* (< Syro-Aramaic ܩܪܣܐ / *qarsā* – cf. *Mannā* 705b) (*biting coldness* – with regard to [a] the *together drawn* = *contracted* water by freezing, [b] the *gathered* = *contracted* limbs – under the influence of cold – making someone *to huddle up, to shiver with cold*); the variant قرص / *qaraṣa* (*to pinch* – by *gathering* = *pressing* the skin *together* between two fingers < Syro-Aramaic

296 Cf. on this subject Ǧawād ʿAlī, المفصّل في تاريخ العرب قبل الإسلام / *al-mufaṣṣal fī tārīḫ al-ʿarab qabl al-ʾislām* [*A Comprehensive History of Arabs before Islam*], vol. 8, 2nd ed., Beirut-Bagdad, 1978, p. 643; cf. also Alfred-Louis de PRÉMARE, *Les fondations de l'islam. Entre écriture et histoire* [*The Foundations of Islam. Between Scripture and History*], Paris, 2002, p. 57 ff.: *La saga des Quraysh* [*The Saga of the Quraysh*]).

ܩܪܨ / *qraṣ* – cf. C. Brockelmann, *op. cit.*, 699b; *Mannā* 707a); in spoken Arabic of the Near East قريش / قريشه / *qarīš* / *qarīše* (= Syro-Aramaic ܩܪܝܫܬܐ / *qrīštā*, ܩܪܘܫܬܐ / *qrōštā*, ܩܪܫܬܐ / *qraštā* – as passive participle rather than *qrāštā* [cf. C. Brockelmann, *op. cit.*, 701a], *colostrum – the first coagulated milk of mammals*); the latter in Northern Mesopotamia, pronounced *qārīše*, means a *belt* (serving to *gather* the garments); the same meaning in New Eastern Syriac ܩܪܝܫܐ (*qarīšā*) – pronounced: *qayīšā;* with regard to freezing cold ܐܬܩܪܫ / *eṯqreš* : *to huddle up = to shiver with cold.*

From the Syro-Aramaic variant ܩܪܨ / *qraṣ* in its figurative sense (*to press*) is finally derived Arabic قرصان / *qurṣān* – actually *qarṣān* (*corsair*, *pirate*) < Syro-Aramaic ܩܪܨܢܐ / *qarṣānā* = ܩܪܣܢܐ / *qarsānā* – cf. *Mannā* 706a: مخاصم . مشاجر /*muḫāṣim*, *mušāğir* (*adversary*, *fighter*). The original meaning of the Syro-Aramaic verbal root (*to press > to extort*) makes the etymology of *corsair* (= *extortioner*) from Syro-Aramaic more probable than from Italian *corsaro* or middle Latin *cursarius.*[297]

As far as the word *pirate*, synonym of *corsair*, means a *bandit*, the Syro-Aramaic verbal root ܦܪܛ / *praṭ* with the meaning *to break*, *to tear* (cf. *Mannā* 609a, 2: شقّ . مزّق / *šaqqa*, *mazzaqa*) makes its etymology from the latter more plausible than from Latin *pirata* or Greek *πειρāτής* (allegedly from the root *πειράω*, *to undertake*, *to attempt*, *to try*). In Mandaic (*Mandaic Dictionary* 379a) the verbal root PRṬ (*praṭ*) has also the sense of *to make a breach*, and in some Syro-Arabic dialects of Northern Mesopotamia has *paraṭ* the sense of *to pluck out, to tear away, to rip off*, *to pull out*. It is therefore presumably not a simple re-borrowing from Greek when C. Brockelmann (*Lexicon Syriacum* 595b) compares Syro-Aramaic ܦܪܛܐ / *prāṭā* (rather *parrāṭā* = modern Arabic نشال / *naššāl* [*pickpocket*]) to Greek *πειρāτής* : *"praedo maritimus"* (*pirate*).

---

297 The same may concern the homonym *corset*, the function of which suggests a possible derivation from the Syro-Aramaic verbal root ܩܪܨ /*qraṣ* (*to press*), that makes more sense than from French noun *corps* (*body*); unless *corset* is rather composed of the Latin nouns *corpus* and *sēdēs* (< *sedeō* / *sēdō*), i.e.: *"body-fit"*.

Some examples of mistranscribed Syro-Aramaic letters

As to the mistranscription of Syro-Aramaic letters from an originally in *Garshuni /Karshuni* written Koranic text, the Koran offers a number of such into the Arabic writing system falsely transcribed Syro-Aramaic letters. Such typical mistranscriptions concern (among others) the two similar letters of the Syriac alphabets ܕ / *d* (with a lower point) and ܪ / *r* (with an upper point), that not only have been occasionally confused between each other, as seen above, but the basic form of which has also led to mistake them as an Arabic و /*w*.

These findings are not owing to any early Koran manuscripts, since the same mistakes are found there; they are much more the result of the philological analysis of the Koranic contexts, as it will be shown by the following examples.

a) As an Arabic و / *w* mistaken Syro-Aramaic ܕ / *d* (The suspected word is underlined).

(Sura 8:2): انما المومنون الذين اذا ذكر اللـــه <u>وجلت</u> قلوبهم

Bell (I 162) translates: "The believers are those whose hearts <u>*thrill with fear*</u> when Allah is mentioned". Though the intended meaning has been approximately found out from the context, the spelling <u>وجلت</u> (traditional reading *wağalat*), from an imagined verbal root وجل / *wağila* with a likewise imagined irregular imperfect يوجل / *yawğalu*, is nevertheless mistranscribed. The meaning concluded from the context, *to be scared, to be afraid*, can namely only be confirmed, if we read the Arabic و / *w* as a Syro-Aramaic ܕ / *d* and the ـجـ / *ğ* without dot as a ـحـ / *ḥ*, according to the well-known Syro-Aramaic verbal root ܕܚܠ / *dḥel* = Arabic دحل / *daḥala* = خاف / *ḫāfa* (*to be afraid* – cf. *Mannā* 145b). The *Lisān* (XI 239a) transmits this meaning cited by *Shammar*, who said:

سمعت علي بن مصعب يقول لا <u>تدحل</u> بالنبطية أي لا <u>تخف</u>

(*I heard Alī b. Muṣʿab saying: "lā tadḥal" in Nabatean means "lā taḫaf" = "be not afraid"*). The mistranscribed <u>وجلت</u> قلوبهم / <u>*wağalat*</u> *qulūbu-hum* is hence to be rectified as <u>دحلت</u> قلوبهم / <u>*daḥalat*</u> *qulūbuhum* (whose hearts <u>stand</u> <u>in fear</u> = in reverence). The same is to apply to Sura 22:35.

Accordingly, the three further identical passages are to rectify as follows: (Sura 15:52) انا منكم وجلون (traditional reading: *innā* [properly: *inna*] *minkum waǧilūn*) = انا منكم دحلون (to read: *dāḥilūn* – as present participle) (*we are afraid of you*); (Sura 15:53) قالوا لا توجل (traditional reading: *lā tawǧal*) = لا تدحل (to read: *lā tadḥal* [*be not afraid*]) – as confirmed by the *Lisān*, by what means the Koran is discharged from an unjustified anomaly imputable to the Arab grammarians and philologists; (Sura 23:60) وقلوبهم وجلة (traditional reading: *wa-qulūbuhum waǧila-tun*) = وقلوبهم دحله (to read: *wa-qulūbuhum dāḥlē* [*their hearts being in fear*], as transliteration of the Syro-Aramaic present participle plural, the end-*h* being an alternative writing of the end-*alif* to designate the plural ending *ē* = ܕܚܠܐ / *dāḥlē* – Arabic to read: *dāḥile* > *dāḥila* – by no means *dāḥila-tun*).

As to this alternative writing, the Koran gives us the following convincing illustration: (Sura 68:43; 70:44) خشعة ابصرهم (traditional reading: *ḫāšiʿa-tan abṣāruhum*); (Sura 54:7) خشعا ابصرهم (traditional reading: *ḫuššaʿ-an abṣāruhum*). Both traditional readings are arbitrary and without any philological foundation, since the historically verifiable Syro-Aramaic orthography leads in both spellings to the sole possible reading: *ḫāšiʿē* (> Arabic *ḫāšiʿa* – not *ḫāšiʿa-tan* and less than ever *ḫuššaʿ-an*) *abṣāruhum* (*their looks down cast* [*in reverence*]).

b) As an Arabic و /w mistaken Syro-Aramaic ܪ /r

There are more examples for the rendering of a Syro-Aramaic ܪ / *r* as an Arabic و /*w*. In Sura 11:70 we find the following example:

فلما را ايديهم لا تصل اليه نكرهم واوجس منهم خيفة

Bell (I 212, 73) translates: "Then when he saw their hands not reaching forward to it, he misliked them and conceived a fear of them".

Though, here too, the underlined word is nearly correctly understood, a verbal root وجس / *waǧasa* is nevertheless unknown in Arabic. The unsettled explanation attempts made hereto by guess in the *Lisān* (VI 253) relate to the presumable understanding of this Koranic passage. *Ibn Sayyidih* is right, when he says: هو عندي أنه على النسب إذ لا نعرف له فعلا (*in my opinion, it is a denominative, because we don't know a verb of it*).

The verbal root is in fact Syro-Aramaic. To reconstruct it, we need only to replace the و /*w* in اوجس /*awğasa* by a Syro-Aramaic ܪ / *r* = Arabic ر / *r* = ارجس /*arğasa*, to have the Syro-Aramaic Verb ܐܪܓܫ / *argeš*. According *Mannā* (723a), this verbal stem means in Arabic: شعر. احسّ / *šaʿara, aḥassa* (*to feel, to perceive*).

Besides, the verb نكرهم (traditional reading: *nakirahum* – rather *nakarahum*) means not *„he misliked them"*, but, as borrowing from Syro-Aramaic ܢܟܪܝ / *nakrī*, according to *Mannā* (448b) under (5): استغرب / *istaġraba* (*to find strange*).

The above cited Koranic vers from Sura 11:70 is hence to understand as follows:

> "Then when he saw their hands not reaching forward to it, he *found them* [= their behaviour] *strange* and *perceived* a fear of them".

14. Misread Arabic Expressions

Sura 17:64

Sura 17:64 offers us one example, among others, of not just Syro-Aramaic but also Arabic expressions that have been misread and/or misinterpreted. Here the context is that God has cast Satan out of Paradise for his refusal to bow down before Adam. Satan asks God for permission to be allowed to abide among men until the Day of Judgment in order to sow confusion[298] among them. God grants him his request and adds:

واستفزز من استطعت منهم بصوتك واجلب عليهم بخيلك ورجلك
وشاركهم في الاموال والاولد وعدهم وما يعدهم الشيطن الا غرورا

Following the Arabic understanding this verse is rendered as follows (here on the basis of Paret's representative translation):

> (Paret 233): "And startle (*wa-stafziz*) with your voice whom(ever) of them you can, pester (*? wa-ağlib ʿalaihim*) them with all of your hosts [note: literally – with your cavalry and your infantry], take part in their wealth and their children (as a partner) and make them promises!" Satan only makes them deceptive promises.
>
> (Blachère and Bell translate accordingly).

Concerning the underlined terms:

(a) That Satan is said to "*startle*" the people with his voice contradicts another Koranic statement according to which Satan "*whispers in the hearts of men*" (Sura 114:5). For the dubious reading استفزز (*istafziz*), the *Lisān* (V 391b) gives the following meaning:

298 The Koranic verb لاحتنكن (*la-aḥtanikanna*) (Verse 62) has been misread; by Paret (233) it has been rendered thus: (*I will with few exceptions*) "do in" (?) [Note: Or … "bring under my sway" (?)] (*his descendants*). The falsely placed upper point of the ـنـ / *n* yields as a lower point ـبـ / *b* the correct reading لاحتبكن (*la-aḥtabikanna*) < Syro-Aramaic ܚܒܟ (*ḥ ak*), *Mannā* (215a): (3) بلبل شوّش .(*balbala, šawwaša*) (*to entangle, to confuse*).

واستفزه: ختله حتى ألقاه في مهلكة (*istafazza-hu : to plunge someone into misfortune through cunning*).
However, the lack of this meaning in the post-Koranic Arabic literature as well as in the vernacular Arabic suggests that the explanation quoted in the *Lisān* is actually made up. Thus, more likely is the assumption that the later points set on both ر /r are superfluous and that the original spelling was استفرر / *istafrir*: "*put to flight*" (i.e.: *avert, turn away from me* – cf. Sura 38:82).

(b) واجلب عليهم "*pester them*" (Blachère: *fonds sur eux;* Bell: *assemble against them*); the corresponding explanation in the *Lisān* (I 269), according to which one, among other things, *attacks somebody shouting*, is here just as unconvincing. On the other hand, the meaning given by the *Lisān* (I 363b) under خلب (*ḫalaba*): خلبه: خدعه (*ḫalaba-hu: to outwit someone*) is appropriate here. Accordingly, the dot below in the جـ / *ğ* should be moved up above (خـ / *ḫ*) and واخلب عليهم (*wa-ḫlub ʿalayhim*) should be read in the modern meaning of وانصب عليهم (*wa-nṣub ʿalayhim*) (*and outwit them*).

(c) بخيلك ورجلك (*bi-ḫaylika wa-rağilika*) supposedly "with your cavalry and your infantry" (Blachère: avec ta cavalerie et ton infanterie; Bell: assemble against them thy horse and thy foot); that the cavalry and the infantry are poorly suited to outwit someone is fairly obvious. Therefore another reading should be considered. Some possibilities for بخيلك (*bi-ḫaylika*) are either بحيلك (*bi-ḥiyalika*) (with your tricks) or, since this word does not occur anywhere else in the Koran in this meaning,[299] بحبلك (*bi-ḥablika or*

299 The expression occurring in Sura 4: 98 لا يستطيعون حيلة (Paret 77: "who dispose of no *possibility* [*ḥīla*]") has nothing to do with the homonymous Arabic word in the meaning of "*trick*." As a loan translation from the Syro-Aramaic expression ܡܨܐ ܚܝܠܐ (*mṣā ḥaylā*) (*Mannā*, 412b: قدر. استطاع) (literally: "*to be capable of a strength*," i.e. "*to have the strength at one's disposal*," a tautology for "*to be able to, to be capable of, to be in a position to*"), it is still today a commonly employed Syriacism in Arabic. That which in modern Arabic is taken to be the feminine ending of حيلة (*ḥīla*) should in the Koran be viewed as a reproduction of the emphatical Syro-Aramaic ending of ܚܝܠܐ (*ḥaylā*). The

ḥibālika) (with your snare) (*Lisān* XI 136b, والحبالة : التي يصاد بها / *wa-lḥibāla: al-latī yuṣādu bi-hā [ḥibāla is that which serves for fishing]* – again, as a Syro-Aramaic loan word, also to be understood here not as the feminine [*ḥibāla^{t}*], but as the transliteration of the masculine Syro-Aramaic ܚܒܠܐ [*ḥablā*]; *Mannā* [216a] [4]: احبولة . شرك . مصيدة / *uḥbūla, šarak, maṣyada* [*trap, snare*], [5]: مكر . مكيدة / *makr, makīda* [*trick, deception*]). Following the Syro-Aramaic meaning, both "trap, snare" and "cunning, deception" are possible.

(d) In the case of ورجلك (*wa-rağilika*) (*your infantry*) one must assume that the ر / *r* is a misread د / *d*, since only ودجلك (*wa-dağalika*) (< Syro-Aramaic ܕܘܓܠܐ /*duggālā*) results in a meaning that makes any sense: "*lying, lies and deception*" (*Mannā*, 137a, ܕܓܠ / *daggel:* كذب /*kaḏḏaba* [*to lie*], 3. مكر . خدع / *makara, ḫadaʿa* [*to deceive, to cheat*]).
This is one among other examples for the mistranscription of a Syro-Aramaic ܕ / *d* as an Arabic ر / *r* from an original text in *Garshuni* / *Karshuni*.

(e) Finally, وشاركهم (*wa-šārikhum*) (*and take part with them*) is still without a meaningful explanation. In *Ṭabarī* (XIV 119 ff.) all the commentators understand this verb in the sense of "*to take part*." In answer to the question as to the way in which Satan would take part in the wealth of people, it is explained that it is in their unlawfully acquired wealth, and in the case of their children: (a) in those born as a result of adultery, and (b) in that one gives them other gods' names (e.g., عبد شمس / *ʿabd šams* "*Servant of the sun = Sun-worshipper*"). What is more likely, however, is the figurative sense of the Syro-Aramaic verb ܣܪܟ (*srak* / *sarrek*), which *Mannā* (515b) renders in Arabic with أولع . أغرى (*awlaʿa, aġrā*) (*to tempt, to seduce*). From this root in Arabic only the nominal form شرك (*šarak*) is known in the meaning "*trick, snare*" (*Lisān*

original Koranic reading was therefore with certainty not *lā yastaṭīʿūna ḥīla^{tan}*, but *haylā*. Besides, for the meaning "*to outwit*" the Koran usually uses مكر (*makar^{a}*).

X 450b): والشرك: حبائل الصائد (*aš-šarak: the snares of the hunter*), which is also mentioned in the cited *ḥadīṯ*: أعوذ بك من شر الشيطان وشركه "*I take refuge in you from the evil of Satan and his snares* or *temptations*" (*wa-šarakihi*). Accordingly, in this passage in the Koran what is meant is not the third Arabic verbal stem شارك (*šāraka*) (*to take part with someone*), but the second Syro-Aramaic verbal stem ܣܪܟ (*sarreḵ*) (*to tempt*). Thus, instead of شاركهم (*šārikhum*)[300] (*take part with them*), شرّكهم (*šarrikhum*) (*tempt them*) should be read.

According to this analysis, the previously cited verse from Sura 17:64 is to be understood in Arabic and Syro-Aramaic as follows:

"Hence <u>avert</u> with your voice whomever you can of them, <u>outwit</u> them with your <u>snare</u> and your <u>lies and deception</u>, <u>tempt</u> them with wealth and children and (to that extent) make them promises – yet nothing but vain illusion does Satan promise you!"

---

300 Here we have an example of a possibly secondarily inserted ا / *ā* that causes a change in meaning. However, the *alif* can also designate a short *a* according to the orthographical tradition of Syro-Babylonian Aramaic (cf. Rudolf Meyer, *Hebräische Grammatik* [*Hebrew Grammar*] I, Berlin, 1966, p. 50 f.; Theodor Nöldeke, *Mandäische Grammatik* [*Mandaic Grammar*], § 3 1); *Syrische Grammatik* [*Syriac Grammar*], § 35). As to the sporadic use of an *alif* for a short *a*, the Koran follows a Syro-Aramaic tradition. This tradition was abandoned in the later classical Arabic, except for some cases, where the *alif* is still taken for a long *ā* as in the suffix of the first personal pronoun, e.g., كتبنا / *katab-na* (*we have written*), the end-*alif* of which is to be read as a short *a*. That the traditional transcription renders it as a long *ā*, is etymologically wrong, since the Arabic personal suffix plural نا /*-na* is nothing but a tertiary remnant of the Syro-Aramaic personal pronoun plural ܚܢܢ /*ḥnan* (< ܐܢܚܢܢ /*enaḥnan* – cf. *Thes.* I 250), enclitical form > ܢܢ /*-nan*, Arabic enclitical form after dropping of the Syro-Aramaic end-*n* > نا /*-na*. That this end-*a* is spoken as a long *ā* before an object suffix, as in كتبناه / *katab-nā-hu* (*we have written it*), is the result of a *compensatory lengthening* (*Ersatzdehnung*), generated by the dropped end-*n*. The explanations of Carl Brockelmann in his *Grundriß der vergleichenden Grammatik der semitischen Sprachen* [*Compendium of the Comparative Grammar of the Semitic Languages*] (I p. 299 f.) as to this pronoun require a more thoroughgoing investigation.

Sura 33:53

A further instance of the misreading of genuine Arabic words is provided to us by Sura 33:53 in the misread word إناه (*ināhu*), which has been misinterpreted as "*cooked* (foods)" (said of a meal) instead of اناثه (*ināṯahu*) "*his wives*" (in referring to the Prophet), and that in a late Medinan text! In the passage in question believers are asked not to enter the houses of the Prophet unless they have been invited for a meal, but then it is said that they are to enter غير نظرين إناه (*ġayra nāẓirīna ināhu*) (as it reads in the modern Koran) "without waiting for its (the *meal's*) *being cooked*," where, if read correctly, it should say: غير نظرين إناثه (*ġayra nāẓirīna ināṯahu*)[301] "without looking at his wives." In the process the Arabic commentators have even deliberately interpreted the unambiguous Arabic verb نظر (*naẓara*) (*to look*) as انتظر (*intaẓara*) (*to wait*) to justify the misreading "*its being cooked*" instead of "*his wives*." In this example it is still a question of a relatively harmless distortion, which our Koran translators have nevertheless not noticed.[302]

---

301 It should be mentioned in this regard, however, that as a rule in Arabic أنثى (*unṯā*) serves as the word for the gender (*feminine* or *female*). On the other hand, in Syro-Aramaic the etymological equivalent ܐܢܬܬܐ / *a*(*n*)*ttā* is used for "*woman*" as well as for "*wife*." The later Arabic readers were evidently no longer aware of this. The same spelling as a plural, although without the personal suffix (اناثا / *ināṯa*ⁿ), is in any case read correctly in six other passages (Suras 4:117; 17:40; 37:150; 42:49,50; 43:19).

302 Thus, Paret translates, or, rather, paraphrases (349): "Ihr Gläubigen! Betretet nicht die Häuser des Propheten, ohne daß man euch (wenn ihr) zu einem Essen (eingeladen seid) Erlaubnis erteilt (einzutreten), und ohne (schon vor der Zeit) zu warten, bis es so weit ist, daß man essen kann (*ġaira nāẓirīna ināhu*)! [You Believers! Enter not the houses of the Prophet without, (if you are invited) to a meal, being granted permission (to enter), and without (already ahead of time) waiting until the time that one can eat (*ġaira nāẓirīna ināhu*)!]". Blachère (452) translates in an equally confusing way: "[*N'entrez point alors*] sans attendre le moment de [*ce repas*]! [(*Do not enter at all*) without awaiting the moment of (*the meal*)]" Bell (II 417) at least notes in reference to his translation, "without observing when he is ready": "As it stands in the text, this is usually taken as referring to the meal, but the grammatical construction of the phrase is difficult...."

15. The Misreading and Misinterpretation of Thematic Contents

Now that it has become clear from the preceding analysis of individual samples of the language of the Koran that already in normal linguistic usage the Koran text has been in part so misread and misinterpreted by Arabic philologists and exegetes, it will no longer be surprising if meanwhile deeply anchored notions in the Islamic tradition, indeed religious contents, have been partially based on an equally misunderstood Koran text. Included among these notions are the *Ḥūrīs* or *Virgins of Paradise*.

The *Ḥūrīs* or Virgins of Paradise

To introduce in the following the notion of the so-called *Ḥūrīs* or *Virgins of Paradise*, which until now has been considered as a specific component of the Koranic presentation of Paradise, the article ḤŪR will be cited from the *The Encyclopaedia of Islam* (Leiden, London, 1971; vol. 3, 581b f.)[303]:

> ḤŪR, plural of *ḥawrāʾ*, fem. of *aḥwar*, literally "the white ones," i.e. the m a i d e n s in P a r a d i s e, the black iris of whose eyes is in strong contrast to the clear white around it. The nomen unitatis in Persian is *ḥūrī* (also *ḥūrī-bihishtī*), Arabic *ḥūrīya.* The explanation of the word found in Arabic works "those at whom the spectator is astounded (*ḥār*ᵃ)" is of course false and is therefore rejected even by other Arab philologists.
>
> These maidens of Paradise are described in various passages in the Kurʾān. In Sūra 2:25, 3:15, 4:57, they are called "purified wives"; according to the commentators, this means that they are free alike from bodily impurity and defects of character. In Sūra 55:56, it is said that their glances are retiring i.e. they look only

303 See also the *Enzyklopaedie des Islām*, vol. 2 (Leiden, Leipzig, 1927) 358 f.

upon their husbands. "Neither man nor d̲jinn has ever touched them"; this is interpreted to mean that there are two classes of them, one like man and the other like the d̲jinn. They are enclosed in pavilions (55:72). They are compared to jacinths and pearls (Sūra 55:58).

Later literature is able to give many more details of their physical beauty; they are created of saffron, musk, amber and camphor, and have four colors, white, green, yellow, and red. They are so transparent that the marrow of their bones is visible through seventy silken garments. If they expectorate into the world, their spittle becomes musk. Two names are written on their breasts, one of the names of Allāh and the name of their husband. They wear many jewels and ornaments etc. on their hands and feet. They dwell in splendid palaces surrounded by female attendants and all possible luxury etc.

When the believer enters Paradise, he is welcomed by one of these beings; a large number of them are at his disposal; he cohabits with each of them as often as he has fasted days in Ramaḍān and as often as he has performed good works besides. Yet they remain always virgins (cf. Sūra 56:36). They are equal in age to their husbands (*ibid.* 37), namely 33 years (al-Baiḍāwī).

These are all very sensual ideas; but there are also others of a different kind. In discussing the Korʾānic "wives" (2:25), al-Baiḍāwī asks what can be the object of cohabitation in Paradise as there can be no question of its purpose in the world, the preservation of the race. The solution of this difficulty is found by saying that, although heavenly food, women etc., have the name in common with their earthly equivalents, it is only "by way of metaphorical indication and comparison, without actual identity, so that what holds good for one may hold for the other also." In another passage (on Sūra 44:54) al-Baiḍāwī observes that it is not agreed whether the *ḥūrīs* are earthly women or not. Likewise Ṣūfī authors have spiritualized the *ḥūrīs* (see especially Berthels, *loc. cit.*).

Sale (*The Koran*, London 1821, *Preliminary Discourse*, p. 134) and others (see Berthels, *l.c.*, p. 287) think that Muḥammed owed the idea of the maidens of Paradise to the Parsis. Dozy (*Het Islamisme*², Haarlem 1880, p. 101, note) has rejected this opinion with the comment that Sale's parsistic source is much earlier than the Korʾān and the relationship is thus the reverse. In the article DJANNA it is suggested that Muḥammed misunderstood Christian pictures of Paradise and that the angels in them are the originals of the youths and maidens of the Korʾān. [Followed by *Bibliography.*] (A.J. Wensinck)

That the notion of the *ḥūrīs* or *virgins of Paradise* in the Islamic tradition can be traced back to a Persian influence has been suggested at the beginning of the article cited above from *The Encyclopaedia of Islam.* It is however not the task of this study to go into the historical circumstances that have led to the creation of this mythological construct. Ascertaining that is better off left to the historians of religion and culture.

The following analysis confines itself to the purely philological interpretation of the passages of the Koran relevant to the so-called *Ḥūrīs* or *virgins of Paradise.* It will show that among the Islamic commentators Baiḍāwī rightly poses the question of the real meaning of these heavenly females. Furthermore, it will confirm the suspicion referred to at the end of the article cited above to the extent that it was not, say, that the Prophet had misunderstood Christian illustrations of Paradise, but rather that the later Islamic exegesis had misinterpreted the Koranic paraphrase of Christian Syriac hymns containing analogous descriptions of Paradise under the influence of Persian conceptions of the mythological *virgins of Paradise*. This analysis is based on the method that was introduced above and explained with the help of individual examples.

The Koran takes as its starting point the axiom that the *Scripture* preceding it (the Old and New Testament) has been revealed. Understanding itself as a component of this *Scripture*, to be consistent it derives from this the claim that it itself has been revealed. In this regard, it emphasizes in no small number of passages, again and again, that it "confirms" (مصدق / *muṣaddiq*) the *Scripture* (e.g. Sura 2:41, 89, 91; 3:3;

4:47; 5:46; 6:92, etc.). To this extent it takes the *Scripture* as its model, for example in Sura 4:82 when it cites as an argument to prove its own authenticity:

ولو كان من عند غير الله لوجدوا فيه اختلفا كثيرا

> "Were it (the Koran) namely not from God, you would find (in comparison to the *Scripture*) many differences (inconsistencies)."

There would be such an *inconsistency*, however, if the likes of the *ḥūrīs*, assumed by the Koran to be an essential feature of its eschatological notions, were not to be found in the *Scripture*. Then the Koran, against its usual assertion, would have thus produced proof that it had not come from God.

Yet in its conclusions the following discussion will concede that the Koran is right. For the Koran is not to blame if, out of ignorance, people have read it so falsely and projected onto it their subjective, all too earthly daydreams. We therefore intend to deal in more detail with the individual verses upon which these so-called *ḥūrīs* or *virgins of Paradise* are based.

Sura 44:54; 52:20

وزوجنهم بحور عين

The starting point for this misunderstanding is in all likelihood these two Sura verses (44:54 and 52:20), where in each case (according to the reading until now) it says: "*wa-zawwağnāhum bi-ḥūr*^{in} *ʿīn*^{in}." Without contesting it, our Koran translators accordingly render this clause as follows:

> (Bell 501,536): "and We have paired them with dark-, wide-eyed (maidens)."

> (Paret 415,439): "Und wir geben ihnen großäugige Huris als Gattinnen…"

> (Blachère 528): "Nous les aurons mariés à des Houris aux grands

yeux." (558) Nous leur aurons donné comme épouses, des Houris aux grands yeux."

On the basis of the following discussion this verse will be understood in the Syro-Aramaic reading as follows:

> "We will *make* you *comfortable under white, crystal*(-*clear*) (grapes)."

It is characteristic of Western Koran research that it has never called into question the diacritical points that were subsequently added to the Koran text and that in each case first determined the suggested letters in an original spelling in need of interpretation. Today the extant, still unpointed early Koran manuscripts provide evidence that these points are not authentic. Nonetheless the conviction has never been challenged that the later pointing was based on an assured oral tradition. A detailed philological analysis, however, will reveal that this is a historical error.

On the Verb زوجنهم (*zawwaǧ-nā-hum*)

In the previously cited verse it should first be noted that in the verb زوجنهم (*zawwaǧ-nā-hum*) two falsely placed points (one above the ر / *r* [= ز / *z*] and one below the حـ / *ḥ* [= جـ / *ǧ*]) have resulted in the misreading "*to marry*." Namely, if we read the original spelling purified, i.e. without these two points, the result is the reading روحنهم (*rawwaḥ-nā-hum*) (according to the context): "we will *let* them *rest*" (as God says with regard to the blessed spirits of the departed in Paradise). This reading finds its justification in the common Syro-Aramaic and Arabic verbal root ܪܘܚ (*rwaḥ*) / روح (*rawaḥ*ᵃ), under whose causative stem *rawwaḥ Mannā* (728a) gives under point (2) the homonymous Arabic meaning: اراح (*arāḥ*ᵃ) (*to let rest*). But the causative stem with the same meaning is also quite common,[304] so that one wonders how Arabic read-

304 Cf., e.g., H. Wehr, *Arabisches Wörterbuch* [*Arabic Dictionary*], 330a, under روح , II: "*to refresh, to revive; to allow to rest, to allow to relax, to give rest and relaxation.*" In any case in modern Arabic the variant ريح (*rayyaḥ*ᵃ) is

ers could have read it wrongly. The reason is presumably that they did not know what to do with the following preposition بـ /*bi-* (*in, with*), which in Arabic is incompatible with this verb, whereas in the meaning "*with*" it is perfectly compatible with the verb زوج (*zawwağ*ª) (*to marry*); therefore in this connection the only possible reading according to the Arabic understanding was "*to marry with*."

On the Meaning of the Preposition بـ / *bi-*

In the process the Arabic philologists with certainty did not think about the meaning of the preposition بـ / *bi-* in Syro-Aramaic. Namely, among the 22 different functions of this preposition, *Mannā* (48a) gives under (20) the following meaning: بين (*bayn*ª) "between, under." In fact, this meaning alone gives the reading روحنهم (*rawwaḥ-nā-hum*) its correct sense: "We will *let* them *rest under* (*between*)" (so-called حور عين *ḥūr ʿīn*) (roughly: "We will *make* them *comfortable, cozy, snug under* such [*ḥūr ʿīn*]).

On the Double Expression حور عين (*ḥūr ʿīn*)

Now because one assumes on the basis of the masculine personal object suffix (*zawwağ-nā-hum*) that it is men who are supposed *to be married*, it was only logical to the Arab commentators that it had in the case of the following double expression, حور عين (*ḥūr ʿīn*), to be a question of female creatures with whom those men were to be married. Whence the necessity to interpret this expression accordingly. The Arabic philologists have correctly understood the Arabic adjective حور (*ḥūr*) (as a plural of the feminine حوراء / *ḥawrā*ʾ) as a borrowing from Syro-Aramaic ܚܘܪ (*ḥwar*) "*to be white*" (ܚܘܪܐ / *ḥewārā* / "*white*"). But on the basis of the presupposed *virgins*, they have likewise understood the following

---

usually used in this meaning, although the Koranic (i.e. Syro-Aramaic) form روح (*rawwaḥ*ª) is common, particularly in the modern colloquial Arabic of the Near East, in expressions like those cited in Wehr روح عن نفسه (*rawwaḥ*ª *ʿan nafsih*ⁱ) (*to relax, to refresh oneself, to be amused*).

عين (*ʿīn*), which is unclear in terms of pronunciation and form, as a description of "*eyes*." Thus there was later derived out of the double expression حور عين (*ḥūr ʾīn*), misinterpreted as "*white big-eyed* (ones)," the expression *ḥūrī*, which never occurs in the Koran, as the name for these imaginary *virgins of Paradise*. In the process the spelling عين (*ʿīn*) was interpreted as the plural form of the feminine adjective عيناء (*ʿaynāʾ*) in the meaning "*big-eyed*."[305]

Yet whether the legendary notion of the so-called *ḥūrīs* or *virgins of Paradise* stands or falls depends on the right or wrong interpretation of this Koranic double expression.

On the Expression حور (*ḥūr*)

With regard to the word حور (*ḥūr*), it has been said already that the Arabic philologists have correctly understood it as the Arabicized plural form of the feminine adjective حوراء (*ḥawrāʾ*) in the meaning of "*white*." But because what it is referring to is not named in the Koran, this had to be imagined. In this context in the Koran there is no talk anywhere of its needing to be, of all things, women or virgins. To be sure, there is mention in two passages of the earthly wives with whom the righteous are to be brought together in Paradise; these are: (a) Sura 43:70:

ادخلوا الجنة انتم وازواجكم تحبرون

> "Enter into Paradise, (therein) shall you be brought together with your wives." [306]

---

305 Cf. *Lisān* XIII 302b: والعين: جمع عيناء ، وهي الواسعة العين (*al-ʿīn* : plural of *ʿaynāʾ*, i.e. a *big-eyed* [one]).

306 In a miscellaneous contribution to the *Zeitschrift für arabische Linguistik* [*Journal of Arabic Linguistics*] (*ZAL*) 29 (Wiesbaden, 1995) 77 f., Michael B. Schub has already correctly identified the origin of the Koranic verb *tuḥbarūnᵃ* from the Hebrew/Aramaic root *ḥḇar* in the meaning of "congregated together." Following the Arabic commentators, Bell (II 496) translates "in gala attire" [note:] or "made happy"; Paret (411) "ergötzt euch (darin)(?) [take delight (therein) (?)]," and Blachère (523) "vous...serez fêtés [you will be entertained]." How-

The Koran also keeps its promise and accordingly presents the pious together with their wives in Sura 36:56:

هم وازوجهم في ظلل على الارائك متكون

"They and their wives lie (reclining) on carpets in the shade."

Quite apart from the fact that with the supposed *ḥūrīs* the Koran would be contradicting *Scripture*, with this latter statement it would also be contradicting itself. After all, with the clear contents of these two verses the Koran is in effect ruling out the existence of any "(female) rivals." Namely, one can well imagine how the earthly wives, in the bliss of Paradise and for all eternity, would be forced to look on helplessly while their husbands enjoy themselves with the putative *virgins of Paradise*. Josef Horovitz has already pointed out this scarcely imaginable contradiction in his article "*Das koranische Paradies* [*The Koranic Paradise*]."[307] Entering into the particulars of the verse cited above, he explains:

> "On the other hand, 43:70-73 is remarkable because there the wives of the pious are also assured admission into Paradise. "Enter into the Garden, you and your wives, to enjoy yourselves.[308] Bowls of gold will pass around among you and cups in which there is that which souls desire and eyes feast upon, and you will abide there forever." The wives are also mentioned in 36:56 and, though there one could in any case also think of the Ḥūris, who according to 44:54 (see above) are indeed given to the blessed departed ones as wives, such an interpretation cannot be upheld

---

ever, it is more likely that the Koranic expression is a direct borrowing from the synonymous Syro-Aramaic ܐܬܚܒܪ / *eṯḥabbar* (*to be led together, to be brought together*).

307 In *Scripta Universitatis atque Bibliothecae Hierosolymitanarum* (Jerusalem, 1923). Here quoted from Rudi Paret, ed., *Der Koran* [*The Koran*] (Darmstadt, 1975) 53-73.

308 See the note above on this expression.

for a passage like 43:70; the invitation to enter Paradise with their spouses can only be directed at the earthly wives."[309]

In spite of this statement, which contradicts the sense imputed to Sura 44:54, Horovitz stops at these findings without daring to take the further step of trying to clarify this obvious contradiction. In fact, it would have sufficed to subject the corresponding passages to a closer philological examination. This may now bring the hoped-for solution to the puzzle.

To conclude with regard to the expression حـور (*ḥūr*), it has now been ascertained that it is formally an Arabic feminine plural adjective, and that this adjective refers to a substantive of the same gender which, although the Koran does not name it here, can be determined from the remaining Koranic description of Paradise.

On the Expression عين (*ʿīn*)

This word, whose singular form in the pronunciation (*ʿayn*) (*eye, well,* etc.) is common to both Syro-Aramaic and Arabic, has been understood in the Arabic exegesis of the Koran as a plural. Yet the two commonly employed plural forms for this in Arabic are عيون (*ʿuyūn*) and أعين (*aʿyun*) (for *eyes* and *wells*, respectively, not to mention أعيان / *aʿyān* for *notables*). Accordingly in the case of this form, which is explained as an additional plural variation occurring only in this Koranic expression عين (*ʿīn*), it may be a question of the graphical rendering of the Syro-Aramaic plural ܥܝܢܐ (*ʿaynē*), though in the Arabicized pausal form (i.e. with the omission of the Syro-Aramaic *emphatic* ending which is foreign to Arabic). Of necessity the only possible pronunciation in Arabic, to make the distinction from the singular (*ʿayn*), would accordingly have been عين (*ʿīn*). This does not mean however that (*ʿīn*), for example, would be an Arabic plural of the substantive عين (*ʿayn*) (*eye*). Whence the necessary assumption in Arabic that one is dealing here with the plural form of the feminine adjective عيناء (*ʿaynāʾ*) in the meaning "*big-eyed*" (woman), as the *Lisān*[310] explains it.

---

309 Paret, ed. *Der Koran* [*The Koran*] 57.

310 As far as that goes, it may be correct that the Arabic عين (*ʿīn*) is the plural of the

In the pronunciation ܥܝܢ (*ʿīn*) the word would be understood in Syro-Aramaic as a *status absolutus* singular (*emphaticus* ܥܝܢܐ / *ʿaynā*).[311] Arguing in favor of the plural is first of all the preceding Arabic plural حور (*ḥūr*) (*white*), by which is explained, according to the Arabic understanding, the following عين (*ʿīn*) as the attributive feminine plural adjective ("*big-eyed*" whites = *ḥūrīs*). For the assumption of an original Syro-Aramaic plural of the substantive ܥܝܢܐ (*ʿaynā*) (*eye*, etc.) that would stand in apposition to the preceding حور (*ḥūr*), the coherence of the Koranic context will be decisive.

The Arabic explanation, according to which the double expression "*ḥūr ʿīn*" would designate the particular gleam of the whites of the eyes as a mark of the beauty of these *virgins of Paradise* does not only contradict Arabic linguistic usage. Namely, when one describes the beauty of eyes, it is said as a rule, and indeed not just in Arabic, "beautiful *black*, beautiful *brown* and beautiful *blue* eyes," but never "beautiful *white* eyes," unless of course one is *blind*. For instance, in the Koran it is also said of Jacob that from all his crying over his son Joseph his eyes have become "*white*" (وابيضت عيناه) (Sura 12:84), i.e. they have been *blinded*. The further explanation given by the Arabic commentators that this *white* particularly emphasizes the beauty of (big) *black* eyes is only an invented makeshift explanation, but one which Bell takes at face-value by translating: "*dark*, *wide-eyed* (maidens)" (whereas Paret and Blachère simply suppress the key expression "*white*").

If for linguistic reasons the meaning "*eyes*" in the sense of *women's eyes* is now to be ruled out, then the imagined *ḥūrīs* or *virgins of Paradise* to which these "*eyes*" until now have referred, disappear *ipso facto*

---

feminine adjective (*ʿaynāʾ*), just as the *Lisān* XIII 302b explains it. Only this meaning has been falsely assigned to the formally identical Koranic orthography. Quotations like the *hadith* إن في الجنة لمجتمعا للحور العين (possible meaning: *In Paradise* [*there will be*] *a meeting with the* "*Ḥūr ʿīn* ") only document the expression that was probably misunderstood in this way from the outset. It follows rather from the explanation given that in the Koranic context it must have been a question of the Syro-Aramaic plural form of the substantive عين (*ʿayn*).

311 Cf. *Thes*. II 2867.

into thin air. Thus, too, would be removed the related contradictions in the Koran and objectivity would be restored to the Koranic statement cited above to the extent that the claim, documented in the *Scripture*, according to which one is neither *married* nor *given in marriage* in Paradise (Mt 22:30; Mk 12:25; Lk 20:35) is now confirmed.

However if the argumentation to this point has shown what the Koranic double expression "*ḥūr ʿīn*" does *not* mean, it still remains to be explained what it really means. In the meantime there is agreement concerning the meaning "*white*" (as the feminine plural) for حور (*ḥūr*). What is thus still to be explained is the relationship to the expression standing in apposition to it, عين (*ʿīn*), whose meaning is not yet certain. To establish this, however, it is first of all necessary to look for a *tertium comparationis.*

The tertium comparationis

This is to be found among what the Koran calls the fruits of Paradise. These include, among others, *date palms* and *pomegranates* (Sura 55: 68) as well as *grapes* (Sura 78:32). These last-mentioned are conspicuously named only in this passage in connection with Paradise, whereas they occur in no fewer than ten passages among the other fruits of the earth and of earthly gardens (Suras 2:266; 6:99; 13:4; 16:11,67; 17:91; 18:32; 23:19; 36:34; 80:28). This is an essential determination in the identification of our metaphorical expression حور عين (*ḥūr ʿīn*). If in fact the grapevine is an essential component of the earthly garden, for which the Koran also uses the same Arabic word جنة (*ǧanna*)[312] borrowed from the Syro-Aramaic ܓܢܬܐ (*gannṯā*),[313] to designate the heavenly Paradise, then in the latter it is even more so the fruit of Paradise *par excellence*. Still, it makes one particularly suspicious that the grapevine is almost never lacking in earthly gardens in the Koran, but is in heavenly gardens, of all places, explicitly named only once.

---

312 Cf. S. Fraenkel, *Aramäische Fremdwörter* [*Aramaic Foreign Words*] 148.
313 Cf., e.g., C. Brockelmann, *Lexicon Syriacum* 122a f.

The Significance of Ephraem the Syrian

An important clue is offered us here by the fourth-century Syro-Aramaic hymns of Ephraem the Syrian (ca. 306-373) "*on Paradise*."[314] A debate over the significance of its vividly described grapevines of Paradise was begun by a book written by the Swedish theologian and Islamic studies specialist Tor Andrae (*Mohammed, sein Leben und Glaube* [*Mohammed: His Life and Belief*] [Göttingen, 1932]). Andrae wanted to prove with this parallel that the Koranic depiction of Paradise had been inspired by those of the Syrian Christian, but he was at the same time advocating the thesis that in Ephraem there are also allusions to the Koranic *virgins of Paradise*. The German Syriologist, theologian and Koran scholar Edmund Beck expressed his opinions on this in an article,[315] from which the following excerpt taken from his introduction (398) should suffice:

> "A closer consideration of this work by St. Ephraem gives me the occasion to express my opinions on the surprising hypothesis that Tor Andrae attaches to his final quotation [pp.71/2]: Wine…is also not lacking in the Christian Paradise, and one can even recognize a furtive suggestion of the virgins of Paradise in Ephraem's words: "He who has abstained from the wine here below, for him yearn the grapevines of Paradise. Each of them extends him a drooping cluster. And if someone has lived in chastity, then they (fem.) receive him in their pure bosom, because as a monk he fell not in the bosom and bed of earthly love."

On the basis of the appended Latin translation of the corresponding Syro-Aramaic passages Edmund Beck contents himself with saying that

---

314 *Des heiligen Ephraem des Syrers Hymnen de Paradiso und contra Julianum* [*The Hymns of St. Ephraem the Syrian De Paradiso and Contra Julianum*], ed. Edmund Beck, in *Corpus Scriptorum Christianorum Orientalium*, vol. 174/175 (Louvain, 1957).

315 "*Eine christliche Parallele zu den Paradiesjungfrauen des Korans?* [*A Christian Parallel to the Virgins of Paradise in the Koran?*]," in *Orientalia Christiana Periodica* XIV (Rome, 1948) 398-405.

in Ephraem it is only a question of a vivid description of the grapevines of Paradise, but by no means of *virgins of Paradise*. He does not take the further step of demonstrating to Tor Andrae that the reversed relationship is the case, namely that in the case of the supposed *ḥūrīs* of the Koran – in agreement with Ephraem's Syro-Aramaic description of Paradise – it is also only a question of *grapes*. That also marked the end of the discussion on the subject.

But not least the internal criteria of the Koran will convince us that with the double expression حور عين (*ḥūr ʿīn*) the Koran is doing nothing more with this metaphor than describing this fruit of Paradise *par excellence in a totally special way* and *emphasizing* it over the other fruits of Paradise, and that by this it finally means nothing more than what Ephraem the Syrian also meant, namely, *grapes*.

Taking as a starting point the Syro-Aramaic expression ܓܘܦܢܐ (*gup̄nā*) (*grapevine*) that Ephraem the Syrian uses in his hymn,[316] it should first be noted that the word is feminine, which is also what led Tor Andrae to see in it an allusion to the *virgins of Paradise*. In the end it was also this that led the Arabic exegetes of the Koran to this fateful assumption.

With this term documented in connection with Christian-Syriac literature of the 4th century in the same context, we would have the *tertium comparationis* we were looking for, the *key word* constituting the referent of its congruent feminine adjective حور (*ḥūr*). The Arabic plural, though, refers to the *grapes* themselves, which the Koran also employs elsewhere in the collective form عنب (*ʿinab*) (twice) and in the plural form اعناب (*aʿnāb*) (nine times) (in Syro-Aramaic, the feminine singular ܥܢܒܬܐ / *ʿenbṯā*).[317] This is made especially clear through the other

316 Cf. Edmund Beck, *loc. cit.*, 400. On ܓܘܦܢܐ (*gup̄nā*) and ܓܦܬܐ (*gp̄ettā*), see, for example, C. Brockelmann, *Lexicon Syriacum* 128b.

317 Cf. *ibid.* 534b. To be doubted is Fraenkel's all too assertive claim in *Aramäische Fremdwörter* [*Aramaic Foreign Words*] (156): "The Arabic language has meanwhile preserved from Proto-Semitic times a large number of genuine words that are related to wine and wine-growing. Thus, for example, كرم and جفن are protected from any suspicion of being a borrowing, likewise عنب ...." The usage of the Koran should suffice to refute this.

metaphors in the Koran that compare grapes with "*pearls*" (Sura 52:24; 56:23; 76:19). Namely, the latter have in common with *white* grapes that they are both *completely white*, which, after all, is known *not* to be the case for the eye.

Surprisingly the *Lisān* (VII 125b) provides us with an Arabic parallel to the borrowed adjective حور (*ḥūr*) in the meaning "*white* (*grapes*)" with the following explanation: البيضة : عنب بالطائف أبيض عظيم الحب "*al-bayḍa*[tu]: (is) a (variety of) white grape with large berries in *Ṭā'if*." The substantivized Arabic adjective البيضة (*al-bayḍa*) (actually البيضاء *al-bayḍā'*) (*the* "*white*") here (as in the Koran) clearly stands for the implied substantive "*grape*."

This in turn is sensibly associated with the equivalent Syro-Aramaic expression, which the *Thes.* (I 1230) gives under the special meanings of the adjective ܚܘܪܐ (*ḥewwārā*) (*white*) in the feminine form under (a): ܚܘܪܬܐ (*ḥewwartā*) ([the] *white* [one]): *vitis species* (*a variety of white grape*).[318]

Solution I

These examples ought to rule out the imagined *virgins of Paradise*, who are not mentioned anywhere in the Koran, as the referent for the substantivized adjective حور (*ḥūr*) "*white*." Not least the اعناب (*a'nāb*) "*grapes*" mentioned repeatedly in the Koran in connection with *gardens* allow one to conclude instead that it is these for which the term حور (*ḥūr*) = "*white*" (*grapes*) stands as a substituted substantive.

Part of the watertight solution to the puzzle, however, is still the explanation of the next expression, عين (*'īn*). Since we had established that this word is perhaps in the plural, as a substantive it can therefore not be understood adjectivally in the sense of "*big-eyed*" since the previously assumed *virgins of Paradise* have been eliminated. Now insofar as the adjective *white* in the Koranic context designates the color, the appearance of the grapes, one should look in Syro-Aramaic for an equivalent descriptive meaning for the noun عين (*'īn*) that follows it in apposition.

---

318 The same is in *Mannā* 229a, under (5): ضرب من الكرم (*a variety of grape*).

The most reasonable explanation seems to be the following cited in the *Thes.* (II 2867) under ܥܝܢ (*ʿīn*):

"valet etiam <u>*aspectus*</u> (*appearance*), *color* (*color*), ܥܝܢܐ ܕܒܪܘܠܚܐ (*ʿaynā ḏ-ḇerulḥā*) (*"eye"* = *coloring, shimmer, gleam of the pearl, of the crystal, of the gem*), Num. XI, 7, Ephr. I, 256 C…; ܥܝܢܗ ܕܚܡܪܐ (*ʿayneh d-ḥamrā*) ("*eye*" of the wine = its "*sparkle*"), Prov. XXIII, 31, Ephr. Opp. Gr. II. 408 D…."[319] (2870, Ap. lexx.): ܥܝܢ ܒܪܘܠܚܐ (*ʿīn berulḥā*) (*"eye"* = *sparkling*, gleaming of the pearl or of the crystal – so-called): ܠܫܘܦܪܐ ܕܚܙܬܗ (*l-šuprā ḏa-ḥzāṯeh*) (*because of its beautiful appearance*). Further *Mannā* 540a, (2): وجه. منظر. لون / *wağh, manẓar, lawn* (*appearance, sight*, color). "

It is moreover interesting to note that the *Lisān* (XIII 302b f.) has also preserved a reminiscence of the Syro-Aramaic meaning in the following expression: وعين الرجل: منظره (*wa-ʿaynᵘ r-rağulⁱ: manẓaruhᵘ*) (*the "eye" of a man = his "appearance"* – actually his *"esteem"*, hence: الأعيان / *al-aʿyān* "the *notables*"[320]), and further on (306a): عين الشيء : النفيس منه (*the "<u>eye</u>" of something = its exquisiteness, <u>treasure</u>* – hence: عينة / *ʿayyina*[321]).

With that the meaning of عين (*ʿīn*) should actually be clear. As a noun standing in apposition to the plural حور (*ḥūr*) "white" (ones) (*grapes*), it has a descriptive function. As such it can be in the singular ("*a gleaming, splendid appearance*" in the meaning "*of gleaming, splendid appearance*") or in the plural (in the sense of "*treasures*"). The

319 For the same meaning in Hebrew, see W. Gesenius, *Hebräisches und aramäisches Handwörterbuch* [*Compendious Hebrew and Aramaic Dictionary*] 582b, (*h*) figuratively speaking: (α) *the eye of the wine*, i.e., *its sparkling in the cup*, Prov. 23:31…; (γ) *sight*; hence, *form, appearance*, Num. 11:7, Lev. 13:5,55. Ezek. 1:4 ff. 10:9, Dan. 10:6.

320 The *Lisān* does not remark that the current plural أعيان /*aʿyān* (*notables*) is derived from this meaning.

321 This feminine form means in modern Arabic "*specimen, sample*". But the original Syro-Aramaic meaning is "*choice, prime, elite, flower*" (= modern Arabic: نخبة / *nuḫba* [*select, choice*], خيرة / *ḫīra* [*the best, choice, elite*]).

spelling عين / *ʿayn* would accordingly have to be in the singular, yet in the plural, rather than *ʿīn* (following the type سفينة / سفن ، *safīna, sufun* and in the style of the commonly used plural form عيون / *ʿuyūn*), it would most likely be *ʿuyun*. The Koran elsewhere uses the two plural forms عيون (*ʿuyūn*) (for *springs, wells*) and اعين (*aʿyun*) (for *eyes*). This would presuppose a singular form عينة (*ʿayna* or *ʿayyina*) respectively, which would be derived from the Syro-Aramaic ܥܝܢܬܐ (*ʿayntā*) (sing.), ܥܝܢܬܐ (*ʿaynāṯā*) (plur.). Namely, the *Thes.* (II 2870) cites the Eastern Syrian lexicographers, who distinguish between ܥܝܢܐ (*ʿaynā*), ܥܝܢ̈ܐ (*ʿaynē*) for living beings and the first-named for things. However, arguing in favor of the Arabic pausal form of the presumed Syro-Aramaic plural ܥܝܢ̈ܐ (*ʿaynē*) is the variant of the Koran text of Ubayy for Sura 56:22 cited in Th. Nöldeke (Bergsträßer-Pretzl) (*GdQ* III 90) with the remark "*quite striking*": وحورا عينا (Arabic: *wa-ḥūr^{an} ʿīn^{an}* = Syro-Aramaic: ܘܚܘܪ̈ܐ or ܥܝܢ̈ܐ : ܘܚܘܪ̈ܬܐ / *w-ḥewwārē* / *w-ḥewwārāṯā* – *ʿaynē* : "*White* [grapes] – *crystal-(clear)* = *Crystal-(clear) white* [grapes]").

Solution II

Inasmuch as the Koran explicitly compares the "*white*(*s*)" (*grapes*) with pearls, the actual sense of عين (*ʿīn*) or (*ʿuyun*) "*eyes*" has also been cleared up. Taking as its starting point the "*sparkle, gleam*" or the "*sparkling, gleaming appearance*" of gems, the Syro-Aramaic expression ܥܝܢ (*ʿīn*), as the *Thesaurus* proves,[322] has itself been transferred to the *gems*. However, because the Koran compares the grapes with "*pearls*," though these are not gems in the proper sense, we can take the alternative meaning given by the *Thes.* "*crystal*" (due to its clarity and its shine) or "*jewel*" as an expression of the "*preciousness*," which in this respect is confirmed by the *Lisān* (عين الشئ : النفيس منه) for the Koranic context.[323]. Now because حور (*ḥūr*) as a designation of "*white*" (*grapes*) is in the plural, the noun عين that follows it in apposition is

---

322 *Thes.* II 2867: ܥܝܢ ܥܓܠܐ (*ʿīn ʿeglā*) *oculus vituli,* gemma quaedam; (with a reference to the East Syrian lexicographers): Ap. lexx. (1) *gemma* (gem).

323 Cf. note 284 above.

logically also to be read as plural, which is indeed confirmed by the traditional reading of the Koran. Accordingly, the Koranic double expression حور : عين (*ḥūr*^un^ *: ʿuyun*) says:

> "*White*" (*grapes*): "*jewels*" (or rather) "*crystals*" = *Crystal-(clear) white* (*grapes*) [instead of: "*dark-, wide-eyed"* (maidens)].

This would explain the syntactic relationship between "*eyes*" [= *crystal-(clear)*] as a nominal adjective and the substantivied adjective "*white*" (*grapes*).[324]

---

324 In a recently by Jan M.F. van Reeth published essay entitled: "*Le vignoble du Paradis et le chemin qui y mène. La thèse de C. Luxenberg et les sources du Coran* [*The Vineyard of the Paradise and the Way leading there. The Thesis of C. Luxenberg and the Souces of the Koran*]" in: *Arabica*, vol. LIII, 4, (Brill) Leiden, 2006, p. 511-524, the author undertakes the task to detect the Christian sources of the Koran. Based on his erudite findings, he supposes a misreading of the double Koranic expression حور عين / *ḥūr ʿīn* (rather *ḥūr ʿuyun*) and proposes instead the emendation كور عنب (*kūr ʿinab*) or خور عنب (*ḫūr ʿinab*) in the sense of "*some quantity of grapes* or *vine*" (*une certaine quantité de raisins, de vin* – p. 515). Indeed, ܟܘܪܐ / *kōrā* designates in Syro-Aramaic a "*dry* or *liquid measure*" of variable size and ܥܢܒܐ / *ʿenbē* "*grapes*"; yet the palaeography allows such an emendation not. For neither within the *ḥiǧāzī* and *kūfī* style nor in the assumed case of a transcription from Syro-Aramaic is a misreading or mistranscription of an Arabic initial كـ / *k* as a حـ / *ḥ* nor a Syro-Aramaic or Arabic final ـب / *b* as a final ـن / *n* conceivable. A comparison of these four letters on the appended copies of the Samarqand codex suffices to exclude normally their confusion. See for example the second copy [CD 0098] following the index, line 4, the initial كـ / *k* and the final ـن / *n* in the word (الر) كعين / *ar-rākiʿīn* [Sura 3:43], and line 5, the dotless final ـت / *t* = ـب / *b* in the undotted first word الغيب / *al-ġayb* [*the invisible*], that can also be read العنب / *al-ʿinab* [*grapes*] but not العين / *al-ʿīn* (or rather *al-ʿuyun*) [*eyes = jewels, crystals*], further the حـ / *ḥ* in the following undotted word نوحيه /*nūḥīhi* [*we inspire it*]. The unconsiderated emendation of these letters, the graphical form of which is unequivocal, would transgress the principle of the *lectio defficilior*. The double expression حور عين / *ḥūr ʿuyun* occurs three times in the Koran (Suras 44:54; 52:20; 56:22); its reading is graphically incontestable and semantically covered through the following expounded context. The task of the philology is to clarify the Koranic text in order to guard the historian of religion against hasty deductions and to provide him with a reliable basis for his far-reaching investigations.

In the history of the Koranic text this significant expression, which served as the inexhaustible source for the mythologized subject of the *ḥūrī* and not just for Arabic popular literature, would thus be restored to its historically authentic dimension thanks to Syro-Aramaic. It helps the Koran to achieve its original inner coherence. That the Christian-Oriental notions of Paradise depicted by Ephraem the Syrian find expression in the Koran can no longer be surprising when one knows that the Christian Syro-Aramaic hymns of Ephraem in the 4th century and afterwards gained such currency beyond the Aramaic speech area of Syria and Mesopotamia that they were even translated into foreign languages such as Greek and Armenian.[325]

Remarkable are to that extent the erudite and to the Bible referring investigations of the author as to his new comparative interpretation of the Sura الفاتحة / *al-Fātiḥa* (p. 519-524). As to the expression غير المغضوب عليهم (*ġayr al-maġḍūb ʿalayhim*) in verse 7, another understanding as the proposed reading from the supposed Arabic verbal root *ʿḍb* in the sense of "*couper*, *transpercer*, *abattre*, *éloigner*" (*to cut*, *pierce*, *strike down*, *take away*) is conceivable without to modify the traditionnal reading, if we start from the Syro-Aramaic sense of the equivalent expression ܪܘܓܙܐ ܕܡܪܝܐ / *rugzā d-māryā* (*the anger of the Lord*), as far as *sinners* (who *transgress* = יפסקון = Koranic يفسقون / *yafsiqūn* the divine law) incur the *divine anger* (cf. *Mannā* 721b, ܐܪܓܙ / *argez*, 1. أغضب / *aġḍaba* [*to anger*], 2. أذنب. أخطأ / *aḏnaba*, *aḫṭaʾa* [*to commit an offense*, *a sin*]). Instead of the proposed understanding: "le chemin de ceux que tu combles de grâce, non de ceux qui sont *anéantis* ou égarés", it should be proposed: "le chemin de ceux que tu combles de grâce, non de ceux *qui se sont attiré ta colère* [= qui ont *transgressé* ta loi] ni de ceux qui se sont égarés [= qui se sont *écartés* de ton *droit chemin*]."

325 Cf. also A. Baumstark, *Geschichte der syrischen Literatur* [*History of Syriac Literature*] (Bonn, 1922) 32 ff.: "The life story of the 'Prophet of the Syrians,' as the grateful admiration of his people called him, began very early on to weave its web around the pious legend. Already purely in terms of volume the mass of what has been preserved under his name in the original and in the variegated dress of foreign languages is overwhelming, without one's even coming close to exhausting what he actually wrote." On the translations, 35 ff.: "Translations of A.'s [Ap(h)rem's = Ephraem's] works already appeared in Greek during his lifetime." Further, on page 36: "One cannot help but be struck to a great degree by how relatively seldom it was for pieces existing in Syriac to come back in Greek translation." .... "Finally, in the best of circumstances one

Additional Relevant Passages

If it has now been established that when the Koran uses the metaphorical expression حور عين (*ḥūr ʿīn*) (or *ʿuyun*), from which the expression *ḥūrī* has been falsely derived, it means the "*white, crystal-clear grapes*" of paradise, it should logically turn out that all of the remaining Koran passages that until now one had connected with the *virgins of paradise* in reality present further descriptions of these very same grapes of paradise, as indeed will be demonstrated by a more detailed philological examination of the following Sura verses: 37:48, 49; 38:52; 55:56, 58, 72, 74; 56:22-23, 34-37. The recurring expression ازوج مطهرة (*azwāǧ muṭahhara*) in the Sura verses 2:25; 3:15 and 4:57 should actually not be included here, but because it has been falsely interpreted, it will be taken up beforehand.

Sura 2:25 (3:15; 4:57)

ولهم فيها ازوج مطهرة

(Bell I 5): 23. "therein also are pure spouses for them, …"

(Paret 9): "Und darin [Note: i.e. in paradise] haben sie gereinigte Gattinnen (zu erwarten)."

(Blachère 32): "Dans ces [jardins], ils auront des <u>épouses purifiées</u>…"

---

would at the least always have to expect that the old translations, during their hundreds of years of use as practical devotional literature, would scarcely be able to escape unintentional distortion and deliberate revision of various sorts." (We have before us such a revision for devotional purposes on, among other things, the topic of Paradise in the Koran.) The Armenian translation of the works of Ephraem is assigned to the 5th century. Later, translations were made by way of Greek into Coptic and into Old Church Slavonic. An Arabic translation, also via Greek, of around 50 pieces by A.[p(h)rem] on ascetic and moral subjects is said to have been completed as late as the year 980 (37).

The Koran does not only apply the expression زوج (*zawǧ*) to people in the sense of "*spouses*," but also to animals and plants in the sense of "*kind, genus, species*." This is made clear from the context of many a verse, such as in Sura 43:12, والذي خلق الازوج كلها , which Paret (407) correctly identifies: "And (he it is) who has created all (possible) *pairs* [note: i.e. *kinds* (of living beings)]." Specifically applied to the plants of the earth (Sura 31:10), وانبتنا فيها من كل زوج كريم , it is here too correctly identified by Paret (339): "And we have caused all manner of magnificent *species* (of plants and fruits) to grow upon it." Further examples can be found in the Suras 20:53; 22:5; 26:7; 36:36 and 50:7.

However, because the Koranic paradise consists of trees, plants and fruits, it is clear that what is meant by ازوج مطهرة (*azwāǧ muṭahhara*) is not "*purified* wives," but

"all manner of species of pure [326] (*fruits*)."

Moreover, that the fruits of paradise are *pure* will be shown in the passages that are yet to be discussed.

Sura 37:48-49

وعندهم قصرات الطرف عين كانهن بيض مكنون

(Bell II 444): 47. "With them are (damsels) restrained in glance, wide-eyed, As they were eggs [Or "pearls"], well-guarded."

(Paret 370): 48: "Und sie haben großäugige (Huris) bei sich, die Augen (sittsam) niedergeschlagen, 49: (unberührt) [Note: or (makellos)] als ob sie wohlverwahrte Eier wären."

326 With "*pure*" the Koran is perhaps rendering one of the meanings of the Syro-Aramaic ܓܒܝܐ (*gabyā*) (*exquisite, noble*), for which *Mannā* (87b) gives, among others, the following Arabic expressions: (3) صفيّ . جيّد. فاضل. طاهر (noble, pure), (4) خالص . كريم . ثمين . فاخر (*sheer, noble, precious, splendid*). However, the actual meaning "*pure*" is also confirmed by Sura 55:56,74, where it is said that nobody before the blessed spirits of the departed has ever "*defiled, soiled*" these grapes.

(Blachère 476): 47/48 "Près d'eux seront des [vierges] aux regards modestes, aux [yeux] grands et beaux, 47/49 et qui seront comme perles cachées."

According to the Syro-Aramaic reading this will be understood as follows:

"They will have (at their disposal) *hanging fruits* (*grapes*) (*for the picking*), *jewels*(-like), as were they *pearls* (yet) *enclosed* (in the shell)."

On the Expression قصرات الطرف (*qāṣirat^u ṭ-ṭarf^i*)

Before one can here determine a fitting meaning for the first expression قصرات (*qāṣirāt*), the second طرف (*ṭarf*) must first be explained. Now that *ḥūrīs* are out of the question, it would be nonsensical to want to speak of their (*demurely lowered*) "*eyes*," as this word has been previously understood in Arabic. What is thus sought is a meaning that goes well with *grapevine* or *grapes*.

Here the Syro-Aramaic synonym ܛܪܦܐ (*ṭarpā*) (with the original meaning "*leaf, foliage*") proves helpful. For the meaning we are seeking the *Thes.* (I 1525) lists under ܛܪܦ (*ṭarrep̄*) *folia decerpsit, racemavit* (*to pick* [*clean*] *the leaves* or *the grapes*), with the following example: ܘܠܐ ܕܢܛܪܦ ܟܪܡܐ (*wālē d̲a-ntarrep̄ karmā*) (*we must pick* [*clean*] *the vineyard* or *the wine leaves*). In addition to this there is in *Mannā* (297) under (4): قطف . قطع . جنى الورق و الثمر (*to pick the foliage* or *the fruits*). Finally, in New East Syriac ܛܪܦܐ (*ṭarpā*) is documented in the meaning (a) *leaf, foliage,* (b) *small branch.*[327]

This leads us first of all to the meaning of the *small branches laden with foliage and grapes* of the grapevine. However, insofar as the denominative ܛܪܦ (*ṭarrep̄*) can also mean "*to pick*," the Koran offers us two parallel passages (Sura 69:23 and 76:14) in which it is said that the

327 Cf. Arthur John Maclean, *A Dictionary of the Dialects of Vernacular Syriac* (Oxford, 1901) 114b: ܛܪܦܐ / *ṭerpâ*: (1) *a leaf,* (2) *a branch.*

(*fruits*) *to be picked* (قطوفها / *quṭūfuhā* < ܩܛܦ / *qṭap̄*) hang down low. This meaning should be assumed for طرف (*ṭarf*).

With this last meaning, قصرات (*qāṣirāt*) should then produce an adequate sense. For the Syro-Aramaic verb ܩܨܪ (*qṣar*) *Mannā* (696b) gives under (2): قصر . خفض (*qaṣṣara, ḫafaḍa*) (*to make short, to lower*). This corresponds to the meaning assumed by our Koran translators, however with regard not to "*lowered eyes*," but to "*lowered*," i.e. "*low-hanging*" (and to that extent easy-to-pick) branches. A parallel expression occurs in Sura 69:23 with قطوفها دانية (*quṭūfuhā dāniya*) (*its fruits are <u>near</u> to be picked,* i.e. within easy reach) (< Syro-Aramaic ܕܢܐ *dnā*).[328]

A similar thought is contained in the expression وذللت قطوفها تذليلا (*wa-ḏullilat quṭūfuhā taḏlīlā*) (*and its fruits are quite easy to pick*).[329] Thus for the expressions وعندهم قصرت الطرف the parallel passages from Sura 69:23 and 76:14 suggest the following understanding:

> "By them (will be) low-hanging branches (laden with fruit)."

The next word عين (*ʿīn*) could here stand for the Syro-Aramaic plural ܥܝܢܐ (*ʿaynē*). The dropping of the emphatic ending would be caused by the Arabic transcription. Besides the meaning "*gleam, shimmer,*" especially of gems, it has already been explained that the term can also designate the *gem* itself or a *jewel.*[330] Accordingly, the double verse cited above from Sura 37:48-49 is to be understood as follows:

> "By them (will be) <u>*fruits*</u> (*grapes*) <u>*hanging down*</u>, (like) <u>*jewels*</u>, as were they <u>*enclosed*</u> <u>*pearls*</u> (still in the shell)."

The final expression بيض (*bayḍ*^{un}), which Paret has rendered according to the Arabic understanding with "*eggs*," Blachère and Bell (in addition

---

328 Cf. *Mannā* 153b, ܕܢܐ (*dnā*): دنا . قرب. (*danā, qaruba*) (*to be near*).

329 Cf. Mannā 148b, ܕܠܠ (*dallel*) (2): هوّن . سهّل (*hawwana, sahhala*) (*to facilitate, to make easy*).

330 *Thes.* II 2867, Ap. lexx. (1) *gemma* (*gem, pearl*); furthermore, at 2870, Ap. lexx., the Arabic المها (*al-mahā*) ("<u>*pearls*</u>" as well as "<u>*crystal*</u>") is given, among other terms, by *Bar Bahlūl* and *Bar ʿAlī* for ܥܝܢܐ العين (*ʿaynā / al-ʿayn*). With this expression, the Koran has once again handed down to us an interesting detail pointing to the Syrian-Mesopotamian region.

to "*eggs*") have correctly conjectured as "*pearls*," though not on the basis of the actual Arabic meaning. In fact, in *Ṭabarī* (XXIII 57 f.) the majority of the commentators explain the expression in the meaning of "*like an unshelled egg*," although the interpretation as "*pearl*" is also advocated once. *Ṭabarī* himself, however, pronounces himself in favor of the former, the majority opinion. However, the parallel passage from Sura 52:24 كانهم لؤلؤ مكنون "as if they were enclosed pearls," suggests the latter meaning. Like لؤلؤ (*luʾluʾ*) (*pearls*), بيض (*bayḍ*) too is a collective noun, which is indicated by the singular form of the verb. On the basis of the Arabic understanding, one can in fact understand "*eggs*" under بيض (*bayḍ*). The *Lisān* does indeed document the feminine form بيضة (*baiḍa*) in the sense of "*white*" to designate a *variety of white grapes*, but not to designate *pearls*. Once again, it is only via Syro-Aramaic that we arrive at this meaning to the extent that the *Thes.* (I 606), with a reference to the Eastern Syrian lexicographers, designates both the ܒܪܘܠܐ (*berūllā*) and ܒܪܘܠܚܐ (*berulḥā*) *margarita* (*pearl* as well as *crystal*) as "*white*": *Albo limpidoque colore est,* ܚܘܪ ܘܨܠܘܠ (*ḥewwār wa-ṣlōl*) (white *and clear*); hence the Syrians explain ܒܪ̈ܘܠܚܐ (*berulḥē*) as ܡܪ̈ܓܢܝܬܐ ܚܘܪ̈ܬܐ (*marganyāṯā ḥewwārāṯā*) *margaritae albae* (*white pearls*). Accordingly, just as in the case of "*white*" (*grapes*) (حور / *ḥūr*), with the Arabic collective noun بيض (*bayḍ*) the Koran is also designating "*white*" (*pearls*) following the equivalent Syro-Aramaic designation.

Sura 38:52

وعندهم قصرت الطرف اتراب

(Bell II 454): "With them are (females) restrained in glance, of equal age."

(Paret 378): "während sie gleichaltrige (Huris) bei sich haben, die Augen (sittsam) niedergeschlagen."

(Blachère 486): "tandis qu'auprès d'eux seront des [*vierges*] aux regards modestes, d'égale jeunesse."

As opposed to both of the prior verses (37: 48-49), in the present verse only the expression اتراب (*atrāb*) has been added. This expression could of course not fail to help spur on the fantastic imagination of the *ḥūrīs* to yet another adequate property. For, although one knew about the "*big-eyed ḥūrīs*" that they were to that extent "*cute*," they still lacked one characteristic: in addition to that they had to be "*young*." And so one hit upon the idea that this misunderstood Arabic expression had to mean something like "*of the same age*," from which there resulted the meaning "*forever young*."[331] Subsequent commentators then even pinned their age down to the symbolic figure of *thirty-three*. So much for the *history of the development* of the expression اتراب (*atrāb*).

It is in the meantime clear that all the commentators were so taken with the idea of the *ḥūrīs* that for them anything else was out of the question. Yet it is astonishing that they have paid so little attention to the Koranic context. Namely, two verses further (54) it is said in regard to the supposed *ḥūrīs:* ان هذا لرزقنا ما له من نفاد "This is our (heavenly) nourishment (رزقنا / *rizqunā*), it (will be) inexhaustible." The Koranic statement is actually clear and excludes every possible figment of the imagination. In excess of *food* and *drink* there is nothing in Paradise.

The Koran confirms this statement in several passages, where it is said among others to the pious: "*Eat* and *drink* (كلوا و اشربوا / *kulū wa-š-rabū*) (Suras 52:19; 69:24; 77:43),[332] enjoy (the fruit) of your toil". Furthermore, it should be noted that even in later Medinan Suras the believers are never promised more than "*gardens* [properly *bowers*], *under which rivers flow*".[333] Not even in the Medinan verse (3:169) referring to those killed for the cause of Allah *ḥūrīs* are mentioned. Instead it is said about them (Bell I 62, 163): "Count not those who have been killed in the way of Allah as dead, nay, alive with their Lord, *provided for*"

331 *Ṭabarī* XXIII 174 f. also gives these interpretations: *They are equal, equal in age, of the same age; they do not treat each other with hostility; they are not envious of each other; they are not jealous of each other.*

332 Cf. also Suras 37:46; 38:51; 47:15; 76:21.

333 Cf. Suras 2:25; 3:15,136,195,198; 4:13,57,122; 5:12,85,119; 9:72,89,100; 10:9; 13:35; 14:23; 16:31; 18:31; 20:76; 22:14,23; 29:58; 39:20; 47:12,15; 48:5,17; 57:12; 58:22; 61:12; 64:9; 65:11; 66:8; 85:11; 98:8.

(عند ربهم يرزقون / *ʿinda rabbihim yurzaqūn* – with fruits of paradise). Consequently, even with the expression اتراب (*atrāb*) the Koran is describing nothing more than those same fruits, which are adduced by the Syro-Aramaic lexicon. For even with the expression اتراب (*atrāb*) the Koran is describing nothing more than those same fruits taught us by the Syro-Aramaic lexicon.

Under ܛܪܒܐ (*tarbā*) the *Thes.* (4495) refers to the loan word in Arabic (today no longer in use) ثرب (*ṯarb*), first of all with the meaning *adeps* (*fat*), and further down with the meaning *pulpa pomorum* (*fruit pulp, flesh*), as well as the adjectival ܛܪܒܢܝܐ (*tarbānāyā*) *pinguis, adiposus* (here: *fleshy, juicy*). The same can be found in *Mannā* (848b): ܛܪܒܐ (*tarbā*) (2) شحم الرمان وغيره من الأثمار (*flesh of pomegranates and other fruits*), and adjectivally ܛܪܒܢܐ (*tarbānā*), ܛܪܝܒܐ (*trī͟bā*), in Arabic أثرب (*aṯrab*).

And thus the "*same-aged*" (or *eternally young*) *ḥūrīs* are transformed into "*fleshy, juicy*" (*fruits*). In Syro-Aramaic the verse cited above from Sura 38:52 is thus to be understood as:

"Among them (will be) *juicy fruits hanging down*."

Through the actual sense of the attributive adjective اتراب (*atrāb*) (*fleshy, juicy*) it is clear from the context of this verse that with طرف (*ṭarf*), as determined from the Syro-Aramaic expression, what is in fact meant are "*fruits ripe for the picking*."[334]

334 Though the Koran here uses طرف (*ṭarf*) as a collective noun, it also has the plural اطراف (*aṭrāf*) in two other passages; in Sura 13:41 it says: اولم يروا انا ناتي الارض ننقصها من اطرافها (in Paret's translation [205]):
„Haben sie denn nicht gesehen, daß wir über das Land kommen, indem wir es an seinen Enden kürzen (*?Nanquṣuhā min aṭrāfihā*) (und damit ihren Machtbereich einschränken?)?" ["Have they not seen that we come over the land by shortening its ends (*?Nanquṣuhā min aṭrāfihā*) (and thus reduce the area of their power?)?"]
With اطراف (*aṭrāf*) here, however, it is not "*ends*" that is meant, but the "*fruits*" of the earth that God "*decreases*" as punishment. Namely, with ننقصها (*nanquṣuhā*) the Koran is reproducing the Syro-Aramaic ܚܣܪ (*ḫassar*) or ܐܚܣܪ (*aḥsar*), for which *Mannā* (254b) (2) gives in Arabic نقص . قلل (*naqqaṣa, qallala*) (*to reduce, to decrease*). The same applies for Sura 21:44. Likewise, the expression

Sura 55:56

فيهن قصرت الطرف لم يطمثهن انس قبلهم ولا جان

(Bell II 551): "In them are (damsels) of restrained glance, whom deflowered before them has neither man nor jinn."

(Paret 448): "Darin [Note: D.h. in den Gärten (Mehrzahl)] befinden sich (auch), die Augen (sittsam) niedergeschlagen, weibliche Wesen, die vor ihnen [Note: D.h. vor den (männlichen) Insassen des Para-dieses, denen sie nunmehr als Gattinnen zugewiesen werden] weder Mensch noch Dschinn (*ǧānn*) entjungfert hat."

(Blachère 570 f.): "Dans ces jardins seront des [*vierges*] aux regards modestes que ni Homme ni Démon n'aura touchées, avant eux."

The result of the ensuing analysis will show that this verse is to be understood Syro-Aramaically as follows:

"Therein (are found) *drooping fruits* (*ripe for the picking*), which neither man nor genius (i.e. an *invisible being*)[335] before them has ever *defiled*."

ناتي الارض (*naʾtī l-ʾarḍᵃ*) is not Arabic "*we come over the land*," but Syro-Aramaic ܢܝܬܐ ܠܐܪܥܐ (*naytē l-arʿā*) (modern Arabic = نؤتي الارض /*nuʾtī l-ʾarḍᵃ*) "*we cause the earth to be of use, to be fruitful, to come to fruition, to bear fruit*"; cf. *Mannā* 45b: ܐܝܬܝܬ ܐܪܥܐ ܥܠܠܬܐ (*aytyaṯ arʿā ʿallāṯā*) . اثمرت اغلت الارض (*aṯmarat, aġallat al-arḍ*) (*the earth* '*is fruitful,*' *bears fruit*). According to this, the verse reads: „Sehen sie denn nicht, daß wir die Erde (ihren Ertrag) bringen lassen (und dabei) ihre Früchte verringern (können)?" ["Do they not see that we allow the earth to produce (its yield) (and at the same time) (are able) to reduce its fruits?"]

335 The original meaning of the Syro-Aramaic verbal root ܓܢ / *gann*, ܓܢܐ / *gnā*, Hebrew גנן / *ganan* > *gnan* (1. *to hide*, 2. *to protect*) suggests that "*genius*" (as a "*hidden*" = *invisible* being) is etymologically derived rather from Syro-Aramaic than from Greek γεννάω > Latin *genō* < *gignō* (*to engender*, *to bear*). Of the same etymology is Arabic جنة /*ǧanna* < Syro-Aramaic ܓܢܬܐ / *gannᵊṯā* (*garden* > *paradise* – grammatically a passive participle) as a "*protected place*". The most likely interpretation of the Koranic plural جنات / *ǧannāt* would be that of

Joining the previously explained expressions in this verse is the new (negated) verb لم يطمثهن (*lam yaṭmiṯhunna*). With "*to deflower*" (or *to touch*) our Koran translators have followed the meanings proposed by *Ṭabarī* (XXVII 150 f.), while *Ṭabarī* himself has repeated the commentators' interpretation of this verse, according to which the *ḥūrīs* restrict their glances to their husbands, i.e. wish for themselves nobody else but him.

Of all the expressions connected with the imaginary *ḥūrīs*, it can be said that with the understanding of "*deflower*" the pinnacle has been reached. Anyone who reads the Koran with a bit of understanding is really compelled at this point to throw up his hands in despair. But the Koran as a holy scripture is not responsible for the insinuations that human ignorance has imagined into it. The Syro-Aramaic reading of these passages will help us to better understand the original meaning of the Koran according to its historical-linguistic context.

To blame for this is first of all the ignorance of the true etymology of the verbal root طمث (*ṭamiṯ*^{a}) in Arabic. We have already seen in the case of اترفوا (*utrifū*) (Sura 11:116) that the Arabic philologists have thought that the Syro-Aramaic verbal prefix ܐܬ / *eṯ-* was a radical, out of which the root ترف (*tarif*^{a}) (in addition to the synonymous رفه / *rafuh*^{a}) then falsely emerged in Arabic. With طمث (*ṭamiṯ*^{a}) we are presented with a situation in which the Syro-Aramaic feminine suffix ܬܐ / *-ṯā* of the adjective ܛܡܐܬܐ (*ṭmāṯā* / *ṭammāṯā*) (*impure*) has likewise been thought to be a radical, out of which the Arabic verb طمث (*ṭamiṯ*^{a})

the single (vine) *arbours* as "*shaded places*", under cover of which the pious are said to rest (just the same sense as the Arabic word خيمة /*ḫayma* [*tent, bower*]; cf. Sura 55:72: حور مقصورت في الخيام [*White* (grapes) *hanging in* (wine) *bowers*]; etymologically, خيمة /*ḫayma* is derived from the root حمى / *ḥamā* [*to protect*], the خ / *ḫ* being a vernacular Eastern Aramaic pronounciation of the ح / *ḥ*, this root beeing again a phonetical variant of the Syro-Aramaic verbal root ܥܡܐ / *ʿmā* [*to cover, to hide*]; cf *Mannā* 547b). S. Fraenkel, *Die aramäischen Fremdwörter im Arabischen* [*The Aramaic Foreign Words in the Arabic Language*], was indecisive as to this etymology, when he noticed (p. 30): "Unklarer Herkunft, aber durch äthiop. haimat (Dillm. 610) als *echt* erwiesen ist خيمة [*Of not clear origin, yet through Ethiopian haimat* (Dillm. 610) is خيمة / *ḫayma* proved as *genuine*]."

emerged as a denominative.[336] This arises not only from the feminine present participle طامث (*ṭāmiṯ*) (said of a woman when she has her period) listed by the *Lisān* (II 165b), but also from the listed meanings that coincide with those of the Syro-Aramaic verb ܛܡܐ / ܛܐܡܐ (*ṭammā*) (*Thes.* I 1484), although with some shifts in meaning. Of course, an etymologically equivalent Arabic root طمئ (*ṭamiʾa*) given by both the *Thesaurus* and Brockelmann, is not listed by the *Lisān*, which is an argument in favor of its having also been borrowed from the Aramaic.

Now whereas the Syro-Aramaic root actually means "*to be impure*," one has related the Arabic denominative to menstruation and naturally connected this with the idea of *blood.* So if a woman says "I am طامث (*ṭāmiṯ*)" (for *I have my period*), in Arabic one has understood "I am *bloody*," whereas in Syro-Aramaic this meant "I am *impure*." In Arabic usage, this notion was also logically applied to the transitive, thus resulting in the meaning "*to deflower*." The comparison between the *Lisān* and the *Thes.* shows clearly that with the meaning "*to deflower*" one has a concrete imagination of *blood* in the Arabic usage, whereas in Syro-Aramaic one understands this in the figurative sense of "*to render impure, to defile, to dishonor*."

And hence this fateful misunderstanding occurred in the Koran where the verb لم يطمثهن (*lam yaṭmiṯhunna*) is used transitively. By that in Arabic, especially with regard to the imaginary *ḥūrīs*, one was thus only able to understand "*to deflower*," whereas in Syro-Aramaic it means "*to render impure, to defile*." What moreover reinforced the Arabic commentators in their notion that the *grapes* of Paradise were *women* is precisely the feminine personal suffix هن / *-hunna*, which according to the rules of Arabic grammar can refer only to rational living beings, i.e. exclusively to women, whereas the Koran in accordance with

336 This fact has previously been noticed by R. Dozy, *Die Israeliten zu Mekka* [*The Israelites in Mekka*], Leipzig-Haarlem 1864, p. 182, note 7: "As to امراة طامث (*imra'a ṭāmiṯ*) it must be noticed that طامث (*ṭāmiṯ*) is not an Arabic word that were derived from a root طمث (*ṭāmiṯa*), it is טמא (*ṭamā* / *ṭmā*), the usual term for *impure* in Levitic sense; the last letter is a feminine ending."

the rules of Syro-Aramaic does not always make this distinction in the case of the feminine.[337]

Finally, one should not fail to mention in favor of the Arabic commentators that *Ṭabarī* (*loc.cit.*) also explains طمث (*ṭamiṯ*[a]) in the meaning of "*to touch,*" as Blachère likewise translates it. With reference to the *white grapes* of Paradise, this understanding would be correct. However, with regard to the intended *ḥūrīs* this expression is only a euphemism.

Thus the previously cited verse is to be understood according to the Syro-Aramaic reading as proposed at the outset.

The related Verse 58, as correctly translated by Paret (449), ["They are (so radiantly beautiful), as if they were hyacinths and corals. / Sie sind (so strahlend schön), wie wenn sie aus Hyazinth und Korallen wären."], accordingly refers not to the *ḥūrīs*, but to the *grapes* and the other *fruits* of Paradise.

Sura 55:70, 72, 74

فيهن خيرات حسان / حور مقصورات في الخيام
لم يطمثهن انس قبلهم ولا جان

(Bell II 552): 70. "In them are (damsels) good and beautiful, 72. Wide-eyed, restrained in the tents, 74. Whom deflowered before them has neither man nor jinn."

(Paret 449): 70: "Darin befinden sich gute und schöne weibliche Wesen. 72: Huris, in den Zelten abgesperrt (so daß sie den Blicken von Fremden entzogen sind). 74: (Weibliche Wesen) die vor ihnen weder Mensch noch Dschinn (*ǧānn*) entjungfert hat."

---

337 Thus, for example, in Sura 12:43 it is said of the seven fat cows devoured by seven lean ones: يأكلهن سبع عجاف (*ya'kulu-hunna* – as they were *women*), instead of classical Arabic – like a singular: يأكلها (*ya'kulu-hā*). In like manner, it is said of the seven withered ears of corn يابسات (*yābisāt*) (as a sound feminine plural for *reasonable beings* [للعاقل / *li-l-ʿāqil*], i.e., *women*) and not يابسة (*yābisa* – like a feminine singular [لغير العاقل / *li-ġayr al-ʿāqil*] for *not reasonable beings*). So, too, in numerous other passages of the Koran.

(Blachère 570 f.): 70 “Dans ces jardins seront des [*vierges*] bonnes, belles, 72 des Houris, cloîtrées dans des pavillons, 74 que ni homme, ni Démon n’aura touchées, avant eux.”

First of all, to comment on the individual words:

Verse 70: The words “good” and “beautiful” do not refer to “(damsels)” (Bell) or “female creatures” (Paret), who are not even mentioned in the Koran. Paret’s understanding of this has been falsely concluded from the feminine ending of the preceding adjective (which according to Arabic grammar is restricted to *rational living creatures*).

(a) The Arabic adjective خيرات (to be read *ḫayyirāt* rather than *ḫayrāt*) stands for Syro-Aramaic ܓܒܝܬܐ (*gaḇyāṯā*), for which the *Thes.* (I 636 f.) gives the meaning *electus* (*choice*). The Arabic meanings that the *Mannā* (87b) gives for this are revealing: (3) جيد . فاضل. طاهر (*good, excellent, pure*), (4) كريم . ثمين . فاخر (*noble, precious, first-rate*), (5) خيار الشىء (*that which is choice*). This last meaning is meant here with regard to the “*choice* (*heavenly fruits*).” Also interesting, however, is the first definition listed under (3) طاهر (*pure*), which makes clear the real meaning of the supposed “*purified wives*” (Suras 2:25; 3:15; 4:57), where what is really meant, however, are “*choice fruits of every sort*.” Meaning (4) كريم (*precious*), which the Koran uses as a synonym in this context (e.g. Suras 8:4; 26:7; 31:10), further confirms this meaning.

The Syro-Aramaic expression helps us moreover to deduce another word characterized as *obscure* in the Koran. In Verse 25 of the Mary Sura, namely, it says: “Shake the trunk of the palm so that they رطبا جنيا will fall down to you.” Paret (249) translates the two words read as *ruṭaba*^{n} *ǧanīya*^{n} as “fresh dates.” In his *Commentary* (329) he remarks (19, 25): “The expression *ǧanī*(*yan*) actually means ‘(freshly) picked,’ which does not fit here.” In reality, however, Syro-Aramaic ܪܛܒܐ (*raṭḇā*) / ܪܛܝܒܐ (*raṭīḇā*) means everything “*fresh and green*” (see *Thes.* II 3893 f.; *Mannā* 737a: رطب . اخضر. نضر). Therefore it is accordingly not “*dates*” that are meant, but *“fresh*” (*fruits*). In the adjective that follows جنيا the upper dot has been falsely set. Setting it lower results in the reading جبيا (*ğabīya* according to the rhyme, but really *ğabāyā*). Namely, as a transliteration of the Syro-Aramaic ܓܒܝܐ (*gḇayyā*) it means "*choice.*" And thus these two adjectives do not mean "*fresh dates*," but "*fresh, choice*" (*fruits*).

(b) The second Arabic adjective حسان (*ḥisān*) is to be understood as a synonym of the first. As the lexical equivalent of the Syro-Aramaic ܛܒܐ (*ṭāḇā*), namely, it results in exactly the same meaning, which *Mannā* (277b) cites under ܛܒܐ (*ṭāḇā*) with the following Arabic expressions: خيّر . جيّد . حسن . فاضل . كريم . فاخر . ثمين . Here too the Syro-Aramaic expression confirms the Arabic equivalents appearing in the Koran خيرات (*ḫayyirāt*), حسان (*ḥisān*), and كريم (*karīm*) in the meaning of "*excellent, choice.*" That this adjective refers to the indicated fruits is clear from the Koranic context.

Thus, in the above-mentioned Verse 70 "*good and beautiful female creatures*" are out of the question. The verse should instead be understood in this way:

"Therein (are found) choice, excellent (*fruits*)."

The problem of Verse 72 is relatively easy to solve when you know that the Arabic word خيمة (*ḫayma*) means not only "*tent*," but also "*bower.*" However, questionable figments of the imagination arise when Paret translates the verse in this way: "Houris cloistered in tents (so as to be withdrawn from the sight of strangers)." In accordance with the expressions explained above and recurring in this verse, this verse should instead be understood Syro-Aramaically as follows:

"White (grapes) hanging in wine bowers."

Interesting in this respect is the parallel with Ephraem the Syrian considering that in what was quoted above he likewise speaks of grapevines of paradise that present *hanging grapes* to the righteous one.

As a repetition of Verse 56, Verse 74 has actually been clarified. In context the Verses 70, 72, and 74 from Sura 55 are thus to be understood Syro-Aramaically as follows:

70. “Therein (are found) *choice, first-rate* (*fruits*),

72. White (grapes) hanging in (wine) bowers,

74. which neither man nor genius has ever *besmirched*“

Sura 56:22-23

وحور عين كامثل اللؤلؤ المكنون

(Bell II 555): 22. “And (maidens) with dark, wide eyes, like pearls treasured – …”

(Paret 450): 22. “Und großäugige Huris (haben sie zu ihrer Verfügung), 23: (in ihrer Schönheit) wohlverwahrten Perlen zu vergleichen.”

(Blachère 572): 22 “[*Là seront*] des Houris aux grands yeux, 22/23 semblables à la perle cachée, …”

This double verse has actually already been clarified and only needs to be repeated:

22: “*White* (*grapes*), *jewels*, 23: Like pearls that are (still) enclosed (in the shell).”

Sura 56:34-37

وفرش مرفوعة / انا انشانهن انشاء
فجعلنهن ابكارا / عربا اترابا

(Bell II 555): 33. “And carpets raised. 34. Verily We have produced them [The houris of Verse 22] specially, 35. And made them virgins, 36. Loving and of equal age, …”

(Paret 450): 34: “und dick gepolsterten [Note: W: erhöhten] Betten. 35: (Und Huris stehen zu ihren Diensten.) Wir haben sie regelrecht geschaffen [Note: W: entstehen lassen] 36: und sie zu

Jungfrauen gemacht, 37: heiß liebend (*ʿuruban*) und gleichaltrig, …"

(Blachère 573): 33/34 "[couchés sur] des tapis élevés [au-dessus du sol], 34/35 [Des Houris] que nous avons formées, en perfection, 35/36 et que nous avons gardées vierges, 36/37 coquettes, d'égale jeunesse, …"

In this verse is the culmination, as though in an apotheosis, of the mythological notion of the so-called houris. It is not easy to straighten out this crooked train of thought, but we intend to make the attempt and examine the individual words.

On Verse 34: Here the only word that needs to be explained is فرش (*furuš*), which as an Arabic plural can if fact mean either "mattresses, beds" or "carpets." In this meaning it corresponds to the Syro-Aramaic ܦܪܣܐ (*prāsā*), from which it is derived. But beyond that, this Syro-Aramaic word has, among others, the following meaning given by *Mannā* (611b): (4) مظلة . خيمة (*tent, bower*). In this respect it can be understood as a synonym of the Arabic خيام (*ḫiyām*) (*tents, wine bowers*) occurring in Sura 56:72 above. The following participle مرفوعة (*marfūʿa*) (*raised*) also refers to this, which results in the meaning: *"raised [or high-climbing] wine bowers"* (and not *"thickly upholstered beds"* or *"carpets raised above the floor"*).

On Verse 35: Here the Arabic verb انشأ (*anšaʾa*) is lexically equivalent to the Syro-Aramaic ܐܘܥܝ (*awʿī*) (or to the synonym ܐܫܘܚ *ašwaḥ*), the Arabic equivalent of which *Mannā* (313b) gives as follows: انبت . اخرج (*to cause to grow*), (2) انشأ . اصدر (*to provide, to create*). From this it becomes clear that here the Koran means انشأ (*anšaʾa*) in the sense of انبت (*anbata*) (*to cause to grow*). In this way this verse also adds itself seamlessly to the one preceding it:

34. "*raised* (high-climbing) *wine bowers*; 35. these we have *had grow tall*."

On Verse 36: Supposedly God has made the *ḥūrīs* into "*virgins*." Yet both in Arabic and in Syro-Aramaic the meaning of the expression بكر (*bikr*) is not primarily "*virgin*," but first of all "*first work*" as well as *"first born."* However, in particular in Syro-Aramaic it has the meaning we need here, which *Mannā* (64a), under ܒܟܪܐ (*bakkārā*), defines in Arabic as follows: (2) باكورة . اول الثمر خاصة (*first works, in particular first fruits*). This means that the precondition of all of the previously listed qualities (*pure, crystal-clear, choice, first-rate*) is this: as *first fruits* the heavenly fruits include in themselves the above-mentioned advantages. Thus Verse 36 is:

"We have made them into *first fruits*."

On Verse 37: That God supposedly had made the *Ḥūrīs* "passionately loving" and "of equal age" is naturally one of the high points of this mythological conception.

It is no accident that the Koranic spelling عربا, which is considered unexplained to this day, has been misread as *ʿuruba*^{n}. As an unexplained term, it could be explained at one's discretion. But then if the *ḥūrīs* were "*young* and *pretty,*" they still lacked one property: in addition to this they had also to be *"passionately loving,"* since nothing would be more boring in Paradise than a cool beauty.

Yet it is a question precisely of *this* property in the case of the misread word عربا (*ʿuruba*^{n}), which would be correctly read in Syro-Aramaic as ܥܪ̈ܝܐ (*ʿarrāyē*) (*cold, ice-cold*), and should accordingly be read in Arabic as عريا (probably *ʿarāyā* or *ʿarāyē*). That the heavenly fruits are "*choice*" as well as "*chilled"* is substantiated by the Koran in Verses 42-44, where it is said on the contrary of those who are on the *left* (that is, of the damned) that they will be in the heat of fire, where they will receive nothing لا بارد ولا كريم (*lā bārid wa-lā karīm*) *cool* nor *choice.*

The next word اترابا (which is to be read *aṯrāba*^{n}) has already been discussed above. Accordingly, Verse 37 no longer refers to *ḥūrīs* that would be "*passionately loving* and *of equal age,*" but of heavenly fruits that are "chilled and juicy."

To sum up, according to the Syro-Aramaic reading, the Verses 34-37 of Sura 56 should now be understood as follows:

> 34. "(They will have) high-climbing (wine) bowers, 35. these we have *had grow tall,* 36. and made into *first fruits,* 37. *chilled* and *juicy.*"

Sura 78:33

This verse offers us a kind of *second selection* on the subject *ḥūrī* in the Koran. Verses 31-34 may be cited in this connection:

أن للمتقين مفازا / حدائق واعنبا
وكواعب اترابا / وكاسا دهاقا

> (Bell II 630): 31. "Verily, for the pious is a place of felicity, 32. Orchards and vineyards, 33. And full-breasted (ones) of equal age, 34. And a cup overflowing, ..."

> (Paret 497): 31: "Die Gottesfürchtigen (dagegen) haben (großes) Glück (*mafāz*) zu erwarten, 32: Gärten und Weinstöcke, 33: gleich-altrige (Huris) mit schwellenden Brüsten 34: und einen Becher (mit Wein, bis an den Rand) gefüllt (*dihāq*)."

> (Blachère 633): 31 "En vérité, aux Hommes pieux reviendra [*au contraire*] un lieu convoité, 32 des vergers et des vignes, 33 des [*Belles*] aux seins formés, d'une égale jeunesse, 34 et des coupes débordantes; ..."

Verses 32 and 34 show that the pious will have *gardens* and *wine bowers* as well as *brimming wine cups*. In this context one has to wonder how the houris (who are not named) suddenly appear with swelling bosom (Paret) or as "full-breasted" (Bell). Here the misinterpreted expression كواعب (*kawāʿib*) is genuinely Arabic. In *Ṭabarī* (XXX 18) it is explained by mutual agreement as "*buxom women.*" The *Lisān* (I 719a) explains the verb كعب as follows: كعب الإناء وغيره : ملأه (ka[cc]ab[a] *means, in speaking of a vessel or whatever: to fill it*). In Arabic one seems to have transferred this meaning to women's breasts. The meanwhile generally accepted notion of the *ḥūrīs* appears to have so fired the imagination of the commentators that this property has now also been ascribed to the "*young, pretty*" and "*passionately loving*" *virgins of Paradise*.

Yet this interpretation, which is unworthy of the Koran, is driven *ad absurdum* by the Koranic context itself. To the extent that the اترابا (*atrāba*ⁿ or *aṯrāba*ⁿ) following كواعب (*kawāʿib*) was explained as "*juicy*" (*fruits*), it can already no longer be a question of "*full-breasted* (*ones*) *of equal age*." Only "*fruits*" can be meant by this expression, if need be, such fruits considered as "*full vessels*." This understanding is suggested namely by other Koran passages, for example, in Sura 43:71, where there is talk of *golden platters and goblets*, and in Sura 76:15, of *silver vessels and chalices*. To be sure, the connection with *goblet*, *chalice* or *cup* is also present in this context, but nothing is said about bowls. Thus it is here more reasonable to assume that the two consecutive adjectives refer to grapes (or other fruits).

Therefore the expression كواعب (*ka-wāʿib*), misinterpreted as "*swelling breasts*," should also now be understood in Arabic in the context of the verses 78:31-34 cited above as follows:

> 31. "The pious (will) (in days to come) (have) a place of felicity:[338] 32. Gardens and *grapes*, 33. and (indeed) lush, succulent (*fruits*), 34. and a brimming-full[339] (wine) cup."

---

338 Arabic مفاز (*mafāz*) at first suggests a loan translation from a nominal form of the Syro-Aramaic root ܢܨܚ (*nṣaḥ*) (*Thes.* II 2437: [1] *to shine, to beam;* [2] *to flourish, to become famous;* [3] *to win, to triumph*). For the nominal form ܡܨܨܚܢܘܬܐ (*maṣṣḥānūṯā*), *Mannā* (461b) gives in the case of the causative stems ܐܨܨܚ (*aṣṣaḥ*) and ܢܨܨܚ (*naṣṣaḥ*) the following Arabic equivalents, among others: (3) مجّد . أسعد (*maǧǧada, asʿada*) (*to glorify, to delight*); (4) نصر . ظفر (*naṣara, ẓaffara*) (*to bestow victory on, to help to triumph*). The Koran renders the latter meaning with the synonymous noun مفاز (*mafāz*), but what it means by that in this context is the former (*happiness, splendor*). As a *nomen loci* it thus seems justified to render مفاز (*mafāz*) following the Syro-Aramaic semantics as a "*place of bliss* or *of splendor*." Although Bell captures the proper meaning with his translation (*place of felicity*), as opposed to the original Arabic meaning of فاز (*fāza*) (*to be victorious*), he does not give his reasons for doing so. Analogously, the other derivations of فاز (*fāza*) (فوز / *fawz* / فائزون / *fāʾizūn*) occur-

This concludes the philological analysis of the complex of themes surrounding the *ḥūrīs* or *heavenly virgins* in the Koran. May the efforts taken in this regard to arrive at a linguistically sound understanding be of assistance in lessening the discrepancy between the Koran as it is to be understood historically and the previous understanding of the text.

These philological conclusions constitute a *terminus post quem* (= *a quo*) as to the so-called *old Arabic poetry* and the *Hadith*-literature, in so far as the theme of the *ḥūrīs* or *heavenly virgins* they refer to is the product of the later Koran commentators of the ninth and tenth century.[340]

The subject that now follows, the *boys of Paradise*, is not as serious as that of the *ḥūrīs*, although it too contradicts to a certain extent the conception of Paradise in the *Scripture*.

---

ring in the Koran are to be understood in each case by taking into account the Syro-Aramaic semantics.

339 *Mannā* (139a) alone lists the expression دهاقا (*dihāq*), which is still considered uncertain, under the root ܕܗܩ (*dhaq*) (nominal form ܕܗܩܐ / *dhāqā*) with the Arabic meaning ملأ. اترع . اهرق (*malaʾa, atraʿa, ahraqa*) (*to fill, to fill to overflowing, to pour*).

340 This is one historical criterion that would confirm that Taha Hussein was right in suspecting partly the authenticity of the old Arabic Poetry (cf. Ṭāhā Ḥusayn, من تاريخ الأدب العربي / *min tārīḫ al-ʾadab al-ʿarabī* [*From the History of the Arabic Literature*], vol. 1-3, 2nd ed., Beirut, 1975-1978, vol. 1, العصر الجاهلي والعصر الاسلامي / *al-ʿaṣr al-ǧāhilī wa-l-ʿaṣr al-islāmī* [*The pre-Islamic and the Islamic Period*], chapter III (p. 79-124): الشك في الشعر الجاهلي / *aš-šakk fī š-šiʿr al-ǧāhilī* [*Doubts about the pre-Islamic Poetry*], chapter IV (p. 127-181): أسباب نحل الشعر / *asbāb naḥl aš-šiʿr* [*The Causes of the Forgery of Poetical Works*], chapter V (p. 185-247): شعر منحول وشعراء مزعومون / *šiʿr manḥūl wa-šuʿarāʾ mazʿūmūn* [*Forged Poetical Works and Pretended Poets*]. A linguistic-historical analysis of this Poetry would furnish further criterions.

16. The Boys of Paradise

Now that the dream is gone of the *ḥūrīs* or *virgins of Paradise*, some may seek consolation in the conception of the remaining *boys* of Paradise, because there is allegedly also talk of such in the Koran. For this we need to look individually at the three verses in which they are named, that is, Sura 76:19, 56:17 and 52:24.

Sura 76:19

ويطوف عليهم ولدن مخلدون اذا رايتهم حسبتهم لولوا منثورا

(Bell II 624): 19. "Round amongst them go boys of perpetual youth, whom when one sees, he thinks them pearls unstrung."

(Paret 493): 19: "Ewig junge Knaben (*wildānun muḫalladūna*) machen unter ihnen die Runde. Wenn du sie siehst, meinst du, sie seien ausgestreute [Note: Oder: ungefaßte (*?manṯūr*)] Perlen (so vollkommen an Gestalt sind sie)."

(Blachère 629): 19 "Parmi eux circuleront des éphèbes immortels tels qu'à les voir tu les croirais perles détachées."

Two expressions are crucial for the proper understanding of this verse: (a) the noun ولدن (*wildān*), and (b) the participial adjective مخلدون (*muḫalladūn*) (both in plural).

Only Paret draws attention to the dubious meaning of these parenthesized expressions. In so doing he has rightly put in question the existence of "*boys of perpetual youth*" in Paradise, whereby the Koran, moreover, would deviate in a further point from the conception of Paradise in the *Scripture*. That this, though, is in fact not the case, the following philological analysis will attempt to prove.

First of all it was established from a purely formal point of view that the participial form مخلدون (*muḫalladūn*) only occurs twice in the Koran and, indeed, precisely in connection with these "*eternal boys*," whereas the forms خالدون (*ḫālidūn*) and خالدين (*ḫālidīn*) occur 25 and 45 times, respectively, in the same meaning of "*eternally living*." This is no accident. If the Koran conspicuously makes this distinction, there must be a reason for it.

The next suspicious element is the circumstance that in this verse as well as in Verse 52:24 the Koran compares these *boys* to "*pearls*." This causes one to sit up and take notice since the Koran, after all, at other times compares "*white grapes*" to "*pearls*," as the analysis of the *ḥūrīs* has shown.

We would thus have two important clues to help us solve the riddle. But here, if one considers the meaning of the central expression upon which everything depends, the task is not that easy. In other words, how can one make "*boys*" into "*grapes*"? Specifically, the word ولدان (*wil-dān*) has not been misread; it is genuinely Arabic and as such rules out other interpretations.

Yet here, too, the Syro-Aramaic proves helpful. Under the etymologically corresponding ܝܠܕܐ (*yaldā*) (*child; that which has been born*) the *Thes.* (I 1594) in fact lists for the expression ܝܠܕܐ ܕܓܦܬܐ (*yaldā ḏa-ḡp̄ettā*) the following references from the New Testament: *Mt.* 26:29, *Mk.* 14:25, and *Lk.* 22:18. These three passages refer to the Last Supper at which Christ took leave of his disciples. In this context it is said that after Christ had blessed the bread and distributed it among his disciples, he raised the chalice, gave thanks and passed it to his disciples, saying (according to the *Pšiṭṭā* from Mt. 26:28): "This is my blood (that) of the new testament, which is shed for many for the forgiveness of sins. But I say unto you (now follows the Syro-Aramaic citation from Mt. 26:29):

ܕܠܐ ܐܫܬܐ ܡܢ ܗܫܐ ܡܢ ܗܢܐ ܝܠܕܐ ܕܓܦܬܐ: ܥܕܡܐ ܠܝܘܡܐ
ܕܒܗ ܐܫܬܝܘܗܝ، ܥܡܟܘܢ ܚܕܬܐ ܒܡܠܟܘܬܗ ܕܐܒܝ

(*d-lā eštē men hāšā men hānā yaldā ḏa-ḡp̄ettā ʿdammā l-yawmā ḏ-ḇeh eštīu[hī] ʿamḵōn ḥaṯṯā ḇ-malkūṯeh d-aḇ[ī]*).

"I will not drink henceforth from this "*child*" of the vine, since I will drink *it* new with you in my Father's kingdom."

The Christian symbolism of the wine of Paradise can probably be traced to these well-known words from the Last Supper. Also based on this are the Christian notions of Ephraem the Syrian concerning the grapevines of Paradise. Finally, traceable to this are the falsely understood *ḥūrīs* and the correctly understood *white grapes* of the Koran.

With the expression ܝܠܕܐ ܕܓܦܬܐ (*yaldā / da-gpettā*) (literally) "*child*" (= *product*) *of the grapevine*, it is then the "*fruit*" or the "*juice*" of the grapevine that is meant. *Mannā* (310 f.) first gives this meaning under ܝܠܕܐ (*yaldā*) in Arabic as follows: (3): ولد . نتاج . ثمرة (*child, product, fruit*), and under ܝܠܕܐ ܕܓܦܬܐ: بنت الكرمة . خمرة ("*daughter of the vine*," *wine*). The Arabic rendering as the feminine بنت (*bint*) (*daughter*) (for masculine ܝܠܕܐ / *yaldā* [*child, product*] is probably best viewed as an assimilation to خمرة (*ḫamra*) (< Syro-Aramaic masculine ܚܡܪܐ / *ḥamrā*)[341] (*wine*), which is taken to be feminine in Arabic.

With the meaning "*fruit*" (or "*juice*") the Syro-Aramaic now lends the Koranic expression ولدن (*wildān*) a meaning that is, in contrast to the prior understanding ("*boys*"), adequate to the metaphor "*pearls*." At the same time proof would be furnished for the parallel to "*white grapes*," which are compared to "*pearls*."

If this is so, then how is the active verb, يطوف عليهم (*yaṭūf*^{u} *ʿalay-him*) "*there go around* (*among them*)," to be explained?

Here it must first be pointed out that in three other passages in the Koran this verb is used in the passive voice; these are the Sura verses 37:45, 43:71, and 76:15. There what is said is يطاف عليهم (*yuṭāf*^{u} *ʿalay-him*) "*it is passed around to them*." Hence here the active verb is not absolutely to be understood as personified either. However, in the hymn cited above (234), Ephraem the Syrian tells us who it is who *passes around* the fruits and beverages of Paradise. There in fact it is said of the grapevines of Paradise that *each of them holds out a drooping cluster* to the righteous one. The Koran also transfers this notion to the beverages

341 This is another example of a Syro-Aramaic masculine *emphatic* ܐ / *-ā* ending which is taken to be feminine in Arabic. Whence, too, the in itself erroneous explanation that there are in Arabic two forms for "*wine*," one masculine خمر (*ḫamr*) (as a *pausal form*) and one feminine خمرة (*ḫamra*). This has had as a result that the masculine خمر (*ḫamr*) can also be feminine (cf. H. Wehr, *Arabisches Wörterbuch* [*Arabic Dictionary*]). In his *Aramäische Fremdwörter* [*Aramaic Foreign Words*] 160 f., S. Fraenkel has not drawn attention to these two variants.

of Paradise. For in the bliss of Paradise one is freed from earthly efforts. Here one need not trouble oneself about food and drink: the fruits and beverages themselves offer to the righteous.

This is why the active verb يطوف (*yaṭūf*[u]) is accordingly applied to the fruits and beverages of Paradise. This therefore does not imply that the task should be assigned to "*boys of eternal youth*." The expression "*boy*," moreover, has been falsely derived from the secondary meaning of the Koranic ولدن (*wildān*). Primarily the root means ولد (*walad*[a]) "*to give birth to, to produce*." In Arabic, the now familiar secondary meaning "*boy, lad*" has developed from the noun ولد (*walad*), a meaning, though, that the Syro-Aramaic ܝܠܕܐ (*yaldā*) does not have.

For the Koranic expression ولدن (*wildān*) this is already reason enough not to adopt the Arabic secondary meaning "*boy*," or even less "*young man*," for that matter.

The meaning of the participial adjective مخلدون (*muḫalladūn*), which Paret renders as "*eternally*" (*young*), could be applied without any problem to the fruits of Paradise to the extent that one can assume that these would be just as eternal as Paradise itself. However, we have established that this passive participle (of the second stem), which occurs only twice in the Koran, does not without reason stand out in opposition to the active participle (of the first stem), which occurs 70 times. Under this special form one should therefore expect to find a special meaning.

The following are some of the marks of quality attributed to the fruits of Paradise in the Koran: They are *first fruits*, to the extent that they are *choice*, *pure*, *white*; like *jewels* they are, among other things, compared to *pearls*; they are furthermore *lush* and *juicy*.

However, an equally essential characteristic has been previously overlooked in the Koran. That these fruits and beverages are *iced* can be at least indirectly inferred from the two-fold occurrence of the Arabic adjective بارد (*bārid*) (*cold, cool*) (Sura 56:44, 78:24). There, though, it is said of the Damned in Hell that they will receive nothing *cool*, but only *hot* things (to eat or to drink). With regard to Paradise itself, however, the expression بارد (*bārid*) is never used.

The reason for this is that the corresponding expressions are Syro-Aramaic. One of them has already been identified (cf. 256 above) with

عريا = ܥܪܝܐ *ʿarrāyē* *"cold, iced"* (fruits or beverages) (in Sura 56:36 misread as عربا *ʿuruban*). A second synonym can be found in the misread spelling currently under discussion, مخلدون. That is to say, here the upper dot of the خـ / *ḫ* has been falsely placed. Namely, with the lower point جـ / *ǧ* it yields the likewise Arabic but meaningful reading مجلدون (*muǧalladūn*),[342] *"iced"* (*fruits*).

Now, inasmuch as the "*iced fruits*" that "*pass*" themselves "*around*" to the righteous are compared with *pearls*, it can be inferred that what is meant by these fruits are *white grapes*. As opposed to the "*enclosed pearls*" (still in the shell) (Sura 37:49; 52:24; 56:23), it is likely that what is meant by the participial adjective employed here منثورا (*manṯūran*) is instead pearls that are "*scattered*" (or "*unmounted*") (Paret), *loose*, rather than connected to each other in a chain, and hence "*dispersed*" *pearls*.[343]

The hitherto misread and as "*boys of eternal youth*" misunderstood ولدن مخلدون (*wildān muḫalladūn*) is therefore in the context of Sura 76:19 to be understood as follows according to the Syro-Aramaic reading:

> "Iced fruits (grapes) pass around among them; to see them, you would think they were (loose) dispersed pearls."

The verses that now follow should also be understood accordingly.

---

342 The *Thes*. (I 724) cites under ܓܠܝܕܐ (*glīḏā*) *glacies* precisely these two expressions as synonyms: ܥܪܝܐ ܘܓܠܝܕܐ (*ʿaryā wa-ḡlīḏā*) (*cold, icy cold*), ܒܝܘܡ ܥܪܝܐ ܘܓܠܝܕܝܐ (*b-yūm ʿarrāyā wa-ḡlīḏāyā*) (*on a cold and icy day* = *on a freezing cold day*).

343 With reference to the Syrian lexicographers, the *Thes*. (I 2486) cites under aph. ܐܬܪ (*attar*), besides the borrowed Arabic word نثر (*naṯara*) (*to cause* fruits *to fall individually* by shaking a tree), the meaning قطف (*qaṭafa*) (*to pick*). In current Arabic usage in the Near East the nominal form is نثر (*naṯr* / *natr*) "*fallen fruit, windfall.*" Applying the meaning of "*pick*" to لولوا منثورا (*luʾluʾan manṯūrā*), say, in the sense of (freshly) *harvested pearls*, would appear, however, to be a bit too daring, since there is no evidence of such a use.

Sura 56: 17-19

يطوف عليهم ولدن مخلدون / باكواب واباريق وكاس من معين
لا يصدعون عنها ولا ينزفون

(Bell II 554): 17. "While round them circle boys of perpetual youth, 18. With goblets and jugs, and a cup of flowing (wine), 19. From which they suffer neither headache nor intoxication."

(Paret 450): 17: "während ewig junge Knaben (*wildānun muḫal-la-dūna*) unter ihnen die Runde machen 18: mit Humpen (*akwāb*) und Kannen (voll Wein?) und einem Becher (voll) von Quell-wasser (zum Beimischen?), 19: (mit einem Getränk) von dem sie weder Kopfweh bekommen noch betrunken werden."

(Blachère 572): 17 "Parmi eux circuleront des éphèbes immortels, 18 avec des cratères, des aiguières et des coupes d'un limpide breuvage 19 dont ils ne seront ni entêtés ni enivrés."

It is not the "boys of eternal youth" that circle "with tankards, jugs, and cups," but rather:

17. "*Ice-cold* (*grape*)*juices* circle among them 18. *in*[344] goblets, pitchers and a cup *from* a spring 19. from which they neither get headaches nor *tire*.[345]

344 In Arabic the preposition بـ / *bi* means both *with* and *in* because the Koran does not always distinguish between بـ / *bi* and في / *fī* and the homonymous Syro-Aramaic preposition ܒ / *b* can have both meanings.

345 Here the Syro-Aramaic ܐܬܪܦܝ (*eṯrappī*) is meant (*Thes.* II 3961): *remisse egit, segnis fuit* (*to tire, to become listless*). The Koranic lettering has been misread. Instead of لا ينزفون (*lā yunzifūn*) it should read يترفون (*yuṯrafūn*) This Syro-Aramaic root has nothing to do with the Arabic نزف (*nazafa*) (*to bleed*).

Sura 52:24

ويطوف عليهم غلمان لهم كانهم لولو مكنون

> (Bell 536): 24. "Around them circle attendants of theirs, as if they were pearls treasured."

> (Paret 439): 24: "Und Burschen, die sie bedienen (*ġilmānun la-hum*), (so vollkommen an Gestalt) als ob sie wohlverwahrte Perlen wären, machen unter ihnen die Runde."

> (Blachère 558): 24 "Pour les servir, parmi eux circuleront des éphèbes à leur service qui sembleront perles cachées."

With the plural غلمان (*ġilmān*)[346] the Koran is here obviously using a synonym of ولدان (*wildān*). The renewed comparison with pearls makes this especially clear and rules out the meaning, assumed here, of "*lads*."

Our three translators have at any rate had trouble with the syntactic classification of لهم (*la-hum*), which they have apparently understood as dative in the sense of "*belonging to them*." That's not the case here. The prefix لـ / *la* should instead be understood simply as an intensifying Arabic particle. The personal pronoun هم (*hum*) accordingly functions as a copula of the subsequent relative clause. For the verse cited above, then, the following understanding is produced:

> "Among them circle *fruits* *that* *are* (*so*) as if they were pearls (still) *enclosed* (in the shell)."

With this philological analysis an explanation has also been provided for the "*perpetually young boys*," in which it was previously thought one could see the "*youths of Paradise*." Accordingly, one can no longer with Josef Horovitz accuse the Koran of having "images of banquets in Paradise looking more like imitations of the descriptions of poets than like the depictions of lived scenes based on one's own experience" (*loc. cit* 65).

---

346 Cf. C. Brockelmann, *Lexicon Syriacum*, 528a: ܥܠܝܡܐ (*ʿlaymā*) (Arabic غلام) (*ġulām*) 1. Puer (*child*).

Through the philologically based misinterpretation, until now, of both the *ḥūrīs* or *virgins of Paradise* and the *youths of Paradise*, one can gauge the extent to which the Koranic exegesis has become estranged vis-à-vis the original Christian symbolism of the wine of Paradise.

17. THE ANALYSIS OF INDIVIDUAL SURAS

While the preceding examples have shown that individual misread or misinterpreted expressions have affected the understanding not only of a given word, but also of entire sentences and their interconnected contents, this applies to an even greater extent for entire Suras that have previously been so misread that, as a result, they have been given a fundamentally different sense. This may be illustrated on two succinct examples.

Sura 108

الكوثر / *"al-Kawṯar"*

The following interpretation of the Arabic Koran exegesis of this short Sura as presented in this article from the *Encyclopaedia of Islam* (vol. 2, Leiden, Leipzig, 1927) may serve as an introduction.

> "KAWTHAR, a word used in Sūra 108:1 after which this Sūra is called *Sūrat al-Kawthar*. Kawthar is a *faw'al* form from *kathara*, of which other examples occur in Arabic (e.g. *nawfal*; further examples in Brockelmann, *Grundriss der vergleichenden Grammatik*, I 344). The word, which also occurs in the old poetry (e.g. the examples in Ibn Hi-shām, ed. Wüstenfeld, p. 261, and Nöldeke-Schwally, *Geschichte des Qorāns*, I 92), means "abundance" and a whole series of Muslim authorities therefore explain al-Kawthar in Sūra 108:1 as *al-Khair al-kathīr* (see Ibn Hishām, *op. cit.*.; al-Ṭabarī, *Tafsīr*, XXX 180 f.). But this quite correct explanation has not been able to prevail in the *Tafsīr*. It has been thrust into the background by traditions according to which the Prophet himself explained Kawthar to be a river in Paradise (see already Ibn Hishām, p. 261 below, and notably al-Ṭabarī, *Tafsīr*, XXX 179), or Muḥammad says that it was a pool intended for him personally and shown to him on his ascension to Paradise (see al-Ṭabarī, *Tafsīr*, XXX 180), which latter view al-Ṭabarī considers the most authen-

tic. Even the earliest Sūras (77:41; 88:12 etc.) know of rivers that flow through Paradise, but it is not till the Medīna period that they are more minutely described, notably in, Sūra 47:15: "there are rivers of water which does not smell foul: rivers of milk the taste whereof does not change; and rivers of wine, a pleasure for those that drink, and rivers of clarified honey." These rivers correspond to the rivers of oil, milk, wine and honey, which had already been placed in Paradise by Jewish and Christian eschatology; the only difference is that Muḥammad replaced oil by water; in Arabia pure water was not to be taken for granted and besides it was necessary to mix with the wine of Paradise (see Horovitz, *Das koranische Paradies*, p. 9). When, after the Prophet's death, eschatological explanations of the "abundance" of Sūra 108:1 began to be made, al-Kaw<u>th</u>ar was identified as one of the rivers of Paradise and when we find in one of the versions quoted in al-Ṭabarī's *Tafsīr* that "its water is whiter than snow and sweeter than honey" or "and its water is wine," etc. we have obviously an echo of Sūra 47:15. But they did not stop at simply transferring these Koranic descriptions to the Kaw<u>th</u>ar but the imagination of later writers gave the river of Paradise a bed of pearls and rubies and golden banks and all sorts of similar embellishments. According to a later view (see *Aḥwāl al-Qiyāma*, ed. Wolff, p. 107) all the rivers of Paradise flow into the *Ḥawḍ al-Kaw<u>th</u>ar* which is also called *Nahr Muḥammed* , because, as we have seen above, it is the Prophet's own." (J. Horovitz)

Before going into the philological analysis of this Sura, which has been made into a legend in the Islamic tradition, it would be good first of all to give the Koranic text and its understanding on the basis of the Arabic exegesis with the traditional reading.

انا اعطينك الكوثر / فصل لربك وانحر / ان شانئك هو الابتر

(*innā aʿṭaynāka l-kawṯar* / *fa-ṣalli li-rabbika wa-nḥar* /
inna šāniʾaka huwa l-abtar)

These three verses are rendered according to the Arabic understanding as follows:

(Bell II 681)[347] 1. "Verily, We have given thee the abundance;[348] 2. So pray to thy Lord, and sacrifice. 3. Verily, it is he who hateth thee who is the docked one."[349]

(Paret 519): 1: "Wir haben dir die Fülle gegeben. 2: Bete darum (*fa-ṣalli*) zu deinem Herrn und opfere! 3: (Ja) dein Hasser ist es, der gestutzt [Note: D.h. ohne Anhang (*? abtar*). Oder: schwanzlos, d.h. ohne Nachkommen (?)] ist [Note: Oder (als Verwünschung): Wer dich haßt, soll gestutzt (oder: schwanzlos) sein!]."

(Blachère 668): 1 "En vérité, Nous t'avons donné l'Abondance.[350] 2 Prie donc en l'honneur de ton Seigneur et sacrifie ! 3 En vérité, celui qui te hait se trouve être le Déshérité!"

The explanation of this short Sura has caused Koran scholars in the East and the West a great deal of trouble. Even a summary of the nearly eleven pages of attempted interpretations in *Ṭabarī* (XXX 320-330) would be taking things too far. In any case, this would only serve as an example of how falsely the Koran text has been in part interpreted by the Arab exegetes. Nevertheless Paret devotes just under two pages to it

347 (Introductory remarks): "SURAH CVIII: This looks like a fragment, but it is difficult to find a suitable context for it. The rhyme might indicate a position in LXXIV – after v. 39 (?). That, however, necessitates a fairly early date, and the reference to sacrifice is difficult to explain, unless we are prepared to assume that Muhammad continued to take part in heathen rites in Mecca. Otherwise it seems necessary to assume that the Surah is Medinan. It is, in any case, an encouragement to the prophet under insult."

348 (Note 1): "*Al-kauthar*, from the root meaning 'many,' is interpreted as meaning much wealth, or by others as referring to the number of his followers; others again take the word as the proper name of a river or pool in Paradise."

349 (Note 2): "Mutilated," "having the tail cut off," probably in the sense of having no son. The word has presumably been applied to Muhammad by an enemy."

350 (Note 1): "*al-Kawṯar* 'l'Abondance.' Ce thème, d'un emploi rare, est une épithète substantivée. Ce sens est ressenti par tous les commt., mais la tradition (cf. Buh) prétend que ce terme désigne un des fleuves du Paradis."

in his *Kommentar* [*Commentary*] (525-527). As an introduction (525) he remarks on the subject: “Harris Birkeland has published an extensive interpretation of this short, but difficult Sura (*The Lord Guideth: Studies on Primitive Islam*, Oslo 1956, pp. 56-99).”

The following explanation of the individual words will show that all of the previous efforts were love’s labor’s lost.

1. The expression selected as the title of the Sura الكوثر (*al-kawṯar*) is the transliteration of the Syro-Aramaic ܟܘܬܪܐ / *kuttāra*, which is the nominal form of the second stem ܟܬܪ / *kattar* (*to persevere*). This verbal root (**kṯar*) is found in both languages, the Arabic root كثر / *kaṯura* (*to be much, many*) referring to quantity, while the Syro-Aramaic counterpart ܟܬܪ / *kṯar* (*to remain, to last*) merely refers to quantity of time, i.e. duration. In the Koran this Syro-Aramaic meaning occurs only occasionally, e.g. in Sura 20:33, 34: كي نسبحك كثيرا / ونذكرك كثيرا / *kay nusabbiḥaka kaṯīrā / wa-naḏkuraka kaṯīrā* “that we may *constantly* glorify Thee and make *constantly* remembrance of Thee”.[351] The medial و / *waw* in كوثر (*kawṯar*) is *mater lectionis* for short *u*, as is normal according to Syro-Aramaic spelling. The word should therefore be interpreted as *kuttār* as in Classical Syriac ܟܘܬܪܐ / *kuttārā* or Western Syriac *kūṯārā*[352] (*constancy, persistence, steadfastness*). The fricative *ṯ* (pro-

351 Although Bell here translates the adverb كثيرا (*kaṯīrā*) according to modern Arabic usage as “*often*,” the Syro-Aramaic semantics and the context suggest the meaning “*constantly*.” Another example of the Syro-Aramaic meaning can be found in Sura 56:32,33, wherein the believers are promised وفكهة ممنوعة ولا مقطوعة لا كثيرة (*wa-fākiha kaṯīra, lā maqṭūʿa wa-lā mamnūʿa*) “*And fruit profuse, Not cut off and not forbidden*” (Bell). The Arabic verb منع / *manaʿa* (*to forbid*) is, however, only one possible equivalent of the Syro-Aramaic verb ܟܠܐ / *klā* (see *Mannā* 337b), the more common meaning being “*to cease, to come to an end*” (*Mannā*: 5. توقف / *tawaqqafa*, 6. انتهى / *intahā*). Moreover, قطع / *qata'a* here does not mean (as in modern Arabic) “*to cut off*," but according to the wider Syro-Aramaic semantics “*to cease, to come to an end, to be used up*.” A preferable translation of the whole verse would therefore be: “*and constant(ly available) fruit, never ending nor running out*.” The latter meaning is furthermore attested in Sura 38:54: ان هذا لرزقنا ما له من نفاد (*inna hāḏā la-rizqunā mā lahu min nafād*) “*this is our provision, of it is no failing*” (Bell).

352 Cf. *Thes.* I 1859 f., ܟܘܬܪܐ (*kuttārā / kūṯārā*) (1) *mora*, *expectatio*, στηριγμός,

nounced as *th* in English "*thing*") of the canonical Koranic reading (*kawṯar*) reflects the Western Syriac pronunciation after the gemination of consonants was generally dropped. Since such a *mater lectionis* is uncommon in the Koran, the Arabic philologists interpreted this *mater lectionis* as the non-syllabic part of the diphthong *aw*, thus reading the form as *kawṯar* (= *fawʿal*). The corresponding Arabic form of the Syro-Aramaic "*kuttārā*" would be تكثير (*takṯīr*).[353]

This uncommon form *kawṯar* ought to have aroused the scepticism of the commentators. It is also no accident that the word has never made its way into Arabic in the meaning of "*abundance*." This is also, as it is

---

duratio, *fixitas*. Further, in *Mannā* 360b, ܟܘܬܪܐ *(kuttārā)*, ܟܬܪ (*kattar*) (2): دام . استمر . ثبت . بقي / *dāma, istamarra, ṯabata, baqiya* (*to last, to continue, to persist, to remain*).

353 The و / *waw* in the irregular form *kawṯar* could also be justified as an element serving to dissolve the following gemination. However, for such a reading there is no evidence. A parallel case of Syro-Aramaic nominal forms of the second stem can be found in Sura 78:28: وكذبوا بايتنا كذابا (*wa-kaḏḏabū bi-ʾāyātinā kiḏḏābā*) (Bell: *And they counted Our signs false utterly*), and 78:35: لا يسمعون فيها لغوا ولا كذابا (*lā yasmaʿūna fīhā laġwan wa-lā kiḏḏābā*) (Bell: *In which they will hear neither babble nor accusation of falsehood*). The form *kiḏḏābā* is an erroneous reading and reflects Syro-Aramaic ܟܘܕܒܐ / *kuddāḇā*, in this case, however, without *mater lectionis* for the short vowel *u*. The equivalent truly Arabic nominal form of the second stem كذّب / *kaḏḏaba* is تكذيب / *takḏīb*, as in Sura 85:19: بل الذين كفروا في تكذيب (*bali l-laḏīna kafarū fī takḏīb*) (Bell: *Ney, those who have disbelieved are engaged in counting false*). A similar same case is attested of the Syro-Aramaic second stem verb ܢܚܬ / *naḥḥeṯ*, of which the correct nominal form would be ܢܘܚܬܐ / *nuḥḥāṯā*. In Sura 19:24 the form occurs twice, in the first case as the false Arabic reading من تحتها / *min taḥtihā* (Bell: *from beneath her*), which should be read as Syro-Aramaic "*min nuḥḥātihā*," i.e. "*right after her accouchement*," and in the second case as the erroneous Arabic reading تحتك / *taḥtaki* (Bell: *beneath you*) for Syro-Aramaic "*nuḥḥātaki* – *your accouchement*." See above, p. 127 ff., for the discussion of the passage from Sura 19:24. A remnant of this Syro-Aramaic form in today's Arabic is found in the specific (and abnormal) word كتّاب / *kuttāb* (*Koran school* or *elementary school* – plural: كتاتيب / *katātīb*), that morphologically could be taken for the plural of the Arabic singular كاتب / *kātib* (*writer*, *author*). But actually, it is the Syro-Aramaic infinitive of the second stem كتّب / *kattaba* (*to make write* = *to teach the art of writing*), corresponding to the Arabic infinitive تكتيب / *taktīb*.

often the case, why it is regarded as the name of a river in Paradise and, among other things, is still used today as a woman's name (with the actually Syro-Aramaic meaning of "*Constantia*").

2. The same meaning is expressed by the borrowing from Syro-Aramaic صل / *ṣalli* (*pray*). On the other hand, the word that has been understood in Arabic as "*slaughter,*" وانحر / *wa-nḥar*, has been misread. What is meant here in connection with "*to pray*" is the Syro-Aramaic root ܢܓܪ / *ngar* (*to wait, to hold out, to persist*).[354] The only meaning from this root that has entered into the Arabic borrowed form نجر / *nağar*ª is the meaning "*to plane.*" In the Koran, however, it is the first meaning that is meant. Therefore, Arabic وانجر / *wa-nğar* (*and persist – in prayer*) should be read here. The Koran employs in this connection among other things the synonymous root صبر / *ṣabar*ª (< ܣܝܒܪ / *saybar*). Parallels are offered here by Sura 19:65: فاعبده واصطبر لعبادته (*so worship him and wait in his worship*) and Sura 20:132: وامر اهلك بالصلوة واصطبر عليها (*command your family to pray and persist therein*). Furthermore, with the lexically equivalent Arabic verb دام على / *dāma ʿalā* (in modern Arabic داوم على / *dāwama ʿalā*) (*to persist in something, to do something constantly*), it is said in Sura 70:23 of those who pray: الذين هم على صلاتهم دائمون (*who say their prayers constantly*).

3. As a further adapted transcription of Syro-Aramaic ܣܢܐܟ / (*sānāḵ*)[355] (*your hater = enemy, adversary*) in Arabic, the Koranic شانئك (*šāniʾaka*) has been understood correctly as "*your hater.*" In the Christian Syriac terminology, Satan is referred to, among other things, as a "*misanthrope*" – hence an "*adversary*" – in contrast to God, who is referred to as ܪܚܡܢܐ (*raḥmānā* > Arabic رحمن / *raḥmān*) "*one who loves mankind*" (*philanthropist*).

4. Finally, the root بتر (*batar*ª) (*to break off, to amputate*), based on the Arabic elative الابتر (*al-abtar*), is a metathesis of the Syro-Aramaic

354 Cf. *Thes.* II 2284 ff.: ܢܓܪ /*ngar* (1) *longus fuit, productus, extensus est* (*to continue, to go on and on*); (2) *patiens, longanimis fuit* (*to be patient, to have patience*), اصطبر . صبر . تمهل .

355 Cf. *Thes.* II 2668 ff; actually Arabic *šāniyaka.*

ܬܒܪ (*tḇar*), for which *Mannā* (829a) gives us the following Arabic meanings: (2) انكسر . انسحق (*to be broken, defeated, destroyed*), (3) فرّ . انهزم (*to make a dash for freedom, to be put to flight*).

Excursus
On the Etymology of the Arabic Root أعطى / *aʿṭā*

The result of the philological analysis of the individual expressions is that, except for the form, *scarcely one word in this Sura is of Arabic origin*. In the end, the only verb considered to be genuinely Arabic, أعطى / *aʿṭā* (*to give*), will prove to be, etymologically (by the shifting of the *hamza* to *ʿayn* and the resultant emphasizing of the ܬ /*t*), a secondary dialectal formation of Syro-Aramaic ܐܝܬܝ / *aytī* (*to summon, to bring*). This is already clear from the Koranic use of these two roots. In other words, while the Arabic root عطى / *ʿaṭā* occurs a total of 13 times in the Koran, the instances of the root borrowed from the Syro-Aramaic ܐܬܐ /*eṯā* > Arabic اتى /*atā* (*to come*), with all its derivatives, are countless. The Arabic form أعطى /*aʿṭā* (*to give*) corresponds to the Syro-Aramaic *Afʿel* ܐܝܬܝ / *aytī* (*to summon, to bring*). The equivalent Arabic form would be أتى / *ʾatā* > *أأتى > *ʾaʾtā*, a form which would violate the phonotactical rule in Arabic, which does not allow two consecutive *hamza*, especially when the second one is *vowelless*.[356] To circumvent this rule, the second hamza was replaced by the acoustically most similar phoneme *ʿayn*. As the place of articulation of the *ʿayn* is pharyngeal, the following consonant was consequently pharyngealized, i.e. it became emphatic *ṭ*. These phonetic replacements thus resulted in the secondary Arabic verb أعطى /*aʿṭā* (*to give*), the radicals of which, however, have no counterparts in any other Semitic language. C. Brockelmann, *Lexicon Syriacum*, gives the

---

356 The *Lisān* (XII 24b f.) quotes as sole exception the plural of إمام (*ʾimām*) = أئمة (*ʾaʾimma*) (where the second *hamza*, however, is not *vowelless*) and explains nevertheless that this form with two *hamza*, according to the philologists of Kufa, is an exception and not a norm (شاذ لا يقاس عليه), since the most Koran readers read أيمة (*ʾayimma*). Hence he concludes that "two successive radical *hamza* never occurred" in Arabic:

فلهذا لم يأت في الكلام لفظة توالت فيها همزتان أصلا البتة !

etymological correlatives of the Syro-Aramaic verbal root ܥܛܐ / *ʿṭā* (520a) (1. *delevit, evertit* / *to efface, to cancel, to exterminate*) as follows: Hebrew עטה (*ʿaṭā*) *velavit* (*to veil*), Arabic غطا (*ġaṭā*) *texit* (*to cover*), Accadean *eṭū obscurum esse* (*to be obscure*). These etymological correlations make clear that the Arabic verb أعطى /*aʿṭā*, in the sense of *"to give"*, is not genuine Arabic, but a secondary derivation from the Syro-Aramaic verbal root ܐܬܐ (*eṯā*) > Arabic أتى (*atā*) > IVth stem *أأتى (*'a'tā*) > أعطى (*ʾaʿṭā*).

The last sceptics may be convinced by the following evidence quoted in A. Jeffery, *Materials for the History of the Text of the Qur'ān*, 146 (codex of Ubai b. Ka'b), Sura 20:36, where the canonical reading أوتيت (*'ūtīta*) (in the context – literally: "*you are given" your request* = *your request is granted*) is transmitted in this old codex as أعطيت (*ʾuʿṭīta*). Hence: أوتيت (*'ūtīta* < *'*u'tīta*) = أعطيت (*ʾuʿṭīta*).[357]

---

357 This is not the unique secondary Arabic formation from a Syro-Aramaic verbal root. The Koran offers us two further secondary derivations from the Syro-Aramaic verbal root ܐܬܐ /*eṯā*: 1. From the IInd intensive stem ܐܬܝ / *attī* (*to bring*) (by secondary sonorization of the *t* > *d*) > Arabic أدّى / *addā* (in the Koran in the meaning *"to bring, to give back"* in the following passages: Suras 2:283; 3:75 [2x]; 4:58; in the vernacular Egyptian Arabic ادّيني / *əddīnī* means means = اعطني /*aʿṭinī* [*give me*]); 2. from the most used Syro-Aramaic *Af'el* stem ܐܝܬܝ / *aytī* in the sense of *"to bring"*, the Koran forms by monophthongization of the diphthong *ay* > *ā* the IVth Arabic stem آتى / *'ātā* (formally equal to the IIIrd stem), as it is attested in numerous passages with the same meaning. A further secondary derivation is to be found in the today's spoken Arabic of Irak, where for example the imperative form انطيني /*ənṭīnī* (*give me*) shows its derivation from the Syro-Aramaic intensive stem ܐܬܝ / *attī* (imperative ܐܬܝܢ / *attī-n[ī]*) after the dissolution of the gemination of the medial radical by insertion of a preceding نـ /*n*, as it can be observed in a number of Arabic verbs borrowed from the Eastern (Mesopotamian) vernacular Aramaic, as it is relatively frequent e.g. in Mandaic (cf. Th. Nöldeke, *MG*, § 68).
This phenomenon can help to clarify the etymology of the Hebrew (and Old Aramaic) verbal root נתן / *n-t-n* (*to give*) as a secondary formation from Eastern Aramaic with a secondary first and third radical from the second intensive stem אתא / *attā* > *antā* + the enclitic object suffix of the first person singular *–n(ī)* or plural *–n* = *אנתני or *אנתן / *antān(ī)* / *antān*, thereby accent-shifting on the last syllable and consequently dropping of the unaccented initial radical (א)נתן /

From the preceding discussion the following reading and understanding has now resulted for Sura 108 according to the Syro-Aramaic reading:

انا اعطينك الكوثر / فصل لربك وانجر / ان سانيك هو الابتر

(*inna aʿṭaynāk^{a} l-kawṯar* or *al-kuttār* / *fa-ṣalli li-rabbik wa-ngar* / *in sānīk^{a} huwa l-abtar*)

1. "We have given you the (virtue of) <u>constancy</u>;
2. so pray to your Lord and <u>persevere</u> (in prayer);
3. your <u>adversary</u> (the devil) is (then) the <u>loser</u>."

Christian Epistolary Literature in the Koran

This brief Sura is based on the Christian Syriac liturgy. From it arises a clear reminiscence of the well-known passage, also used in the *compline* of the Roman Catholic canonical hours of prayer, from the First Epistle General of Peter, Chapter 5, Verses 8-9 (according to the *Pšiṭṭā*):

(a)ntān > נתן / *natān* > *ntān* (hence no spirantization of the originally geminated ת / *t* after the vocalized secondary נ / *n*).
The end- ܠ / *l* in the parallel Syriac variant ܢܬܠ / *n-t-l* is the enclitic preposition ܠ / *l* marking the dative (or indirect object), by analogy with the verb ܝܗܒ ܠ / *ya(h)ḇ l-* (*to give "to" someone*). This formation has been nearly recognized by Stade (according to Th. Nöldeke, *MG* 52, note 6: in *Lit. Centralbl.* 1873 Nr. 45, p. 1418), who, however, sees in this end-*l* (as well as Nöldeke) an assimilation of the end-*n* of the previous form, that Nöldeke regards as a former original one. But in reality, both variants are parallel secondary formations depending on the use of the original verb: a) *attā* as ruling the accusative (or direct object), b) *attī* as ruling the dative by means of the preposition ܠ / *l*.
While C. Brockelmann does not quote this irregular form in his *Lexicon Syriacum*, *Mannā* and the *Thesaurus* adduce it in alphabetical order under ܢ /*n*. *Mannā* (470b) explains the fictitious verbal root *ܢܬܠ / *ntal* as (مماث / *mumāt*) (*died out*); the *Thes.* (II 2480) explains it as *verbum defectivum* and compares it to Hebrew נתן / *natan* and Eastern Aramaic נתן / *ntan* beside נתל / *ntal* (without further etymological explanation). In his *Syrische Grammatik* [*Syriac Grammar*], p. 128, Th. Nöldeke refers only to נתן / *n-t-n* as root of the Syro-Aramaic infinitive ܡܬܠ / *mettal*, without further explanation.

8 “Wake up (Brothers) and be vigilant, because your *adversary* the *devil*, as a roaring lion, walketh about, seeking whom he may devour: 9 Whom *resist steadfast* in the faith.”

From this first evidence of Christian epistolary literature in the Koran it now becomes clear that it has previously been a mistake to connect the text of Sura 108 with any of the enemies of the Prophet Muḥammad, not to mention with the expressions the Koran has been accused of using in this regard, expressions which are unworthy of it. This text is without a doubt pre-Koranic. As such it is a part of that *matrix out of which the Koran was originally constituted as a Christian liturgical book* (*Qəryānā*), and which as a whole has been designated in Western Koran studies as the “*first Meccan period*.”[358] The address in the second person in this as in other Suras is moreover not necessarily directed at the Prophet himself. Rather, as is customary in liturgical books, each believer is addressed in the second person.

As in the Roman Catholic *compline*, one can easily imagine these three verses as an introduction to an earlier Syro-Aramaic hour of prayer. Bell’s suspicion that it is a fragment from Sura 74 cannot be ruled out, since this Sura as well as Sura 73 with their call to bedtime prayer, i.e. to the *vigils*, read in part like a *monastic rule*.[359] Whence there too the hitherto unrecognized Syro-Aramaisms, the explanation of which is being reserved for a future work.

Sura 96

A second prime example of a largely misunderstood text is Sura 96. In the Islamic tradition this is held to be the beginning of the prophetic revelation. Serving as the title is a keyword selected from the text, العلق

358 Cf. Nöldeke-Schwally, *GdQ* I 74-117.

359 Cf. Tor Andrae, *Der Ursprung des Islams und das Christentum* [*Christianity and the Origin of Islam*] (Uppsala, 1926) 139: “*The eschatological piety of the Koran is thus very closely related to the religious viewpoint predominant in the Syrian churches before and at the time of Muhammed. This Syrian piety is actually a monastic religion...* .”

(*al-ʿalaq*), which until now has been falsely translated by "*Clotted Blood*" (Bell), "*Der Embryo*" (Paret), and "*L'Adhérence*" (Blachère). For purposes of comparison the following rendering of Paret's translation (513 f.) ought to be sufficient.

Sura 96:1-19

العلق / *"al-ʿAlaq"*

1: "Recite in the name of your Lord who has created, 2: has created man out of an embryo! 3: Recite! Your Lord is noble like nobody in the world [Note: literally, the noblest (one) (*al-akramu*)], 4: (He) who [Note: (Or) Your Lord, noble like nobody in the world, is the one who] taught the use of the calamus-pen [Or who taught by means of the calamus-pen], 5: taught man what (beforehand) he did not know.

6: No! Man is truly rebellious (*yaṭġā*), 7: (for) that he considers himself his own master (*an raʾāhu staġnā*). 8: (Yet) to your Lord all things return (some day) [literally: To your Lord is the return].

9: What do you think, indeed, of him who 10: forbids a slave [Or: a servant (of God)] when he is saying his prayers (*ṣallā*)? 11: What do you think if he (i.e., the one?) is rightly guided 12: or commands one to be God-fearing? 13: What do you think if he (i.e., the other?) declares (the truth of the divine message) to be a lie and turns away (from it)? (That the latter is in the wrong should be clear.) 14: (For) Does he not know that God sees (what he does?) 15: No! If he does not stop (doing what he is doing) we will surely seize (him on Judgment Day) by the forelock, 16:a lying, sinful forelock. 17: May he then call his clique (*nādī*)! 18: We shall (for our part) call the henchmen (of Hell) (*? az-zabāniya*). 19: No! Prostrate yourself (rather in worship) and approach (your Lord in humility)!"

The discussion of the underlined expressions will first of all be carried out verse by verse.

Verse 1: Borrowed from the Syro-Aramaic ܩܪܐ (*qrā*), the Arabic verb قرأ (*qaraʾa*, although originally probably *qarā* like *banā* and *ramā*), has for the most part taken over the meaning "*to read*" from Syro-Aramaic. Elsewhere, the Koran furnishes evidence of the meaning "*to teach*" once in Sura 87:6, سنقرئك فلا تنسى (*sanuqriʾuka*, which should actually be read *sanuqrīka*), which is rendered as follows by Paret (507): "We will cause you to recite (revelatory texts). You will now forget nothing (thereof)." Under ܐܩܪܝ (*aqrī*) *Mannā* (698b) gives the meaning "*to teach*" in Arabic with علّم (*ʿallam*[a]). Accordingly, what is meant by this verse is: "We will teach you (in a way) that you will not forget."[360]

The correct interpretation of the expression اقرا باسم ربك (*iqraʾ* [actually *iqrā*] *bi-smi rabbika*) is of crucial importance for the historical appraisal of this Sura, which Islamic tradition has declared to be the beginning of the prophetic revelation. In this regard, Nöldeke refers (*op. cit.* 81) to Hartwig Hirschfeld, who, in pointing to the frequent occurrence in the Bible of the Hebrew expression קרא בשם יהוה (*qrā b̲-šem Yahwē*), had translated the Koranic expression correctly with "proclaim the name of thy Lord!" The explanation given by the Arabic grammarian Abū ʿUbaida – that قرأ (*qaraʾa*) means as much as ذكر (*d̲akara*) "to call (upon)" here – proves to be equally correct, despite the fact that it is rejected by Nöldeke with the comment: "But قرأ never has this meaning." For that, he refers to M. J. de Goeje in the glossary to *Ṭabarī* where قرأ بشئ is said to mean "he read in something." Thus,

360 The phrase that is cited in Nöldeke-Schwally, *GdQ* I 33, قرأ على فلان السلام and قرأ فلانا السلام (*to greet someone*) can certainly be traced back to the Syro-Aramaic expression ܩܪܐ ܫܠܡܐ (*qrā šlāmā*), as given in the *Thes.* (II 3713) and explained with *salutavit*. The same is in *Mannā* 698: ܩܪܐ ܫܠܡܐ ܥܠ (*qrā šlāmā ʿal*): سلّم . قرأ سلاما على . The *Lisān* (XV 174a ff.) lists under the root قرا (*qarā*) (with the variants قرو / *q-r-w* and قرى / *q-r-y*) a whole series of no longer common expressions in modern Arabic that can only be explained on the basis of their Syro-Aramaic origin. One of them is, for example, قرى الضيف (*qarā ḍ-ḍayf*), which the *Lisān* (179b) conjecturally explains with "*to honor a guest*," but which in Syro-Aramaic means "*to call = to invite*" *a guest*. Also interesting are the further forms such as إنه لمقرى للضيف ومقراء as well as إنه لقريّ وإنها لقريّة للأضياف , whose form already betrays their Syro-Aramaic origin.

Nöldeke took as his model for the explanation of this early Koranic expression its later misunderstood use in Arabic, instead of tracing it back to its Syro-Aramaic (or Hebrew) origin. The fact is that the equivalent Syro-Aramaic expression taken from Biblical usage ܩܪܐ ܒܫܡ ܡܪܝܐ (*qrā b̲-šem māryā*) (with and without ܒ / *b*) has in general become a *technical term* for "*to pray, to hold divine service*."[361] But as for how the preposition ܒ / *b-* is to be explained, it is simply to be understood here as follows: *Call: "In the name of the Lord!"* One does this particularly at the beginning of a prayer or a divine service, and indeed it was this that was also replaced later on in the recitation of the Koran by the parallel formula بسم الله الرحمن الرحيم (*b̲i-smⁱ l-lāhⁱ raḥmānⁱ raḥīm*) (*In the name of God, the compassionate, the merciful*).

Nöldeke has also not noticed that this expression, though not with the borrowed verb قرا (< ܩܪܐ / *qrā*), but with the lexically equivalent Arabic verb دعا (*daʿā*) (*to call, to invoke*), is documented in connection with the preposition بـ / *bi-* in this meaning in a verse[362] attributed to *Waraqa ibn Nawfal* (ورقة بن نوفل) (cousin of *Ḫadīǧa*, the first wife of the Prophet),[363] which runs as follows:

---

361 Cf. *Thes.* II 3713: ...ܩܪܐ ܒܫܡ (*qrā b̲-šem*) *proclamavit nomen ejus*; *vocavit, invocavit Deum*. Furthermore in *Mannā* 698: ܩܪܐ ܒܫܡ ܡܪܝܐ (*qrā b̲-šem māryā*) نوّه باسم الرب . صلى . سجد. عبد الرب (*to invoke God's name, to pray, to worship, to worship God*). G. Lüling, *Über den Ur-Qur'ān* [*About the Original Qur'ān*], p. 30; *A Challenge to Islam for Reformation*, p. 32, was right in confirming this understanding by Gustav Weil and Hartwig Hirschfeld.

362 *Aġānī* III 16, cited from: Ǧawād ʿAlī, *al-Mufaṣṣal fī tārīḫ al-ʿArab qabl al-Islām (Exhaustive History of the Arabs Before Islam)*, vol. 6, Beirut, ³1980, p. 651.

363 In the article WARAQA b. Nawfal b. Asad al-Qurašī in the *Shorter Encyclopaedia of Islam* (Leiden, 1934, 631) it is reported that Waraqa "encouraged and possibly influenced the Prophet in the first years of his mission" (in Mecca). As a Christian "he was abstemious, knew Hebrew, studied the Bible, and had written down" (i.e. translated) "the Gospels" (probably one Gospel) allegedly in the Hebrew alphabet. It was he "who found Muḥammad as a child when he strayed from his nurse." He is also the one who "warmly approved" of the first marriage of the Prophet to Waraqa's cousin *Ḫadīǧa.* The (Islamic) tradition admits that Waraqa was nonetheless never converted (to Islam).

أقول إذا صليت في كل بيعة تباركت قد أكثرت باسمك داعيا

"I say whenever I pray in a church[364]: 'Be you praised, full oft *I call* [with] *your name'*!"

There can accordingly be no doubt that the introductory formula اقرا باسم ربك (*iqra' bi-sm^i rabbik^a*) has the equivalent Syro-Aramaic sense and is to be understood as a call to prayer. Indeed, the subsequent context of the entire Sura argues for this as well. To understand from this a call to *read in a book* is simply without any objective foundation. The previous interpretation rests solely on the later Arabic exegesis's misunderstanding of the use of this *Syriacism*.

The logical conclusion is that the view held by the Arabic tradition, according to which the angel Gabriel had with this *formula* called upon the Prophet to read, even though the Prophet could not read, is a later pious legend growing out of this very same misunderstanding. The Sura is, as a whole, a thematically presented call to worship, as the other misunderstood expressions will show.

Verse 2: About the expression علق (*ʿalaq*) Blachère (657) remarks correctly that it seems originally to have been a noun derived from the verb *ʿalaqa*, "*to stick, to cling*." To that extent, he is doubting the interpretation "*clots of blood*" of the Arab exegetes, which Paret, in turn, interprets as "*embryo*." With the corresponding translation, "*adhérence*" (*adhesion*), however, he is nonetheless not able to explain the actual meaning of this metaphorical expression. This is because here, too, the *tertium comparationis* can only be determined by way of the Syro-Aramaic. Add to this that the *Thes.* (II 2902) cites for us under ܥܠܘܩܐ (*ʿālōqā*) (for which it gives the loan word in Arabic علقة / *ʿalaqa* "*leech*") the following commentary from the Syrian lexicographers, who, besides

---

364 Arabic بيعة (*bīʿa*) has already been recognized by S. Fraenkel, *Aram. Fremdwörter* [*Aramaic Foreign Words*] 274, as a borrowing from Syro-Aramaic ܒܝܥܬܐ (*bīʿtā*) (*egg, dome = church*); the plural بيع (*biyaʿ*) occurs in the Koran in Sura 22:40. The expression is still common today among Arabic-speaking Christians in the Mesopotamian region.

the *leech* named after this property, also explain the following with this *nomen agentis* “*clinger*”:

ܐܘ ܛܝܢܐ ܘܠܝܫܐ ܕܕܒܩܝܢ ܒܐܝܕܐ ܘܥܣܩܝܢ ܠܡܬܬܫܝܓܘ

(*aw ṭīnā w-layšā d-dāḇqīn b-īḏā w-ʿasqīn l-mettšīḡū*)

The expression “*clinger*” designates either a “*leech*” “or the clay or dough that sticks to one’s hand and is difficult to wash off.”[365]

With that, the expression علق (*ʿalaq*) would be explained, since the property “*sticky*” is indeed used by the Koran in connection with “*clay*,” in one instance, in Sura 37:11: انا خلقنهم من طين لازب “we have created you out of sticky[366] clay.” Adapted to the rhyme, the Koran is here using the synonymous Syro-Aramaic expression familiar to it. With من علق (*min ʿalaq*) what is meant in Arabic is لازب = من طين عالق (out of something *sticky* = *sticky clay*).

Verse 3: For the Arabic elative (absolute superlative) referring to God, الاكرم (*al-akram*), the meaning also common in modern Arabic, “*honorable, admirable*,” is actually adequate, especially since it is here precisely a question of the worship of God in the church service.

Verse 4: Because God has taught man بالقلم (*bi-l-qalam*) “*with the calamus reed-pen*,” surely the most plausible explanation is the *knowledge revealed through the scripture*.

---

365 As a Syro-Aramaic substratum *al-Munǧid fī l-luġa wa-l-aʿlām*, Beirut 1987, 526b, has recorded the expression العلق (*al-ʿalaq*) in the meaning الطين الذي يعلق باليد (*aṭ-ṭīn al-laḏī yaʿlaq bi-l-yad*) (*the clay that sticks to one’s hand*). This meaning is missing in the *Lisān*.

366 Even though the meaning of the Arabic لازب (*lāzib*) “*sticky, clinging*” is actually clear, Paret (368) translates “of pliant [literally, consistent] clay,” [“aus geschmeidigem (W: konsistentem) Lehm”], Blachère (475) “of solidified clay,” [“d’argile solidifiée”]; and Bell (II, 443), approximately, “of clay cohering.”

Verse 6: There begins at this point in the Sura, with كلا (*kallā*),[367] which has been misread in Arabic and misunderstood abruptly in the context as "*No!*", a series of three adverbs, all of which mean the Syro-Aramaic ܟܠܐ (*kullā*) and which are, depending on the context, to be understood positively in the sense of "*everything*," but negatively in the meaning of "*not at all.*" In this verse the كلا (Syro-Aramaic *kullā* in the sense of Arabic كلّيا *kullīya*ⁿ) belongs with the preceding ما لم يعلم (*mā lam yaʿlam*), because in the Koran the sentence does not necessarily end with the rhyme. Hence this كلا is to be drawn into Verse 5, so that this verse will then be: "he taught man what he did <u>not</u> know <u>at all</u>."[368]

Secondly, Paret translates the verb طغى (*ṭaġā*) with "*aufsässig sein* [*to be rebellious*]" (Blachère: "L'homme … est <u>rebelle</u>"; Bell: "man <u>acts presumptuously</u>"). Except for the secondary غ / *ġ* there is, in itself, nothing Arabic about this verbal root.

Excursus
On the Etymology of the Verbal Root طغى (ṭaġā)

This verb is unusual in any Arabic dialect. Its use in modern Arabic is due exclusively to this misread Koranic word. The etymological Arabic equivalent is in fact the verbal root ضاع / *ḍāʿa* (generated by sonorization of the Syro-Aramaic emphatic ܛ / *ṭ* > ض /*ḍ* with simultaneous sound-shifting). The Arabic ع / *'ayn* in ضاع / *ḍāʿa* makes clear that the diacritical point in طغى / *ṭaġā* has not any justification and that the original spelling طعى / *ṭaʿā* renders truly the Syro-Aramaic verbal root ܛܥܐ /*ṭʿā*.

The etymology is covered by the original meaning of both verbal roots (cf. C. Brockelmann, *Lexicon Syriacum* 282a, ܛܥܐ /*ṭʿā* 1. *erravit* [*to go astray*]) = Arabic ضاع /*ḍāʿa* (*to get lost*). According to the classical correspondence table of the Semitic sounds in C. Brockelmann's

---

367 Paret begins the sentence with "*Nein!*"; Blachère sees in it a warning: "*Prenez garde!*". Like Paret, Bell understands "*Nay.*"

368 The same sense has the Syro-Aramaic adverbial expression ܠܓܡܪ / *la-ḡmār* (*Mannā* 112b: ابدا. قط. بتة / *abadan, qaṭṭ, batta*; C. Brockelmann, *Lexicon Syriacum* 121b: *absolute, omnino* [*absolutely, completely, ever/never*]).

Syrische Grammatik [*Syriac Grammar*] (p.15), the Arabic ض /*ḍ* can only correspond with a Syriac ܥ / *ʿayn*. A classical example is Syriac ܐܪܥܐ /*arʿā* = Arabic ارض /*arḍ* (*earth*). This is the classical rule. But that in the multiplicity of the Arabic (or common Aramaic) dialects a Syro-Aramaic emphatic *ṭ* can become occasionally an Arabic *ḍ* by sonorization, this phenomenon has hitherto not been considered in the Semitic philology. A first example we had with Syro-Aramaic ܛܪܦ (Eastern Aramaic *ṭrap*) > Arabic ضرب (*ḍaraba* [*to strike*, *to hit*]), from which there are three variants that illustrate the transition from Syro-Aramaic ܛ /*ṭ* into the Arabic ض / *ḍ*: a) طرف (*ṭarafa* < Western Syro-Aramaic ܛܪܦ / *ṭrap̄* = *ṭraf*) (*to hit, to touch the eye with something*) (*Lisān* IX 213b, 11f.); b) طرب (*ṭariba* < Eastern Syro-Aramaic ܛܪܦ / *ṭrap* – with sonorization of the *p* > *b*) (to be *touched* emotionally = *to be moved*, *to be delighted*); c) finally with sonorization of the emphatic ط /*ṭ* > ض /*ḍ* = ضرب (*ḍaraba*) (*to strike*).

The Koran offers a further example of a sonorized Syro-Aramaic emphatic ܛ /*ṭ* with the secondary Arabic verbal root ضرّ (*ḍarra*) (*to harm, damage*) < Syro-Aramaic ܛܪܐ (*ṭrā*) (*to strike*, *to push* – 7 further variants in C. Brockelmann), that C. Brockelmann, *Lexicon Syriacum* 287a, compares with the actually from Syro-Aramaic truly borrowed Arabic Verb طرأ (*ṭaraʾa*), the *tertiae hamza* of which is nothing but a fictitious pronunciation imagined by the Arab philologists. Not only the apparent restriction of this verb to the first stem and its semantics field to one general meaning (*to break in*, *overtake*, *befall*) shows that it is borrowed, but also the fact that the Arab lexicographers did not observe that its VIIIth stem إضطرّ (*iṭṭarra* /*uṭṭurra*) (*to be forced, compelled*), according to its original meaning, does not fall under the root ضرّ (*ḍarra*) (*to damage*), but under طرأ (*ṭaraʾa* = *ṭarā*), according to the meaning of Syro-Aramaic ܛܪܐ (*ṭrā*) (*to push away*, *to repel*) and its reflexive stem ܐܬܛܪܝ (*eṭṭrī*). That the secondary Arabic form ضرّ (*ḍarra*) is derived from the Syro-Aramaic ܛܪܐ (*ṭrā*), shows C. Brockelmann (*op. cit.*) by the same specific meaning quoted under 6.: *offendit* (*to harm*).

The second element that shows the perplexity of the Arab Koran readers is the variable reading of the alternative writing of the nominal form of the verbal root ضرّ (*ḍarra*), depending on its spelling with or without the Syro-Aramaic emphatic ending *ā* of the *status emphaticus*. Apart from the reading *ḍarr* (*harm*, *damage*) as antonym of نفع (*naf ͨ*) (*use*, *benefit*), the Koranic spelling ضر (without the emphatic end-*ā*) is read *ḍurr(u/i/a)* (derived from the IInd Syro-Aramaic intensive stem ܛܪܝ / *ṭarrī*, verbal noun ܛܘܪܝܐ / *ṭurrāyā*) (19 times in the Koran in the sense of *distress*, *adversity*). When, on the other hand, the same word is written with the Syro-Aramaic emphatic end-*ā* ضرا (properly: *ḍurrā* – with dropping of the unaccented *y* of the Syro-Aramaic word before the end-*ā* – as in قران < Syro-Aramaic ܩܪܝܢܐ / *qəryānā* / *qəryān* > Arabic *qurān* / *qur'ān*) or with the Arabic article الضرا (etymologically: *aḍ-ḍurrā* < ܛܘܪܝܐ / *ṭurrāyā*) (both spellings 9 times), this spelling is read with an added *hamza* after the end-*ā* as الضراء (*aḍ-ḍarrāʾu*), as though this spelling were etymologically different.

On the Origin of the Arabic End-Hamza

In his "*Grundriß der vergleichenden Grammatik der semitischen Sprachen* [*Compendium of the Comparative Grammar of the Semitic Languages*]" (I 593, C.a.), C. Brockelmann supposes a verbal class *tertiae hamza*, according to the classical Arabic grammar, when he says: "Als 3. Radikal war ʾ schon im altarab. Dialekt des Ḥiğāz nach *i* und *u* zu *ĭ* und *ŭ* geworden…[As 3rd radical, the ʾ (= *hamza*) had become already in the old Arabic dialect of Ḥiğāz *ĭ* and *ŭ* after *i* and *u* …]".

But in fact, what C. Brockelmann says about the Hebrew (*op. cit.* 594 b.), Syriac and Assyrian (594 c.) as to the "*dropping*" of the III ' (*tertiae hamza*), is likewise to apply on the so-called (post-Koranic) *Old Arabic*. For the Koranic orthography has no graphical sign for a final *hamza*. Spellings as اتوكوا (*atawakkaw* [*I lean*] – same spelling in both codices of Samarqand and British Library Or. 2165 – traditional reading: *atawakka'u*) (Sura 20:18) let suspect a hypercorrect late emendation according to the classical Arabic grammar. As to the supposed III ' (*tertiae hamza*), the end-*alif* in the Koranic spelling has been erroneously regarded as a *hamza*-bearer. From Syro-Aramaic borrowed verbs, as e.g. قرا (*to read*) and برا (*to create*), are not to be read *qara'a* and *bara'a*, but – according to the Syro-Aramaic pronunciation: *qarā* and *barā*. Except some onomatopoetic verbs in Arabic, as تأتأ / *ta'ta'a* (*to stammer*), طأطأ / *ṭaʾṭaʾa* (*to bow one's head*) and the glottal stop in spoken Arabic in لأ / *la'*, *la'a* = *lā* (*no*), perhaps also in the case of a softened ع / *ʿayn* as in بدأ / *bada'a* < بدع / *badaʿa* < methatesis of Syro-Aramaic ܥܒܕ / *ʿḇaḏ* (*to create*),[369] it can be said that with regard to the Koranic orthography the Koran does not know a III ' (*tertiae hamza*).

Much graver is however the addition of the by no means justified *hamza* after an end-*alif*, as far as such an *alif* in Syro-Aramaic can designate at least three different categories:

a) The ending of a *status emphaticus* masculine (be it a noun or an adjective), as e.g. شفاء (traditional reading: *šifāʾun* – Suras 10:57; 16:69; 17:82; 41:44) < Syro-Aramaic ܫܦܝܐ / *šep̄yā* or *šp̄āyā* (*clearness*, *purity*); the same Syro-Aramaic form ܗܕܝܐ / *heḏyā* or *hḏāyā* = Arabic هدى / *hudan* or هداية / *hidāya* (*leading*, *guidance*) shows how arbitrary the traditional different reading of the alternative spelling of these both words in Sura 41:44 (هدى وشفاء) as *"hudan wa-šifā'an"* is, since both words, according to the same Syro-Aramaic origin, are to read likewise as *"hudā wa-šifā"* (after dropping of the unaccented Syro-Aramaic *y* before the emphatic end-*ā*).

   The superfluous end-*hamza* can also distort a genuine Arabic adverb, as in Sura 12:16, where it is said of Joseph's brothers: وجاو اباهم عشاء يبكون (Bell I 219: *They came to their father in the evening, weeping*), whereas the adverb *"in the evening"* occurring four times in the Koran (Suras 19:11,62; 30:18; 40:46) as عشيا (*ʿašīyan*) and not عشاء (*ʿišāʾan*), should had call the attention of the Arab readers to the fact, that the latter original spelling, without the

---

369 This sense is attested in the Koran in Sura 2:117 and 6:101: بديع السموت والارض / *badīʿ as-samāwāt wa-l-arḍ* = Syro-Aramaic ܥܒܕ ܫܡܝܐ ܘܐܪܥܐ / *ʿāḇeḏ šmayyā w-arʿā* (*Creator of the heaven and the earth*). The secondary Arabic verb بدأ / *badaʾa*, with the secondary common meaning "*to begin*", has in the Koran partially the original meaning of "*to create*", as it arises e.g. from Sura 7:29: كما بداكم تعودون / *kamā badākum* or *bada'akum taʿūdūn* (*As He created you, you will turn again*) (Bell I 139 translates: "As He *began* you, ye will come again").

end-*hamza*, was to read غشا يبكون (*ġiššan* *yabkūn*) *"fallaciously weeping"*.

b) All cases of the Arabic feminine elative with an end-*alif* reflect truly the ending of the Syro-Aramaic *status absolutus* feminine with an end-*ā* and are consequently to read without the superfluous end-*hamza*, as, e.g., صفرا (*yellow*) in Sura 2:69, that is to read adequately *ṣafrā* (as in spoken Arabic) and not صفراء (traditional reading: *ṣafrāʾu*). The early Arab grammarians were obviously aware of this morphology, in so far as they declared such an ending as ممنوع من الصرف / *mamnū' min aṣ-ṣarf* (*banned as to the inflection* = *indeclinable*). Later grammarians may have interpreted this rule as *partially declinable* (rendered in the Western Arabic grammars by the term *diptotic*) and added to this purpose the fictitious end-*hamza*. This concerns as well the following plural endings.

c) The plural ending, corresponding to the Arabic plurals of the types: فعلاء / *fuʿalāʾ* and افعلاء / *afʿilāʾ*, are to value same wise. All these unjustified additions are an invention of the Arab philologists subsequent to the creation of the classical Arabic grammar in the second half of the eighth century and later. As far as such forms occur in the Arabic poetry, this linguistic-historical criterion would provide a *terminus post quem* (= *a quo*) as to the origin of the corresponding poetical works. Further morphological formations of the classical Arabic grammar, borrowed from Syro-Aramaic, will be demonstrated with some examples from the early Arabic poetry in a forthcoming study.

Continuation of Sura 96:6

Since it became now clear that طغى (*ṭaġā* = *ṭaʿā*) (with all other Koranic derivations) is a borrowing from the Syro-Aramaic ܛܥܐ (*ṭʿā*), its meaning can consequently be found among the equivalent semantics field appropriate to this context. It follows from the context that the meaning to be retained is the one cited in *Mannā* (289b f.) under (6) نسى (*nasiyᵃ*) (*to forget*). Accordingly, this verse does not say "man is *rebellious*," but "man *forgets*."

Verse 6: First of all, the result of the above misunderstood ليطغى (*la-yaṭġā*) was that the particle following it, ان, was misread as *ʾan* (*that*) instead of *ʾin* (*when*). The personal suffix for the verb رءاه (*raʾ-hu* – properly: *rā-hu*) has been correctly understood reflexively from the context. This usage happens by chance, of course, not to be Arabic, but Syro-Aramaic.[370]

Secondly, however, in the case of the next verb استغنى (*istaġnā*), it is not "*considers himself his own master*" that is correct, but rather the alternative that Bell proposes (II 667) in note 4: "he *has become rich*."

The verses 6-7 are accordingly:

"In truth, man *forgets* *when* he sees that he *has become rich*."

Verse 7: In the first place, it should now be clear that this understanding yields a conjunction أنّ (*anna*) (*that*) introducing a dependent clause. The hitherto misunderstood context, however, has caused the syntactical unity of this sentence construction to be so torn apart that one made this dependent clause into an independent main clause introduced by the intensifying particle إنّ (*inna*).

Secondly, from this misunderstanding the need arose to interpret the Arabic verbal noun الرجعى (*ar-ruǧʿā* – rather *ar-raǧʿā*) in no other way than the general sense of "*return to your Lord*." If one considers the new understanding, however, then this "*return*," referring to the "*man who has become rich*," is to be understood as the "*return*" or "*repatriation*" of this circumstance unto God, which man "*forgets*" to the extent that he, in accordance with a familiar human experience, no longer thinks

370 Cf. Th. Nöldeke, *Syrische Grammatik* [*Syriac Grammar*] § 223: "The personal pronouns must also express the reflexive wherever this function is not already performed by the verbal form… . That is, very often one uses ܢܦܫܐ (*napšā*) "soul," and less frequently ܩܢܘܡܐ (*qnōmā*) "person" with the personal suffixes for the exact expression of the reflexive relationship. . . ." In Arabic the only way to express the reflexive is by means of the equivalent expressions نفس (*nafs*) and حال (*ḥāl*). Accordingly, إن رءاه (*in raʾā-hu* – properly: *rā-hu*) in Arabic should have properly been إن رأى نفسه (*in raʾā nafsahu*).

about praying. Verses 6-8 are thus directly concerned with the subject of this Sura and should be understood as follows:

> 6. "In truth, man *forgets,* 7. *when* he sees that he *has become rich,* 8. *that* (this) is *to be returned unto* your Lord."

Whereas until now it was a question of a man become wanton who fails to pray out of personal conviction, in the sequence which now follows the Koran addresses the external influence of an unbeliever who wants to stop a devout man (a *servant of God*) from praying. In the process, the verses 9-14 consist syntactically of two previously completely overlooked conditional clauses, the first formulated as a question and the second as a counter-question. From Paret's translation, the previous confused understanding is evident. Nevertheless, first of all, as an introduction to the syntactic structure, the individual elements will be analyzed.

Verse 9: From the perspective of the Arabic understanding, the particle أ *ʾa* prefixed to the verb ارءيت (*a-raʾayt^a^* – properly: *a-rayt^a^*) in Verses 9 and 11 cannot be understood otherwise than as an interrogative particle. This understanding excludes a subsequent conditional clause, but exposes at the same time the disharmony of the syntactic period.

Excursus
(*a*) *On the Meaning of the Particle* أ / *ʾa*

This problem cannot be overcome without the help of Syro-Aramaic. For only the Syro-Aramaic can give us information about the genesis of the Arabic interrogative particle أ / *ʾa*, which until now has been considered *classical*. In his study on the subject Bergsträsser[371] naturally starts from the classical assumption and contents himself with a descriptive

371 Gotthelf Bergsträsser, *Verneinungs- und Fragepartikeln und Verwandtes im Kurʾān. Ein Beitrag zur historischen Grammatik des Arabischen* [*Negative and Interrogative Particles in the Koran: A Study of the Historical Grammar of Arabic*] (Leipzig, 1914) 89-100. Concerning ارايت (3-91) he says laconically: "Subordinate clauses are occasionally inserted after *a*, but then the *a* is usually repeated. The text causes more difficulties here than elsewhere...."

reproduction of the opinions of the Arabic grammarians. Nobody seems to have realized till now, however, that, on the basis of the Koranic usage, the Arabic interrogative particle أ / *ʾa* has only grown secondarily out of the Syro-Aramaic particle ܐܘ (*aw*) through the omission of the ܘ *w*. Evidence for this is provided by the Koranic usage itself. For example, it can be determined that the original particle أو / *aw* occurs as an interrogative particle in conjunction with the negative particle لا (اولا *awᵃ-lā*) three times and with لم (اولم *awᵃ-lam*) 33 times, whereas, with 78 occurrences, the usage with the monophthongized particle أ / *ʾa*, for instance, ألم (*a-lam*), clearly predominates.

The *Lisān* (XIV 55b) cites *al-Farrāʾ*, who explains the و / *w* of the Koranic interrogative particle أولم (*awᵃ-lam*) as an "*isolated* wāw" to which the interrogative particle أ / *ʾa* was added (إنها واو مفردة دخلت عليها ألف الاستفهام). Hence the awareness that this interrogative particle is not of Arabic origin is lacking among all of the Arabic philologists. The other uses of the particle أو / *aw* in the Koran also coincide to a large extent with that of the homonymous Syro-Aramaic ܐܘ / *aw*.[372]

Thus, for example, the Koranic use of the monophthongized particle أ / *ʾa* has found its place in Arabic as a conjunction introducing an apodosis expressing uncertainty or doubt, especially after corresponding negative verbs, as in لا أدرى أ (*lā adrī ʾa*) or لا أعلم أ (*lā aʿlamᵘ ʾa*) (*I do not know whether*...) (cf., e.g., Sura 72:10,25). As a rule this is felt to be an indirect interrogative particle. From one's feeling for the language, however, one can already no longer recognize this function as soon as, instead of the Arabically naturalized secondary particle أ / *ʾa*, the original

372 Cf. *Thes*. I 47, particula (1) distinctiva; (48) (2) interrogativa, *num, an, ne.* The Hebrew particle ה (*ha*) that Brockelmann associates with the Arabic interrogative particle أ (*ʾa*) in *Arabische Grammatik* [*Arabic Grammar*] § 86, note (a), would suggest a sound shift from *ha* to *ʾa*. But the parallel use of أو (*ʾaw*) and أ (*ʾa*) as an interrogative particle in the Koran would seem to verify the creation of the latter through the monophthongization of the Syro-Aramaic particle ܐܘ (*aw*). This, however, does not rule out the possibility that the former was also first created through a sound shift of the demonstrative particle ܗܘ (*haw*) to ܐܘ (*ʾaw*).

Syro-Aramaic particle ܐܘ / *aw* occurs. An example of this is provided by Sura 3:128:

ليس لك من الامر شئ او يتوب عليهم او يعذبهم فانهم ظلمون

Paret (55) renders this verse as follows:

> "– it is not for you (to decide) the matter – or to turn again to them (mercifully) or (else) to punish them. They are (indeed) wrongdoers."

The *Lisān* (XIV 55a) explains the particle أو / *aw* here in the sense of "*until* he takes pity on them" or "*unless* God takes pity on them" (حتى يتوب عليهم وإلا أن يتوب عليهم). However, according to the Syro-Aramaic understanding of the conjunction ܐܘ / *aw* the verse says:

> "It should be *a matter of indifference* to you whether (God) takes pity on them or dooms them to death (by fire): they are (in any case) wrongdoers."

(*b*) *On the Usage of the Particle* أ / *ʾa in the Sense of* إن / *in* (*if*)

The list that the *Thes.* (I 48) supplies, by way of the East Syrian lexicographers, on the usage of the Syro-Aramaic conjunction ܐܘ (*aw*) is interesting in this regard. Under the eight occasionally occurring functions *Bar Bahlūl* gives the meaning ܐܢ (*ēn*) (*if*). This in turn coincides with the explanation provided by *Kisāʾī* (953-1002), cited in the *Lisān* (XIV 55a), that أو (*aw*) may also occur *conditionally* (قال الكسائي وحده : وتكون شرطا).

The Solution of Verses 9 to 14

On the basis of this excursus, the following new interpretation emerges for these verses:

9-10. The first ارءيت is to be understood in the sense of إن رأيت (*in raʾayt*^{a}) (*if* you see). Accordingly, the double verse runs:

"*If* you see one who (wants) to stop a worshipper (of God) (from praying) when he is praying...."

11-12. The second ارءيت is to be understood as a question in the sense of "*to think*": "do you (*then*) think *that*...." Accordingly, the falsely read إن (*in*) must be read as أن (*an*). As a result, this double verse reads as an *apodosis*:

"do you (*then*) think *that* he is on the right path or *is thinking pious thoughts*?"

13-14. Parallel to Verse 9, the repeated ارءيت is in turn to be read إن رأيت (*in raʾayt*^{a}) (*if you think*), followed once more by أن (*an*) (*that*) instead of إن (*in*) (*if*), and understood as a counter-question with a protasis and apodosis:

"*If* (on the other hand) you think *that* he is denying (God) and turning away (from Him), *then* does he not know that God sees *everything*?"

15. What is meant by the second كلا is again Syro-Aramaic ܟܠܐ (*kullā*) (in the sense of كل شيء / *kull*^{a} *šay*ʾ) (*everything*); as an object it belongs to the preceding verb.

The particle لئن (falsely *la-ʾin*, actually to be read *l-ēn*) consists of the intensifying Arabic particle لـ / *la-* and the Syro-Aramaic conjunction ܐܝܢ (*ēn*).[373] This form occurs 61 times in the Koran. Older Koranic manuscripts should provide evidence of the full spelling لاين (= *l-ēn*). The *little peak* considered as a ـيـ / *y carrier* was, contrary to the Koranic (i.e., Syro-Aramaic) pronunciation, subsequently occupied by a *hamza*. In the canonical version of the Koran, this orthography (أفإين / *af-ēn* < ܐܦ ܐܝܢ / *āp̄ ēn*) is documented twice (Suras 3:144 and 21: 34).

The Arabic verb لنسفعا (*la-nasfaʿa*^{n}) certainly does not mean "*to seize*." In the *Lisān* (VIII 157b f.) the meaning is given correctly as لطم

373 The *Thes*. (I 249) gives the spelling ܐܝܢ (*ēn*), in addition to ܐܢ (*ēn*), as *Chaldean*; the first spelling also appears at times in Christian Palestinian (250): ܐܝܢ. For this: "Est ubi scriptum est ܐܝܢ..."

(*laṭam*^{a}ˁ) and ضرب (*ḍarab*^{a}ˁ) (*to strike*). On the other hand, the explanation that follows, وسفع بناصيته: جذب وأخذ وقبض ("*to seize*" by the "*forelock*"), is based on the false understanding of "*forelock*." What is meant by "*to strike*," however, is "*to punish*" in a figurative sense (in modern Arabic usage, as well). It is likely that here as an exception the final ا /-*ā* stands, in place of the final ن /-*n*, to mark the *energicus*, which requires the pronunciation as with *nunation*. A parallel to this is provided by Sura 12:32 (وليكونا / *wa-l-yakūna*^{n}ˁ).[374]

It is astounding that, of our Koran translators, not one has objected to the expression "*forelock*" (Paret "*Schopf*," Blachère "*toupet*"). Yet, what is meant here by the spelling ناصية (except for the secondarily inserted ا / *ā*) is Syro-Aramaic ܢܨܝܐ (*naṣṣāyā*). For this, the *Thes.* (II 2435) first gives the meaning: *contentiosus, rixosus* (*contentious, quarrelsome*) (said of a woman, as in Prov. 21:9,19; 25:24). From the Syrian lexicographers it then cites, in addition to further Syro-Aramaic synonyms, the following Arabic renderings: مخاصم . مقاوم (*opponent, adversary*).

But more amazing than this is the discovery that, over and over again, even the *Lisān* (XV 327) explains the root نصا (*naṣā*), documented in earlier Arabic, as a denominative of ناصية (*nāṣiya*), presumably misunderstood in Arabic as "*forelock, shock of hair*," even though the *ḥadīṯ* of *ʿĀʾiša* that it cites actually makes the Syro-Aramaic meaning clear. Namely, therein *ʿĀʾiša* is recorded as saying: لم تكن واحدة من نساء النبي تناصيني غير زينب (*none of the wives of the Prophet quarreled with me except for Zaynab*). Although the *Lisān* then explains this as: أي تنازعني وتباريني (i.e. "*she quarreled with me, she opposed me*"), it traces this explanation back to the circumstance that in doing so the two women, so to speak, "*got into each other's hair*" (وهو أن يأخذ كل واحد من المتنازعين بناصية الآخر), or more exactly, "*seized* each other *by the scruff of the neck*." It can be seen from this how little the later Arabic philologists have understood the earlier Syriacisms and Aramaisms.

---

374 Cf. W. Diem, *Untersuchungen zur frühen Geschichte der arabischen Orthographie* [*Studies in the Early History of Arabic Orthography*], III.: *Endungen und Endschreibungen* [*Endings and Their Spellings*], in *Orientalia*, vol. 50, 1981, § 193, 378. But actually, this orthography goes back to an Eastern Syro-Aramean (Babylonian) tradition.

The following understanding therefore results for Verse 15:

"If he does not stop, we will (severely) punish the adversary."

In the same way as for ناصية (*nāṣiya*, but actually *naṣṣāyā*), the apparent feminine ending for كذبة (*kāḏiba*, actually *kaddāḇā*) and خاطية (*ḥāṭiʾa*, actually *ḥaṭṭāyā*) is nothing other than the phonetic rendering of the Syro-Aramaic *emphatic* ending. Therefore, Verse 16, modeled on Verse 15, is to be understood as follows:

"The denying, sinful adversary."

17. The expression ناديه (*nādiyahu*), which occurs here, must be redefined. The "*clique*," as Paret translates the expression in the modern Arabic sense of "*club, association*," (Bell: "*council*"; Blachère: "*clan*"), is out of the question. Inasmuch as the facultative medial ا / *alif* in ناديه, according to the Eastern Syro-Aramean orthographical tradition, can occasionally designate a short *a*, the spelling yields the Syro-Aramaic ܢܕܝܗ (*naḏyeh* or *naddāyeh*). As a *nomen agentis* this form leads us to the intensive stem ܢܕܝ (*naddī*), whose primary meaning the *Thes.* (II 2291) gives as "*commovit, concussit, terrefecit*" (*to agitate, to shake, to scare off*). Applied to the *idols* that are probably meant here, this would result in the meaning "*of the one who arouses fear*" (i.e. whom one *fears* as a god). The *Thes.*, however, then refers to a further form: "Partic. ܡܢܕܐ (*m-naddē*) vide infra." The expression that is found further down (2292) ܫܟܝܪܬܐ ܘܡܢܕܝܬܐ (*šḵirtā wa-m-nad-daytā*) ([something or someone] *disgusting and repulsive*) brings us closer to the sense we are seeking. The Arabic meanings that are cited by *Mannā* (431b) under ܐܢܕ (*aneḏ*) are informative: (2) مقت . ابغض (*to hate, to detest*), (3) رذل . نبذ (*to reject, to disown*), (6) نجّس . قذر (*to make dirty, to besmirch*), (7) ارعب . افزع (*to scare away, to frighten*). All these meanings lead namely to the "*unclean spirit*" or "*idols*" designated with synonymous expressions in Syro-Aramaic (cf., e.g., *Thes.* I 1490, under ܛܢܦܐ *ṭanpā* "*impurus, immundus*"; *ἀκάθαρτος* de daemonibus, Matt. 10:1,...; further under ܛܢܦܘܬܐ / *ṭanpūṯā : pollutio, res quae polluit = idolum*, Exod. 8:26, Deut. 7:26, Jer. 32:34; de *idolatriis*, Deut. 20:18...; in connection with this, the following expression [1491], documented in the Koran

with انداد [*andād*],[375] ܢܕܝܕܘܬܐ [*nḏīḏūṯā*] [*impurity*] also becomes a designation for ܦܬܟܪܐ [*pṯaḵrē*] [*idols*], etc.).

Thus, with the *tertium comparationis* discovered via Syro-Aramaic, Verse 17 is to be understood as follows:

"May he then call upon his *idols* [literally: *impure ones*]!"

18. The expression الزبانية (until now pronounced *az-zabāniya*)[376] is still considered a puzzle. The misreading of the preceding verbal form in the first person plural سندع (*sa-nadᶜu*) is of course responsible for one's seeing in this incomprehensible expression in Arabic the "*henchmen*" (of hell) that God will allegedly *call in*. However, if we transcribe the original spelling (without the secondary ا / *ā*) into Syro-Aramaic, the result is the reading ܙܒܢܝܐ (*zaḇnāyā*). As the adjective from ܙܒܢܐ (*zaḇnā*) (*time*), this simply gives us, according to the *Thes*. (I 1079) under ܙܒܢܝܐ (*zaḇnāyā*), the meaning: *temporalis, temporarius, haud aeternus* (*temporal, transitory, not eternal*). This designation is a perfect match for the (*transitory*) "*idols*" of the (God-) *denying adversary*. It is to this extent only logical that the verbal form سيدع is to be read in the third person (*sa-yadᶜu*). This results in the following understanding for Verse 18: "… he will (only) call upon a[377] transitory (*god*)!"

---

375 The translation of the Koranic plural انداد (*andād*) by (*gods*) "*of his own kind*," as our Koran translators render it, trusting in the Arabic commentators (e.g. Paret at Sura 2:22), is therefore false.

376 In Jeffery, *Foreign Vocabulary* 148: "The guardians of Hell."

377 This would be justified as an *appellative* by the word determined by the Arabic article ال / *al.* The Koran, however, does not always orient itself according to the Arabic norm, and so it often happens that the Koran also leaves out an article required by Arabic, as in Sura 95:5, ثم رددنه اسفل سفلين, where what is seen in Arabic as an indeterminate (and therefore as a *false*) genitive of the *status constructus* is considered as determinate (and as *correct*) in Syro-Aramaic. Variations in both directions are to be observed in the Koran, so that criteria of Arabic as well as of Syro-Aramaic grammar must be taken into account depending on the context. Cf. for example the variants in the old codices edited by Arthur Jeffery, *Materials for the History of the Text of the Qur'ān*, Leiden 1937, p. 178 (Codex of Ubai b. Ka'b), Sura 95:5, where سفلين (*sāfilīn*) is transmitted with the article ال / *al* : السافلين (*as-sāfilīn*), "as Ibn Mas'ūd." The

19. Although the third and last كلا can be read in Arabic as *kallā* (*no*) in connection with, and as intensifying, the negative imperative that follows it, in Syro-Aramaic (*kullā*) it has the meaning of "(*not*) *at all*."

In addition to the actual Syro-Aramaic meaning of "*to bow*" (as an external sign of respect), one should also assume for the Arabic borrowed verb سجد (*sağad*^{a}) (< ܣܓܕ / *sgeḏ*) the metaphorical meaning of "*to worship God*" (*Thes*. II 2522, "metaph. *adoravit* Deum").

The Arabic borrowed verb اقترب (*iqtarab*^{a}) has in this context a quite particular content that the general Arabic meaning "*approach*" (without object or reference) is not able to provide. As a translation of Syro-Aramaic ܐܬܩܪܒ (*eṯqarraḇ*) the *Thes*. (II 3724) gives us (in particular as a *reflexive* or *intransitive* verb) the specific meaning that fits here, as follows: "spec. <u>*celebrata est liturgia*</u> (*to celebrate* the *liturgy*); it. <u>*Eucharistiam accepit*</u> (*to receive* the *Eucharist*). The latter meaning is logically to be assumed provided that one as a believer takes part in the *celebration of the Eucharist*. The term points in any case without a doubt to the participation in the "*sacrifice of the mass*," in the "*celebration of the Eucharist*" or in the "*communion liturgy*."

Those that this unambiguous explanation shocks are invited to refer to the Arabic dissertation mentioned in the Foreword (ix, note 4) (part I, chapter 4, "*Religious Customs and Rites Among Christian Arabs Before Islam*," 89).

In sum, the result of this philological discussion is the following reading and understanding for Sura 96 according to the Syro-Aramaic reading:

العلق
(*al-ʿalaq*) The Clay (Literally: the "*sticking*")
اقرا باسم ربك الذى خلق
(*iqrā b-ism*^{i} *rabbik*^{a} *l-laḏī ḫalaq*)
1. <u>*Call*</u> the name of your lord who has created,
خلق الانسن من علق
(*ḫalaq*^{a} *l-insān*^{a} *min ʿalaq*)

---

same occurs in the following Sura 96:16 : "He read الناصية الكاذبة الخاطئة (*an-nāṣiya al-kāḏiba al-ḫāṭiʾa*). So Abū Ḥaṣīn."

2. (who) has created man from *<u>sticky</u>* (*clay*);

اقرا وربك الاكرم

(*iqrā wa-rabbak^a l-akram*)

3. *<u>call</u>* (indeed)[378] your *<u>most admirable</u>* Lord,

الذى علم بالقلم

(*al-laḏī ʿallam^a bi-l-qalam*)

4. who has taught by the reed pen (i.e., the *scripture*),

علم الانسن ما لم يعلم كلا

(*allam^a l-insān^a mā lam yaʿlam kullā*)

5. has taught man what he did *<u>not</u>* know *<u>at all</u>*.

ان الانسن ليطعى

(*in* or *ēn : al-insān^u la-yaṭʿā*)

6. Verily, man *<u>forgets</u>*,

إن راه استغنى

(*in* or *ēn rā-hu staġnā*)

7. *<u>when</u>* he sees that he has *<u>become rich</u>*,

أن الى ربك الرجعى

(*ann^a ilā rabbik^a r-rağʿā*)

8. *<u>that</u>* (this) is *<u>to be returned</u> <u>to</u>* your Lord.

اريت الذى ينهى

(*a-rayt^a l-laḏī yanhā*)

9. *<u>If</u>* you *<u>see</u>* one who (wants) to stop[379]

عبدا اذا صلى

(*ʿabd^an iḏā ṣallā*)

10. a worshipper (of God) (from praying) when he is praying,

اريت أن كان على الهدى

(*a-rayt^a an kān^a ʿalā l-hudā*)

11. do you think (perhaps) *<u>that</u>* he is on the right path,

او امر بالتقوى

(*aw amar^a bi-t-taqwā*)

---

378 Namely, in Arabic the conjunction و / *wa* also has an *explicative* function, including that of a more detailed explanation.

379 Syro-Aramaic ܟܠܐ (*klā*) is the supposed lexical equivalent for Arabic نهى (*nahā*). For this, *Mannā* (337b) cites in Arabic, besides نهى . نفى (*nahā, nafā*) (*to forbid*), also صدّ . عاق (*ṣadd^a, ʿāq^a*) (*to hinder, to hold back*).

12. or is even[380] thinking pious thoughts?[381]
اريت أن كذب وتولى
(*a-rayt^{a} an kaḏḏab^{a} wa-tawallā*)
13. *If* you (on the contrary) *think that* he *is denying* (God) and turning away (from Him),
الم يعلم بان الله يرى كلا
(*a-lam yaʿlam bi-ann^{a} llāh^{a} yarā kullā*)
14. (then) does he not know that God sees *everything*?
لين لم ينته لنسفعا بالناصيه
(*l-ēn lam yantahi la-nasfaʿan bi-n-nāṣiya* or *naṣṣāyā*)
15. If he does not stop (doing that), (one day) we shall punish the *adversary* (severely),
ناصيه كذبه خاطيه
(*nāṣiya kāḏiba ḫāṭiya* or *naṣṣāyā kaddāḇā ḥaṭṭāyā*)
16. the *denying*, wicked *adversary*!
فليدع ناديه
(*fa-l-yadʿu nādiya-hu* or *nadya-hu*)
17. May he call (then) on his (whoever) *idol*—
سيدع الزبانيه
(*sa-yadʿu z-zabāniya* or *zabāniyē*)
18. (in doing so) he will call on *transitory* (gods)!
كلا لا تطعه
(*kullā lā tuṭiʿhu*)

380 Among the eight different aspects (ܦܪܨܘܦܐ /*parṣōpē*) of the Syro-Aramaic conjunction ܐܘ (*aw*) that *Bar Bahlūl* names, the *Thes.* (I 48) cites the "*intensifying*" meaning designated with ܝܬܝܪ (*yattīr*). This conjunction is also used with such a meaning in the Koran, in Sura 37:147, where it is said of Jonas وارسلنه الى مائة الف او يزيدون "and we dispatched him to one hundred thousand *or (even)* more." The Arabic philologists have noticed this nuance (see *Lisān* XIV 54b).

381 The single meaning of the Arabic borrowed verb أمر (*amar^{a}*) "*to command*" does not do justice to the present context. It is not a question of "*commanding*," but rather of the "beliefs" or "convictions" upon which the action is based. To that extent the meaning given by *Mannā* (26a) in Arabic under (4) for the Syro-Aramaic ܐܡܪ (*emar*) ارتأى (*irtaʾā*) (*to think, to consider, to ponder*) is appropriate.

واسجد واقترب
(*wa-sğud wa-qtarib*)
19. You ought <u>not</u> to heed him <u>at all</u>,
perform (instead) (your) divine service[382]
and take part in the liturgy of Eucharist.

According to this understanding, Sura 96 proves to be a unified composition having as its overall content a call to take part in the divine service. As such it has the character of a ܦܪܘܡܝܘܢ (< προοίμιον / *prooemium*) introducing the Christian Syriac liturgy, which was replaced in the later Islamic tradition by the فاتحة (*fātiḥa*) (< Syro-Aramaic ܦܬܚܐ / *pṯāḥā*) (*introductory prayer*). That this liturgy is *Communion* is indicated by the final Syro-Aramaic term. An important task in the history of religion would be to find out which pre-Islamic Christian Syrian (or possibly Judaeo-Christian) community this was.

Now, if the Arabic tradition considers this to be the oldest Sura, one must concede that it is right to the extent that this Sura is, in any case, part of that *nucleus of the Koran*, the *Christian Syrian origins* of which cannot be ignored. Whether this is also the first that was revealed to the Prophet is probably based on a later legend grown out of the misinterpretation of the opening verse. Arguing in favor of its being very probably pre-Koranic, i.e., much more pre-Islamic, is its language, hitherto perceived as mysterious and puzzling. For it is precisely this language with its unadulterated expressions that reveals to us its venerable origins.

One such expression is the Arabic اقترب (*iqtarab*[a]) borrowed from the Syro-Aramaic verb ܐܬܩܪܒ (*eṯqarraḇ*). As a *technical term* of the Christian Syrian liturgy it gives us a valuable, hitherto unexpected insight into the origins, not only of the oldest parts of the Koran in terms of the history of religion. For only this expression opens our eyes to a parallel occurring in what is held to be the last Sura revealed, Sura 5 (*The Table*), a parallel whose actual importance in terms of the history of religion has in a similar way been ignored until now. Between this *term* and the "*table*" that Jesus, the son of Mary, requests of God in Sura

382 Literally: Bow (instead) (to honor God). As a *terminus technicus*, سجد (*sağad*[a]) here means "*to hold divine service*."

5:114, تكون لنا عيدا لاولنا واخرنا "that it may become ours as *liturgy*,[383] for the first and the last of us," and which, in Verse 115, God sends down from heaven, threatening any who would *deny* it (فمن يكفر *fa-man yakfur*) with the severest of all punishments (فاني اعذبه عذابا لا اعذبه احدا من العلمين) (*him I shall punish in such a way as I shall punish no man*), there exists a connection insofar as both clearly allude to the *liturgy of Communion*, whose importance was misjudged in later Islam and has since been totally forgotten. This central item in the Christian components of the Koran is, in any case, of eminent importance in terms of the history of religion.

If any should doubt, however, the importance of the Christian Syriac liturgical term اقترب (*iqtarab*ᵃ) (< ܐܬܩܪܒ / *etqarrab*) (*to take part in the liturgy of Communion, to receive the Eucharist*), they may refer to the Arabic dissertation mentioned in the Foreword (p. iii, note 4) where the author (89), in the fourth chapter of the first part of her work, "*Religious Customs and Rites of Christian Arabs Before Islam*," refers to the Arabic compilation الأغاني (*al-Aġānī*) (vol. II 107) of *Abū l-Farağ al-Isfahānī* (d. 356 H./967 A.D.), who reports of عدي بن زيد (*ʿAdī ibn Zayd*) (d. circa 590 A.D.) and هند بنت النعمان (*Hind bint an-Nuʿmān*) (d. after 602 A.D.) how they went on Maundy Thursday into the church of *al-Ḥira* (located southwest of the Euphrates in modern-day Iraq) " ليتقربا " (*li-yataqarrabā*) "*to take part in the celebration of the Eucharist*" (or *to receive the Eucharist*).

In the corresponding passage in the كتاب الأغاني (*Kitāb al-aġānī*)[384] (*Book of Songs*) *Abū l-Farağ al-Iṣfahānī* (d. 967) cites the traditional

---

383 The true meaning of the term عيد (*ʿīd*), which occurs as a *hapax legomenon* in the Koran, has until now been overlooked. Brockelmann, *Lexicon Syriacum* (515b), explains the derivation of Arabic عيد (*ʿīd*) in the meaning "*feast*" as the phonetic rendering of the common Aramaic pronunciation of ܥܐܕܐ (*ʿēḏā* > *ʿīḏā*). As a faithful rendering of the Syro-Aramaic ܝܥܕܐ (*ʿyāḏā*), however, the Koranic term has accordingly, in addition to the original meaning of "*practice, custom*," the meaning of "*liturgy*," which is clear here from the Koranic context. Cf. also the *Thes.* II 2827: Valet etiam ܝܥܕܐ (*ʿyāḏā*) *ritus, caeremonia* (*rite, ceremony*).

384 Vol. II, 1st edition (Cairo, 1928) 129.

account of the pre-Islamic Christian Arab poet *ʿAdī ibn Zayd* living in *al-Ḥīra* according to which he had gone on Maundy Thursday into the church of *al-Ḥīra* ليتقرّب (*li-yataqarrab*) "*to take part in the celebration of the Eucharist*" (or *to receive the Eucharist*) On this occasion, he wanted to see *Hind*, the daughter of the last of the Laḫmids' kings of *al-Ḥīra*, النعمان / *an-Nuʿmān III* (580-602), who had gone to the aforementioned church تتقرّب (*tata-qarrab*) "*to take part in the celebration of the Eucharist.*"[385]

Thus, this *liturgical term* is already historically documented in the 6th century even from the Arab side as a Syro-Aramaic ecclesiastical term of the Christian Arabs of Syria and Mesopotamia.

---

385 This term is still used among the Arabic speaking Christians of the Near and Middle East.

18. Résumé

The importance of the Koran in terms of the history of religion and cultural history is a generally acknowledged fact. Although its role as a mediator between a more than thousand-year Aramean civilization and the Arabic culture it ushered in has been recognized, the Aramaic language's share in the process has not been sufficiently appreciated.[386] That is why opinions have differed ever since on the interpretation of its contents and of its mysterious language. This is first of all due to the interwoven composition of the Koran text, but secondly to the linguistic approach of the Arabic Koran exegesis, which from the beginning can

386 The findings made in the meantime as to the *Relics of Syro-Aramaic letters in Early Koran Codices in Ḥiǧāzī and Kūfī Style*, mentioned above and partially shown in this study, provide a further concrete evidence for the existence of a proto-Koran written in *Garshuni* / *Karshuni* (i.e. Arabic with Syriac letters) corroborating the intimate connection between the Koran and the Syro-Aramaic culture. This may confirm the assumption expressed byYehuda D. Nevo and Judith Koren in their collective work: *Crossroads to Islam. The Origin of the Arab Religion and the Arab State*, Amherst, New York (Prometheus Books), 2003, p. 328, especially note 2:

"We cannot tell if the resulting Arabic texts were actual *translations* of the original Syriac ones; more probably they were formulations in Arabic of Judaeo-Christian ideas known from Syriac texts."

That with *al-inǧīl* (the *Gospel*), mentioned in the Koran, the Syriac *Diatessaron* (the so-called *Gospels Harmony*, a chronological disposition of the four Gospels arranged by the Syrian Tatianos, presumably in the second half of the second century) is meant, Jan M.F. van Reeth says in his essay "*Le Coran et ses scribes* [*The Koran and its Scribes*]" in: *Acta Orientalia Belgica* (published by the Belgian Society of Oriental Studies, ed. by C. Cannuyer, A, Schoors, R. Lebrun), vol. XIX, *Les scribes et la transmission du savoir* [*The Scribes and the Transmission of Knowledge*], ed. by C. Cannuyer, Bruxelles, 2006, (p. 67-81), p. 73, 21 ff.:

"Ce constat s'ajoute à la théorie de Luxenberg tout en la renforçant: le livre sacré que lisait la communauté de Muḥammad, était un livre en syriaque [*This conclusion is to be added to the theory of Luxenberg, reinforcing it: the holy book that was read by the community, of which* Muḥammad *was a member, was a Syriac book*]."

be characterized as unsuccessful. It was this that was finally decisive in steering the interpretation of the Koran in a direction that was not intended by the Koran at all.

I. The Language of the Koran

The Arabic philologists themselves realized that the language that the Koran calls *Arabic* for the first time differs essentially from the later Classical Arabic language, the *ʿArabīya*. Contrary to the earlier assumption of a dialect of Arabic spoken in Mecca, the present study has shown that, insofar as the Arabic tradition has identified the language of the Koran with that of the *Qurayš*, the inhabitants of Mecca, this language must instead have been an *Aramaic-Arabic hybrid language*. It is not just the findings of this study that have led to this insight. Namely, in the framework of this study an examination of a series of *ḥadith* (sayings of the Prophet) has identified Aramaisms that had either been misinterpreted or were inexplicable from the point of view of Arabic.

This would lead one to assume that Mecca was originally an Aramean settlement. Confirmation of this would come from the name *Mecca* (*Macca*) itself, which one has not been able to explain etymologically on the basis of Arabic. But if we take the Syro-Aramaic root ܡܟ (*mak*, actually *makk*) (*lower, to be low*) as a basis, we get the adjective ܡܟܟܐ (*mākkā*) (masc.), ܡܟܟܬܐ (*mākktā*) (fem.), with the meaning of "(the) *lower* (one)." Topographically, this adjective would designate a place located in a *low-lying area* or in a *valley*, which indeed is also the case for Mecca. As opposed to this ܪܡܐ (*rāmā*) (masc.), ܪܡܬܐ (*rāmtā*) (fem.) "(the) *high* (one)" (*the upper one*) designates a place located on a *rise*, a *hill* or a *mountain*.[387]

However, because the *Thes*. (II 2099 ff.) usually gives the figurative sense for this root, this should also be taken into consideration. For instance, among other things the *Thesaurus* (2100) cites the expression ܕܘܟܝܬܐ ܡܟܟܬܐ (*dūkkyātā mākkātā*) with the explanation: *agri minoris*

387 Thus, for example, the city located near the Syrian border in modern-day Jordan, الرمثا (*ar-Ramtā*) = Syro-Aramaic ܪܡܬܐ (*rāmtā*).

pretii (*low-quality farmland*). This meaning would find confirmation in Sura 14:37; there namely Abraham says:

ربنا اني اسكنت من ذريتي بواد غير ذي زرع عند بيتك المحرم

"Lord, I have <u>settled</u> (some) of my offspring in a <u>barren valley</u> near your holy house."

Thus both Syro-Aramaic meanings would fit Mecca and would at the same time suggest that it was an early Aramean settlement.[388] The

---

388 As for بكة (allegedly: *Bakka*) in Sura 3: 96, although until now this has been taken to be a second name for Mecca, in reality it is here a question of a misread verbal form. The verse from Sura 3: 96 runs:

ان اول بيت وضع للناس للذي <u>ببكة</u> مباركا وهدى للعلمين

This has been understood by our Koran translators as follows:

(Bell I 54): 90. "The first house founded for the people was that at <u>Bakka</u> [*I.e.* <u>Mecca</u>], a blessed (house) and a guidance to the worlds."

(Paret 52): „Das erste (Gottes)haus, das den Menschen aufgestellt worden ist, ist dasjenige in <u>Bakka</u> [Note: D.h. <u>Mecca</u>], (aufgestellt) zum Segen und zur Rechtleitung für die Menschen in aller Welt (*al-ʿālamūn*)."

(Blachère, 88): 90/96 En vérité, le premier temple qui ait été fondé, pour les Hommes, est certes celui <u>situé</u> à <u>Bakka</u> [Note 90: Autre forme de *Makka* = la Mekke], [*temple*] béni et Direction pour le monde (ʿâlamîn).

Thus, our Koran translators are following, without hesitation, the interpretation given in *Ṭabarī* (IV 9 f.), according to which this word, inexplicable from the point of view of Arabic, has therefore to be (applying the tried and true method) a second name for Mecca. As justification, *Ṭabarī* etymologically derives this word from the (no longer commonly used) Arabic verbal root بك (*bakka*) (*to press, to push*) and applies this to the district of the *Kaʿba* around which the pilgrims "*pressed*" in circling it. The name *Bakka* would thus designate the shrine, whereas *Makka* would designate the surrounding houses, i.e., the city itself, and not, as others believed, the other way around.

In the case of the misread spelling ببكه (supposedly *bi-Bakka* = "*in Bakka*"), it is in fact a question of the Syro-Aramaic verbal root ܬܟ (*tāḵ*) in the *paʿʿel* form, ܬܝܟ (*tayyeḵ*), whose meaning *Mannā* (832b) renders in Arabic under (4) as حدد (*ḥaddada*) (*to surround*), سيج (*sayyağa*) (*to enclose*), احاط (*aḥāṭa*) (*to surround with a wall*). The *Thes.* (II 4406f.) refers, among other things, to Deuteronomy 12:8, where it is said that in building a house its roof should be surrounded by a balustrade ܬܝܟܐ (*tyāḵā*). The only word preserved from this root in Arabic is the substantive تكة (*tikka*) (dialectally دكة / *dikka* / *dəkke*) (*a cloth*

Aramean origin of Medina has already been identified by S. Fraenkel (*Aramäische Fremdwörter* [*Aramaic Foreign Words*] 280).

Now, if according to Sura 42:7 the Koran has expressly given the Prophet the task of proclaiming the Koranic message to the *metropolis* (ام القرى) (namely *Mecca*) and its *surrounding area* (ومن حولها), one can assume that the Meccans also correctly understood this message. To this extent the Koran did not intend its language for those Arabs who laid out another Arabic language around a century and a half afterwards. This essential circumstance explains historically why the later Arabs no longer understood this Koran Arabic.

What widened the gap even more, however, is the lack of reference to the *Scripture* in the Arabic exegesis of the Koran. Historical reasons must have led the later Islamic tradition to renounce the *Scripture*, the heeding of which by the believers is assumed as *a matter of course* by the Koran in the words from Sura 3:119: تومنون بالكتب كله (*tuʿminūna bi-l-kitābi kullihi*) "you believe, indeed, in the *entire Scripture*." At the same time consideration of the *Scripture* would have been more capable

---

belt, waistband), about which *Ibn Durayd* (*Lisān* X 406b) says: لا احسبها إلا دخيلا وإن كانوا قد تكلموا بها قديما (*I consider it a foreign word even though it was used earlier*).

It is therefore no surprise if the later Arabic readers of the Koran were unable to suspect a Syro-Aramaic root behind the spelling ببكه. From this arose the need to see in it (as so often) an undocumented epithet for Mecca. In the process (assuming this were also true), instead of the here misread preposition بـ / *bi-*, the Arabic في / *fī* (*in*) would have been more expected. Transliterated into Syro-Aramaic, however, this spelling yields the reading ܬܝܟܗ (*taykeh*) = Arabic: تيّكه (*tayyakahu*) = سيّجه (*sayyağahu*), أحاطه (*aḥāṭahu*) (*he fenced it off, built a wall around it*), in which case the figurative sense منعه (*manaʿahu*) (*he protected it, made it* therefore *into a protected district*) (*Mannā*, *loc. cit.*, under 2) is also possible. This results in the following reading for Sura 3: 96:

ان اول بيت جعل للناس للذي تيكه مباركا وهدى للعلمين

"The first shrine that was erected for the people is the one that He has fenced off (*enclosed*) as a holy (literally: blessed) (district) and (as) right guidance for the people."

This reading is confirmed by the subsequent verse 97, in which it is said that the place of residence (مقام = ܡܩܡܐ / *m-qāmā*) of Abraham was located in this (district): ومن دخله كان امنا "and whoever enters it enjoys protection."

of contributing substantially to the understanding and clarification of the language of the Koran than the systematic reference to the so-called *Old Arabic poetry*, which has in many cases driven the exegesis further off the track than before such reference.

Other inferences could also be drawn concerning the origin of the language of the Koran, but it would be premature to do so on the basis of these individual findings since theses based on such grounds could prove to be fallacious. Only a comprehensive philological explanation of the text of the Koran would provide an objective foundation for further conclusions.

II. The Oral Tradition

The unsuspected extent of the misreading that has come to light in connection with numerous Koran passages raises the question of the authenticity of the previously alleged oral Arabic tradition. In view of this, the thesis advocated so far in this regard can no longer be upheld. On the contrary, this necessitates the assumption from the beginning of a text transmitted in writing. The early Koran manuscripts still extant today in defective Arabic script make it clear even to a non-specialist that without a reliable oral tradition such a text would not have been easy to decipher even for a learned Arab. It is therefore understandable that the later Arab exegetes and philologists who had endeavored for generations to achieve a reasonably coherent reading of the Koran text were not up to the task inasmuch as they took as their starting point an understanding of language based on a written Arabic that was first standardized around the second half of the 8th century. This makes the numerous misreadings and misinterpretations of the Koran text comprehensible.

This determination, however, will have more impact on Koran studies than on Islamic studies. The task of Islamic studies will continue to be the concern with Islam as it has developed historically. For Koran studies, however, the task set is another. For it can now already be stated that the Koran exegesis in East and West has started out from historically false assumptions. This is evidenced not least by the Western Koran translations whose authors, though they always endeavored anew to shed some light on the obscurities of the language of the Koran, could not conjure more out of it than the Arabic language as such was able to give.

III. Arabic Philology

This refers, above all, to the Persian *Sībawayh* (d. circa 796) as the founder of the grammar of the Arabic written language still valid today for standard modern Arabic. The Arabic philologists call their written language *al-ʿArabīya.* In Western Arabistics it is designated as *Classical Arabic*. Essentially, this claim is traced back to the literary language's preservation of three case endings from the hypothesized *proto-Semitic*, but also to the other sounds lost in colloquial Arabic, apart from particular syntactic structures.

In the course of their work, the Arab philologists based their reflections on the one hand on the *Koran*, as the first written monument, and on the other hand on the so-called *Old Arabic poetry*. Insofar as the latter, however, was not fixed in writing, one relied on the accepted oral tradition of the Arabian nomads, who, in particular, it was presumed, had preserved the so-called *hamza*, the stop in a medial or final position, from prehistoric times. But because a reliable oral Arabic tradition was likewise assumed for the Koran as well, the defective script of which – except for the original *matres lectionis ū* and *ī* – had no vowel signs at all, once it was fixed according to the model of the so-called *Old Arabic poetry*, the course for the future was set. For the correct understanding of the Koran text, this circumstance was of crucial and, at the same time, of fateful historical significance.

For whereas one knew until now that the *hamza* and partly the *alif* had been inserted later on into the text of the Koran as a *mater lectionis* for long *ā* and the other vowel signs, one was nevertheless convinced that this had occurred on the basis of a reliable oral tradition. Beginning from the assumption of the downright phenomenal memory of the *Arabs*, who supposedly had orally preserved an impressive quantity of poetical works, one assumed as a matter of course that this was also the case for the Koran, not only because it was the first, but even more so because it was the *holy Scripture* of the Arabs.

However, to this day nobody has dared to take seriously into consideration the occasionally expressed suspicion[389] that the Koran text was *misread* and *distorted* not only by the introduction of the vowel signs, but especially by the subsequently inserted *diacritical points* that first established the *original consonant script.*

IV. The Historical Error

The findings of this first study, however, force one to conclude that the previous thesis of a reliable oral transmission of the text of the Koran stemmed from a mere legend.

According to the examples presented here, if the Arab philologists and commentators have even misread genuinely Arabic expressions, the only possible conclusion regarding the oral transmission of the Koran is obvious. If such a tradition existed at all, it must be assumed that it was interrupted fairly early on. In any case, the least conclusion that one can draw from this is that it has considerable gaps.

V. The New Reading of the Koran

If the above philologically underpinned analysis has demonstrated that on the basis of both philological and objective criteria the Koran text has

---

389 Karl Vollers, for instance, in the conclusions of his work *Volkssprache und Schriftsprache im alten Arabien* [*Vernacular Language and Written Language in Ancient Arabia*] (184), voiced the opinion that "the way in which the Koranic language, which is based on imitation, is praised by posterity as genuine *ʿArabīya* should be labeled by the historian as *counterfeiting*." To correct a Koran text that has been misread in numerous passages, a critical edition of the oldest Koran manuscripts, as advocated, for example, by R. Blachère (*Introduction au Coran* 196) and from which he expects insights into the origins of the Arabic language, is certainly desirable. Yet, read properly, the basic form of the canonical Cairo edition of the Koran is already sufficient in itself to enable one to make far-reaching conclusions regarding this.

been misread and misinterpreted to a degree hitherto considered unimaginable, then the inevitable consequence is the need for a fundamentally new reading of the Koran. The findings of the present study have created the prerequisites for such a reading.

From this results an essential finding of this study, according to which the hitherto scarcely perceived importance of Syro-Aramaic lexicography has turned out to be crucial not only in providing evidence of actual Aramaisms (or Syriacisms) but also and especially in the determination of even the Arabic vocabulary of the Koran. To this extent it may not be too audacious to hope that with the method on which this work has been based the way has now been cleared for the creation of a new glossary of the Koran.

Literature Cited

ʿAbd al-Bāqī, Muḥammad Fuʾād. *al-Muʿǧam al-mufahras li-alfāẓ al-Qurʾān al-karīm* (*Koran concordance*). Beirut, 1945.

ʿAlī, Ǧawād, *al-Mufaṣṣal fī tārīḫ al-ʿArab qabl al-Islām* (*Exhaustive History of the Arabs before Islam*). 3rd ed. Vol. 6. Beirut, Baghdad, ^{3}1980.

Ahrens, Karl. *Christliches im Qoran* [*Christian Elements in the Koran*]. In: *ZDMG* 84 (new series, Vol. 9) Leipzig, 1930. 15- 68.

Andrae, Tor. *Der Ursprung des Islams und das Christentum* [*Christianity and the Origin of Islam*]. Uppsala, 1926.

Bā-l-Ḥāǧǧ Ṣāliḥ - al-ʿĀyub, Salwā. *al-Masīḥīya al-ʿarabīya wa-taṭawwurātuhā min našʾatihā ilā l-qarn ar-rābiʿ al-hiǧrī* / *al-ʿāšir al-mīlādī* [*Arab Christianity and Its Development from Its Origin to the Fourth Century of the Hegira / Tenth Christian Century*]. Diss. U Tunis I, 1995. Beirut, 1997.

Baumstark, Anton. *Geschichte der syrischen Literatur* [*History of Syrian Literature*]. Bonn, 1922.

Beck, Edmund. "Eine christliche Parallele zu den Paradiesjungfrauen des Korans? [A Christian Parallel to the Virgins of Paradise in the Koran?]" *Orientalia Christiana Periodica*. Vol. 14. Rome, 1948. 398-405.

Bell, Richard. *A Commentary on the Qurʾān*. 2 vols. Manchester, 1991.

Bell, Richard. *Introduction to the Qurʾān*. Edinburgh, ^{2}1958.

Bell, Richard, trans. *The Qurʾān* : Translated, with a Critical Rearrangement of the Surahs. Vol. 1. Edinburgh, 1937. Vol. 2. Edinburgh, 1939.

Bergsträsser, Gotthelf. *Verneinungs- und Fragepartikeln und Verwandtes im Qurʾān: Ein Beitrag zur historischen Grammatik des Arabischen* [*Negative and Interrogative Particles and Related Forms in the Koran: A Study of the Historical Grammar of Arabic*]. Leipzig, 1914.

Beyer, Klaus. *The Aramaic Language*. Göttingen, 1986.

Biblia Hebraica. Ed. Rudolf Kittel. 7th ed. Stuttgart, 1951.

Blachère, Régis, trans. *Le Coran, traduit de l'arabe* [*The Koran Translated from Arabic*]. Paris, 1957.

Blachère, Régis. *Introduction au Coran* [*Introduction to the Koran*]. Paris, 1947.

Brockelmann, Carl. *Arabische Grammatik* [*Arabic Grammar*]. 14th ed. Leipzig, ^{14}1960.

Brockelmann, Carl. *Kurzgefasste vergleichende Grammatik der semitischen Sprachen* [*A Concise Comparative Grammar of the Semitic Languages*]. Berlin, 1908.

Brockelmann, Carl. *Grundriss der vergleichenden Grammatik der semitischen Sprachen* [*Outline of the Comparative Grammar of the Semitic Languages*]. Vol. 2. Berlin, 1913. Hildesheim, 1961.

Brockelmann, Carl. *Lexicon Syriacum* [*Syriac Lexicon*]. 2nd ed. Halle, ^{2}1928.

Brockelmann, Carl. *Syrische Grammatik* [*Syriac Grammar*]. Leipzig, ^{8}1960.

Burgmer, Christoph (ed.), *Streit um den Koran. Die Luxenberg-Debatte. Standpunkte und Hintergründe* [*Dispute about the Koran. The Luxenberg-Debate. Standpoints and Backgrounds*], 3rd ed., Berlin 2006.

Déroche, François and Sergio Noja Noseda. *Bibliothèque Nationale de France*: Sources de la transmission du texte coranique [Sources of the Transmission of the Text of the Koran]. Vol. 1. Les manuscrits de style *ḥiǧāzī* [Manuscripts in the *ḥiǧāzī* Style]. Le manuscrit arabe 328(a) de la Bibliothèque Nationale de France [Arabic Manuscript No. 328(a) in the Bibliothèque Nationale de France]. Paris (Bibliothèque Nationale de France), 1998.

Diem, Werner. *Untersuchungen zur frühen Geschichte der arabischen Ortho-graphie* [*Studies on the Early History of Arabic Orthography*]. I. *Die Schreibung der Vokale* [*The Writing of the Vowels*]. In: Orientalia, new series, vol. 48, 1979, 207-257; II. *Die Schreibung der Konsonanten* [*The Writing of the Consonants*]. Vol. 49, 67-106; III. *Endungen und Endschreibungen* [*Endings and Their Spellings*]. Vol. 50, 1981, 332-383.

Drewes, A. J. *The Phonemes of Lihyanite*. In: *Mélanges linguistiques offerts à Maxime Rodinson* (Supplément 12 aux comptes rendus du groupe linguistique d'études chamito-sémitiques). Paris (offprint, n. d.). 165 ff.

EI (1): *Enzyklopaedie des Islām*. 4 vols. Leiden, Leipzig, 1913-1936 (Supplementary vol., 1938).

EI (2): *The Encyclopaedia of Islam*. 8 vols. Leiden, London, 1960-1995.

Ephraem Syrus. *Hymnen de Paradiso und contra Julianum* [*Hymns of Paradise and Contra Julianum*]. Ed. Edmund Beck. In: *Corpus Scriptorum Christianorum Orientalium*. Vol. 174, Scriptores Syri, Tomus 78, Louvain, 1957.

Fischer, A. "Der Wert der vorhandenen Koran-Übersetzungen und Sura 111 [The Value of the Existing Koran Translations and Sura 111]." In: *Berichte über die Verhandlungen der Sächsischen Akademie der Wissenschaften zu Leipzig. Philologisch-historische Klasse*. 89th vol. 1937. No. 2, 3-9.

Fraenkel, Siegmund. *De vocabulis in antiquis Arabum carminibus et in Corano peregrinis* [*On the Foreign Words in Old Arabic Poetry and in the Koran*] . Leiden, 1880.

Fraenkel, Siegmund. *Die aramäischen Fremdwörter im Arabischen* [*Aramaic Foreign Words*]. Leiden, 1886. Hildesheim, New York [2]1982.].

Geiger, Abraham. *Was hat Mohammed aus dem Judenthume aufgenommen?* [*What Did Mohammed Take Over from Judaism?*]. 2nd ed. Leipzig, [2]1902. Osnabrück, 1971.

Gesenius, Wilhelm. *Hebräisches und aramäisches Handwörterbuch über das Alte Testament* [*Concise Dictionary of Old Testament Hebrew and Aramaic*]. Berlin, Göttingen, Heidelberg, [17]1959.

Gilliot, Claude, «*Informants* », in: *EQ* II, p. 512-518 (*Encyclopaedia of the Qur'ān*, I-V, General Editor Jane Dammen McAuliffe, Leiden 2001-2005). Id. «*Les "informateurs"* juifs et chrétiens de Muḥammad. Reprise d'un problème traité par Aloys Sprenger et Theodor Nöldeke [*The Jewish and Christian "Informants" of Muḥammad. Resumption of a Problem Treated by Aloys Sprenger and Theodor Nöldeke*] », in : *JSAI*, 22 (1998), p. 84-126.

Grohmann, Adolf. *Arabische Paläographie* [*Arabic Paleography*]. Vol. 1. Vienna, 1967. Vol. 2. Vienna, 1971.

Healy, John F. *The Early History of the Syriac Script. A Reassessment.* In: *Journal of Semitic Studies* XLV/1 *Spring 2000*, p. 55-67.

Horovitz, Joseph, *Jewish Proper Names and Derivatives in the Koran*. Ohio, 1925. Hildesheim, 1964.

Horovitz, Joseph. *Koranische Untersuchungen* [*Koranic Studies*]. Berlin, Leipzig, 1926.

Ibn Warraq (ed.), *What the Koran Really Says. Language, Text & Commentary*, Amherst, New York, 2002.

al-Iṣfahānī, Abū-l-Farağ. *Kitāb al-Aġānī.* Vol. 2. Cairo, 1928.

Jeffery, Arthur. *The Foreign Vocabulary of the Qur'ān.* Baroda, 1938.

Jerusalemer Bibel. Eds. Diego Arenhoevel, Alfons Deissler, and Anton Vögtle. 1968. 15th ed. Freiburg, Basel, Vienna, 15 1979.

Luxenberg, Christoph, *Weihnachten im Koran* [*Christmas in the Koran*] (Sura 97), see Burgmer, Christoph (ed.), *Streit um den Koran. Die Luxenberg-Debatte. Standpunkte und Hintergründe* [*Dispute about the Koran. The Luxenberg-Debate. Standpoints and Backgrounds*], 3rd ed., Berlin 2006, p. 62-68; see further "*imprimatur*" I / 2003, p. 13-17.

– *Noël dans le Coran* [*Christmas in the Koran*], see: Anne-Marie Delcambre, Joseph Bosshard (ed.) et alii, *Enquêtes sur l'islam. En hommage à Antoine Moussali* [*Inquiries about Islam. In Homage to Antoine Moussali*], Paris (Desclée de Brouwer), 2004, p. 117-134.

– *Der Koran zum „islamischen Kopftuch"* [*The Koran on the „Islamic Veil"*] (Sura 24:31), see: Burgmer, Christoph (ed.), (*op. cit.*), p. 83-89; see further in "*imprimatur*" IV / 2004, p. 72-75.

– *Le voile islamique* [*The Islamic Veil*], see: Yves Charles Zarka, Sylvie Taussig, Cynthia Fleury (ed.), *L'Islam en France* [*Islam in France*], in: Cités (Revue) Hors Série, Paris (Presses Universitaires de France) 2004, p. 665-668; see further there: *Quelle est la langue du Coran ?* [*Which is the Language of the Koran?*], p. 661-665.

– *Neudeutung der arabischen Inschrift im Felsendom zu Jerusalem* [*New Interpretation of the Arabic Inscription within the Dome of the Rock in Jerusalem*], see Ohlig, Karl-Heinz / Puin, Gerd-R. (ed.), *Die dunklen Anfänge* [*The Obscure Beginnings*], Berlin 2005, 2006, 2007, p. 124-147.

– *Relikte syro-aramäischer Buchstaben in frühen Korankodizes im ḥiğāzī- und kūfī-Duktus* [*Relics of Syro-Aramaic letters in Early Koran Codices in Ḥiğāzī and Kūfī Style*], see Ohlig, Karl-Heinz (ed.), *Der frühe Islam* [*The Early Islam*], Berlin 2007, p. 377-414.

Maclean, Arthur John. *A Dictionary of Vernacular Syriac*. Oxford,1901.

Mannā, Jacques Eugène. *Vocabulaire Chaldéen-Arabe* [*Vocabulary of Chaldean Arabic*]. Mosul, 1900.Reprinted with a new appendix by Raphael J. Bidawid. Beirut, 1975.

b. Manẓūr, Abū l-Faḍl Ğamāl ad-Dīn Muḥammad b. Mukarram al-Ifrīqī al-Miṣrī. *Lisān al-ʿarab* ["*Tongue*" *of the Arabs*]. 15 vols. Beirut, 1955.

Mingana, Alfons. *Syriac Influence on the Style of the Kur'ān*. In: *Bulletin of John Rylands Library*. Manchester, 1927. 77- 98.

al-Munğid fī l-luġa wa-l-aʿlām. 29th ed. Beirut, 29 1987.

Nevo, Yehuda D. and Judith Koren, *Crossroads to Islam: the origins of the Arab religion and the Arab state*, Amherst, NY, 2003.

Nöldeke, Theodor. *Beiträge zur semitischen Sprachwissenschaft* [*Essays on Semitic Linguistics*]. Strasbourg, 1904.

Nöldeke, Theodor. *Neue Beiträge zur semitischen Sprachwissenschaft* [*New Essays on Semitic Linguistics*]. Strasbourg, 1910.

Nöldeke, Theodor. *Geschichte des Qorâns* [*History of the Koran*]. Göttingen, 1860.

Nöldeke, Theodor and Friedrich Schwally, *Geschichte des Qorāns*. Vol. 1. *Über den Ursprung des Qorāns* [*On the Origin of the Koran*]. 2nd ed. Leipzig, 1909. Vol. 2, *Die Sammlung des Qorāns* [*The Collection of the Koran*]. 2nd ed. Leipzig, 1919; Vol. 3. Ed. Gotthelf Bergsträßer and Otto Pretzl, *Die Geschichte des Korantextes* [*The History of the Text of the Koran*]. 2nd ed. Leipzig, 1938. Hildesheim, 1961.

Nöldeke, Theodor. *Zur Grammatik des classischen Arabisch* [*On the Grammar of Classical Arabic*]. In the appendix: The handwritten supplements in Theodor Nöldeke's personal copy, revised and provided with additions by Anton Spitaler. Darmstadt, 1963.

Nöldeke, Theodor. *Kurzgefasste syrische Grammatik* [*Concise Syriac Grammar*]. 2nd ed. Leipzig, 1898. Reprint of the 2nd ed. In the appendix: The handwritten supplements in Theodor Nöldeke's personal copy and a register of the references. Ed. Anton Schall. Darmstadt, 1977.

Nöldeke, Theodor. *Mandäische Grammatik* [*Mandean Grammar*]. Halle an der Saale, 11875. Photomech. reprint of the 1875 edition. In the appendix: The handwritten supplements in Theodor Nöldeke's personal copy. Ed. Anton Schall. Darmstadt, 1964.

Nöldeke, Theodor. *Die semitischen Sprachen* [*The Semitic Languages*]. 2nd ed. Leipzig, 21899.

Ohlig, Karl-Heinz / Puin, Gerd-R. (ed.), *Die dunklen Anfänge* [*The Obscure Beginnings*], Berlin 2005, 2006, 2007, p. 124-147. *Relikte syro-aramäischer Buchstaben in frühen Korankodizes im ḥiǧāzī- und kūfī-Duktus* [*Relics of Syro-Aramaic letters in Early Koran Codices in Ḥiǧāzī and Kūfī Style*], see Ohlig, Karl-Heinz (ed.), *Der frühe Islam* [*The Early Islam*], Berlin 2007, p. 377-414.

Ohlig, Karl-Heinz / Puin, Gerd-R. (ed.), *Die dunklen Anfänge. Neue Forschungen zur Entstehung und frühen Geschichte des Islam* [*The Obscure Beginnings. New Researches on the Rise and the Early History of Islam*], Berlin 2005, 2006, 2007.

Ohlig, Karl-Heinz (ed.), *Der frühe Islam. Eine historisch-kritische Rekonstruktion anhand zeitgenössischer Quellen* [*The Early Islam. A Historic-Critical Reconstruction on the Basis of Contemporary Sources*], Berlin, 2007.

Paret, Rudi. *Der Koran. Übersetzung*. 2nd edition. Stuttgart, Berlin, Cologne, Mainz, 21982.

Paret, Rudi. *Der Koran. Kommentar und Konkordanz* [*The Koran: Commentary and Concordance*]. Stuttgart, Berlin, Cologne, Mainz, 1971.

Paret, Rudi, ed. *Der Koran*. Wege der Forschung [Directions of Research]. Vol. 326. Darmstadt, 1975.

Prémare, Alfred-Louis de, *Les fondations de l'islam. Entre écriture et histoire* [*The Foundations of Islam. Between Scripture and History*], Paris, 2002.

– *Aux origines du Coran – questions d'hier, approches d'aujourd'hui* [*Towards the Origins of the Koran – Questions of Yesterday, Today's Approaches*], Paris, 2004.

Qur'ān karīm. Cairo, 1972.

Reeth, Jan M. F. van, *Le vignoble du Paradis et le chemin qui y mène. La thèse de C. Luxenberg et les sources du Coran* [*The Vineyard of Paradise and the Way that Leads Tthither. The Thesis of C. Luxenberg and the Sources of the Koran*] in: *Arabica*, tome LIII/4, Leiden, 2006, p. 511-524.

Reeth, Jan M.F. van, *Le Coran et ses scribes* [*The Koran and its Scribes*] in: *Acta Orientalia Belgica* (published by the Belgian Society of Oriental Studies, ed. by C. Cannuyer, A, Schoors, R. Lebrun), vol. XIX, *Les scribes et la transmission du savoir* [*The Scribes and the Transmission of Knowledge*], ed. by C. Cannuyer, Bruxelles, 2006, p. 67-81.

Rosenthal, Franz. *A Grammar of Biblical Aramaic*. Wiesbaden, 1963.

Rudolf, Wilhelm. *Die Abhängigkeit des Qorans von Judentum und Christentum* [*The Dependence of the Koran on Judaism and Christianity*]. Stuttgart, 1922.

Sfar, Mondher, *Le Coran, la Bible et l'Orient ancient* [*The Koran, the Bible and the Ancient Orient*], Paris, 1998.

– *Le Coran est-il authentique ?* [*Is the Koran Authentic?*], Paris, 2000.

Sokoloff, Michael. *A Dictionary of Jewish Palestinian Aramaic*. Ramat-Gan, ^{2}1992.

Smith, Payne, ed. *Thesaurus Syriacus*, Tomus I. Oxonii, 1879. Tomus II. Oxonii, 1901.

Speyer,Heinrich. *Die biblischen Erzählungen im Qoran* [*The Biblical Stories in the Koran*]. Breslau (?), 1931. Hildesheim, 1961.

Spitaler, Anton. "Die Schreibung des Typus صلوة im Koran. Ein Beitrag zur Erklärung der koranischen Orthographie [The Writing of the Type صلوة in the Koran: A Contribution to the Clarification of Koran Orthography]." In: *Wiener Zeitschrift für die Kunde des Morgenlandes* [Vienna Journal of Oriental Studies]. 56th vol. Festschrift for Herbert W. Duda. Vienna, 1960.

Syriac Bible (63DC). United Bible Societies. London, 1979.

aṭ-Ṭabarī, Abū Ǧaᶜfar Muḥammad b. Ǧarīr. *Ǧāmiᶜ al-bayān ᶜan ta'wīl al-Qur'ān* (*Koran commentary*). 30 parts in 12 vols. 3rd ed. Cairo, 1968.

Vollers, Karl. *Volkssprache und Schriftsprache im alten Arabien* [*Vernacular Language and Written Language in Ancient Arabia*]. Strasbourg, 1906.

Wansbrough, John, *Quranic Studies. Sources and Methods of Scriptural Interpretation*, Amherst, New York, 2004.

Wehr, Hans. *Arabisches Wörterbuch für die Schriftsprache der Gegenwart* [*Arabic Dictionary for the Written Language of the Present Day*]. 5th ed. Wiesbaden, ^{5}1985.

Wehr, Hans. *A Dictionary of Modern Written Arabic* (Arabic-English), ed. by J. Milton Cowan, 4th ed. Wiesbaden, 1979.

Wild, Stefan. *Das Kitāb al-ᶜAin und die arabische Lexikographie* [*The Kitāb al-ᶜAin and the Arabic Lexicography*]. Wiesbaden, 1965.

Zayn ad-Dīn, Nāǧī. مصور الخط العربي (*Muṣawwar al-ḫaṭṭ al-ᶜarabī*) (*Illustrated Presentation of Arabic Writing*). Baghdad, 1968.

مصدق muṣaddiq *249*
صراط ṣirāṭ *53, 226*
s. also: سراط sirāṭ
صرع ṣara^{c}a *172*
اصطره aṣṭuruhu *236*
s. also: اضطره aṭṭarruhu
بمصيطر bi-muṣayṭir *235*
المصيطرون al-muṣayṭirūn *233*
235
صعقا ṣa^{c}iqa^{n} *164*
صعقة ṣā^{c}iqa *165*
اصلح aṣlaḥa *196*
صل ṣalli *296*
الصيحة aṣ-ṣayḥa *165*
الصاخة aṣ-ṣāḫḫa *165*

ض

الضر aḍ-ḍurr *209, 310*
الضرا aḍ-ḍarrā(^{ɔ}) *310*
ضرب ḍarab^{a} ***209**, 308, 316*
ضرب **ḍaraba** *209, 308*
ضاع ḍā^{c}a *308*
اضطرم iṭṭarama *176*

ط

طرا ṭarā (ṭara^{ɔ}a) *309*
اضطر iṭṭarra / uṭṭurra *17*
236, 309
اضطره aṭṭarruhu *236*
s. اصطره aṣṭuruhu
طرب ṭariba
طرف ṭarf *267, 271, 308*
طعام ṭa^{c}ām *192*
طغى ṭaġā *307, 311*
طعى ṭa^{c}ā *308*
ليطغى la-yaṭġā *311, 321*
طاغية ṭāġiya(tun) *48*
طمث ṭamiṯa *273, 275*
كالطود ka-ṭ-ṭawd *83*
كالطور ka-ṭ-ṭūr *83*
يطوف yaṭūf^{u} *286, 289*
طين لازب ṭīn lāzib *306*

ع

عـ ^{c}ayn *42, 101, 164*
187, 255, 262, 309
عبدا ^{c}ibādan *28*
s. also: لبدا libadan
عتل **^{c}utull** *76*
عتم ^{c}attama *182*
اعجز a^{c}ǧaza *118*
إعجاز i^{c}ǧāz *69*
أعجمي a^{c}ǧamī *109, 111, 112*
عدّل ^{c}addala *196*
عربا ^{c}uruba^{n} *278, 280, 288*
عريا ^{c}arāyā *280, 288*
عصى ^{c}aṣā *187*
معاصيا mu^{c}āṣiya^{n} *189*
عاقر ^{c}āqir *219*
أعطى a^{c}ṭā *298*
عطى ^{c}aṭā *298*
s. also: اتى atā
علّم ^{c}allam^{a} *303*

ن

انبت	anbata	*279*
فانتبذت	fa-ntabaḏat	*138*
نثر	naṯar^{a}	*288*
ناديه	nādiyahu	*318*
ناصية	nāṣiya	*317*
نحت	naḥata	*131, 139*
نحتك	nuḥḥātaki	*147*
نحيت	naḥīt	*129, 130*
وانجر	wa-nǧar	*297*
وانحر	wa-nḥar	*293, 296*
ينزفون	yunzifūn	*289*
نسى	nasiy^{a}	*311*
نسيا	nasya^{n}	*138, 214, 217*
نسير	nusayyir^{u}	*151*
انشأ	anšaʾa	*279*
نشر	našara	*195*
ننشز	nanšuzu	*195*
نصا	naṣā	*317*
نظر	naẓara	*163, 191,* ***246***
انتظر	intaẓara	*246*
ننقصها	nanquṣuhā	*271*

ه

هذى	haḏā	*117*
هزأ	hazaʾa	*118*
هلا	hallā	*199*

و

اوجس	awǧasa	*240*
لا توجل	lā tawǧal	*240*
وجلة	waǧila	*240*
وجلون	waǧilūn	*240*
وحى	waḥā	*125*
أوحى	awḥā	*125*
وضع	waḍaʿa	*133, 189*
وقود	waqūd	*174*
ولـد	walada	*133, 286*
ولد	walad	*133, 286*
ولدن	wildān	*284,* ***287****, 290*

ي

ياجوج	Yaǧūǧ	*88*
يسر	yassara	*123*
يورية	**Yawrīya**	*90*

s. also: التورية at-Tawrāt

Koran codex of Samarqand (CD 0024)

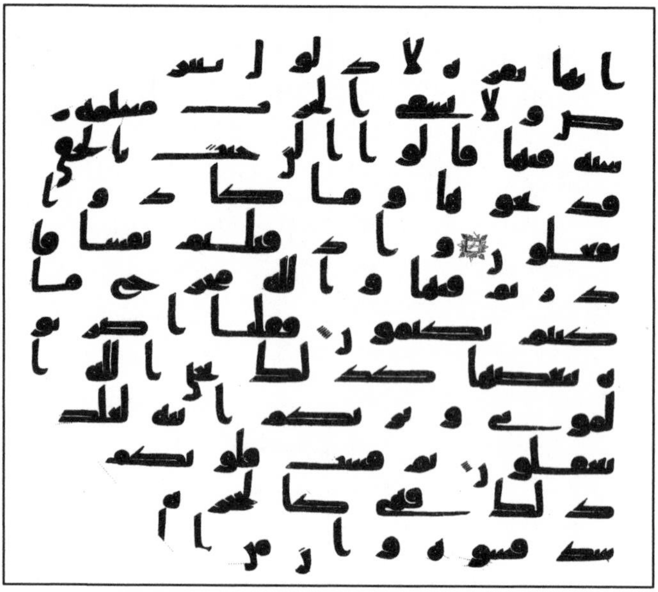

Koran codex of Samarqand (CD 0098)

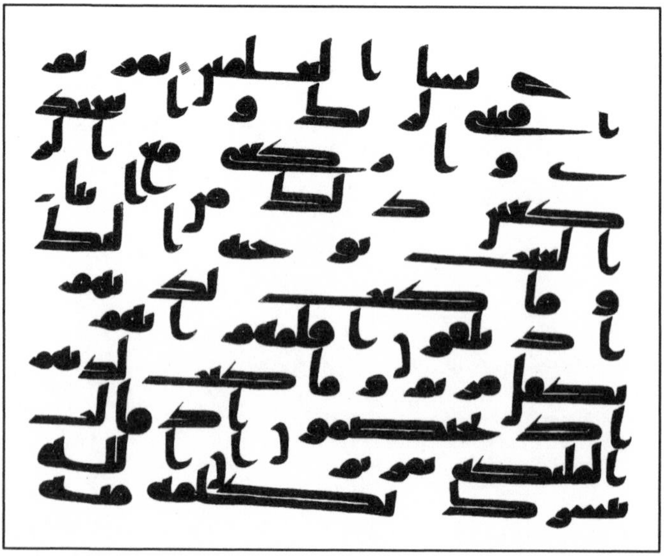

Koran codex of Samarqand (CD 0585)

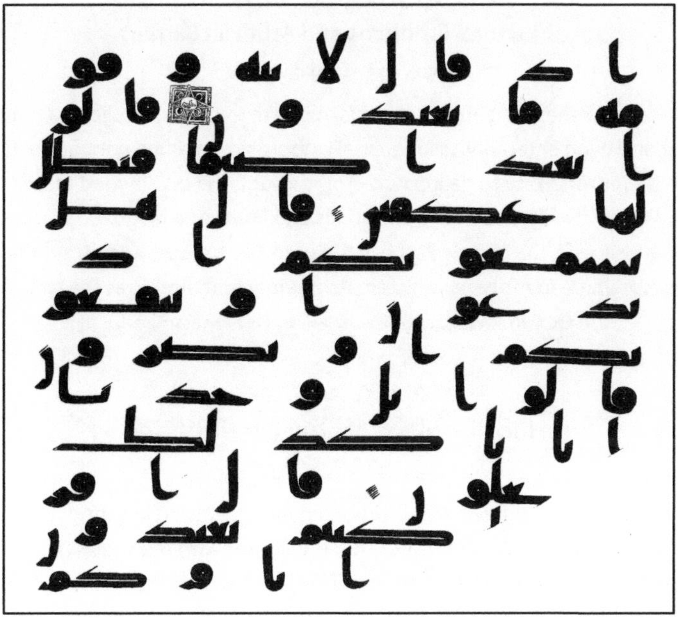

SAMARKANDSKII KUFICHESKII KORAN – Coran coufique de Samarcand écrit d'après la tradition de la propre main du troisième Calife Osman (644–656) qui se trouve dans la Bibliothèque Impériale Publique de St. Petersbourg. Edition faite avec l'autorisation de l'Institut Archéologique de St. Petersbourg (facsimile) par S. Pissaref. St. Petersbourg. 1905

Robert Marzari

Arabic in Chains

Structural Problems and Artificial Barriers.

ISBN 978-3-89930-119-9

"What distinguishes Marzari's work is his ability to explain complicated matters in clear and even entertaining language. Linguists often cut a poor figure here, given their propensity to gallop non-stop through the brushwood of grammar. Not so Marzari. He illustrates the potentials and limits of a language that over 300 million Muslims in the Middle East call their mother tongue, aside from the many others elsewhere in Africa as well as in Asia, who recite Arabic as the language of the Qur'an." Wolfgang G. Schwanitz / Der Tagesspiegel, Berlin

Abit Yasar Kocak

Handbook of Arabic Dictionaries

ISBN 978-3-89930-021-5

This book is a brief guide to Arabic dictionaries. It aims on assisting learners of Arabic to cope with the difficulties that encounter with the various dictionary movements over centuries: Madrasah al-Taklîbât, a school established by al-Khalîl; Madrasah al-Kâfiyyah, a school born out of the expansion of the poetry under the dominance of the "sacî" (rhymed prose); and Al-Madrasah al-Abdjadiyyah.

Amr Hamzawy (ed.)

Civil Society in the Middle East

ISBN 978-3-89930-027-7

The internal Arab, Iranian and Israeli debates on civil society in the 1980s and 1990s have only partly found their way into Western studies on the issue. An analysis of the discursive structures of the local debates, which represents the major objective of the current edited volume, may help shifting the nexus of the academic discussion to Middle Eastern perceptions and actors. Amr Hamzawy analyses the Arab sociological and political discussion on civil society, depending on the intellectual literature of the last ten years. Asghar Schirazi distinguishes in his contribution between three central intellectual currents in Iran: Islamist, leftist, and liberal, each of which can be further subdivided. The article of Angelika Timm explores the historical development of the Israeli civil society and addresses some important spheres of civil activities.